HOW TO
cheat
IN
Photoshop CS3

The art of creating photorealistic montages

Steve Caplin

ELSEVIER

AMSTERDAM • BOSTON • HEIDELBERG • LONDON • NEW YORK • OXFORD
PARIS • SAN DIEGO • SAN FRANCISCO • SINGAPORE • SYDNEY • TOKYO
Focal Press is an imprint of Elsevier

Focal
Press

Focal Press is an imprint of Elsevier
Linacre House, Jordan Hill, Oxford OX2 8DP, UK
30 Corporate Drive, Suite 400, Burlington, MA 01803, USA

First published as *How to Cheat in Photoshop* 2002
Reprinted 2002, 2003
Second edition 2004
Third edition 2005
Reprinted 2006
First published as *How to Cheat in Photoshop CS3* 2007

British Library Cataloguing in Publication Data
A catalogue record for this book is available from the British Library

Library of Congress Cataloging-in-Publication Data
A catalog record for this book is available from the Library of Congress

ISBN–13: 978-0-240-52062-9

For information on all Focal Press publications visit our website at www.focalpress.com

Book design and cover by Steve Caplin

Printed and bound in Canada

07 08 09 10 11   11 10 9 8 7 6 5 4 3 2 1

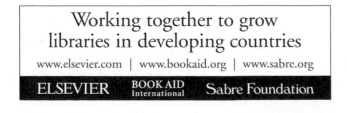

Contents

How to cheat, and why

The truth about cheating

I've used the word 'cheating' in the title of this book in two ways. The most obvious is that I'm describing how to make images look as much as possible like photographs, when they're not. In this sense, it simply means creating photographic work without the need for a studio.

The other sense of 'cheating' is finding shortcuts to help you work more quickly and more economically. Too often you'll see Photoshop techniques explained using long-winded, complex operations that take an age to complete. Wherever possible, I've used quicker solutions to achieve the same results. For the artist on a deadline, the difference between a perfect work of art and one that's turned in on time means the difference between a happy client and one faced with a blank page in the next day's newspaper.

Workthroughs and examples

Each workthrough in this book is designed as a double page spread. That way, you can prop the book up behind your keyboard while going through the associated file on the CD. Some of the workthroughs take the form of case studies, where I dissect an illustration I've done as a commissioned job; many of the sections open with one of my illustrations as a real-world example of the technique I'm talking about. One reason I've used my own artwork is that I know how it was created, and have the original files to take apart.

Messing about in Photoshop can be the most fun you can have without breaking the law, and it's tempting to experiment with filters and special effects. But it's not until you produce an illustration to a specific brief that you realize the issues and problems involved – and then find a way around them. Almost all the techniques I describe in this book have been learned out of necessity; there's nothing like a tight deadline to concentrate the mind. Adrenaline is sometimes the best drug there is.

At the end of each chapter you'll find an Interlude, in which I discuss an issue of relevance to the Photoshop artist. Think of them as light relief.

Photoshop terminology

In Photoshop 7, a collection of layers in a folder was called a Layer Set, and using one layer to mask those above it was called Grouping. In Photoshop CS, the word Grouping was replaced with the cumbersome 'Make a Clipping Mask';

in Photoshop CS2 the term Layer Set was replaced with the word Group. I've updated all the references so they apply to the latest version; and I've used the term 'clipping' to refer to making a clipping mask with the underlying layer. It's bound to cause some confusion for those using earlier versions, but it was necessary to update the terminology as the program has evolved.

What's on the DVD?

I've included most of the workthroughs in this book on the DVD, so that after reading about them you can open up the original Photoshop files and experiment with them for yourself. I've reduced the image sizes to make them more manageable, so you'll find yourself working with screen resolution images. There are also some movies showing specific techniques in action.

In a few cases, I haven't been able to provide the examples on the DVD. These tend to be workthroughs that are case studies, in which I've used images of politicians and other celebrities for whom it was impossible to get clearance to include them for electronic distribution. All the other images have been either photographed by me or generously provided by the various image libraries concerned, to whom I owe a debt of gratitude. For full details of what's included, see the back pages.

Spelling and metaphors

I've tried to use American spelling wherever possible. First, because we're more used to reading US spelling in England than Americans are to reading English spelling; and second, because Photoshop is an American product. Initially I tried not to use any words that were spelled differently in the two languages, but I found it impossible to get through the book without mentioning the words 'color' and 'gray'. My apologies if I've employed any phrases or vernacular that don't work on both sides of the Atlantic. It's a wide ocean, and some expressions don't survive the journey.

Going further

Visit the book's website at www.howtocheatinphotoshop.com and you'll find the user forum. This is where you can post questions or problems, and exchange ideas with other readers: you can also take part in the weekly Friday Challenge, to pit your wits against a wide variety of Photoshop users.

Steve Caplin
London, 2007

Acknowledgments

This book is dedicated to Carol, of course.

I'm immeasurably grateful to the following:

Marie Hooper of Focal Press, for her patience and persistence

Davd Huss, for technical read-throughs

Keith Martin, for helping me create the keyboard shortcuts font

David Asch, Atomicfog, Baby Biker, Becky Fryer, Ben, Ben Mills, BigVern, Bob, Char, Chris Berry, Chris Martin, Dave Cox, Deborah Morley, David Urquhart, Dek_101, Dirtdoctor23, Eyal Fitoussi, hi-liter, James, John White, Josephine Harvatt, KateW, Glen, Gordon Bain, Marty Guyer, Michael Sinclair, Neal, Paul, Paul2007, Pauline, photosynth, Pierre, Raffy, Rufus, Stefan, Steve Hill, Steve Mac, Ted Eggs, 2bfree, Toby, Tom, uk2usadaz, Vibeke, Vicho, Wayne, Whaler, and all the other regulars on the Reader Forum who have made writing this edition so enjoyable.

Adobe Systems Inc., for making Photoshop in the first place.

I'm indebted to the art editors of the newspapers and magazines who commissioned the artwork I've used as examples in this book:
Jonathan Anstee, Dave Ashmore, Dan Barber, Kevin Bayliss, Andy Bodle, Julian Bovis, Roger Browning, Zelda Davey, Miles Dickson, Robin Hedges, Paul Howe, Lisa Irving, Alice Ithier, Ben Jackson, Jasmina Jambresic, Hugh Kyle, Alix Lawrence, Fraser McDermott, Garry Mears, John Morris, Doug Morrison, Lawrence Morton, Martin Parfitt, Mark Porter, Tom Reynolds, Caz Roberts, Caroline Sibley, Matt Straker and Richard Turley.

A couple of the tutorials in this edition have previously been published, in a slightly different form, in the magazines MacUser and Total Digital Photography. My thanks to their editors for allowing me to repurpose my work here.

Many of the images in this book are from royalty-free photo libraries. Their websites are:

Able Stock	www.ablestock.com
Bodyshots	www.digiwis.com
Corel	www.corel.com
Hemera	www.hemera.com (digital image content © 1997-2002 Hemera Technologies Inc. All rights reserved.)
Photodisc	www.photodisc.com (digital images © 2001 PhotoDisc/Getty Images)
PhotoObjects	www.photoobjects.net
Photos.com	www.photos.com
Rubber Ball	www.rubberball.com (all images © Rubber Ball Productions)
Stockbyte	www.stockbyte.com

How to use this book

I doubt if any readers of this book are going to start at the beginning and work their way diligently through to the end. In fact, you're probably only reading this section because your computer's just crashed and you can't follow any more of the workthroughs until it's booted up again. This is the kind of book you should be able to just dip into and extract the information you need.

But I'd like to make a couple of recommendations. The first four chapters deal with the basics of photomontage. There are many Photoshop users who have never learnt how to use the Pen tool, or picked up the essential keyboard shortcuts; I frequently meet experienced users who have never quite figured out how to use layer masks. Because I talk about these techniques throughout the book, I need to bring everyone up to speed before we get onto the harder stuff. So my apologies if I start off by explaining things you already know: it'll get more interesting later on.

The techniques in each chapter build up as you progress through the workthroughs. Frequently, I'll use a technique that's been discussed in more detail earlier in the same chapter, so it may be worth going through the pages in each chapter in order, even if you don't read every chapter in the book.

A CD icon on a page indicates that the Photoshop file for that tutorial is on the CD, so you can open it up and try it out for yourself. The Movie icon indicates that there's an associated QuickTime movie on the CD.

If you get stuck anywhere in the book, or in Photoshop generally, visit the Reader Forum, accessed through the main website:

www.howtocheatinphotoshop.com

This is where you can post queries and suggestions. I visit the forum every day, and will always respond directly to questions from readers. But expect other forum members to weigh in with their opinions as well! It's also a great place to meet other Photoshop users, and to take part in the weekly Friday Challenge – of which you'll see a few examples in this edition.

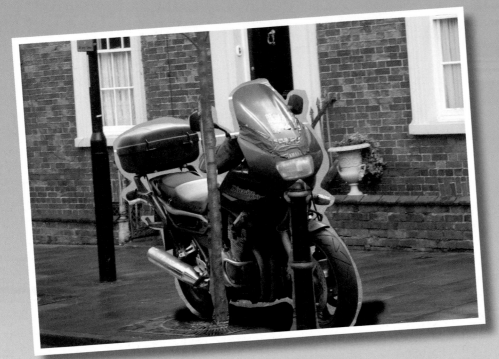

■ There are only three elements in this simple montage: the background, the bike, and its shadow. But there's a world of difference between the crudely selected version, top, and the careful cutout, right. Making accurate selections is the key to working in Photoshop successfully.

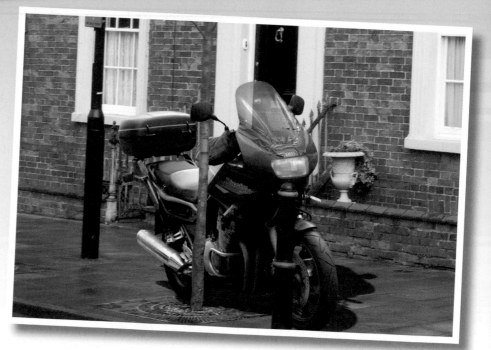

1

Natural selection

THE TECHNIQUES described in this book assume you
have a reasonable working knowledge of Photoshop.
In later chapters, we'll discuss ways of working that
involve modifying selections, and using both QuickMask
and the Pen tool to create Bézier curves. The first part
of this chapter will serve as a refresher course on these
fundamental techniques for those who already know
them, and will introduce the concepts for those who have
not yet experimented with them.

Later on, we'll go into more detail on how to work with
and modify layers and colors without having to pick up
a brush first: there are many techniques, such as those
for changing colors selectively, that can be accomplished
entirely by means of dialog boxes.

Selection: the fundamentals

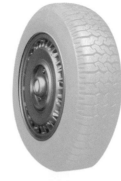

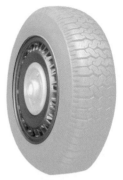

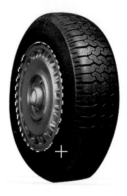

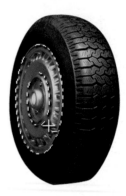

ALL PHOTOSHOP WORK begins with making selections. Shown here are some of the basic keyboard shortcuts that every Photoshop user should be able to use as second nature: even if you hate learning keyboard commands, you owe it to your productivity and your sanity to learn these.

Temporarily accessing the Move tool, using the shortcut shown in step 8, works when any other tool is active – not just the selection tools. This makes it easy to move any layer around while painting, selecting or using type, without having to reach for the toolbar.

1 Normal drawing with the Marquee tool is from corner to corner. But if you're using the Elliptical Marquee, it's hard to conceive where the 'corner' might be. Hold down ⌥ *alt after* you begin drawing to draw from the center outwards. The selected region is shown above, in each case.

2 If you hold ⌥ *alt before* you draw a second selection, you will remove this selection from the original one. Be sure to press this key before you begin drawing, or you'll simply draw from the center. Here, we've deselected the center of the hubcap, leaving just the rim.

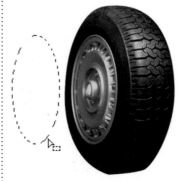

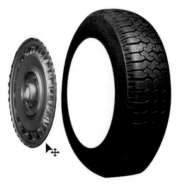

6 If you drag a selected area with a selection tool active (Marquee, Lasso etc), you'll move the selected region but not its contents.

7 To access the Move tool temporarily, hold ⌘ *ctrl* before you drag. Now, the selection itself will be moved when you drag it.

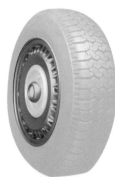

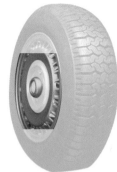

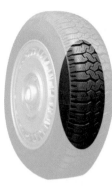

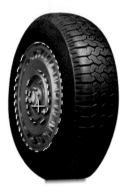

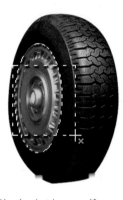

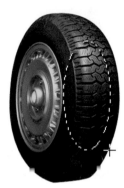

3 Holding *alt* subtracts from the selection, but holding *Shift* adds to it. Again, be sure to hold the key before you begin drawing. By holding this key down, we're able to add back the middle knob on the hubcap from the section we'd previously deselected.

4 Here's what happens if we combine the two keys. Holding *alt Shift* intersects the new selection with the previous one, resulting in just the overlap between the two. Here, the original elliptical selection is intersected with the new rectangular selection.

5 A little-known modifier is the Space bar, which performs a unique task: it allows you to move a selection while you're drawing it, which is of enormous benefit when selecting areas such as the ellipse of the hubcap. Here, we've used the technique to move the selection over to the side.

HOT TIP

Selections can be nudged with the arrow keys, as well as being dragged into position – useful for aligning them precisely. One tap of the arrow keys will move a selection by a single pixel. If you hold the *Shift* key as you tap the arrow, the selection will move by 10 pixels at a time. If you also hold *ctrl* you'll move the contents, rather than just the selection boundary.

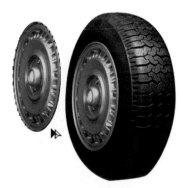

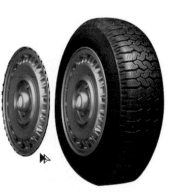

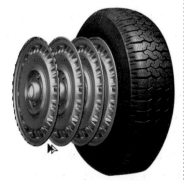

8 Holding down *alt* as well will move a copy, leaving the original selection where it was – but be sure to hold the modifier before dragging.

9 To constrain the movement to exactly vertical or horizontal, hold the *Shift* key after you've started to drag the selection.

10 You can continue to make several copies by releasing and holding the mouse button while holding the *alt* key down.

SHORTCUTS
MAC WIN BOTH

5

The Lasso and Magic Wand

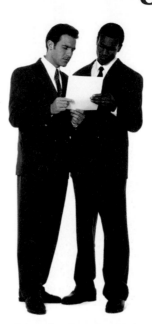

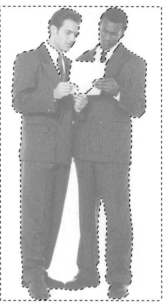

THE LASSO MAY WELL have been the first selection tool to be seen in a digital paint program, having put in its initial appearance 20 years ago, but these days it's far from being the ideal tool. Clumsy and inaccurate to draw with, it's best reserved for tidying up selections made in other ways, as we'll see here.

There is one surprising use for the Lasso tool, however, and that's for tracing straight lines – thanks to a little-known keyboard shortcut. We'll look at this technique in steps 6 and 7.

The Magic Wand tool is a great all-purpose tool for selecting areas of a similar tonal range, and is widely used for removing simple backgrounds. Its tendency to 'leak' into areas you don't want selected, however, means you have to pay close attention to what's actually been selected – and be prepared to fix it afterwards.

1 This straightforward scene should be an ideal candidate for Magic Wand selection: after all, it's on a plain white background. But even simple selections can have their pitfalls.

2 Begin by clicking in the white area outside the two figures. (Note that the main image has been knocked back so we can see the selection outlines more clearly.)

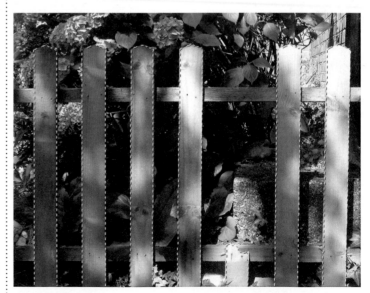

6 Although the Lasso tool may seem the obvious choice when drawing freehand selections, it can also be used to select objects made of straight lines, such as this fence. Hold the ⌥ *alt* key and then click once at each corner of each vertical post, clicking additionally from the bottom of one to the bottom of the next. You can also use the Polygonal Lasso tool to do this job on its own, without holding the modifier key.

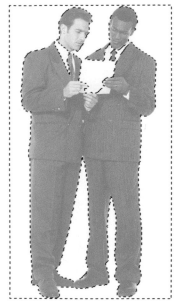

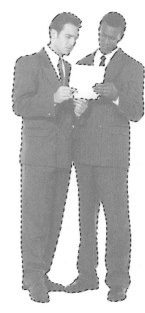

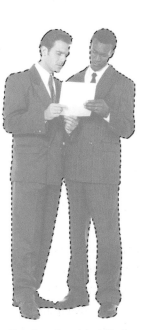

3 The area between the men's legs was not included in the original selection, so we need to hold the *Shift* key and click there to add it to our selection area.

4 So far, we've selected everything except the bodies. We need to inverse the selection, by pressing ⌘ *Shift* *I* *ctrl* *Shift* *I*, to select the bodies themselves.

5 Note how the original Magic Wand selection 'leaked' into the paper and the shirt collars. This is easily fixed by holding *Shift* as we add those areas with the Lasso tool.

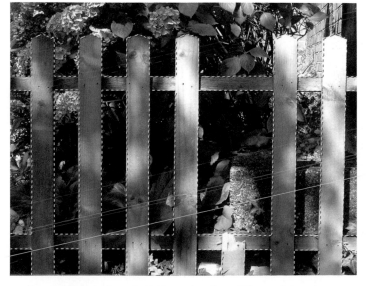

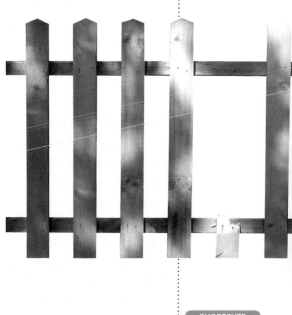

7 Now to add the horizontals. Hold the *Shift* key and then, after clicking the first corner point, add the ⌥ *alt* key and continue to click each corner as before. Be sure not to hold ⌥ *alt* before beginning to click or its effect will be to subtract the new selection from the old one, rather than adding to it – see the previous page for details on how these modifier keys work. The fence will now be fully selected.

QuickMask 1: better selection

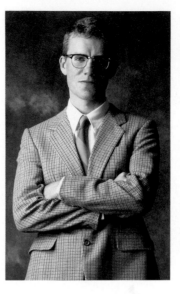

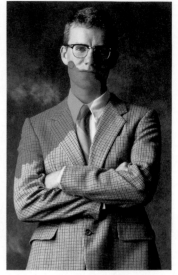

QUICKMASK IS THE MOST POWERFUL tool for creating selections in Photoshop. It uses a red overlay to show the selected area, allowing you to see the image through it; when you leave QuickMask mode, the painted area will be selected.

In QuickMask, painting with black will add to the selection and painting with white will subtract from it (as long as you're set up as described below). This makes it easy to trace around any object: it's far quicker and more controllable than the Lasso tool, and in situations such as the one shown here it's the best solution.

The default setting is for QuickMask to highlight the masked (unselected) areas with a red overlay, leaving the selected areas transparent: I find it far preferable to work the other way around, so that the selected areas are highlighted. To change the settings, you need to double-click the QuickMask icon (near the bottom of the toolbar, just below the foreground/background color swatches) and use the settings shown above.

1 This image would be tricky to select using the Lasso tool, and impossible with the Magic Wand – the background and foreground are just too complex. Press **Q** to enter QuickMask mode so we can begin.

2 Using a hard-edged brush, begin to trace around the inside of the figure. You don't need to paint the whole figure in one go, so take it at your own pace and let the mouse button up every now and again to take a break.

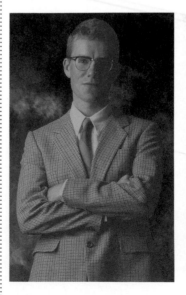

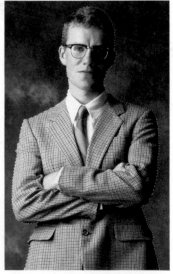

6 With the basic outline selected, we can address the detail. Lower the brush size using **[** until you have a size that's small enough to paint in the outline detail comfortably.

7 Now the outline is selected, leave QuickMask by pressing **Q** again, and the selection will be shown as a familiar 'marching ants' outline. You can now press **⌘ J** **ctrl J** to make a new layer from the selection.

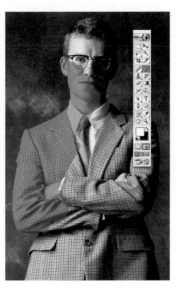

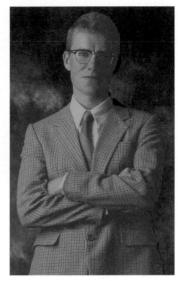

3 It's easy to make a simple mistake when painting the outline, such as going over the edge by accident – as I've done at the elbow here. Don't simply press Undo, or you'll lose the whole brush stroke; there's a better way to correct the error.

4 To paint out the offending selection area, change the foreground color from black to white (the keyboard shortcut to do this is **X**). Paint over the mistake, then press **X** again to switch back to black to paint the rest of the selection.

5 You don't need to worry too much about fine detail at this stage – just get the basic figure highlighted. Fiddly areas, such as around the ear and the collar, can be left till later.

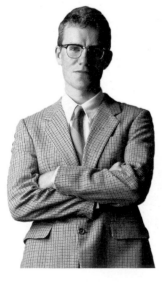

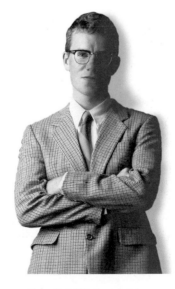

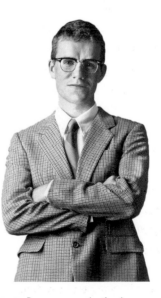

8 When the background is removed, we can see more clearly that the right side of the image is in really deep shadow – too deep to work with. Again, we can use QuickMask to select the shadow area.

9 Enter QuickMask again by pressing **Q**, and this time change to a soft-edged, larger brush. When we paint over the shadows now, we're creating a soft-edged selection; then leave QuickMask with **Q** again.

10 Because our selection has a soft edge, we can use any of the standard Adjustments to lighten up the shadow area (I've used Curves here) without showing a hard line between the changed and unchanged areas.

SHORTCUTS
MAC | WIN | BOTH

QuickMask 2: tips and tricks

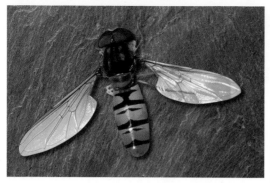

QUICKMASK IS THE BEST TOOL FOR making complex selections, especially of natural or organic objects where there are no hard, straight edges. By switching between large and small brushes, it's easy to trace even the most fiddly of objects with a little patience.

It all becomes more interesting when we look at using shades other than pure black and white to paint the mask. By painting with gray, we create a mask which is semi-transparent: the darker the shade, the more opaque the resulting selection will be. This technique is of particular benefit when selecting objects such as this fly, which has an opaque body and legs but semi-transparent wings. Building that transparency into the selection makes the whole effect far more convincing when we place the fly on a new background: the lowered opacity makes it look far more as if it belongs in its new surroundings.

1 Enter QuickMask mode with **Q**. Begin by using a hard-edged brush to trace around the main body of the fly. Don't worry about the legs at this stage – we'll add them in later. Remember that if you make a mistake, you can always swap the foreground color to white and paint it out.

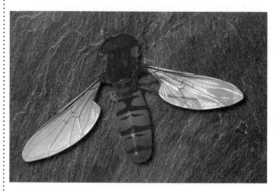

4 Now for the legs. Switch to a much smaller (but still hard-edged) brush, and trace each leg carefully. You can change brush sizes by using **]** to go to the next size up, and **[** to go to the next size down.

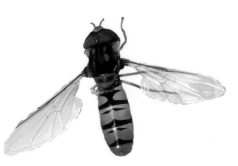

7 Now exit QuickMask by pressing **Q** again, and press **⌘ J** **ctrl J** to make a new layer from this selection. When we hide the underlying layers, we can see a few small errors: a bit of background has crept into the wings.

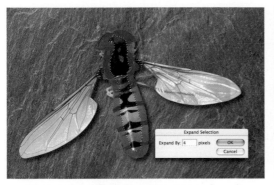

Expand Selection

Expand By: 4 pixels OK

Cancel

2 We could just paint in the middle of the body – but with a large selection, that would take a while. Here's a shortcut: use the Magic Wand tool to select the middle portion, then expand that selection (Select menu) by, say, 4 pixels to make sure the edges are covered.

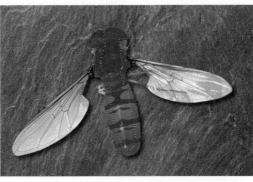

3 Now fill that new selection with the foreground color (the shortcut for doing this is ⌥ ← _alt_ ←) and then deselect (⌘ D _ctrl_ D) to remove the Magic Wand selection. This is a useful technique for large images in particular.

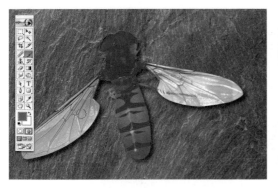

5 Before painting the wing area, we need to switch from black to a dark gray color to give the wings their transparency. Choose a gray from the Swatches palette, and, with a bigger brush, paint over the wings.

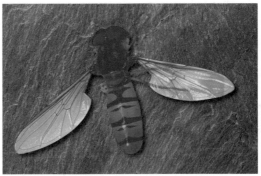

6 The wings may need to be semi-transparent, but those fine legs shouldn't be – so switch back to black (press _D_) and, with a small brush, paint in the legs where they're seen through the wings.

HOT TIP

Why didn't we simply paint with a lower brush opacity in step 5, rather than switching to gray? Because if we had, we would have to have painted the whole of each wing in a single brushstroke, without interruption. Otherwise, the new stroke would overlap the old one, creating a darker area (and so a stronger opacity) in the intersection.

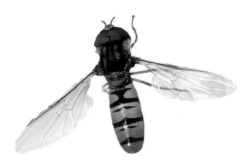

8 The easiest way to fix this is simply to erase the offending areas with a hard-edged Eraser. If you prefer, you could go back to QuickMask and tidy it up there, but it generally isn't worth the extra effort.

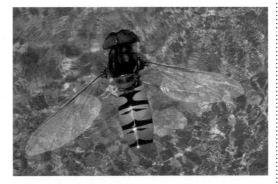

9 Because we selected the wing area using built-in transparency, we can partially see through them when we place the fly on a different background, adding greatly to the realism of the scene.

SHORTCUTS

MAC WIN BOTH

QuickMask 3: transformations

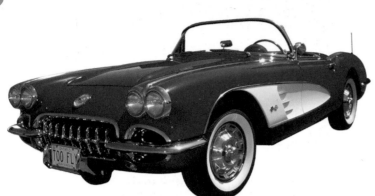

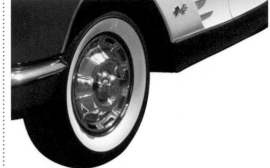

1 The hubcap on this car is a perfect circle photographed from an oblique angle. The Elliptical Marquee tool, however, only works on an orthogonal axis – there's no way to make it draw at an angle, as would be required here.

AS WELL AS USING PAINTING TOOLS, you can use any of the standard transformation tools within QuickMask. This can make it easier to select tricky areas, such as the angled hubcaps on this sports car. Even though the hubcap is an ellipse, the angle at which it's been photographed makes it impossible to select with the standard Elliptical Marquee tool. QuickMask, however, makes short work of the problem.

QuickMask can be used for creating all kinds of shapes from scratch. Hard-edged rectangles and smooth circles can be combined to build lozenge shapes far more quickly than toying with the radius settings of the Shape tools, for example.

There are many more uses to QuickMask than are shown here. Get into the habit of using it for your everyday selections, and you'll find it quickly repays the effort.

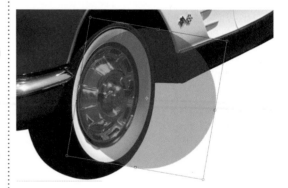

4 Enter Free Transform mode by pressing ⌘ T ctrl T, and selection borders will appear around the circle – no need to make an additional selection first. Drag the circle so one edge touches the edge of the hubcap, and rotate it to roughly the right angle.

7 Here's a simple and quick way to make a lozenge shape to exactly the size you want. First, draw a rectangle of the right height, and press **Q** to enter QuickMask. Choose the Elliptical Marquee tool, and position the cursor just inside the top of the rectangle; hold the **Shift** key and drag to the bottom edge of the rectangle.

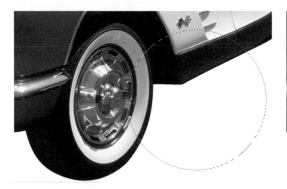

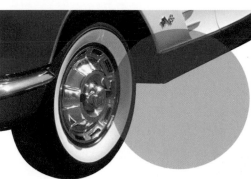

2 To begin, use the Elliptical Marquee tool to draw a circle anywhere on the image (hold the *Shift* key as you draw to constrain the ellipse to a circle). If you can't find the Elliptical Marquee tool, click and hold on the regular Marquee tool in the toolbar and it will pop open for you.

3 Now enter QuickMask mode by pressing *Q*. The circle you just drew will appear as a solid red circle, which will show us exactly where our selection edges lie in the illustration.

You might wonder why we bother using QuickMask to make this selection, rather than using Photoshop's Transform Selection tool. The answer is that it's really quite hard to make out an accurately positioned border when it's composed of a row of marching ants; using QuickMask, however, shows us the selection as a solid block of red, which makes it much easier to see through to the underlying image.

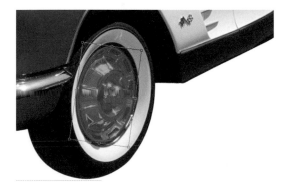

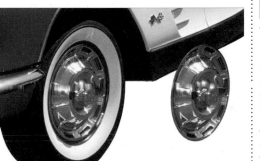

5 Now pull in the opposite handle so it touches the opposite rim of the hubcap, and do the same with the top and bottom edges. At this point, you may need to adjust the angle of rotation of the ellipse so it matches the hubcap perfectly.

6 With the ellipse perfectly positioned, press *Enter* to leave Free Transform, then press *Q* once again to leave QuickMask mode. You can now move the hubcap, or make a new layer from it.

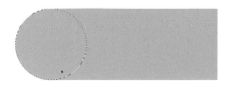

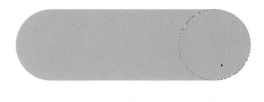

8 Assuming you started and ended in the correct place, your circle should now be exactly the same height as the rectangle. Release the mouse button before letting go of the *Shift* key, then switch to the Move tool (press *V*) and hold *alt* to move a copy as you drag the circle to the end of the rectangle; add *Shift* to move it horizontally.

9 Now release and then hold the *alt* key once again, and hold *Shift* as you drag the circle to the other end of the rectangle. When you leave QuickMask (by pressing *Q* again) you'll be left with a perfect lozenge selection, which you can then fill or stroke as you wish.

The Quick Selection tool 1

MAKING SELECTIONS AUTOMATICALLY has been the wish of every Photoshop artist since photomontage began. Now, with Photoshop CS3, that dream has taken a giant step towards reality.

The new Quick Selection tool is a fast, easy way to remove the background from just about any person or object. It won't work for every situation; sometimes, the difference between foreground and background elements are just too hard to be discerned automatically, especially if both are complex, fiddly subjects.

Here, we'll look at the basics of using this most useful of tools in a straightforward situation. On the following pages, we'll go on to show how to work with more difficult images.

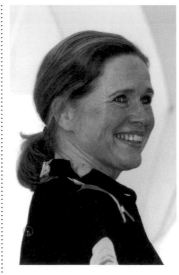

1 This photograph of the actress Liv Ullman has been taken against a plain background. It would be an easy task to select and remove it using the old Magic Wand tool; but even in situations as basic as this, the Quick Selection tool has added advantages.

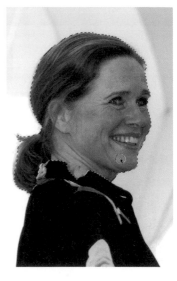

2 Begin by choosing the tool from the toolbox. The keyboard shortcut is **W**, which doubles as the key for the Magic Wand; press **Shift W** to toggle between the two. Start by dragging the tool across the head and hair, and selection outlines will appear.

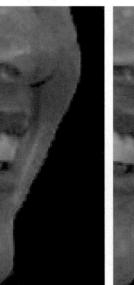
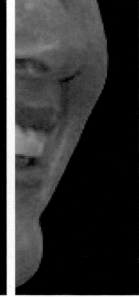

IMAGE: RITA MOLNÁR, LICENSED UNDER CREATIVE COMMONS

An Auto-Enhance checkbox on the Options bar produces smoother results automatically – but takes longer to process each brush stroke. These enlargements show an unedited selection with Auto-Enhance off (left) and on (right).

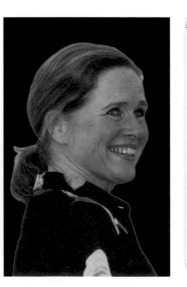

6 Clicking the center one of the five viewing modes at the bottom of the palette allows us to see the cutout against a black background. Now, we can see that there's a strong white fringe not previously noticeable.

Refine Selection Edge — Radius: 1.0 px — Contrast: 0 % — Smooth: 3 — Feather: 1.0 px — Contract/Expand: -60 %

7 To remove that fringe, we need to contract the selection; we do this using the Contract/Expand slider at the bottom. Note that the values are percentages, rather than pixels; here, a value of -60% works well.

14

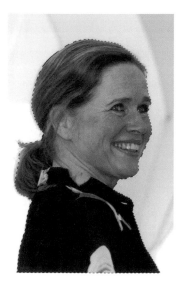

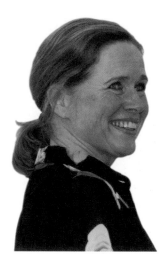

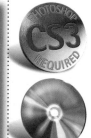

3 The default mode for this tool is to add to the existing selection. So when you go on to drag over the clothing – not forgetting that splash of pale color at the bottom – the selection will increase to include that area. Selection was never this easy!

4 We could stop there, and work with the selection as it stands. But the Quick Selection tool has some extra tricks up its sleeve that will make the cutout that much more effective. To continue, press the Refine Edge button on the Options bar.

5 These are the default settings. Click the small triangle button at the bottom for a description of how each slider affects the selection. By default, the image is shown cut out against white, but there are other viewing options.

Get used to viewing each of your selections against both black and white backgrounds to be sure that they will work on any background on which you later place the cutout. It would have been all too easy to simply accept the initial view against white; when placed on a dark background, the image would have looked very phoney.

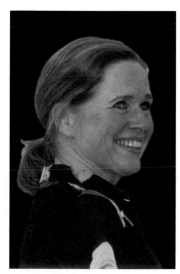

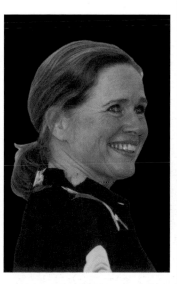

8 Once we've contracted the selection area, we can see that the white fringe has entirely gone. But in doing so, we're left with a slightly fuzzy outline that now needs to be tightened up.

9 To get rid of that fuzziness, we can use the Contrast slider. This tightens the selection area, producing a less feathered appearance. You can see the effect as you drag the slider; here, a value of around 28% works for us.

10 This is the result of applying both the Contract/Expand and the Contrast sliders to the selection. Press OK to dismiss the dialog, which will result in an image with a standard 'marching ants' selection.

15

The Quick Selection tool 2

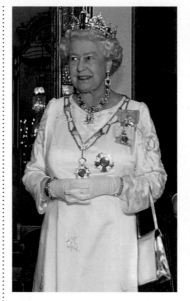

ON THE PREVIOUS PAGES, we looked at the basics of the Quick Selection tool, using a straightforward image for our demonstration. Here, we'll explore the methods for dealing with a far more difficult cutout.

This photograph of The Queen of England is just about the hardest image we could choose for an automated cutout. The complexity of the dress and crown are matched by a fiddly, detailed background: it would be hard to expect Photoshop to cope with this image as easily as others.

And, to be frank, it can't quite manage it. But it does get very close, with only a small amount of hand editing required to finish the job. It's a rather more fiddly process than we saw previously, but this is still the quickest way to cut a complex figure from its background.

Throughout this tutorial, we'll be showing selections in QuickMask mode. This is not how they appear when working with the Quick Selection tool, but are far easier to discern on the printed page.

1 Begin by using the Quick Selection tool with a medium sized brush – with a radius of around 50 pixels – and drag it through the head and body to see what the first pass comes up with.

2 The results aren't great, as this QuickMask view shows. The crown and half the body are missing entirely; Photoshop has seen the chain as a dividing line, and treated it accordingly. Refinement required!

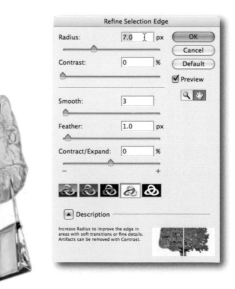

6 Even after our additional Lasso selection, we can still use the Refine Edge dialog to enhance the image. Here's how it stands so far: rather fuzzy around the edges.

7 To recapture some of the fine detail, we need to raise the Radius. Drag the slider to the right: here, a setting of around 7 pixels works well, as we'll see.

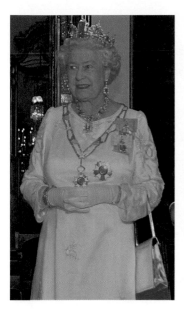

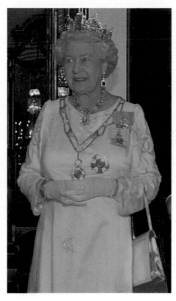

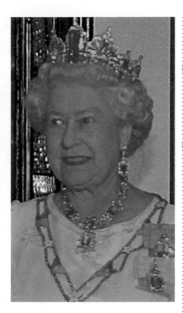

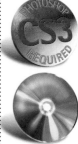

3 Continue to drag with the same brush in unselected areas. By default, the Quick Selection tool will add to an existing selection. Here, the wall behind the head has been selected as well; we'll deal with that next.

4 To remove areas from a selection, hold ⌥ *alt* as you drag with the brush. At this point, it's worth switching to a far smaller brush: around 10 pixels is sufficient. Drag in the wall as required.

5 No amount of automatic adding and removal will capture fine detail such as the top of this crown. Zoom in, switch to the Lasso tool and hold *Shift* as you drag around those fiddly areas by hand to include them.

The trick is getting to know just how much you can expect from this tool. It might just have been possible to achieve this cutout with no Lasso work at all, but the time taken would have been disproportionate to the value of the finished result. Sometimes it's best to augment automation with a little hand finishing.

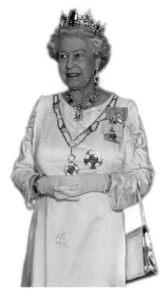

Refine Selection Edge

Radius:	7.0	px

Contrast: 65 %

Smooth: 3

Feather: 1.0 px

Contract/Expand: 0 %

OK
Cancel
Default
☑ Preview

Press P to toggle the preview of the edge refinements. Press F to cycle through the preview modes, and X to temporarily view the image.

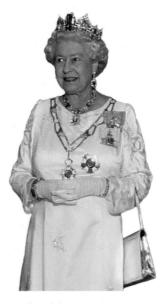

8 The trouble with increasing the radius is that we increase the fuzziness as well. We've smoothed out the lumps, but at the expense of clarity in the cutout.

9 Once again, turn to the Contrast slider to tighten up that over-smooth edge. A high contrast setting – around 65% – is needed here to counteract that large radius.

10 And here's the final result. A bit of a fiddle, for sure; but the cutout is convincing and reasonably accurate, and was achieved with minimal pain.

Refine Edges: going further

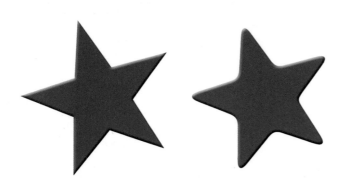

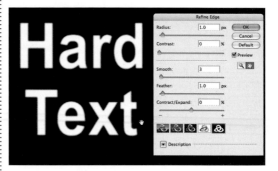

1 Begin by creating your text. It will appear on a new layer, as always. Here, we've used plain old Arial Bold. No need to rasterize the layer, since we'll be using a new layer later anyway.

S O FAR, WE'VE LOOKED AT the Refine Edges dialog purely as an add-on to the new Quick Selection tool. But there's far more to it than that: it can be used in combination with any of the selection tools to tighten up selections – and to loosen them.

The red star above was made using Photoshop's Shapes tool, with a bevel added later. The softer purple star was created in just a few seconds by modifying the outline of the red star using Refine Edges. This is a shape which would have been tricky to create by any other means!

Here, we'll look at using Refine Edges to make round-edged text. It's useful when we want to make lettering that appears to be made of stone, neon, or a natural material; even the most basic fonts can be turned into something special using this method.

4 Click the final icon at the bottom of the Refine Edges palette to view the selection as an Alpha Channel. Now, we can see how the default settings affect the outline: it's softened it, making it a little blurry.

7 The further you drag the Feather slider, the more rounded the edges will become. Where you stop is up to you: it's possible to soften the lettering so much that it's barely legible – which may, of course, be exactly the effect you want.

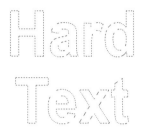

2 Load up the pixels in this layer by holding ⌘ ctrl and clicking on the layer's icon in the Layers palette. The outlines will appear in familiar "marching ants" form. Now, hide the text layer by clicking the eye icon next to it.

3 Bring up the Refine Edges dialog by pressing ⌘ ⌥ R ctrl alt R. Because the layer itself is hidden, we'll see nothing yet: that's because we're looking at a hidden selection on a white background.

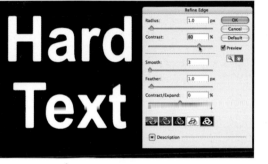

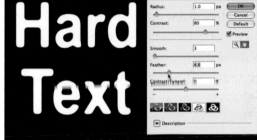

5 To fix that blurriness, increase the contrast. The further you drag this slider to the right, the harder the edge will become. Beware of dragging it too far, or you'll end up with jagged edges; a setting of around 80% works well.

6 Now to soften the lettering. Drag the Feather slider to the right and, as you do so, you'll see the corners of the text rounding off. Although feathering normally softens a selection, the high amount of contrast keeps it hard here.

When extreme amounts of feathering are used, it can easily become impossible to create hard edges, even with the contrast value set to 100%. This was true of the stars used in the introduction to this tutorial: the points were so rounded that they remained soft and fuzzy. The solution: repeat the Refine Edges dialog to tighten up the softness.

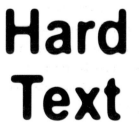

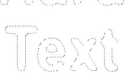

8 When you've got the effect you like, hit OK to dismiss the Refine Edges dialog. You'll be left with the marching ants once more, showing the edges of your selection in the usual way.

9 You can't work on the text layer itself, since it can contain only live text. So make a new layer, and press ⌥ ⌫ alt ⌫ to fill with the current foreground color. You can repeat the process as many times as you like, using the original text layer as a starting point.

The Pen is mightier...

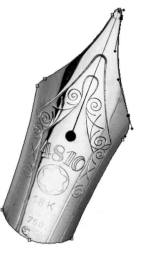

T HE PEN TOOL is one of the key tools
available to the illustrator – not just in
Photoshop but in Illustrator, FreeHand and
many other programs as well.

The Pen tool creates paths using Bézier curves
(named after the French designer who devised
them, so legend has it, to design the outline of
the Citroën 2CV in the 1930s). Bézier curves are
unique in that simple curves can be made to fit
any shape: they're easily editable after they've
been drawn, so you needn't worry about getting
the curve perfect first time around – it can
always be adjusted later.

The paths created by the Pen tool have
another great advantage: they can be used
to define selections which can then be stored
within the document when it's saved. Most of
the cutout objects in royalty-free CD collections
are defined with paths.

The problem is that the Pen tool has the
steepest learning curve of all. Here, and on the
following pages, I'll try to help you get to grips
with mastering the essential tool for making
perfect selections.

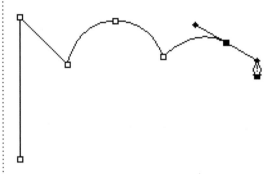

1 To draw straight lines with the Pen tool, simply click
each point. If you want to constrain a line to horizontal,
vertical or 45°, hold down the *Shift* key before clicking the
second point.

4 Because we clicked and didn't drag in step 3, when the
next point is drawn (with a click and drag), the curve
coming out of the back of it joins the previous one with a
hard corner rather than a smooth curve.

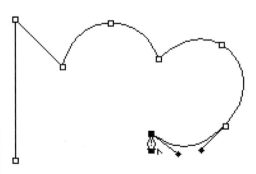

7 If you've clicked and dragged on a point, making a
smooth curve, you can turn it into a corner point instead
by holding *alt* and clicking on the point again. You can
then click and drag on the same point again to make a new
curve from that corner.

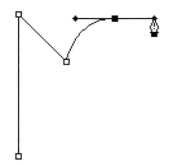

2 If you click and then drag before releasing the button, you'll get a curve. This is the essence of the Pen tool: curves are defined by the anchor points (the dots where you click) and the handles that set their direction and strength.

3 Every time you click and drag, you get a curve; and the point clicked in the previous step shows how the curve operates on both sides of the point. But if you just click without dragging, you make a corner point.

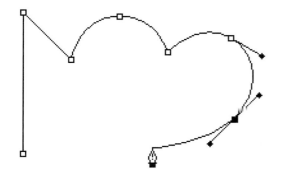

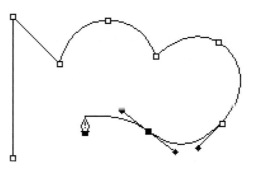

5 The handles operate as tangents to the curve, not crossing it but acting like a surface off which the curve bounces. The points should be placed at positions where the curve changes direction.

6 Sometimes, the handles do appear to cross the curve – but only in cases where the curve is S-shaped, as appears here. The handles are still really tangents to each side of the curve.

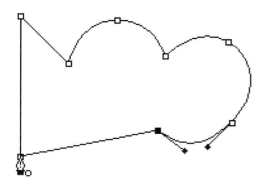

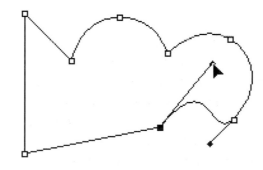

8 When you click on the starting point again, the path will be completed and the anchor points will disappear, showing just the path's outline. You can leave a path open-ended instead, if you like – for example, if you want to stroke it with a painting tool (see pipes and cables in Chapter 12).

9 A path can be adjusted by moving the anchor points, moving the handles, or dragging on the curve itself. Hold ⌘ ctrl to move points with the Pen tool active; or press Ⓐ for the path selection tool – use the filled tool to select an entire path, the hollow version for individual points.

SHORTCUTS
MAC WIN BOTH

The Pen tool by numbers

THE PEN TOOL confuses people more than any other in Photoshop. Here's a step-by-step guide to cutting out a simple object – in this case, a child's toy.

The Photoshop file on the DVD has all the numbers, click points and drag points marked on it, so you can follow the instructions here as you trace around the toy. If you make a mistake, use Undo to go back one point – no need to start again.

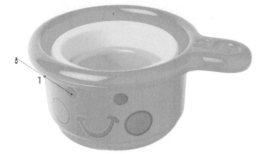

1 Start at the corner point marked 1. Click the pen tool and drag the handle to the red dot to set the direction.

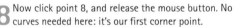
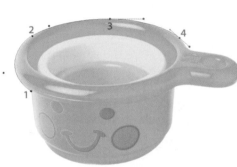

4 Click point 4, and drag just a short way to its red dot: this is a very short curve, so the dot is close to it.

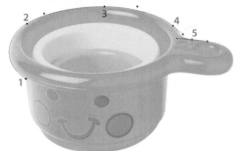

5 Click point 5. The curve will look wrong until you drag to its dot, when the curve behind it will be sorted out.

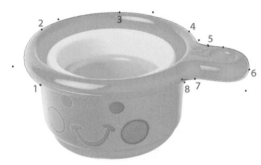

8 Now click point 8, and release the mouse button. No curves needed here: it's our first corner point.

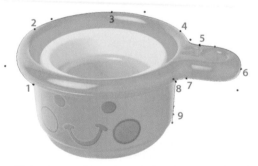

9 Click point 9, and drag downwards a short way to its red dot to start off the next curve.

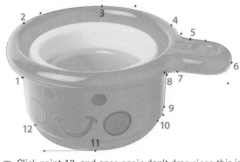

12 Click point 12, and once again don't drag since this is another corner point.

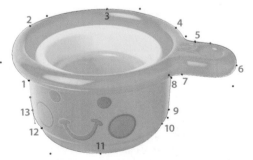

13 Click point 13, halfway round the next curve, and drag to the red dot. Nearly home now!

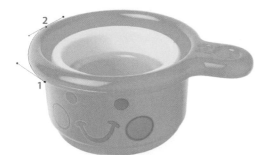

2 Click the point marked 2, and drag to its red dot: this completes the curve behind it, and sets the next.

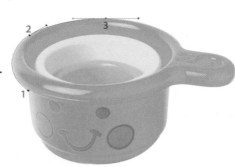

3 Now click point 3, and drag to the red dot. This is the top curve on the toy.

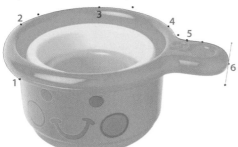

6 Now click point 6, and drag to its red dot: the handles are clearly at a tangent to the curve of the toy.

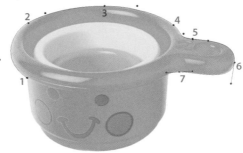

7 Click point 7: once again, it's only a short drag to make the curves both behind and in front of this point.

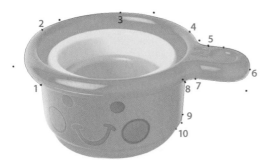

10 Click point 10, but don't drag: once again, this is a corner point, so we don't need a curve here.

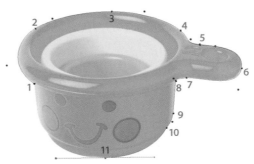

11 Click point 11, right at the bottom, and drag to the red dot to make the large curve along the base.

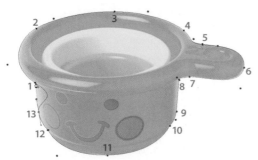

14 Here's what happens when we place the cursor over our starting point: an ugly curve from point 13.

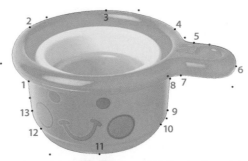

15 Instead, hold _alt_ ⌥ as you click the starting point, to make a corner instead of a curve.

HOT TIP

To make the Pen tool much, much easier to use, make sure it's in Rubber Band mode – this shows you the path you're about to create before you click the tool.

To turn on Rubber Band mode, click the triangle at the end of the Pen Options bar and select it from the pop-up dialog. When you've completed this exercise, try it again without the dots!

SHORTCUTS

MAC WIN BOTH

23

Putting the Pen into practice

ON THE PREVIOUS PAGE we looked at the basics of using the Pen tool using a step-by-step, numbered pattern with all the click and drag points marked. This time, the task is to outline an object without any points on the Photoshop file to show you where to drag to. Of course, you could always just look at the examples here and use the paths shown as a guide.

This is a compound path, in that it includes one element within another. You don't need to do anything to the path within the handle to make it subtract from the main outline: Photoshop will take care of this automatically, as long as the Overlap mode – the final icon of the set of four – is selected from the Path Modes buttons on the Pen Options bar.

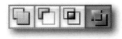

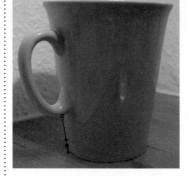

1 Begin by clicking the first point just below the mug's handle, then click and drag down a short way at the bottom of the straight section.

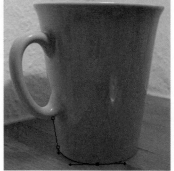

2 Now click and drag at the bottom of the curve: keep your drag horizontal, so it makes a tangent to the curve.

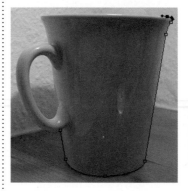

6 Complete this small curve by clicking and dragging just around the corner. Keep the drag parallel to the mug once more.

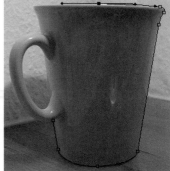

7 Now click and drag at the middle of the top of the mug. This is the mid-point of the curve that makes the mug rim.

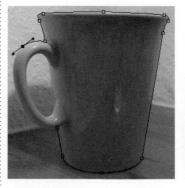

11 Click and drag at the point on the handle where the curve changes direction – just around from the top.

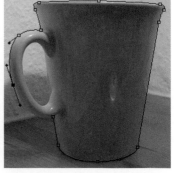

12 Another click and drag, once again where the direction of the curve changes, on the outermost part of the handle.

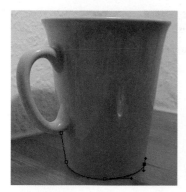

3 Go round the corner, and click and drag a short way up the side of the mug. Drag the handle so that it follows the line of the mug.

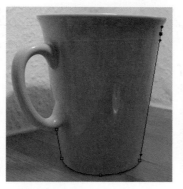

4 Now click at the top of the straight section, and drag a short distance to create the start of the curve that follows.

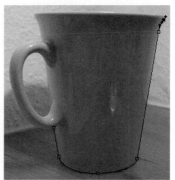

5 Click and drag at the beginning of the lip at the top of the mug: only a short drag is needed to make this curve.

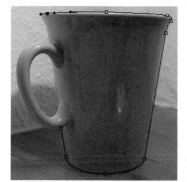

8 Click and drag again at the edge of the rim, just before the lip curve begins.

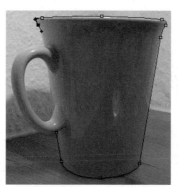

9 Now click and drag once more just around the lip, again keeping the drag parallel to the side of the mug.

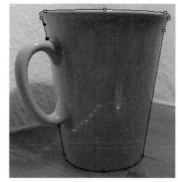

10 Now click at the top of the handle, but don't drag this time: there's a sharp corner here, and we don't want a curve at this point.

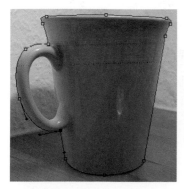

13 Click on the starting point and drag into the mug – it's the back of the handle that defines the curve behind it.

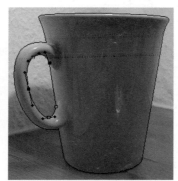

14 Follow the same process to make the inside of the handle, remembering to make corner points where the handle joins the mug.

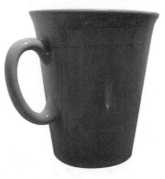

15 With the path complete, you can turn it into a selection using ⌘ Enter ctrl Enter; inverse the selection and delete the background.

SHORTCUTS
MAC WIN BOTH

Losing the edges

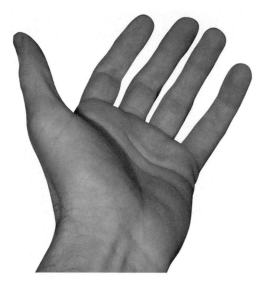

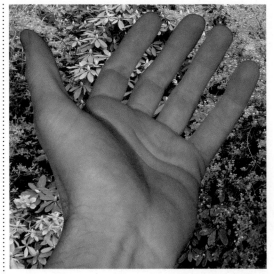

W HETHER YOU ISOLATE AN OBJECT from its background using the Magic Wand tool, or by loading a pre-drawn path, you'll frequently find a slight fringe of the background color surrounding the layer. This is due to the anti-aliasing technique used in Photoshop to ensure a smooth edge.

There are two built-in methods for removing this fringe – Defringe and Remove White Matte. Neither does the job perfectly; here, we'll look at the effects of both these techniques, and at a couple of extra methods that I find work more effectively.

All these techniques assume that the cutout object – the hand, in this case – is on a separate layer from the background.

1 When placed against a complex background such as this foliage, the white fringe on the hand is hard to discern: there's so much visual detail going on behind it that the eye is distracted.

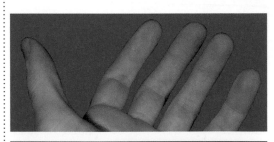

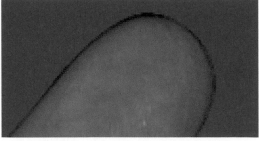

4 The next alternative is Remove White Matte, also found in the Matting menu. Once again, this gets rid of the white area automatically, but tends to result in an unnaturally dark edge on the remaining pixels.

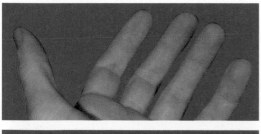

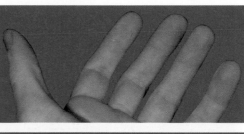

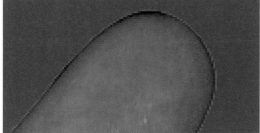

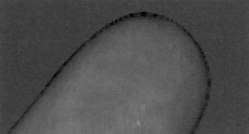

2 Placed against a plain background, we can now see the white fringe more clearly. The lower picture, detailing the tip of the forefinger, shows an enlarged view of the image so that we can see the effect of the different operations we're about to perform.

3 The first method of removing the white is Defringe, found under Layer/Matting. Entering a figure of 1 pixel in the dialog removes the white by sampling the colors just inside the radius specified, and pushing those colors outwards to replace those already there. It gets rid of the white, but is a little clumsy: we tend to get hard blocks of unwanted color this way.

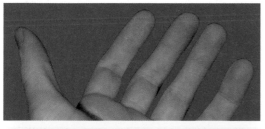

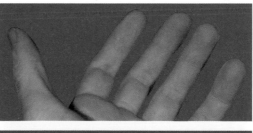

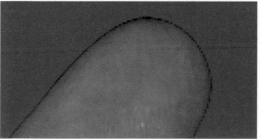

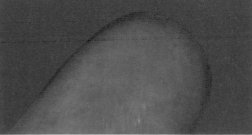

5 My preferred method is to load the layer's selection by ⌘ ctrl clicking on the name, then inverse the selection using ⌘ Shift I ctrl Shift I. Expand the selection by one pixel (Select menu) and then delete – which has the effect of removing a single pixel from all the way round the image. Write an Action to perform this task with a keystroke!

6 There are times when deleting a pixel all the way round doesn't work. In these cases, you need to take a more painstaking approach: lock the transparency of the layer using / and then, using a small soft-edged brush, paint around the edge of the layer, sampling the adjacent colors with the Eyedropper tool frequently as you go.

SHORTCUTS
MAC WIN BOTH

27

Lock and load

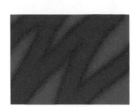

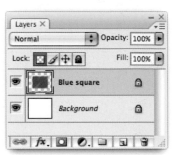

L OCKING TRANSPARENCY is an essential capability to learn, as it allows you to paint on a layer without affecting transparent areas. It's a feature we'll be using throughout this book.

Loading selection areas is another shortcut that you'll see used again and again in the chapters that follow, and it's important to understand how it works. In the example here, we're working on a document that includes three playing cards, on separate layers. We want to create a shadow on a fourth layer, above the other three: by loading up the transparency of the underlying card layers, we can achieve our aim with ease. It's worth noting that the shortcuts for adding to and subtracting from selections are the same as those used for standard selections, as described earlier in this chapter.

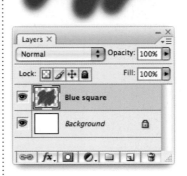

1 Under normal conditions, when we paint on a layer the paint will be applied irrespective of the layer's boundaries, as can be seen here.

2 If we check the Lock Transparency box on the Layers palette, any painting actions are limited to those pixels already present in the layer: they change color, but aren't added to.

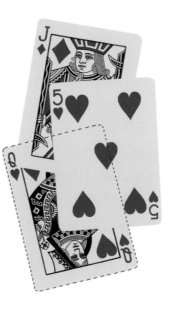

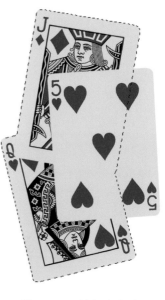

1 Here's another example. Let's load up the Queen of Hearts layer by holding ⌘ ctrl and clicking on the thumbnail in the Layers palette. The outlines show that area selected.

2 We want to add the Jack of Diamonds, so we need an extra key: holding ⌘ Shift ctrl Shift and clicking on its thumbnail will add that layer to the existing selection.

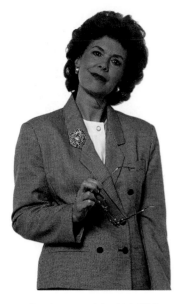

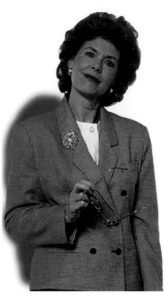

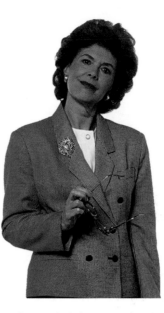

3 So what, you might think. Well, here's a typical example: we want to change the color of this woman's dull jacket into something a little more eye catching.

4 With the Brush tool set to Color mode, we'd expect the color of the jacket to change without affecting the texture. But the color leaks out, polluting the background as well.

5 Once we lock the transparency of the pixels, we can paint our color directly onto the layer without affecting the rest of the artwork; again, only the pixels present are affected.

The shortcut for locking and unlocking transparency is `/`. The trouble is, this is also the shortcut for locking a layer so it can't be painted on, and locking it so it can't be moved. In general, the key will repeat the last action you chose by clicking in the icons on the palette; but if you do find yourself getting a warning that a task couldn't be completed, just go to the palette and uncheck the box.

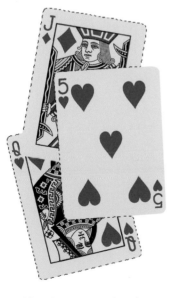

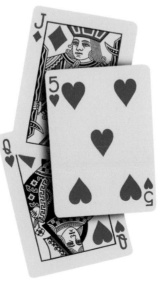

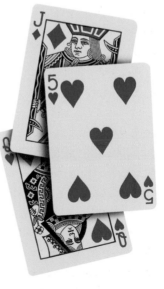

3 We only want to work on the two back cards, so we need to subtract the Five layer. Holding ⌥ ⌘ *alt* *ctrl* while clicking on the thumbnail removes that layer's selection.

4 With our selection made, we can now make a new layer for the shadow and begin to paint – hiding the selection edges first (⌘ H *ctrl* H) so we can see what we're doing.

5 But the Jack has to cast a shadow on the Queen as well. Holding ⌥ ⌘ *alt* *ctrl* while clicking on its name will remove the Jack's selection, and we can add the shadow we want.

Find and replace

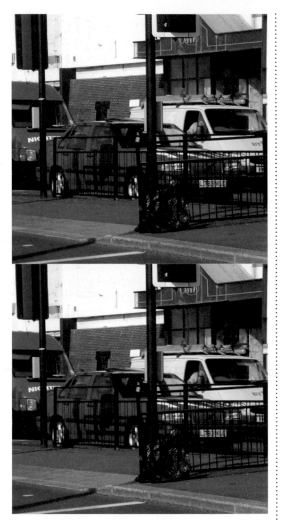

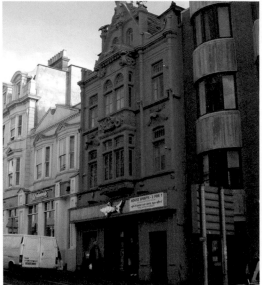

1 The brash blue of this once-elegant Victorian building may not appeal to all tastes. It certainly doesn't appeal to mine, so let's change it to something more environmentally friendly. Choose Image/Adjust/Replace Color to get started.

CHANGING THE COLOR of the car above from red to blue would be an almost impossible task by conventional means: all those railings in the way would make selecting the car something of a nightmare. But by using Replace Color, we can adjust the hue selectively without having to lay hands on a single selection or painting tool.

Replace Color is a hugely powerful tool that turns what would otherwise be a complex task into one that's enjoyable and effective.

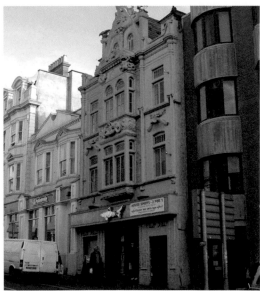

4 To add more colors, hold the *Shift* key and click on an unchanged area, or drag to select a range of colors: that range will be added to the selection, and the color will change in the image. If you select a spot by accident, hold *⌥* *alt* while clicking to deselect that color.

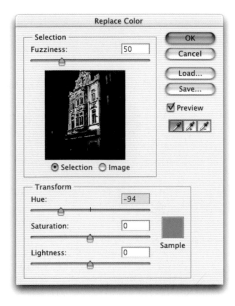

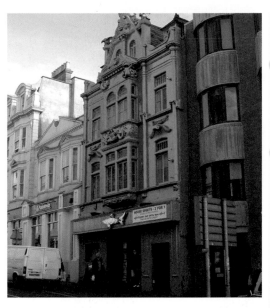

2 By default, the Replace Color dialog shows a monochrome view of what's been selected: white is active, black isn't. By clicking on the image, regions of that color become selected. When you change the Hue value, the image changes to reflect that, as seen in the next step.

3 Here's the result of our initial change, and we're turning the building green. It doesn't matter what color you choose to begin with; go for something bright, so you can see the change. So far, only a portion of the face of the building has changed color.

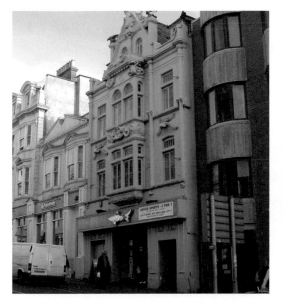

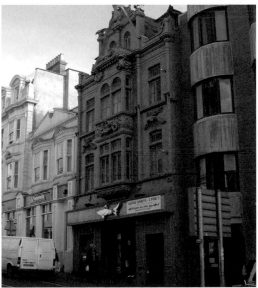

5 Keep adding more color ranges until the entire building is altered. One way of increasing the range of colors changed is to raise the Fuzziness value; but this draws in unwanted colors in the surrounding area, as can be seen in the color change in the windows of the neighboring building.

6 Now we're sure the building is selected, we can change the hue to a shade more in keeping with its surroundings. It may not be painted white like the building to the left of it, but it certainly blends into the street better than it did before.

HOT TIP

There are often areas in the surrounding image that are close to the target color range, and they will get changed as well. One solution is to duplicate the layer, apply Replace Color, and then simply erase or mask the parts you didn't want to change.

SHORTCUTS
MAC WIN BOTH

Color by numbers

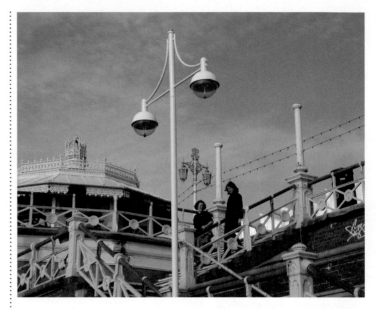

T HE SELECT COLOR
command works in
precisely the same way as the
Replace Color dialog detailed
on the previous page, except
that rather than changing the
hue it returns a selection.

This makes it the ideal
tool for changing elements
such as the sky, as shown in
this example: with the sky
isolated from the original
image, we can paste in any
cloud formation we want to
strengthen and add drama to
the image. Here, we've taken
a sunny day on the Brighton
seafront and made the scene
altogether more doom-laden
simply by replacing the sky
with something a touch more
dramatic.

1 This image shows a complex skyline, with many fiddly elements punctuating the heavens – from the street light to the strings of bulbs stretched between them, to the ornate roof on the building on the left. An impossible job using the Lasso tool: but there's a better way. Choose Select/Color Range to begin the operation.

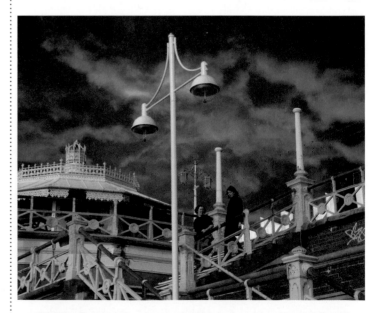

3 With the sky selected, open any other sky you have lying around. Select All (⌘ A / ctrl A) and Copy (⌘ C / ctrl C), then paste it inside the selected area: use Shift ⌘ V / Shift ctrl V or choose Paste Into from the Edit menu. The new sky will be positioned within the selection, and you can move or scale it as required. It will move independently of the area you've just pasted it inside.

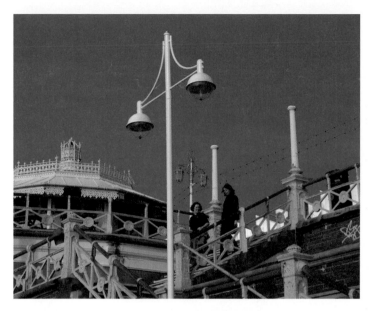

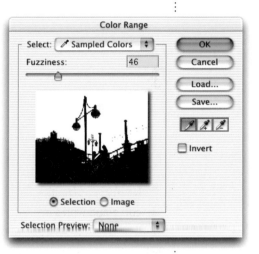

2 The dialog works in the same way as Replace Color: the main difference is that the selected area is shown on the image as a QuickMask selection, although you can change this using the pop-up menu. Use *Shift* and ⌥ *alt* as before, to add and subtract colors to and from the selected range, until the entire sky is selected.

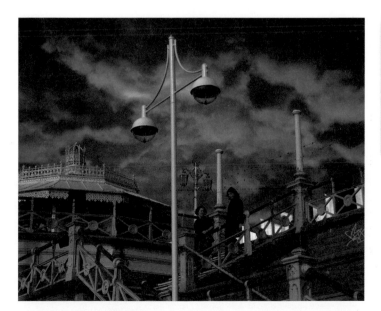

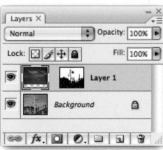

4 Choosing Paste Into creates a layer mask that exactly matches the original selection – see Chapter 3 for more about how to use layer masks. We can now paint on the mask to remove pieces of sky from regions where it shouldn't have appeared, such as halfway up the railings on the left. We'll also take this opportunity to adjust the foreground image to match the new sky's colors.

HOT TIP

If you've performed a Select Color operation and want to repeat it exactly, hold ⌥ *alt* as you select it again from the menu. It will reappear with the same settings already loaded up. Holding this modifier will reload the last settings for any of the color adjustments as well.

Brush-on color

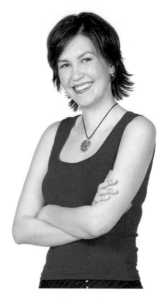

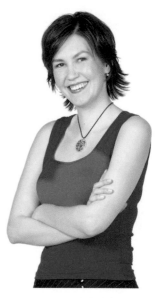

T HE COLOR REPLACEMENT TOOL performs a task almost identical to the Replace Color dialog, discussed earlier in this chapter, but it has one significant advantage: you can paint the new color directly onto the image, without having to go through a dialog first.

In one way, it's simply more satisfying to paint the new color straight on. But there are many other advantages to the new tool: where Replace Color would globally change one color for another, the brush allows us to mix our colors at will. In addition, we can control the area we color with more precision than we could with the dialog.

The settings that determine the way the Color Replacement tool operates are the same as those used by the Background Eraser tool, covered later in this book: take a look at The perfect haircut in Chapter 8 to see how to change the settings for both these tools.

1 Here's our model, wearing a bright red shirt. In color terms, it's pretty close to the skin tones, so the Replace Color dialog would have some difficulty with this image; the Color Replacement Brush is the perfect solution.

2 To begin, choose a color and set a tolerance of around 50%, then paint a test patch. You should watch to see that the color covers all the areas you want, and doesn't leak into unwanted skin regions.

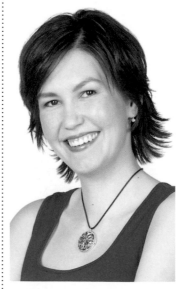

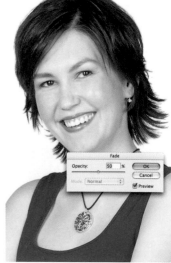

6 Here, we'll use the same tool to change the model's hair color from black to brown. In order to make this process work, you need to complete the whole coloring operation in a single brushstroke. Far too bright – let's fix it.

7 Press ⌘ *Shift* *F* *ctrl* *Shift* *F* to bring up the Fade dialog immediately after brushing on the color: now we can reduce the strength of the last operation by dragging the slider, to make it more realistic.

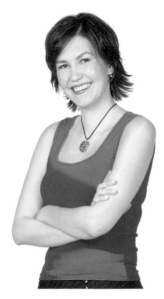

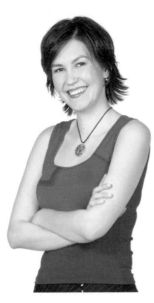

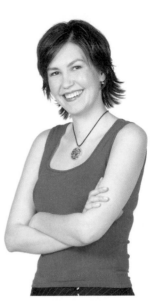

3 Here's what happens if you choose the wrong settings. At the top, too high a tolerance means the skin is being changed along with the shirt; at the bottom, too low a tolerance means not enough of the shirt is changed.

4 Try to change all contiguous areas of color in one go. If you start with a small patch, as we did in step 2, and then carry on with a new brushstroke in the same area you'll get an ugly join which can be hard to get rid of.

5 Because the top half and the bottom half of the shirt are split in two by the arms, we can treat each as a separate region. By coloring each section in one go, we maintain an evenness of color throughout.

HOT TIP

There are three 'sampling' modes for the Color Replacement Brush: Once, which only samples the first time you click; Continuous, which keeps sampling the color beneath the crosshair as you paint; and Background Swatch, which uses the current background color. Once is the most controllable method to use; only choose Contiguous if there are strong variations in shading.

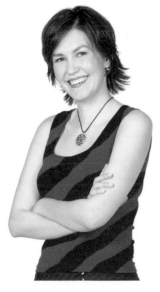

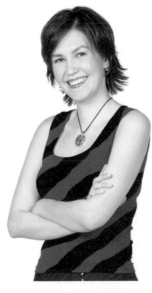

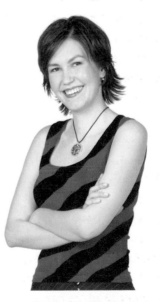

8 In general, you'd want to use a soft-edged brush for this tool. Here, we'll paint tiger stripes onto the shirt by using a hard-edged brush. We'll begin by painting the black stripes, in Color mode.

9 Although the last step changed the color, it didn't make the stripes darker. To do this, we need to change the brush mode to Luminosity instead. Now, when we brush over the changed areas, we make them darker as well.

10 Change the brush mode back to Color, and pick a bright orange. We can now change all the remaining red using the new color, to create this convincing tiger pattern on the shirt.

SHORTCUTS
MAC WIN BOTH

35

The perfect setup

GETTING THE BEST OUT OF PHOTOSHOP means making the application behave the way you want it to. This may mean investing in memory and additional hard disk space, as well as taking care arranging your palettes.

Photoshop needs as much memory as you can give it. RAM is cheaper now than it has ever been: if you're serious about Photoshop, you should be looking at a total system RAM configuration of at least a Gigabyte – more if you can manage it. The more real RAM (rather than Virtual Memory) Photoshop has available to it, the faster it will run.

Even with enormous amounts of RAM, Photoshop will still write huge temporary files. It deletes these when you quit the application, so you're unlikely to notice them, but they can run into hundreds of megabytes. If your main hard disk is used as a 'scratch disk' Photoshop will be reduced to fitting these files in whatever spaces it can find; they'll be so fragmented that the whole process will become slowed down.

The best solution is to buy a second hard disk of at least 4Gb in size, or partition a larger disk, and assign this to be Photoshop's scratch disk – you do this using File / Preferences / Plug-ins and Scratch Disks. Resist the temptation to put anything else on this disk: keeping a large, clean disk spare for the exclusive use of Photoshop will greatly speed up its processing power (to say nothing of reducing fragmentation on your main hard drive).

Even with a clean scratch disk, Photoshop will still have to wade through its large temporary files, particularly if you're working on big images. Get into the habit of using the Purge All command (Edit menu) every time you're sure you won't want to undo what you've just done, use the History palette or paste an item from the clipboard. This will clear out the temporary files, and can often take a minute or so to accomplish – which gives you some idea of how large these files can get.

The interface has changed in Photoshop CS3. You can set up your frequently used palettes by storing them as icons attached to the Layers palette, so they

The toolbar can now be displayed as a single column, rather than double: this saves space so you can see your image more clearly

Dock your frequently used palettes as icons. They'll appear when you click on them, and disappear when you've finished.

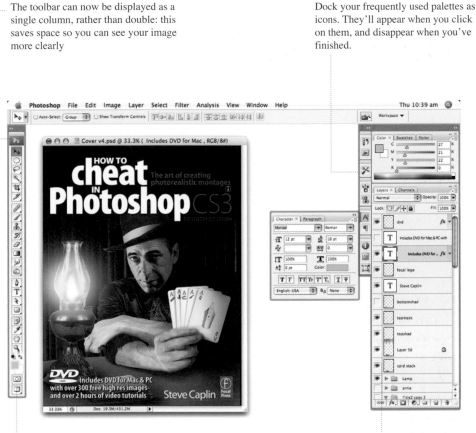

Click this icon to see the image alone against a gray background, or against black with menus hidden: use the F key to cycle through the options.

Don't dock the Layers or Color palettes as icons – you'll need these constantly on view.

can be accessed with a single click; you can set them up in the Preferences dialog so they vanish when you click elsewhere. But if you want to see the image you're working on uncluttered by any screen debris, press the Tab key and all the palettes, including the Toolbar and Options bar, will disappear. Press the Tab key once more to bring them back. Don't put the Layers palette into the Palette Well, since you won't want that to keep disappearing.

If you're working on montages that contain a large number of layers, make new layer groups to hold them. If you want to make a new group from existing layers, the simplest way is to select them and then choose *New Group from Layers* from the pop-up menu on the Layers palette. Remember that you can also duplicate entire groups, which makes it easy to try out multiple variations.

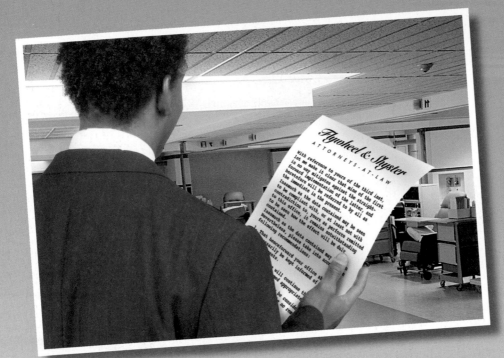

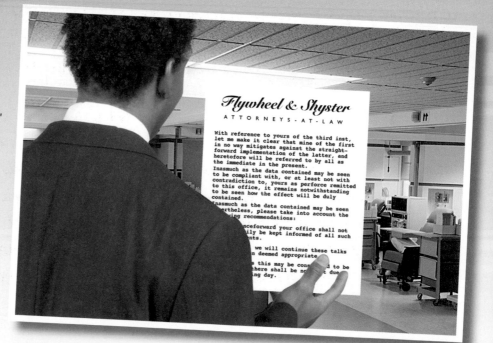

■ Two views over this lawyer's shoulder. The top image shows him holding a realistic sheet of paper; in the bottom picture, he's holding a letter that appears unnaturally stiff, as if it has been pasted onto a sheet of card. Transforming the sheet was the work of just a few seconds, yet can make all the difference when creating a realistic montage.

2 Transformation and distortion

PHOTOMONTAGE IS ABOUT COMBINING images from
a variety of sources. And unless you're very, very lucky,
you'll need to at least change the scale of some of these
images to make them fit with the rest of the picture. You
may also need to distort and modify them in other ways.

Photoshop CS2 brought us Image Warp, a sophisticated
and powerful tool for creating twisted, bulging, curved
and stretched distortions. It's the feature users have
been asking for since Photoshop first appeared. We'll
be looking at how to use it later on in the chapter. First,
though, we'll go through some of the basic concepts
– and some that are not so basic – that make up Free
Transform mode.

The Free Transform tool

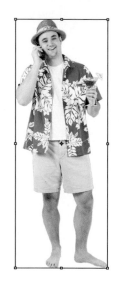

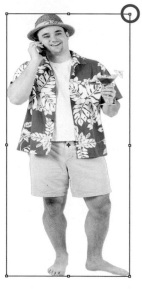

A LL PHOTOSHOP WORK involves distorting layers – whether it's simply scaling them so they fit next to each other, or producing complex perspective distortions to match the view in an existing scene.

Free Transform mode is the key to scaling, rotating, shearing and distorting layers. If just one layer is selected, you'll affect just that layer; but if more than one is selected, the distortion will occur on all the layers simultaneously. Similarly, if a layer set is chosen, then the transformation will affect the entire set in one go.

The Free Transform bounding box has eight handles around its perimeter, and each one transforms the layer in a different way. In addition, you can hold down a variety of modifier keys to change the method of transformation, as detailed here.

1 Enter Free Transform mode by pressing `ctrl` `T` `⌘` `T`. A bounding box will appear around the current layer, or group of layers if more than one is selected. To commit a transformation, press `Return`.

2 If you grab a corner handle and drag it, you'll scale the layer. The corner you drag will move, and the opposite corner remains where it is. Think of the layer as pinned by the corner opposite the one you drag.

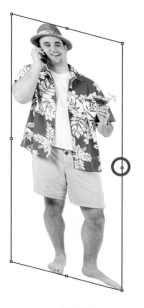

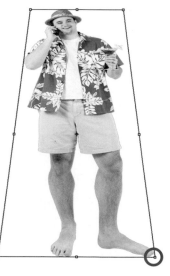

6 If you hold `ctrl` `⌘` as you drag a center side handle, you'll shear the layer. Adding `Shift` forces Photoshop to shear in just the horizontal or vertical dimensions.

7 To create a perspective effect, hold `ctrl` `alt` `Shift` `⌘` `⌥` `Shift` as you drag a corner handle. The direction of drag produces a horizontal or vertical distortion.

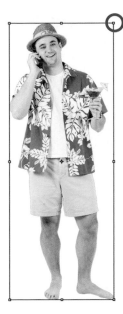

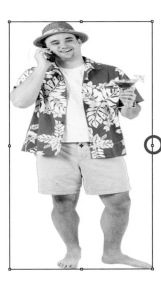

3 Holding the *Shift* key as you drag a corner handle maintains the proportions of the original. Use this when you want to make a layer bigger or smaller, but don't want to change its shape.

4 If you grab a center side handle on the left or right, you'll scale a layer only horizontally. If you grab a top or bottom center handle, you'll scale it vertically.

5 When you position the cursor outside the bounding box and drag, you rotate the layer. The further away from the bounding box you start, the more control you'll get over the rotation amount.

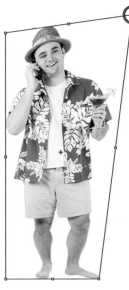

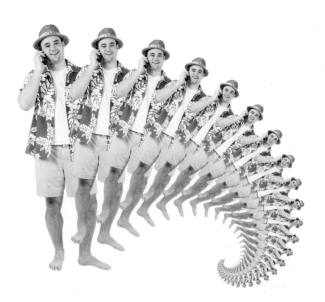

8 Holding just *ctrl* ⌘ as you drag a corner handle distorts the layer in a freeform manner. You can move each of the corner handles to create complex distortions.

9 To repeat the last transformation exactly, press *ctrl* *Shift* *T* ⌘ *Shift* *T*. This can be useful if you distort a layer and then find you should have made some changes to

it first: you can Undo, then perform the transformation again. If you press *ctrl* *alt* *Shift* *T* ⌘ *alt* *Shift* *T*, however, you'll *duplicate* the last transformation, as shown here.

HOT TIP

Scaling by dragging a handle will always 'pin' the transformation at the opposite corner or side handle. But if you hold *alt* ⌥ as you drag, you'll scale around the center instead – that is, around the center marker. You can move this marker anywhere in your artwork to make that the point around which each transformation takes place.

SHORTCUTS
MAC **WIN** **BOTH**

Step and repeat rotation

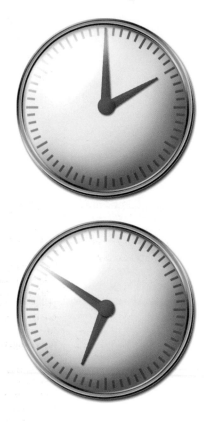

THE STEP AND REPEAT PROCESS mentioned on the previous page can be used to create regular patterns and arrays. The success of the operation depends largely on where you place the center marker: here, we'll demonstrate the techniques by building a simple clock face.

It's easiest to find the center point of the clock if you create two guidelines first, by dragging them in from the rulers (you'll need to show the rulers if you can't see them already). Make a vertical and a horizontal guide so that they cross in the center of the artwork.

Once the basic clock is complete, it's easy to change the position of the hands to make them tell any time you want.

1 Begin by drawing a tiny rectangle, on a new layer, and filling it with color. This will be the starting point for all the ticks around the perimeter of our clock face.

2 Now enter Free Transform. We want to rotate around the center, so grab the center marker (it's easier to get if you hold *alt* ⌥) and drag it vertically downwards.

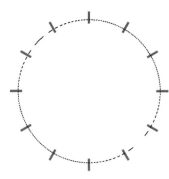

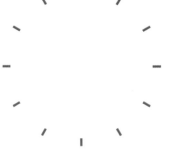

6 Now to make the minute markers. Duplicate the layer, and make an elliptical selection that includes around half of each marker.

7 Now delete to shorten each marker. Here, I've hidden the original hour markers so we can see the difference.

11 Now for the hands. On a new layer, make a simple rectangle and fill it with red. It should be centered on the 12 o'clock position, with its base at the clock center.

12 To make the hand pointed, hold *ctrl* *Shift* *alt* ⌘ *Shift* ⌥ as you drag a top corner handle: this will produce a symmetrical distortion, making a simple triangle.

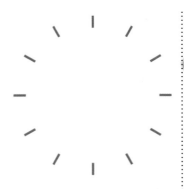

3 Hold **Shift** as you drag outside the bounding box to rotate, and it will jump to 15° steps. We want 30° to mark the hour points on the clock, so move it two steps round.

4 That transformation moved the original marker. Undo, then press **ctrl Shift alt T ⌘ Shift ⌥ T** to repeat the transformation: this time, it will rotate a copy of the original layer.

5 Continue pressing **ctrl Shift alt T ⌘ Shift ⌥ T** another ten times, and each time another marker will be added around the clock face. Then select and merge all the layers.

HOT TIP

It's easy to end up with too many layers using this technique – 60 of them, in fact. So take the opportunity to merge layers together whenever appropriate, by selecting them and choosing Merge Layers from the Layer menu, or pressing **ctrl E ⌘ E**.

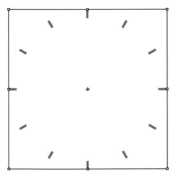

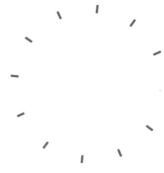

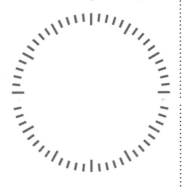

8 Enter Free Transform. We need to rotate by 6° this time, so enter this figure in the Rotate field in the Options bar: △ 6 ° | H: 0.0 ° | V: 0.0 °

9 Here's our shortened minute marker layer, rotated by 6°. (360° divided by 60, the number of minutes in an hour, if you're wondering.)

10 Press **ctrl Shift alt T ⌘ Shift ⌥ T** three times, and all the minutes will appear. The hour markers are shown here again.

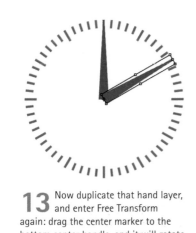

13 Now duplicate that hand layer, and enter Free Transform again: drag the center marker to the bottom center handle, and it will rotate around that point.

14 Before leaving Free Transform, we need to make this hand shorter. So grab the top center handle, and drag it towards the center of the clock: we now have an hour hand.

15 All we need to do now is cover up that ugly join in the center. That's easily done by making a new layer, and filling a circular selection with the same color as the hands.

SHORTCUTS
MAC **WIN** **BOTH**

43

Introducing Image Warp

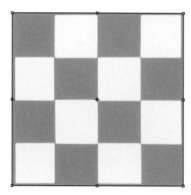

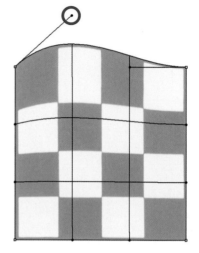

IMAGE WARP IS THE FEATURE Photoshop users had requested more than any other. In the first two editions of this book, I devoted a lot of space to methods of distorting and curving images using the Shear filter, a fiddly and often frustrating process: now that's all history.

Image Warp is a special mode of Free Transform, and it's entered by going into Free Transform mode and pressing the Image Warp button on the Options bar, over on the right.

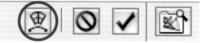

There are several preset modes within Image Warp, which we'll look at shortly. But the default is the versatile Custom mode, which uses an array of control handles to allow the user to distort layers in different ways. Here, we'll begin by examining how the different handles affect the shape of the distortion.

1 When you enter Warp mode, a grid of lines appears. Each of the corner points of the grid has two Bézier handles which change the direction of the line coming from that corner: move these, and you'll turn the straight line into a curve. The image will warp to fit that curve.

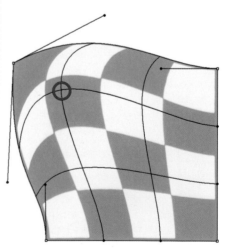

4 There are also four more control vertices, located at the intersections of the grid lines within the grid itself. And again, these operate independently of all the other control points. In total, this makes 24 separate controls with which to distort the grid.

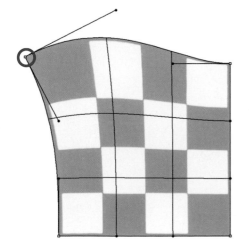

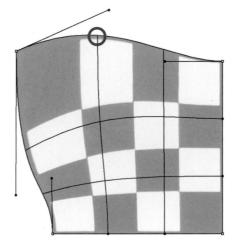

2 As well as moving the handles, you can move the corners themselves. The handles associated with each corner, however, will remain in the same place as you drag the corner – they operate independently of their corners.

3 There are two further control points on each side of the bounding grid. Each of these can also be dragged to create distortions at that point: once again, they operate independently of both the corners and the corner Bézier curve handles.

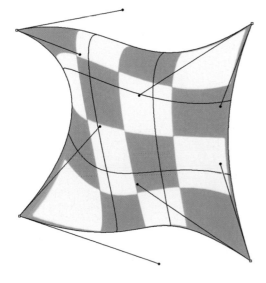

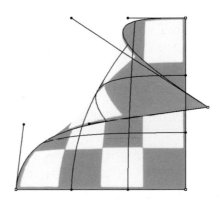

5 By using a variety of these control points together, you can create just about any kind of distortion you want. Unlike third-party plug-ins which have previously attempted this task, the results are perfectly accurate: and the benefit is that you work on the artwork, not through a dialog.

6 You can even distort an image so that it wraps back on itself, producing this page curl effect. This one's great for creating paper distortions. To enhance the effect, add a shadow beneath the curled portion onto the underlying layer. (You may need to split it into two layers first.)

Image Warp in combination

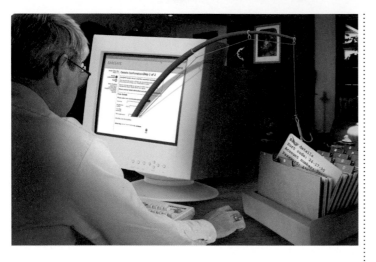

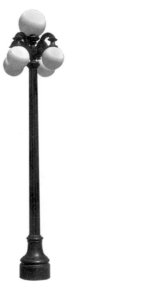

PRESET WARP MODES offer a good range of possibilities: there are plenty of useful presets to help you get started, and they're found in the pop-up menu on the tool's Options bar (it will read Custom by default). Often, however, they don't give us precisely the control we need for a particular job. But Custom Warp can be unwieldy, given so many available control points; the result can just be a confusion of lines and anchors.

In these circumstances, it makes sense to begin with the preset warp mode that best fits the image you're working on, and then switch into Custom Warp mode for fine tuning the effect.

Warps can be used for even the simplest task. The illustration above was for the Sunday Telegraph: the fishing pole was drawn as a straight line, then bent using the Arc preset, fine-tuned with Custom mode.

1 Here's the problem: we want to distort this lamp post so it looks as if the dog is pulling it over. We'll need to attach a lead as well, of course. Before Image Warp, this simple task would have involved a lot of chopping and fiddling about: now, it's a straightforward job.

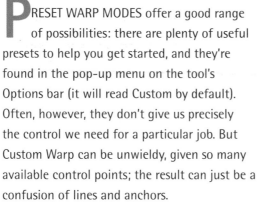

4 On the Tool Options bar is a button that changes the direction of those presets that have directional effects. Press it, and the Rise warp will switch from vertical to horizontal. Drag the control handle, top left, to the angle you want the lamp post to have.

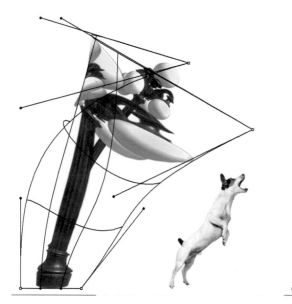

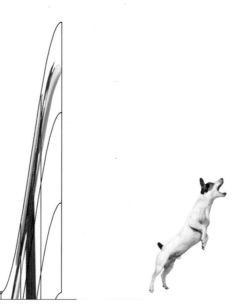

2 Enter Free Transform mode and press the Image Warp button on the toolbar. It would, just, be possible to distort this lamp post using solely the Custom Warp handles, but frankly it's barely worth the bother. You're more likely to get yourself in a terrible mess, such as this one.

3 Instead, we can start with the preset warp that most closely fits our needs. In this case, it's the Rise warp, so choose it from the pop-up list that currently says Custom. You'll notice that the layer disappears off the bottom of the page: we need to change the way Rise bends.

HOT TIP

The trick here is to try to keep the top of the lamp, with the five glass globes, as undistorted as possible. It does involve some fiddling with the anchor points and handles to achieve this: you may find it easier simply to copy the top from the original lamp post, then rotate it and stick it in place afterwards.

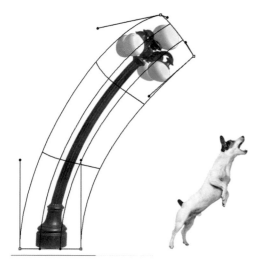

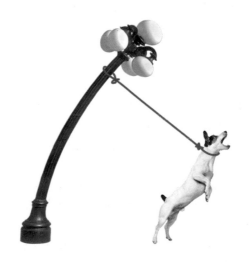

5 Now change the pop-up menu back to Custom Warp, and you'll find that the custom handles reappear around the perimeter – but with the Rise warp still applied. It's now a relatively easy matter to move the top handles and vertices to bend the top of the lamp post over.

6 The dog's leash is created by drawing it as a pen path first. Then, with the path still visible, switch to the Brush tool and choose a small, hard-edged brush: pressing *Enter* will stroke the path with that brush, using the current foreground color.

47

Cloning in perspective

PHOTOSHOP'S CLONE TOOL, sometimes referred to as the Rubber Stamp, has undergone a massive enhancement with CS3. As well as now having the ability to store up to five clone sources per image, we've also been given the capability to rotate and scale our images as we clone them.

None of this would be any use, of course, if we couldn't see what we were doing before beginning the clone operation. So the Clone tool now has the option of showing a ghosted overlay on top of the image, showing exactly where the operation will take its effect.

It's a great improvement, bringing the tool's functionality firmly up to date.

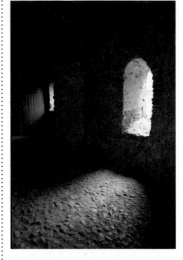

1 Here's our starting image: an old stone building, with a pair of windows casting their light on the ground. We're going to duplicate the near window in perspective, to achieve a seamless blend as it slots into the existing wall.

2 Open the Clone Source palette, and click the Show Overlay button. This will produce a ghosted version of the image to be cloned. Just to be on the safe side, make a new layer so we don't work directly on the base image; and be sure to set the Clone tool to Sample All Layers on the Options bar.

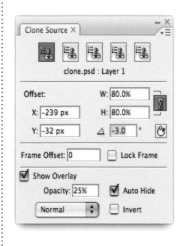

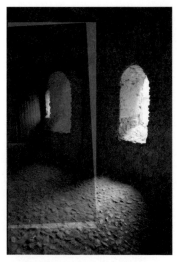

6 The new Clone tool now allows us to rotate the clone source as well. Click in the Rotate field, and press the up and down cursor keys to change the angle: the overlay will rotate as you do so. In this case, an angle of –3.0° produces exactly the right rotation.

7 The overlay now shows the ghosted image to be cloned in place, with the scaling and rotation as we set them. The advantage of the overlay system is clear: we can see exactly what we're going to get before we begin to clone.

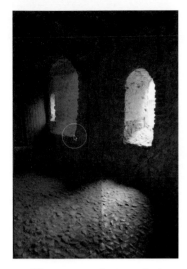

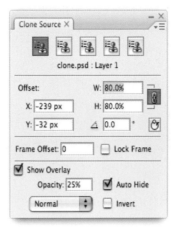

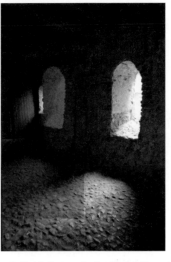

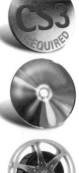

3 When we move the cursor back into the image, we can see the overlay: it follows the cursor around as we move it. Hold ⌥ *alt* and click the bottom right corner of the existing image to mark the clone source. Now click where you want the cloning to begin painting on the image.

4 In step 3, we clicked to mark the point where cloning should begin. Undo that with ⌘ Z *ctrl* Z to remove the first cloning operation: the overlay will stay in place. Because the window is too large for its perspective, we need to reduce it. A scale of around 80% works well here.

5 Here's the result of reducing the scale of our window. This is still the overlay: we haven't started cloning yet. But we can see a problem here. In order to match the perspective in the scene, we need to rotate the cloned copy slightly so that it matches the distortion caused by the camera lens.

Check the Auto Hide button on the Clone Source palette to make the overlay disappear while you're cloning – far easier to see what you're doing that way. In all the numerical fields, you can use the up and down cursor keys to raise and lower the values: hold *Shift* as you do so to change them by ten times, then release the key for fine adjustments.

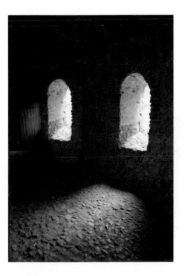

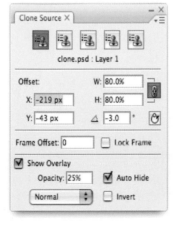

8 Time to start cloning. Choose a brush appropriate to the size of the window, and begin to paint the new one in. When you release the moues button, the overlay will reappear; hold the Space Bar to hide it temporarily.

9 The light cast by the window, as seen in the overlay in step 7, is too far from the window itself, resulting in a poor impression of perspective. So, back in the Clone Source dialog, tweak the Offset numbers in order to bring the light closer to the wall.

10 With the offset corrected, we can now continue to clone the light onto the floor. Because we're using a soft edged brush, the blend is seamless; but it's just as well to clone onto a new layer, so we can edit out mistakes if we need to.

Special effects with cloning

ON THE PREVIOUS PAGES we looked at the basics of using offset, scaling and rotation to introduce the new features in the CS3 Clone tool. Here, we'll examine some of the special effects that can be produced using a combination of these techniques.

All these examples depend on working on a new layer, *behind* the target layer. This is essential to making the techniques work: be sure, also, that you have the Clone tool set to Sample All Layers, or you'll be cloning nothing at all.

This is just a taste of the sort of effects that can be achieved using this powerful, innovative new tool.

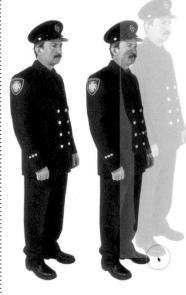

1 Here's a security guard: we'll make a whole row of them. Begin by holding ⌥ *alt* as you click the very bottom of the guard's shoe to set the source point; then click the equivalent point behind him, to set the position.

2 Undo that last click operation, and turn to the Clone Source palette. A scale of around 90% produces the efect we want here; you may wish to fiddle with the offset values as well, to make sure the perspective is right.

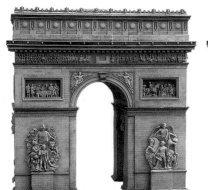

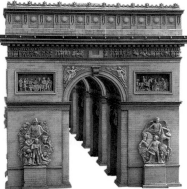

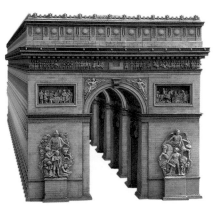

6 We can apply exactly the same principle to architectural images as well. In this case, we'll begin with this view of a triumphal arch that already has some perspective built into it.

7 As with the guard, click the bottom point of the inside of the arch, and adjust the scaling and offsets until the perspective is correct. Each time you apply the Clone tool, you'll create another set of arches behind.

8 We can apply a similar process to the left side of the arch, so that its apparent depth matches that indicated by the arches within. You'll need to set new offset and scale values to make the effect work, though.

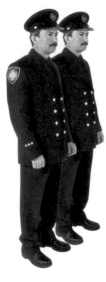

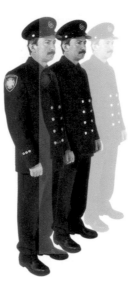

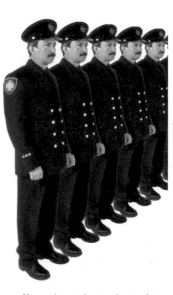

3 On a new empty layer, behind the current (guard) layer, begin to clone the new guard in with a single brush stroke that paints in the entire guard in one step. And there he is, perfectly placed next to the original.

4 When you now release the mouse button, you'll see that the Overlay now updates itself to show a third guard ghosted behind the other two. That's because the Clone tool is now sampling the second guard as well.

5 No need to make new layers: just keep cloning. Each time you clone a guard and release the mouse button, an additional guard will appear on the Overlay. We can make as many as we want, disappearing into the distance.

The key to making these techniques work is to get the perspective right when setting the scale and offset values for the initial cloning operation. There are usually clues in the picture: with the guard, the vanishing points are clearly shown by the eye line and the angles of the bottom rows of buttons on his jacket.

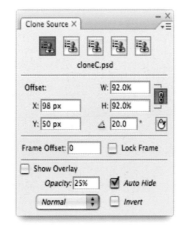

Clone Source ×

cloneC.psd

Offset: W: 92.0%

X: 98 px   H: 92.0%

Y: 50 px   △ 20.0 °

Frame Offset: 0   ☐ Lock Frame

☐ Show Overlay

     Opacity: 25%   ☑ Auto Hide

     Normal   ☐ Invert

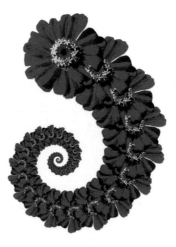

9 Further effects can be obtained by including rotation with scaling. In this example, we'll use this simple cutout of a flower to create a striking graphic image.

10 It can take a little experimentation to get the position and angles right. Here, an angle of 20° with a scale factor of 90% gives us the effect we want.

11 By repeating the cloning process a number of times, we're able to build this spiral of flowers which disappears into the center of the illustration. Simple, but effective.

Transformation in practice

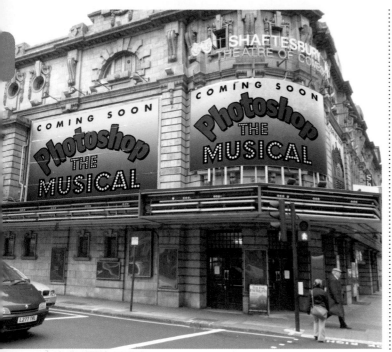

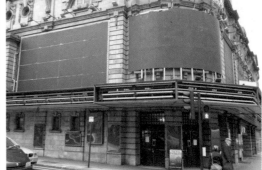

A SINGLE PHOTOMONTAGE JOB can easily include a variety of transformation techniques, and it's important to know which one to use for each task.

However much twisting, turning and stretching you might do during a single Free Transform operation, the final layer isn't rendered until you hit the *Enter* button or click inside the Transform area. This means you can scale up and down, as much as you like, during the process – and it's this that makes difficult transformations much easier to perform.

In this example, we'll look at how we can use two different transformation methods to apply new signs to this closed theater.

1 I was fortunate enough to be passing this theater when it was closed, and the old hoardings had been taken down. True, we could have just covered up any hoardings that were there – but we can make use of those blank posters, as they have a great texture.

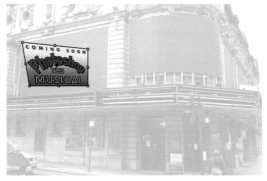

4 Now we'll try to distort the poster to fit the hoarding. With it reduced and placed in the center of the space, we can see the four corners around it: so begin by holding *ctrl* ⌘ as you drag one corner up to fit the corner of the hoarding.

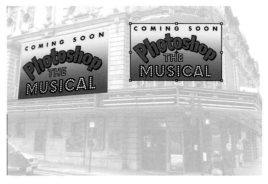

7 Press *Enter* to commit that Free Transform, and make the original poster visible again. This poster needs to be warped to fit that round corner on the theater. Begin by entering Free Transform, and shrink the poster down so it's the correct width for the site.

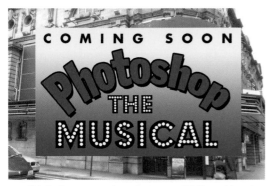

2 This is the poster we're going to use. We'll need it twice during the course of this montage, so remember to duplicate it before distorting it the first time: you can always hide the original while working on the duplicate, but if you don't make a copy you'll have to undo all your work.

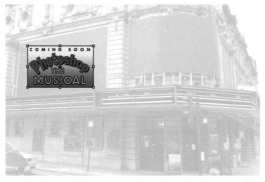

3 I've knocked the background opacity right back so we can see what's going on more clearly. We'll begin with that hoarding on the side: enter Free Transform with ctrl T ⌘ T and shrink the poster down so that all four corners of the site are visible. It doesn't matter that it's too small!

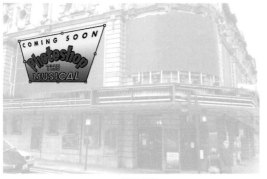

5 Dragging while holding ctrl ⌘ produces a non-symmetric, freeform distortion, which is exactly what we want here. We can now drag the second corner into place at the top right of this hoarding. Don't click inside the Free Transform area yet!

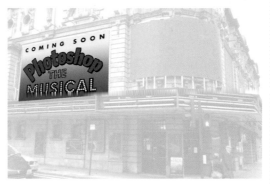

6 Now drag the remaining two corners into place. The job is slightly complicated by the fact that we can't see the bottom right corner — it's obscured by the box on the front of the theater. But we can work out where that point should go by watching how the perspective distorts the poster.

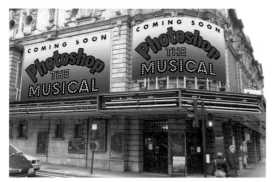

8 As described on the previous page, we need a combination of Warps now: first Arch, to get the basic curve, and then switch to Custom for fine tuning. Here are the two posters, in place, with the background returned to full opacity.

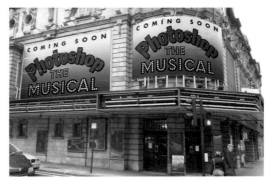

9 By the end of the previous step the posters may have fitted the space, but they didn't look convincing: we couldn't see any shading or texturing. Changing the Layer mode, at the top of the Layers Palette, to Overlay for both posters helps. There's more about Layer modes in Chapter 3.

HOT TIP

Perspective transformation, such as that outlined in steps 3 to 6, is remarkably easy when the target is so clearly defined: you just drag the corners of your object to the corners that are already marked. Perspective isn't always so forgiving, though: there's much more about this thorny topic in Chapter 6.

SHORTCUTS
MAC WIN BOTH

53

The freelance artist

FOR THE FREELANCER, working at home is one of the main attractions of the job. It can also be one of the major drawbacks.

The advantages are plentiful. No need to worry about bus and train times; no commuting; and above all, no office politics. On the down side, there's the problem that you're always at work, even when you're off-duty. In order to complete the first edition of this book I had to rent a flat at the seaside simply to get away from the telephone: it's hard to complete a long-term project when the telephone's constantly offering you short-term work.

When you work at home, it's important that you have a separate room in which to work. Partly it's because you need somewhere you know won't be littered with washing, children's toys and bicycle parts; but mainly, so you can escape in the evening and get back to reality. In the days when I used to have my computer set up in the back of the living room I felt I could never completely get away from it.

I now never work at weekends. It's a golden rule that I break only two or three times a year, and even then it's only when I'm called out to deliver a lecture or seminar. I occasionally have to turn work down that would require me to work over a weekend to meet a deadline, but my sanity is all the better for the restriction.

Try to arrange your workspace so that your desk faces the window, so the light doesn't glare on the screen, and make sure you use sidelights rather than ceiling lights for the same reason. Don't push your desk right up against the wall or window: you'll need to get round the back to plug in cables, and you want to make this as easy as possible.

I'd also recommend renting a water cooler. Partly because water's good for you; but mainly because since I got mine my coffee intake has dropped considerably. And, at the risk of sounding like your mother, I'd also suggest eating lunch now and again. Falling over from hunger at 4.30 in the afternoon will do little to help you meet a 6pm deadline.

There are two main problems with the freelance lifestyle: not having enough work, and having too much. It's hard to decide which is the more onerous: if you don't have enough work, you can always spend the spare time putting up shelves. But if you have too much, at some point you'll get to that dreaded stage when you realize that you'll have to turn a job away.

The first time you turn work down it feels awful: after all, there's a job that needs doing, and if you don't do it they'll get someone else – so what will happen next time? Will they come back to you, or go straight to the person they know could get it done last time? The answer is that if you're any good, people will come back; and if you're too much in demand to do the work one week, they'll be all the more keen next time. But if you take on more than you can handle, you'll do neither job well.

There are many factors that determine whether a freelance artist gets plenty of work: whether your work's any good, whether it's original, whether you can interpret a brief, and so on. But without doubt the strongest factor is this: can you meet a deadline?

Unlike trains, TV shows and your brother's birthday, you can't miss a deadline. Period. If a newspaper phones you at 1pm and requires an illustration delivered by 5pm, then that's the time you have to have it finished. It's no good spending an extra couple of hours turning your illustration into a work of art if the paper's gone to press by the time you've finished: they'll be faced with a blank page, which they'll fill with a stock photograph, and the phone will go strangely silent for the next few weeks.

The tightest deadline I ever had was 45 minutes, for an illustration for the front page of a newspaper: it ended up with me right up against the deadline, asking for an extra ten minutes and being granted five. The next day a quarter of a million copies were distributed around the country, each one showing the bits I hadn't finished yet; the day after that it was lining the bottom of the cat litter tray. So much for posterity.

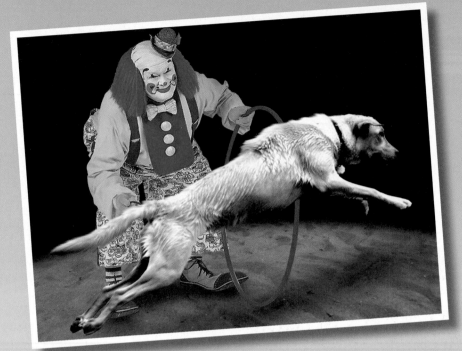

■ A dog jumping through a hoop. Or rather, it isn't; in the original version, above, the dog layer is in front of the clown layer. By making a layer mask for the dog, we can hide that portion of it that overlaps the front half of the hoop, making it appear to be leaping through it. A simple technique, but one that makes all the difference.

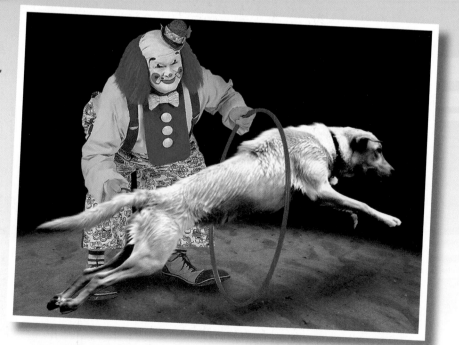

3

Hiding and showing

THE EASIEST WAY of removing part of a layer is to delete it. But deletion is irrevocable: you can't go back later and undelete the lost elements. Using a layer mask, however, forces you into no such constraints. Areas can be hidden, using hard or soft edges, and then painted back into place if the need arises. Layer masks are one of the most powerful devices available to the photomontage artist.

Changing the way two layers interact with each other is also a vital technique to master. Layer interaction may involve altering the blending mode to allow the underlying texture to show through, or selectively hiding parts of a layer depending on its brightness values; you can even hide parts of a layer depending on the brightness of the layers beneath it.

Texture with layer modes

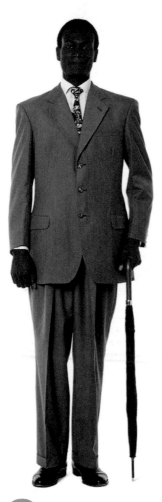

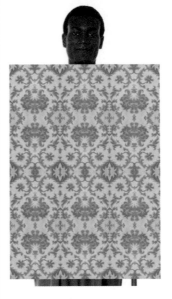

1 The jacket has been separated from the figure and made into a new layer. The texture (a piece of wallpaper) is placed over the top, and completely obscures the jacket.

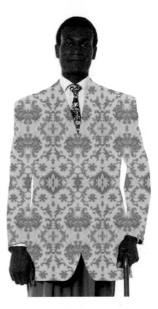

2 We can use the jacket as a Clipping Mask for the layer by pressing ⌥ ⌘ G alt ctrl G (for versions prior to CS2, use ⌘ G ctrl G).

C LIPPING MASKS are the easiest way of constraining the visibility of one layer to that of the layer beneath.

It all gets more interesting when you start to change the mode of the masked layer. (In versions of Photoshop prior to CS, making a Clipping Mask was called Grouping a layer with the one beneath.)

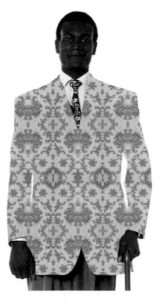

6 Lighten mode is similar to Screen, but with a twist: it only brightens those parts of the underlying layer that are darker than the target layer.

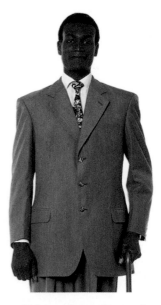

7 Darken mode does the opposite of Lighten. Since the background of the pattern is brighter than the suit color, it has no effect; only the relief on the pattern shows through.

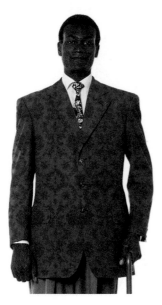

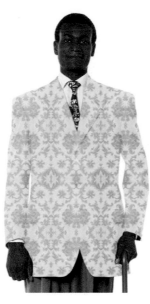

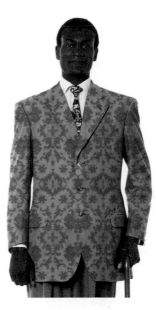

3 Layer modes are changed by selecting from the pop-up menu at the top of the Layers palette. This mode is Multiply, which adds the darkness of the layer to the one beneath.

4 The opposite of Multiply is Screen: this adds the brightness of the layer to the brightness of the layer beneath, resulting in an image that's brighter than either.

5 Overlay mode is a kind of mid-point between Multiply and Screen. It's a more subtle effect than either, and allows the full texture of the jacket to show through.

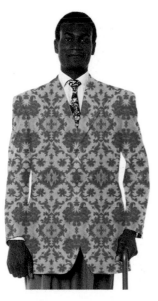

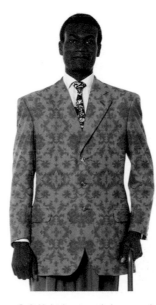

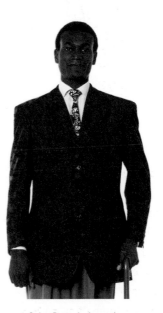

8 Hard Light is a stronger version of Overlay, which increases the saturation of both layers. Some of the underlying layer's detail is often lost using Hard Light.

9 Soft Light is a toned-down version of Hard Light, producing an altogether subtler effect. The textures of the original jacket are clearly visible beneath the pattern.

10 Color Burn darkens the underlying layer, but adds a strong color element to it, producing a deeply hued result that's quite different to any of the others.

HOT TIP

You can use keyboard shortcuts to change layer modes, so you don't have to keep reaching for the pop-up menu. Hold down Shift ⌥ Shift alt while typing the first letter of the mode's name – so use Shift ⌥ M Shift alt M for Multiply, Shift ⌥ H Shift alt H for Hard Light, and so on.

Layer masks 1: intersections

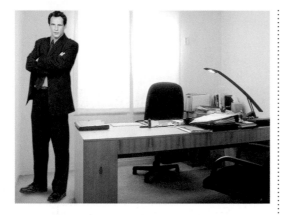

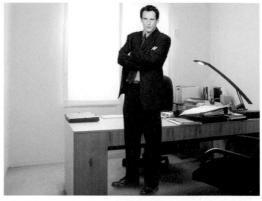

1 When we move the man to the right, we can see the problem: he's in front of the desk, and he needs to be behind it. We could, of course, make a new layer from the desk; but this is a better method.

MOST MONTAGES involve combining objects in such a way that they interact with each other. In the scene above, for instance, the businessman is standing next to his desk; we want to place him behind it. The simplest way of putting him into this scene is to use a layer mask, which allows one object to appear to be simultaneously in front of and behind another.

Painting in black on a layer mask hides the layer; painting in white reveals it again. Although you'd frequently use a brush to paint a layer mask, because this desk is composed of straight edges we'll use the Lasso tool instead to select it, and then fill the selected area with black.

Layer masks have more uses than this, as we'll see later in this chapter: they're one of the most powerful weapons in the photomontage artist's arsenal, and deserve close inspection to see how you can achieve the best results from them.

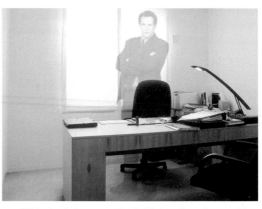

4 With the desk area outlined, fill the selected area with black – use ⌥ *Delete* *alt* *Delete* to fill the area with the foreground color. The mask now takes effect.

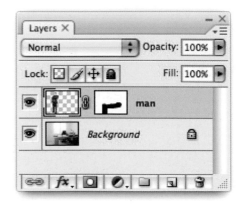

7 The key lies in the little chain icon between the layer and its mask. Click here to remove it; then click on the layer icon, rather than the mask icon, to select it.

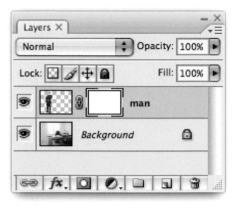

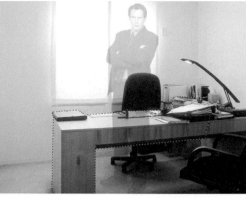

2 Choose Layer > Add Layer Mask > Reveal All. This will make a new, empty mask with the Man layer. When we paint on this mask, black will hide the layer; painting in white will reveal it again.

3 We'll use the Lasso tool to select this desk. It helps to reduce the opacity of the Man layer so we can see the background. Trace the shape of the left half of the desk, holding ⌥ alt as you click with the Lasso.

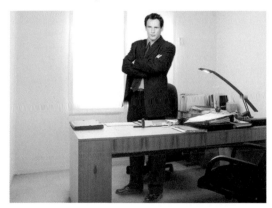

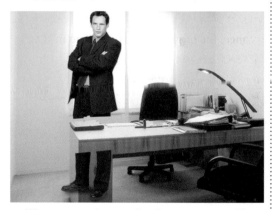

5 When we bring the Man layer back to full opacity, we can see that the mask has done its job: he's now effectively hidden behind the desk.

6 When we move the man, though, we can see a problem. The mask is moving with him, which looks ridiculous. We want to move the layer, while leaving the mask where it is.

HOT TIP

Painting on a mask with black hides the layer; painting with white reveals it. A useful shortcut is to press **X**, which swaps foreground and background colors over. This makes it easy to adjust the mask without having to swap colors in the toolbox.

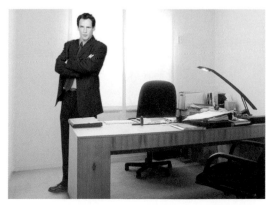

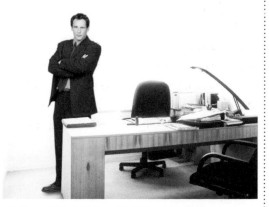

8 Now that the layer is unchained from the mask, we can move the man around – and the mask remains in place. We can position him anywhere behind the desk with ease.

9 Because the background is still a single layer, we can adjust it as we like: here, we've boosted the brightness considerably. The man, of course, remains untouched.

Layer masks 2: transparency

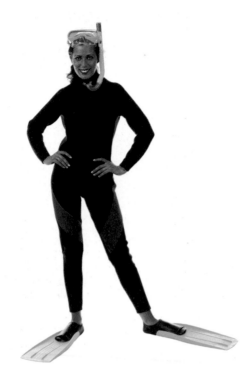

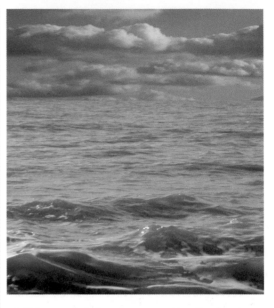

1 This sea and sky have been comped together from two different photographs. The hard line that separates them looks too rigid: this amount of cloud would surely create a hazy effect on the horizon.

PAINTING ON LAYER MASKS with black hides the layer; painting with white reveals it again. But painting with intermediate shades of gray causes the layer to become partially transparent.

Rather than choosing a gray tone, we can simulate gray by lowering the opacity of the brush tool as we paint – which is how the image of the diver's legs as seen through the water is achieved.

As well as lowering the opacity, we can also use a soft-edged rather than a hard-edged brush to paint with. This creates a fading mask, as if we'd feathered a selection and deleted it. But of course, since this is a mask, we can paint the hidden areas back in again at any time – which would be impossible if we'd chosen to delete the area instead.

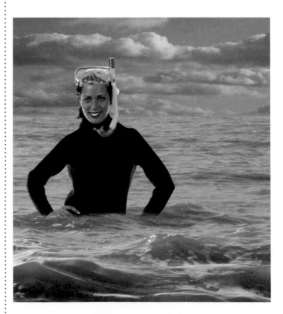

4 Another layer mask is created, this time for the diver. The bulk of her body beneath the waves is simply painted out with a large brush, to hide as much of the unwanted area as possible in one go.

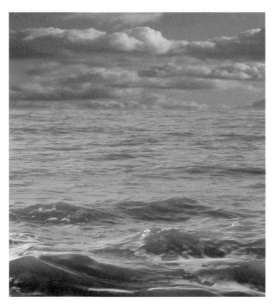

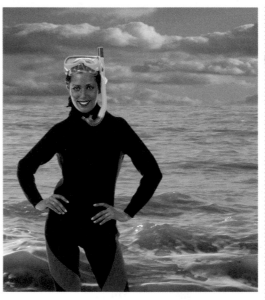

2 After creating a layer mask for the sea layer, I've simply brushed along the horizon using a small, soft-edged brush – holding the **Shift** key down to ensure a straight line as I painted. This creates the effect of a slightly feathered edge along the horizon.

3 Placing a figure in the foreground looks desperately unconvincing: the diver may occupy the same visual space as the background, but there's no sense of her fitting into it.

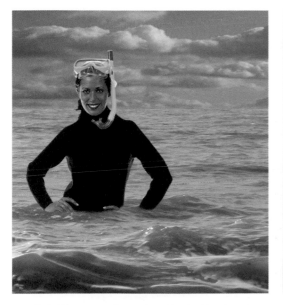

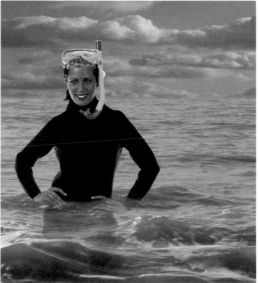

5 Switching to a much smaller, soft-edged brush, and painting with white rather than black, we can begin to paint the figure back in around the water line. By following the contours of the figure as well as those of the waves, we can make her look far more part of the scene.

6 But water is a translucent substance. Still using white, choose a larger brush and set its opacity to just 20%. By painting selectively on the mask below the water line, we can now see a hint of the diver through the sea. I've also used the Wave filter to make the diver's legs ripple slightly.

HOT TIP

When painting layer masks, you may frequently need to change brush size to create fine adjustments. Rather than picking from the pop-up list, use the keyboard shortcut: the **[** key selects a smaller brush, the **]** key selects the next larger one.

SHORTCUTS
MAC WIN BOTH

Layer masks 3: soft edges

ANY OF THE PAINTING tools can be used on a layer mask – not just the Brush. If a tool can be used in a Photoshop layer, it can be used on the mask as well.

This greatly extends the scope of masking, as well as allowing us to create some interesting and unusual effects. Here, we'll use the Gradient tool to produce a softly feathered edge to a bank of cloud, looking just as if we'd removed it with a huge Eraser.

More interesting is the second effect, which uses the Smudge tool to create the mask by bringing in the black around the figures, so that the grass appears to overlap them convincingly.

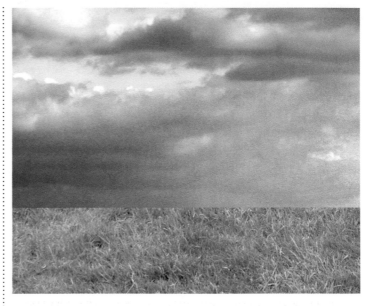

1 A patch of cloud has been placed directly over the top of the grass in this image. The effect is clearly desperately unconvincing, and even raising the horizon line by deleting a section of sky would look like a poor montage. To enhance the misty effect, we'll blend the sky smoothly into the grass.

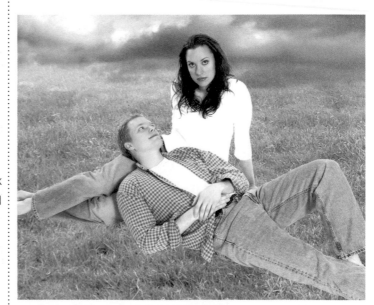

3 This sultry pair seem unaware of the fog rolling in behind them – but we need to make them fit into their environment better. After creating their layer mask, we first hold ⌘ ctrl and click on the icon in the Layers palette, which loads up the area taken up by the pixels in the layer. Then inverse the selection, using ⌘ Shift I ctrl Shift I ; fill the new selection (which includes everything except the couple) with black. You won't see any change: that comes later.

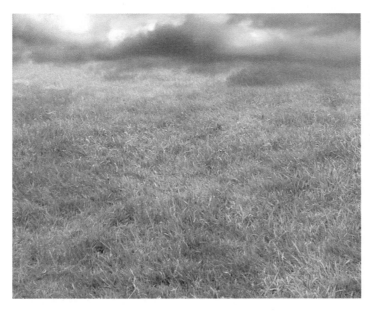

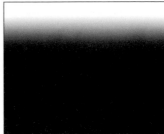

2 After creating a layer mask for the cloud layer, choose the Gradient tool and set it to Foreground to Background, using black and white as the respective foreground and background colors. Now position the Gradient tool at the bottom of the clouds and drag vertically, holding the Shift key down as you do so to create a pure vertical. The result is a smoothly fading mask: the mask itself is shown inset.

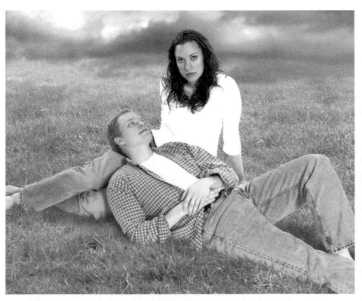

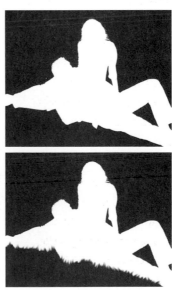

4 The layer mask we just created looks like the inset (above right). Because white is the selected area, the hidden region (black) hides nothing. Now for the interesting bit: using the Smudge tool, gradually streak up the black mask where the bodies touch the ground. Each streak will hide a part of them, and the result will look as if the blades of grass are truly in front of the bodies. The minimal shadow, painted on a new layer behind them, simply adds to the effect.

HOT TIP

Experiment with different brushes and tools on layer masks to see the effect. Using a brush set to Dissolve, for instance, would be a good way of masking these figures if they were lying on sand rather than grass. For less defined background surfaces, try using the Blur tool instead – set it to Darken, or it will have little effect.

SHORTCUTS

MAC WIN BOTH

65

Layer masks 4: smoothing

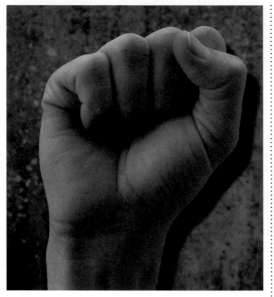

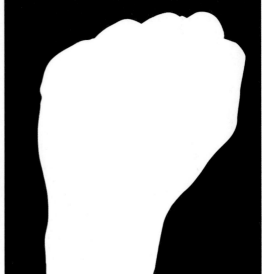

CUTOUT OBJECTS CAN LOOK TOO CRISP, particularly if they've been silhouetted using the Pen tool. This hand appears false against the slightly out-of-focus background: it's an obvious montage that wouldn't fool anyone.

One technique might simply be to feather the edges of the hand. But that's an irrevocable step: anything that has been permanently deleted will be hard to put back afterwards.

A better method is to create a layer mask and adjust that, as shown here. This technique makes it easy to get exactly the amount of edge blurring you need, without having to commit yourself at any stage: you can always discard the layer mask and repeat the process with different settings later.

1 First, hold ⌘ *ctrl* and click on the layer name to load the selection. Make a layer mask and inverse the selection, then fill the inverted area with black. Here's how the mask looks: its crisp edges won't affect the layer yet, since it's only masked what isn't visible anyway.

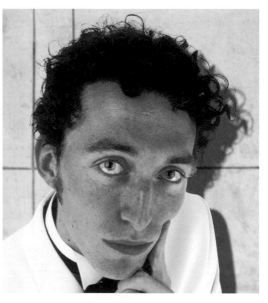

4 This figure suffers from the same problem: the hard edge of that white jacket looks more like plastic than fabric, and his ear is too crisp against the background. Applying the method outlined above will rectify this situation easily.

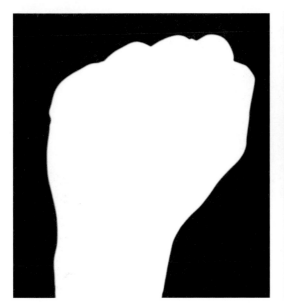

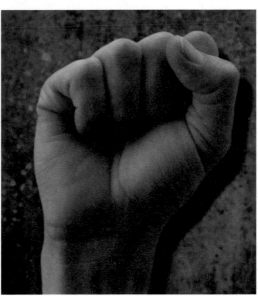

2 Now, with the inverse still selected, feather the selection by using `⌥ ⌘ D` `alt` `ctrl` `D` and specifying the feather amount, then fill with black again. A figure of 1 or 2 pixels will be sufficient. Here's how the mask looks afterwards.

3 Now the hand looks more like it belongs with the background: the edges are softened, without a single pixel having been deleted from the layer itself. If the background changes and you need the hand to be crisp again, simply discard the mask.

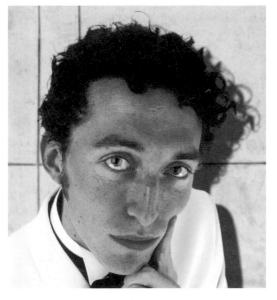

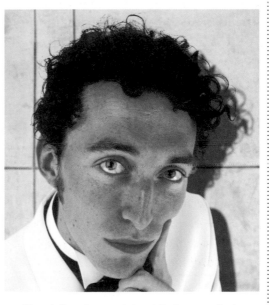

5 So far, so good: the jacket and ear blend in much better with the background. The hair, however, is another matter. Because the original strands of hair were so fine, the new mask has made the individual stray hairs disappear, while the remainder now looks more like a bad wig.

6 The solution, of course, is to set the foreground color to white and simply paint out the mask around the hair edge. It's always worth checking for details like this when using this masking technique, as any fine elements can easily be lost in the process.

Blending 1: fire power

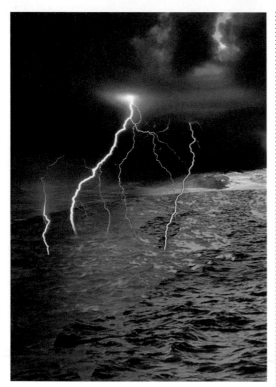

T HE BLENDING OPTIONS feature, tucked away within the Layer Style palette, is one of the most overlooked features in Photoshop. But it's an enormously powerful tool that allows you to hide or show picture elements automatically, without touching a brush or layer mask.

In the image above, for the Sunday Telegraph, I duplicated the background sky complete with lightning, and placed it in front of the globe; then used Blending Options to remove the sky from the front version.

1 Here are the two elements of this montage – the hand holding the gun, and the photograph of the firework which has been rotated to match the gun's angle. Simply changing the mode of this layer to Screen would get rid of the black, but the flame would be pale against a light background – and would become invisible against white.

3 When we zoom in on the image, however, we can see that moving the slider produces a sharp cut-off between what's visible and what's hidden. It's an ugly, stepping effect; in order to make the effect more realistic, we need to look more closely at exactly how that black slider operates.

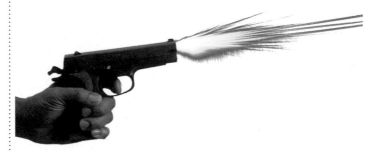

5 Further adjustment of both sliders allows us to set the visibility of this layer exactly as we want it. Now, the left slider is set to 50 and the right slider to 120, which removes exactly the right amount of black without weakening the effect of the rather enthusiastic gunshot.

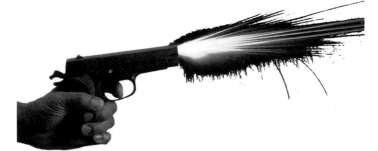

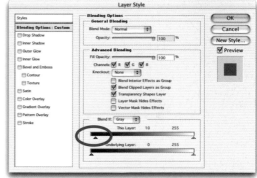

2 Double-click the layer's name or choose Layer/Layer Style/Blending Options to bring up the dialog. It's the bottom section we want to look at, the one headed Blend If. On the This Layer section, drag the black triangle to the right – here, it's at a position of 10 (working on a scale of 0=black to 255=white). This hides everything darker than 10 in the image.

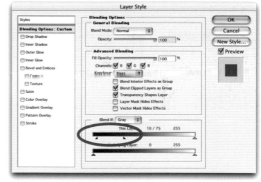

4 What appears to be a single triangle is, in fact, two. Hold down ⌥ *alt* as you drag and it will split into its two sections, which can be manipulated individually. With the left slider still set to 10, we now drag the right one out to a position of 75. This is what happens: everything darker than 10 is hidden, and everything brighter than 75 is fully visible. But now, all the values in between fade smoothly between the two states.

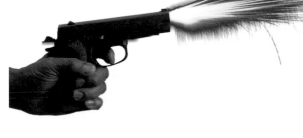

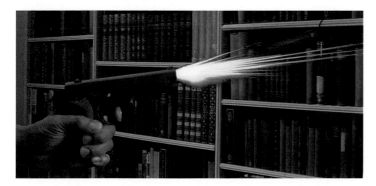

6 When placed against a suitable background (somehow libraries always come to mind when I think of gunshots) the effect is dramatic. I don't believe there's any other way that this flame could have been isolated from its background as convincingly as this in Photoshop.

Blending 2: plane view

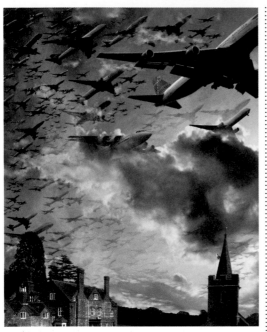

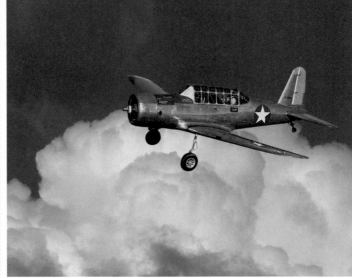

1 In this example, we're going to make the plane fly through the clouds rather than just sitting on top. Working on the plane layer, it's clear that we don't want to hide that layer

depending on its brightness values: unlike the example on the previous page, this isn't simply a case of removing the black element from the target layer.

THIS SECTION DEALS WITH the other half of the Blending Options dialog – the Underlying Layer section. This controls the visibility of the target layer depending on all the layers beneath it, not just the one directly below.

The illustration above was for a Sunday Times Magazine cover, illustrating the crowded state of Britain's air traffic. Rather than creating an Underlying Layer adjustment for each plane, I duplicated the cloud layer to the front and removed the blue sky from that layer: seen through it were not only the planes, but the original sky as well.

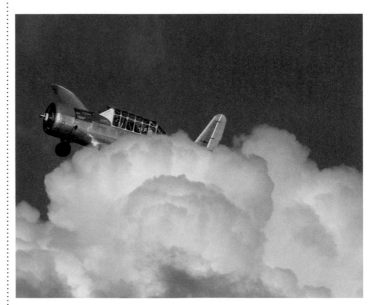

3 Since we're working with blending values rather than with a layer mask, we can move the plane anywhere we want within the artwork and the

effect will still apply. This is a great technique for animation, and works well if you're planning to import Photoshop artwork into After Effects.

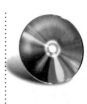

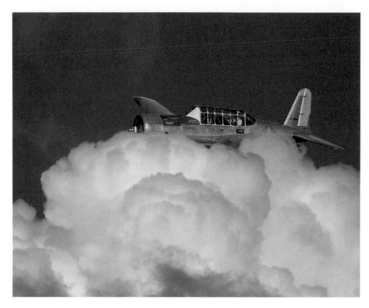

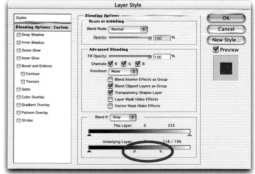

2 Because we want the visibility of the plane to be affected by the presence of cloud in the layer beneath, we need to turn our attention away from the This Layer section

of the Blending Options dialog, and look instead at the Underlying Layer section. This works in exactly the same way, except – as its name implies – the visibility of the target layer

is determined by what's going on underneath. Here, we've dragged and split the right (white) slider rather than the left (black) one, settings of 118 and 167 do the job well.

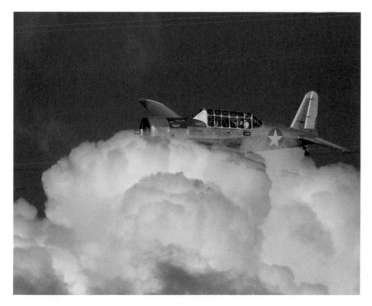

4 Although we hid the plane in the clouds correctly, the overall effect can be made more realistic by allowing a little of the plane to show

through – after all, clouds are not solid objects. This is achieved by dragging the right slider back towards the right, increasing the number: in this instance,

a value of 196 as the white cutoff point is enough to add just a touch of translucence to what would otherwise be over-opaque clouds.

71

Graphics tablets

I SPENT SEVERAL YEARS reviewing graphics tablets for MacUser, praising their capabilities and deriding their shortcomings, while all the time secretly wondering why anyone would use such an awkward device. When each new tablet arrived I'd expect a liberating feeling, hoping that I could finally discard my mouse and sketch as if I was drawing on paper with a pencil. And each time I felt frustrated, because drawing on a tablet while looking up at a monitor is nothing like drawing on paper. And then I realized the problem.

Graphics tablets take a lot of getting used to.

Using a stylus is very different to using a mouse. For one thing, it isn't tied to your computer, which means it can roll around the desk, drop into the waste paper basket and have to be rescued from among a pile of junk mail before it ends up as landfill. The stylus could end up anywhere: at least a mouse can't be more than a cord's length away.

My main problem with the stylus, though, was that although it seemed perfectly adequate for shading and painting, it was too clumsy for web browsing and general use. There's also the problem that while a mouse moves the cursor in the direction you choose – and you can site a mouse anywhere on the mouse pad while you drag it around – the stylus and tablet have a one-to-one relationship with the monitor: the top left corner of the tablet represents the top left corner of the screen. You can't simply position a stylus anywhere you want it and expect it to behave like a mouse.

In theory, I could have used the mouse for some tasks, and the stylus and tablet for others. But the mouse wouldn't work properly on the tablet's surface, and in order to use the tablet I had to place it on top of my mouse mat and then take it away again to use the mouse. So the tablet always ended up sitting on the shelf until the PR agency who'd lent it to me in the first place sent out a courier to pick it up again.

Then I was sent a combined mouse/stylus combination to review. Made by Wacom, it's the cheapest tablet they produce: at a cost of under $100, I fully expected it to be more of a toy than the kind of tool a serious graphic artist would give a second glance.

The first thing that surprised me was the mouse. It was cordless, which felt decidedly modern. True, it was no longer chained to my computer, but at least it couldn't roll off the desk like the stylus. There was no ball to clog up, which meant the regular task of scrubbing my mouse ball and scraping the rollers with a fingernail were finally a thing of the past.

The mouse also had two buttons, which was quite a novelty for a diehard Mac user, although I spent many hours trying to decide what to do with the second button (you can customize it to do anything you like, and even change its function depending on the application you're working in). But best of all, the mouse had a scroll wheel that let me zip through web pages, tear down Word documents and whizz through image libraries without having to click on one of those annoyingly small arrow icons at the corners of windows.

I started using the mouse in earnest, glancing occasionally at the stylus as it perched in its holder at the top of the tablet. Once in a while I'd reach for the stylus when I wanted to perform a task for which variable pressure would be useful, such as painting shadows or using the Dodge and Burn tools.

Gradually, over the weeks, I began to feel more at home with the stylus, and found myself using it increasingly often. Now I find that I'd be lost without it: I take it with me everywhere I take my PowerBook, and if I ever have to give a demonstration where I have to use the mouse that comes with the demo computer, it feels clumsy and awkward.

The upshot of all this is that I now recommend a graphics tablet wholeheartedly to anyone who'll listen, to the extent that I consider them an essential tool.

Just don't expect to take to it immediately.

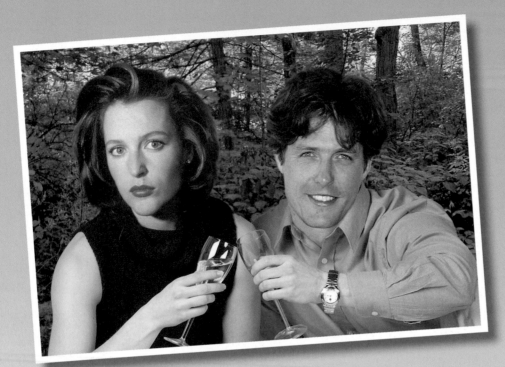

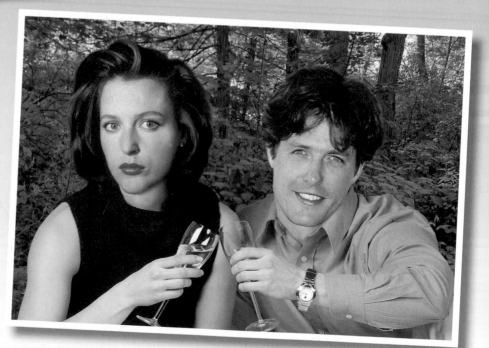

■ Gillian Anderson and Hugh Grant: a match made in heaven, perhaps. But the montage above wouldn't fool even the most news-hungry of tabloid journalists; the pair barely look as if they're on the same planet. Yet it takes only minor adjustment to give the couple the same warm, healthy color that Mr Grant was so conspicuously lacking before.

4

Image adjustment

ONE OF THE COMMON problems facing the montage artist is making skintones match. You might place a head on a different body, and then use a new hand to replace the existing one; the chances are that the colors of each component will be wildly different. In this chapter we'll look at the Curves adjustment, the most powerful tool for correcting color, which can also be used to boost contrast within the image.

We'll kick off this chapter by taking a look at Shadows and Highlights, one of the most powerful adjustment features in Photoshop. It's an enormously satisfying tool to use, as it's capable of providing a quick fix solution to the problem of over-dark and bright areas in a photograph.

Shadows and highlights

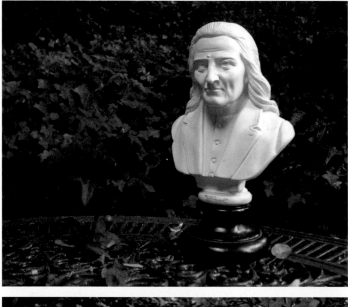

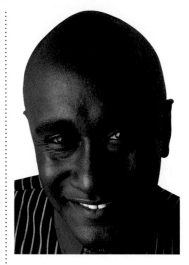

1 This figure has been photographed with strong side lighting. If used in a montage, we'd have to arrange all the lighting in the scene to match it; but with Shadow/Highlight, we can make this image look as if it has been lit from the front.

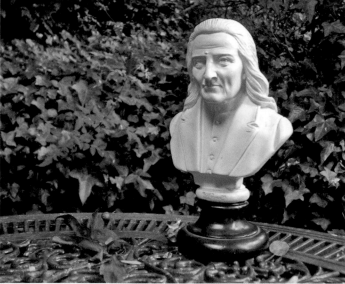

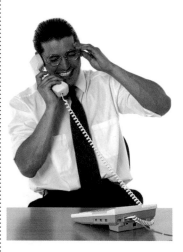

THE SHADOW/HIGHLIGHT ADJUSTMENT is an enormously powerful and time-saving tool. This bust of Liszt (top) has been photographed outdoors against a dark background. Hard to remedy conventionally, the default settings of Shadow/Highlight (bottom) produce great results. The background is duly brightened, and none of the fine bright detail of the bust has been lost in the process.

4 This figure poses the opposite problem. The lighting on the skintones is fine, but the shirt is very bright – it almost disappears against this white background. We'll use Shadow/Highlight once again, but this time we'll turn our attention to the Highlights area rather than the Shadows section.

IMAGES: BODYSHOTS, STOCKBYTE

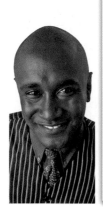

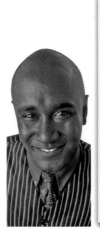

2 The default settings of Shadow/Highlight produce a markedly better image, with much of the detail that seemed to be lost in the shadows being returned to view. Overall, though, we can still see a strong light from his right, leaving the left side of the face in shadow.

3 By increasing the Amount setting in the Shadows dialog from the default 50% to 80%, we're able to balance both sides of the face to give an even lighting overall. The colored lighting still produces a blue sheen on the left, but that can easily be fixed later.

5 To start with, reduce the Shadows amount to zero so there's no change in that area. Now we can increase the Highlights value to, say, 50%, which darkens up the shirt well (but note how that white telephone cord still stands out against the dark tie). The shirt's looking good, but some of the Highlight setting has 'leaked' into the skin, making it too dark and over-saturated.

6 To fix this problem, we need to reduce the scope of the Highlights adjustment. The Tonal Width slider in the Highlights setting has a default value of 50%; by reducing this to just 20%, we're able to limit the range of the effect so that the skintones are not included. Now, the shirt has been reduced in brightness, while the skin has been left pretty much alone.

HOT TIP

Now that Photoshop allows you to customize keyboard shortcuts, it's well worth assigning a custom shortcut to this feature, since it's likely to be one you'll use on almost every image you open. Dodgy lighting was never this easy to cope with!

Learning Curves

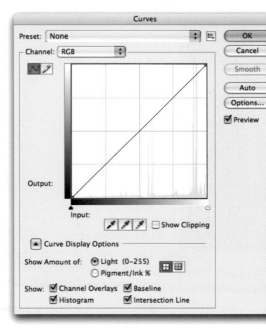

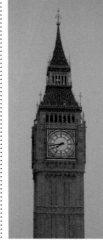

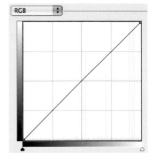

1 When you open the Curves dialog you see, perhaps surprisingly, not a curve but a straight line. As a default, the input values are the same as the output, so there's no change.

HERE ARE MANY WAYS OF ADJUSTING images in Photoshop – Levels, Brightness & Contrast, Hue & Saturation, Color Balance. The most powerful of the lot is Curves, which allows you to make both fine and sweeping alterations in a single dialog.

The Curves dialog is one which confuses many new users, but it's worth getting to grips with. The graph shows how the input values (the original image) translate into the output values (the result of the operation); by subtly tweaking this graph, we can adjust not only the overall brightness and contrast but each of the red, green and blue channels as well.

Using Curves often involves thinking backwards: so if an image is too red, for example, the best fix is often to increase the blue and green components, rather than to reduce the red (which would result in too dark a result). Subtlety is the key: small adjustments are always the best way forward.

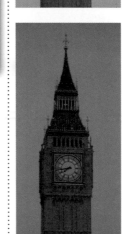

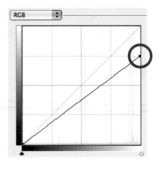

4 As well as clicking in the center, we can also adjust the endpoints. Clicking the top right point and dragging down limits the brightest part of the image, reducing contrast.

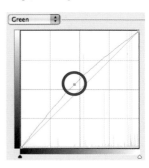

7 We can also adjust each color individually. Choose the color channel from the pop-up menu: we'll correct the red cast by adding green to the image.

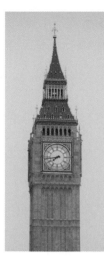

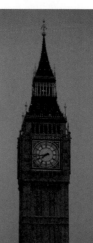

2 By clicking in the center of the line and dragging upwards, we make our first curve. Raising the curve increases the overall brightness of the scene.

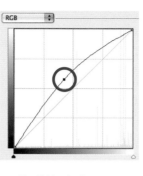

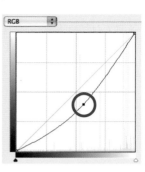

3 Conversely, clicking in the center and dragging downwards lowers the brightness, producing an image that's darker overall.

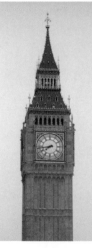

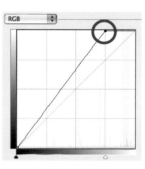

5 If we drag that top right point to the left rather than down, we produce the opposite effect – increasing the contrast of the image. This is a very useful and controllable quick fix.

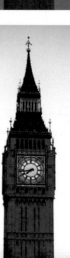

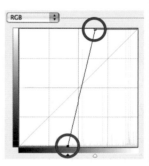

6 By dragging the top and bottom points towards the center, we create a stylized, posterized effect that turns any photograph into more of a graphic object.

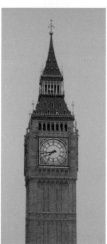

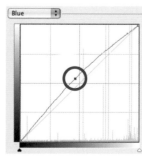

8 To correct our image further, we need to add more blue. Switching to the Blue channel allows us to raise the blue content. But the image is now too washed-out.

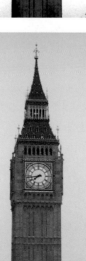

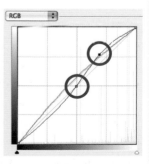

9 Click once in the center of the RGB curve to 'pin' that midpoint; now drag just the top half of the curve to make this S shape, and the result is to increase the overall contrast.

HOT TIP

If you find that Curves behaves in the opposite way for you, make sure the gradient bar beneath the graph is dark on the left and light on the right. If it isn't, click the double-headed arrow in the center and it will be changed for you. To switch between the Red, Green and Blue channels, use ⌘ 1 ctrl 1, ⌘ 2 ctrl 2 and ⌘ 3 ctrl 3.

SHORTCUTS
MAC WIN BOTH

Matching colors with Curves

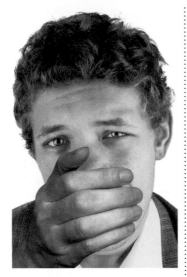

MATCHING COLORS between two photographs is at the heart of the photomontage artist's craft. Variations in lighting can produce enormous differences in color and tonal range, which need to be balanced in order to make a montage work.

While the hand shown here was a reasonably good original digital capture, it looks completely wrong when placed against a face which appears to be a totally different color.

The Curves adjustment is the ideal tool for this job. The process involves several steps, and it's a good way of learning how to manipulate Curves to achieve precisely the results you want.

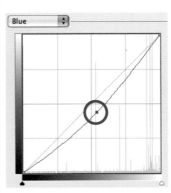

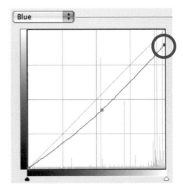

1 At first glance, the hand needs to have much more yellow in order to match the face. There's a problem here: we have access to each of the Red, Green and Blue channels, but there's no yellow. The trick is to think in reverse, taking out colors we don't want rather than adding colors we do.

It's fairly clear, if we look at it this way, that the hand is far too blue. So open Curves (using ⌘ M ctrl M) and switch to the Blue channel using the pop-up menu. Click in the center of the line and drag down slightly to remove that blue cast from the skintones.

2 Removing the blue from the midtones, as we've just done, helped a lot; but we can still see some blue in the highlights, most noticeable in the shine on the backs of the fingers and in the fingernails. To fix this, click on the right side of the curve and drag vertically downwards. This limits the brightest part of the Blue channel, reducing the highlight glare.

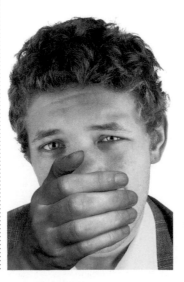

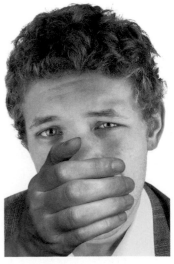

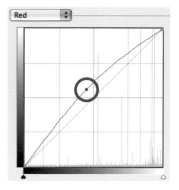

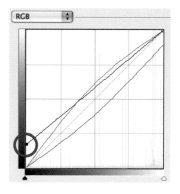

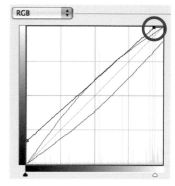

3 So far, so good – but the image still isn't quite the right color. Taking out the blue has left it with a greenish tint. We could simply take out the green, but that would make the whole thing too dark; instead, if we compare it to the face, we see that the face has more red in it. So switch to the Red channel, click in the center of the line and drag upwards slightly to increase the red content in the midtones.

4 The result of the last three operations left us with a hand that is now the right color, but which is too highly contrasted: the shadow on the left of the hand is much darker than anything we can see in the face.

Switch now to the RGB channel, which affects the overall contrast and brightness. Because we want to remove the shadow, we need to click on the extreme left of the line – which marks the darkest point – and drag upwards, to limit the darkness of the layer.

5 Much better – but not quite there yet. By reducing the shadows, we've also left ourselves with a hand which is somewhat lacking in contrast. We can boost this by clicking on the top right corner of the line, and dragging it to the left: the result of this is to compress the tonal range, so boosting the contrast overall. It's important to make only a small adjustment here, as it's easy to go too far. In the end, though, we've got a hand which matches the face almost exactly.

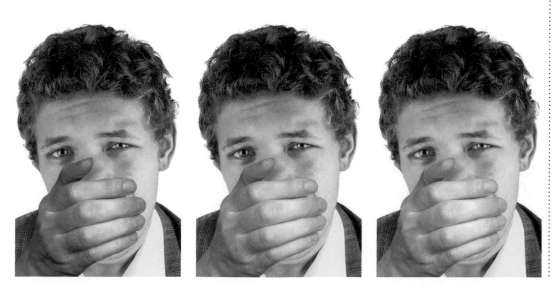

Major color changes

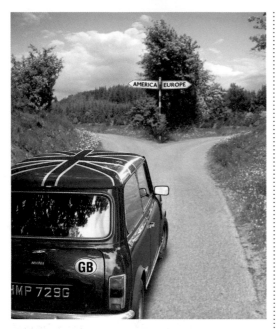

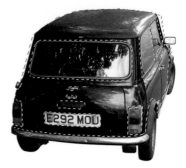

1 Here's the original car photograph, cut out from its background using the Pen tool. There really is no better tool for this sort of job, and mastering it is an essential skill.

2 The next step was to isolate just the black body, again using the Pen tool. On the version on the CD, you'll find that I've done this for you: just load up the Pen path.

WHEN THE GUARDIAN newspaper ran a cover story about whether Britain was moving towards an American or European ideology, they wanted to show Britain at the crossroads. The gimmick was to use a car with a Union Jack painted on the top, as seen in the Michael Caine film The Italian Job.

In order to see the roof, I had to stand on the top of my own car (after driving round the streets looking for a suitable mini) in order to get the correct perspective. Changing the color from the original black, however, is the technique that most concerns us here.

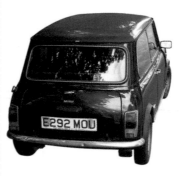

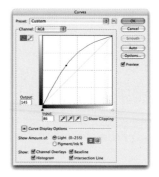

5 A far better solution is to say OK to the Hue/Saturation dialog after you've made the color change, and then use Curves to increase the brightness. By clicking on the midpoint of the RGB curve and raising it, we're able to increase the brightness of the midtones without affecting either the shadows or the highlights for a more natural result.

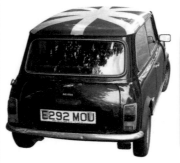

9 With the new layer now isolated, we can apply our blue coloring to it using the Hue/Saturation dialog once again. The procedure is exactly the same as in step 3, using a combination of the Hue and Saturation sliders to achieve exactly the color you want. Beware of increasing the Saturation slider too far, or you'll produce a color that's unprintable.

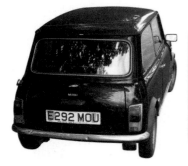

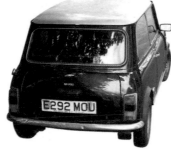

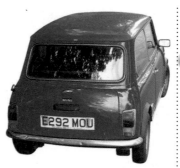

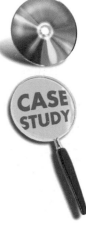

3 Once the body paintwork had been made into a new layer, it needed to be changed from its original black to a strong red. It would have been possible to do this using Curves,

but for an operation like this the Hue/Saturation adjustment is far more suitable. Check the Colorize box, and adjust both the Hue and Saturation sliders to get the right effect.

4 Because the bodywork was too dark, you might think that raising the Lightness slider would be the answer. But this produces a pale, washed-out version of the original.

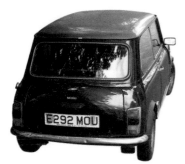

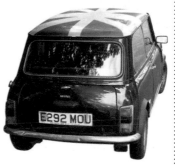

HOT TIP

When color changes are made using Hue/ Saturation it's easy to create colors that look good on screen, but which aren't within the CMYK gamut and will simply die when printed on paper. The solution is to turn on Print Preview mode using ⌘ Y ctrl Y ; toggle this mode on and off when you're working within the dialog, and if you can see a significant change then you're working outside the CMYK gamut.

6 Now for the flag. The roof is selected from the red layer, and made into a new layer; then desaturated using ⌘ Shift U ctrl Shift U .

7 With all the color knocked out of the roof, duplicate the layer (we'll need the original later) and brighten it up to near white, once again using the Curves dialog.

8 Now we can return to the original desaturated roof, and draw our Union Jack outline. This is made into another new layer, and moved on top of the white layer.

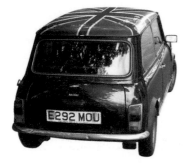

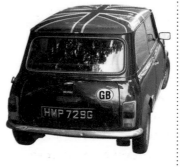

10 The red portion of the flag is created by drawing its outlines, and then deleting that area from the white roof to reveal the red coloring that's already beneath it.

11 For the sake of historical accuracy, I used the number plate from the original film (found by phoning the webmaster of an Italian Job fan website). The lettering was

set in the shareware font CarPlates, which was curved using the Shear filter and then had the EyeCandy Chrome filter applied – still the fastest way of making effective chrome lettering.

SHORTCUTS

Multi-layer enhancement

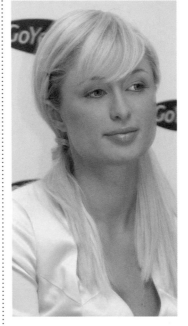

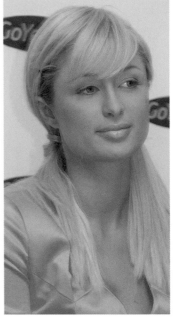

PHOTOSHOP INCLUDES many tools for enhancing images – all the Adjustments, Unsharp Mask, and others. But sometimes working directly on the image layer produces ugly or over-saturated results; by making a duplicate of the layer, we can apply only the adjustments we want and discard those we don't need, simply by changing the layer mode.

1 A snapped photo of Paris Hilton at a press conference: it's dull and lacking in contrast. But a Curves adjustment would change the colors: we only want to boost the contrast, leaving the colors alone.

2 The technique is simple. First, duplicate the layer, and desaturate it using ⌘ *Shift* U *ctrl* *Shift* U. This produces a grayscale version of the image, and serves to show us just how low in contrast it really is.

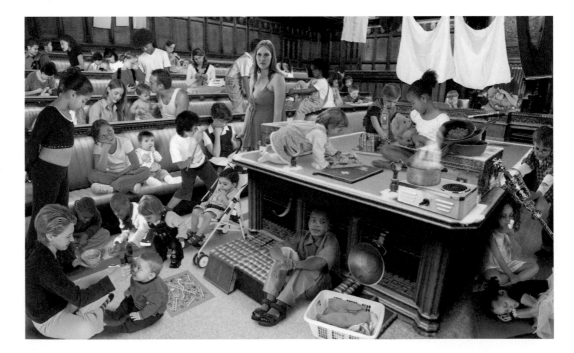

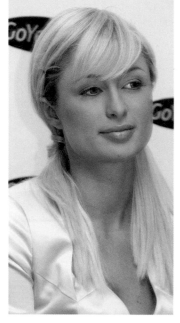

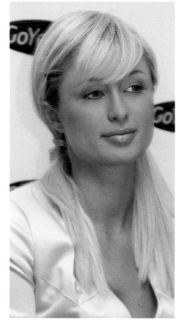

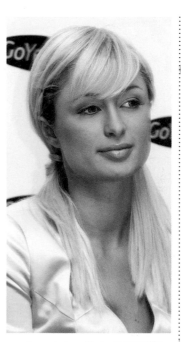

3 The grayscale version may be dull, but we can use it to enhance the color version beneath. Change the mode of this new layer from Normal to Soft Light for a radical difference: plenty of contrast, no color change!

4 To make the eyes and glossy lips stand out, I've duplicated the layer again, and sharpened it a lot with Unsharp Mask – 300% at a 3 pixel radius. Then, using a layer mask, hid all but the target areas.

5 For a starker effect, try changing the layer mode from Soft Light to Hard Light. This produces a harder image altogether; the choice of which to go for depends on the final use to which it will be put.

We can achieve a similar effect using Adjustment Layers. The image below (left) is a poster for the housing charity Shelter, showing the British House of Parliament inhabited by homeless families. To make the image starker (right), I set the colors to default black and white, and added a Gradient Map Adjustment Layer at the top. If I'd left it at that, the result would have been a strong grayscale version of the image; but by changing the mode of this Adjustment Layer to Soft Light, I achieved the stronger result without having to change any of the layers individually.

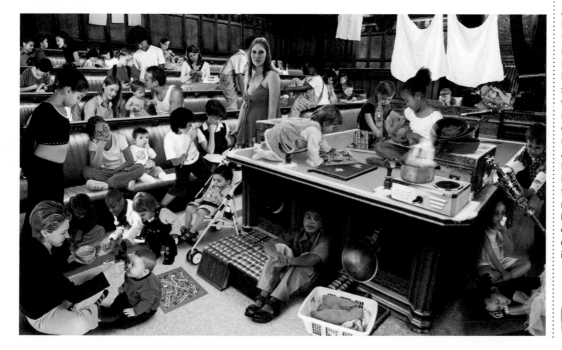

SHORTCUTS
MAC **WIN** **BOTH**

Sharpening: Unsharp Mask

How Unsharp Mask works

SHARPENING MEANS bringing back definition to soft or slightly out-of-focus images. Rather than using the uncontrollable Sharpen and Sharpen More filters, the best way of proceeding is to use the Unsharp Mask filter.

The very name is enough to put you off, let alone the confusing interface. It's the single filter that confuses Photoshop users more than any other. The Unsharp Mask filter works by enhancing border regions between areas of contrasting color or brightness, giving the impression of a more tightly focussed original photograph.

The amount of sharpening you apply depends on the original image – and also on the paper the final image will be printed on. Glossy art paper, such as that used in this book, is capable of reproducing images at high quality; but if your work will end up on newsprint, say, you'll need to sharpen your images twice as much as normal so they don't look fuzzy when they're finally printed.

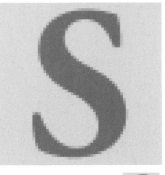

1 Here's our image, shown magnified (above) so we can see the effect. It's simply a dark gray letter placed on a light gray background, with no color to distract the eye.

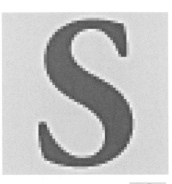

2 Here's the result of applying 100% sharpening with a radius of 1 pixel. The inside of the dark gray is darkened and the inside of the light gray brightened to increase contrast.

The interface

Toggle the Preview on and off to compare the before and after images before committing yourself

Hold ⌥ *alt* and click Cancel to revert

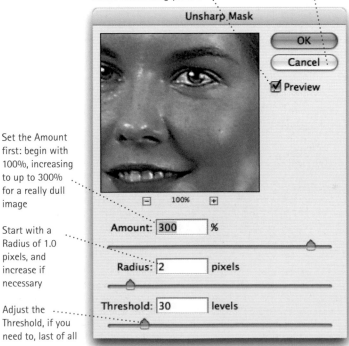

Set the Amount first: begin with 100%, increasing to up to 300% for a really dull image

Start with a Radius of 1.0 pixels, and increase if necessary

Adjust the Threshold, if you need to, last of all

Unsharp Mask

OK
Cancel
☑ Preview

100%

Amount: 300 %

Radius: 2 pixels

Threshold: 30 levels

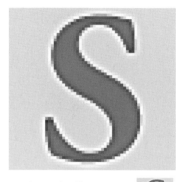

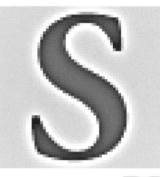

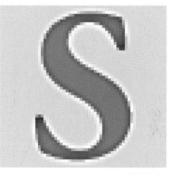

3 Increasing the amount to 200% makes the contrast between light and dark even stronger, producing a much crisper result.

4 When we increase the radius to 2.0 pixels, we can see that the lightening and darkening operation now occupies a wider border around the hard edges – 2 pixels wide, in fact.

5 By increasing the Threshold value, we determined how much of the image is affected by the operation – in this case, the darkening doesn't eat into the gray to such an extent.

Putting Unsharp Mask into practice

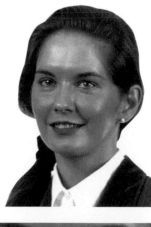

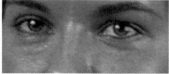

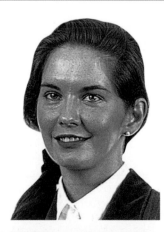

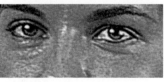

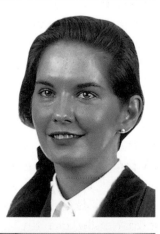

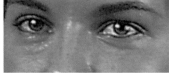

1 Our original image is fairly soft, especially around high contrast areas such as the eyes. There's also little detail visible in the hair, and we can use Unsharp Mask to bring both of these into stronger focus.

2 In this exaggerated example, I've used an amount of 300% with a radius of 2.0 pixels. But note how the skintones have become over-sharpened by this operation: that's the area we want left smooth.

3 This is where the Threshold feature comes into play. By raising this to a level of 30, we prevent the filter from acting on the low-contrast skin area, while still enhancing the contrast in the eyes, mouth and hair.

Natural healing

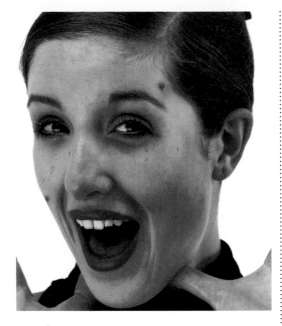

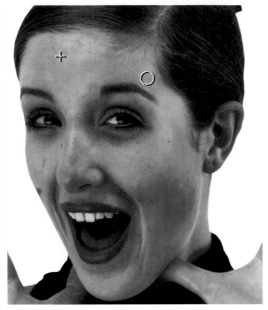

1 To begin, let's take out that large mole above her eyebrow. Hold ⌥ *alt* and click in the middle of the forehead to set the source point, then paint over the mole. The result will look like simply cloning the forehed, until you release the mouse button – then the tool does its magic.

T HE HEALING BRUSH, INTRODUCED IN Photoshop 7, has quickly proved itself to be one of the most popular image correction tools. Far more powerful than the Clone tool, it's able to correct blemishes in images quickly and very easily.

The secret lies in its ability to recognize the inherent texture of the source point, and blend that seamlessly with the lighting around the target area. For getting rid of spots, scratches and wrinkles, there's no better method.

In this typical example, we'll use the Healing brush to remove the moles and spots from this model's face (although, to be fair to the original model, I have enhanced the blemishes to make them easier to see).

The Healing brush works by sampling an area of clear texture to use as a reference point: the forehead is a great choice here, as for most faces, providing a wide expanse of skin uncluttered by facial features or hair.

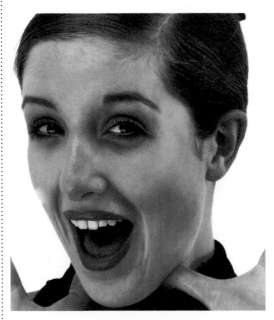

4 When we try to heal the mole on the side of the model's face, however, we run into some difficulty. The tool works by blending the shades of the surrounding area; here, it's read the white background and blended with that.

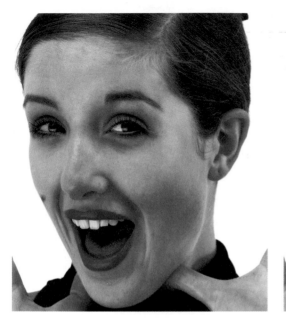

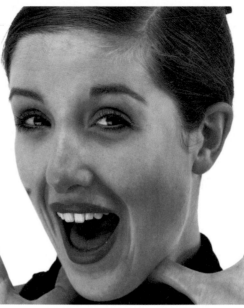

2 You can continue to paint over each additional mole in turn with the Healing brush. No need to reset the source point: the middle of the forehead will be remembered, and will be used for each new painting stroke.

3 The tool is so powerful that we can even take out the hole left by a missing earring. The color here is different, and the ear is in shadow compared to the forehead, but the tool can still patch the hole perfectly using the forehead skintones as the source.

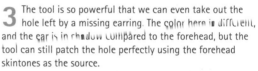

HOT TIP

Although you might think you need to use a soft-edged brush to produce the best blend, in fact the opposite is true: the Healing brush works at its most effective with a hard brush. If you use a graphics tablet, you should choose a brush whose size varies with pressure, rather than opacity.

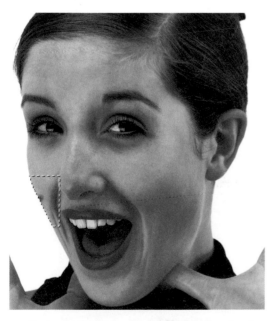

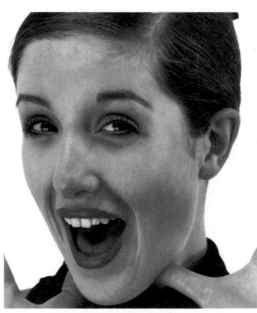

5 To stop the Healing brush looking beyond the edge of the face, we need to tell it where to stop – by making a selection. The easiest way is to make a rectangular selection, and use the Magic Wand to remove the white from it.

6 Now, when we use the Healing brush on that area, it will know not to blend with any colors outside the selected area; and so it removes the mole on the side of the face perfectly.

SHORTCUTS
MAC | WIN | BOTH

Getting started

WHENEVER I SPEAK IN PUBLIC, either in colleges or at computer shows, there are two questions I'm always asked. The first is the question asked of all creative artists: 'Where do you get your ideas from?' (I generally reply that I get them from the local idea store, except for particularly exotic ideas which have to be bought by mail order direct from Paris.) The second, and more pertinent, question is: 'How do you get started in a job like yours?'

This is a much more serious question, and deserves a less flippant response. What students want to hear is that you go to such-and-such a college, do this or that degree, and then apply through a website along the lines of freelancegraphicartist.com (or whatever) and a plum job will land on your plate. In real life, however, things rarely work out that way. For a start, I didn't go to art college, and therefore feel justified in describing myself as an unqualified success. The truth is that like so many people, I fell into what I'm doing by accident. The manager of the wine bar in which I had a job playing the piano left to start a local listings magazine, and I began working on the project with him. He dropped out, I carried on – and the rest is history. This, of course, is the last thing a budding illustrator wants to be told.

There is another way. Some years ago, one of the students on a course I taught got a summer job on the picture desk of a national newspaper. It sounded more glamorous than it was: the job mainly involved filing prints in the paper's unwieldy photographic archive. Then, one day, a photograph needed scanning for inclusion in the paper. She pointed out that she'd done some scanning at college, and was allowed to scan the picture.

A short while later, a picture she'd scanned needed some color correction. As she'd studied Photoshop, she volunteered to make the corrections. Then one day a montage had to be done in a hurry – and once again, she volunteered. Today, she has a thriving design business, which combines creating illustrations in her own very distinctive style with working as a freelance designer on the same newspaper.

This example is just one of the stories of illustrators who have made their careers by being in the right place with the right skills. It's one approach: get yourself a job in the right sort of organization, and if you have any talent people will find out about it. You don't need to be pushy, you just have to make sure those around you are aware of what you can do – and take every opportunity to show them what you're capable of.

To make a career as a freelance artist, you need to prove to prospective clients that you can meet a brief and a deadline. The best way to do this is to show them work you've already had published. Art editors are a cautious bunch in the main, and will be reluctant to be the first to try out an untested artist. With good reason. If you screw up, they'll be left with a hole they'll have to fill at the last minute. But if they've seen that other art editors have trusted you and used you – particularly if they've come back and used you again – then they'll be that much more inclined to put your talents to the test.

So if you're determined to pursue the freelance route, the important thing is to get as much work published as you possibly can. Going straight to national newspapers or magazines may prove to be a frustrating business, and you'll be unlikely to get past the receptionist.

You could begin working for local newspapers and magazines, and offer your services free to charities and local, low-budget publications who would otherwise use a piece of clip-art to fill the space. It may seem demeaning if you're working for nothing, and you may feel that your skills are not appreciated when they're not paid for; but it will get you into print, and that's what matters. The more printed examples of your work you can show, the more likely art editors will be to take you on.

It's also important to evolve your own visual style. While it may be tempting to propose that you can work in any style art editors want, the result will be that they'll never think of you when they want an illustration done; be distinctive, and you'll stick in their minds.

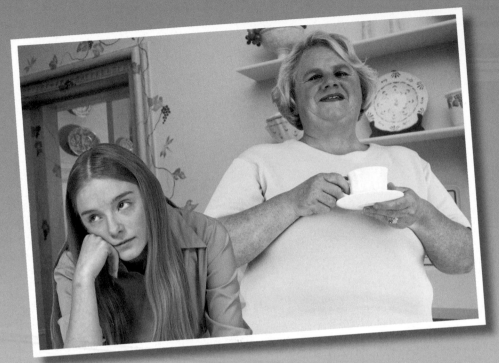

■ Visiting one's grandparents is always a dull chore for an adolescent. But that doesn't mean we need to end up with a dull image. In the top picture, the girl and her grandmother are the same size, in the same plane. Which of them are we supposed to be looking at? The focus is lost. In the lower image, it's clear that we're on the side of the bored girl.

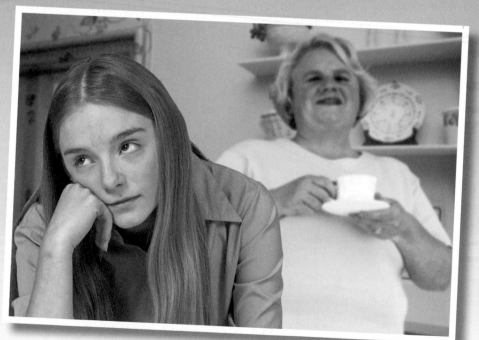

5

Composing the scene

COMPOSITION, as any art historian will tell us, makes the difference between a good picture and a bad one. So it is with photomontage: the position of people and objects within the montage enables us to tell the story we want to tell. As we'll see in the first few examples in this chapter, the relative positions of characters can completely change the message we're putting across.

One way of making a montage look more realistic is to place our characters so that they interact with their background. Films which use a lot of computer-generated imagery, such as Jurassic Park, always go to great lengths to show their subjects part-hidden by foliage and other foreground elements: it's this incorporation within the picture that makes them more convincing.

Location is everything

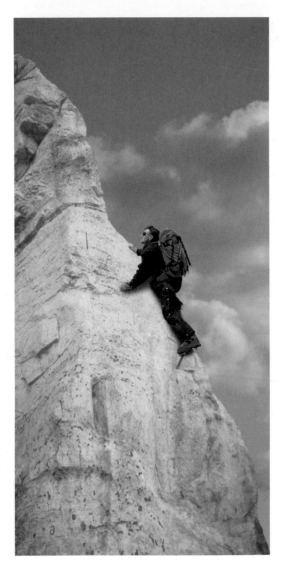

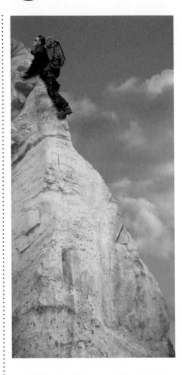

1 With the climber positioned right at the top, we can see how far he's climbed. Our view of the mountain shows the task that he's accomplished to date; but we have no way of telling whether he's just started out, or if he's nearing completion. The rest of the climb may be visible to him, but the viewer is left with no sense of the job that awaits him.

THE WAY AN IMAGE IS CROPPED can have dramatic results in terms of the story being told. Here, we're looking at a montage in which the mountain, the climber and the sky are three separate elements that can be rearranged as we choose; but the same principles apply to cropping an existing image. The fact that this image is composed of three layers simply makes it easier for us to arrange the elements to tell the climber's story as we see it.

As it stands, the image above left shows a mountain climber on a piece of rock. Placed bang in the middle of the frame, the positioning tells us almost nothing about his progress: it's a static picture in which the climber is fixed in place, moving neither up nor down. The strong diagonal of the mountainside,

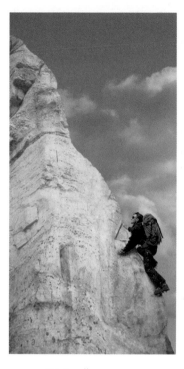

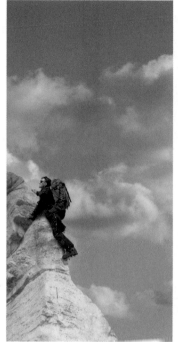

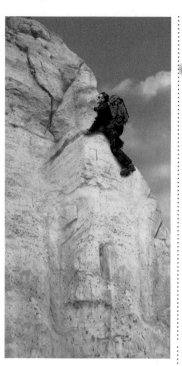

2 Moving the climber to the bottom has the opposite effect. Now we get a good idea of the task in front of the climber, as we can see how far he still has to go. The presence of all that sky, though, positions him some distance up the slope.

3 When we move the mountain down so that the majority of the image is taken up with sky, we get a much stronger impression of the climber nearing the peak. With so much sky around him, we can share his sense of isolation and solitude. All this sky shows us that there isn't another person around for miles.

4 By moving the mountain so that it takes up most of the frame, we position it so that our own viewpoint interacts with the picture. Where before the focus was on the climber, now the viewer can get a sense of the hardship faced. So much rock face highlights the climber's daunting task.

running from top left to bottom right, divides the image neatly in two as it delineates the difference between the land and the sky; but that neatness also takes away all sense of the dramatic.

Cropping a picture enables the viewer to focus on the key image without being distracted by extraneous elements. But it also allows the picture editor, or the digital artist,

to tell the story they want to tell rather than simply reproducing the scene as it originally appeared.

While the use of photomontage in newspapers has attracted much criticism amid claims of it distorting the truth, few readers complain about the way images are cropped – and yet the story is determined as much by cropping as by montage.

Relative values: interaction

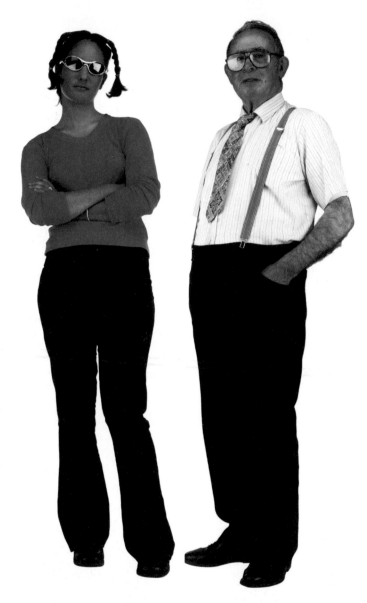

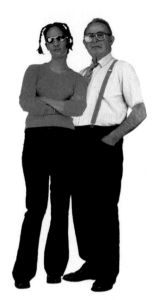

1 Simply moving them closer together so that they overlap helps to establish a link between them. By flipping the girl horizontally, both figures are now angled towards the center of the image.

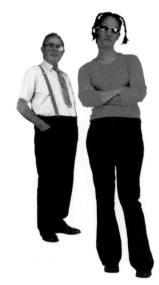

5 Now the tables have been turned. It's the daughter who is in the dominant position, while the father remains distanced from her: like most parents, he's now concerned that she's moving away from him.

COMBINING TWO PEOPLE in a montage entails more than just placing them on the same background. You've got to work out the relationship between them, and position them to tell the story in the best way. The image above shows, let's say, a father and daughter. They may share the same space but the reader gets no hint of how they might interact; by varying their position we can make their relationship clear.

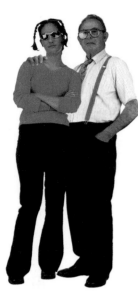

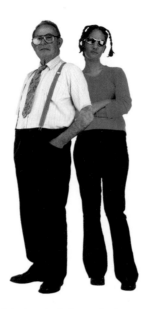

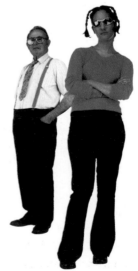

2 A simple additional device such as the hand on her shoulder puts the father in a more protective role. His body language is one of pride with, perhaps, a hint of restraint.

3 Bringing the father to the front still establishes his protectiveness, but now there's a sense that the safeguard is needed: he's shielding her from the viewer, while she is content to take refuge behind him.

4 By moving her towards the back we create an emotional as well as physical distance between them. Flipping her so that her shoulders point away from his accentuates the disparity: she now resents his control.

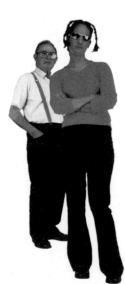

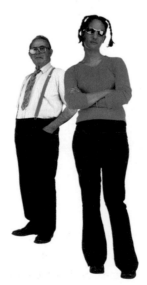

6 When we tuck the father behind the daughter, we strengthen the sense of her supremacy over him. In the previous example, she was merely moving away; now she's beginning to eclipse him.

7 Flipping the father horizontally makes him face away from his daughter metaphorically. His understanding of her is less than in the last example, but her pose shows she's prepared to turn back to him.

8 Flipping the daughter alters her body language as well: the two figures are now opposed, their shoulders pointing in different directions as she now turns her back on him absolutely.

I only have eyes for you

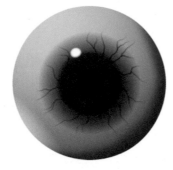

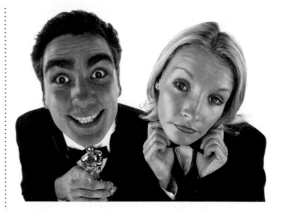

1 With both characters gazing directly at us, there's no contact between them – and we're left with no idea what either of them is thinking.

ON THE PREVIOUS PAGE, WE LOOKED at how changing body position can make a difference to the apparent relationship between people in a montage. But body language is only one way of explaining a relationship: far more subtle – and just as effective – is eye contact.

The photomontage artist often has to work with mugshots of politicians and celebrities, or images from a royalty-free collection. Either way, you're more or less guaranteed that the subjects will be gazing straight at the camera, and probably grinning inanely at the same time. This may suit the needs of the celebrity's publicist, but it's of little help when combining two or more people within a scene.

Here, we've taken a glamorous couple – so glamorous that he's just won an Oscar – and moved their eyes around from frame to frame. Nothing else has been changed, and yet the entire expression alters with the position of the eyes. The nine examples here are just a small part of the infinite range of expressions that can be achieved by simply changing the eyes.

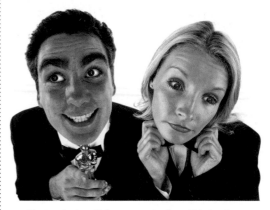

4 He now looks a little over-protective of his trophy, as if someone might be about to snatch it from him: but she's downcast, as if the prize should have been hers.

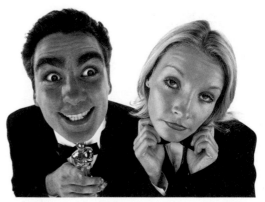

7 He now gazes excitedly into the future – who knows what doors this prize will open? She isn't so much annoyed with him as just plain bored by the whole evening.

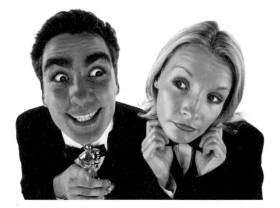

2 He's looking at her hopefully, and the grin has become almost a leer. Her reply is ambiguous, but not wholly negative – she might go along with his plans, she might not.

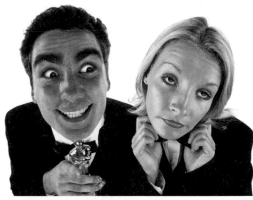

3 His expression hasn't changed, but hers certainly has. No chance for him tonight: she's fed up with the whole idea and can't wait to be rid of him.

HOT TIP

To change the direction a character's eyes are looking in, you need to create two new layers – one for the eyeball, and one for the iris: make a clipping mask for the iris with the eyeball, and you can move it around within the eye. For more about working with eyes, see Chapter 8.

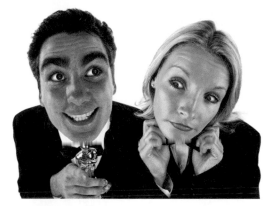

5 Now he's gazing up at his adoring audience – a subtle difference from the previous example. She, however, only has eyes for the trophy.

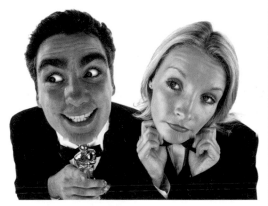

6 Now he's really worried, glancing over his shoulder as if he expects to be mugged – and that grin looks more false than ever. Her mind is somewhere else entirely.

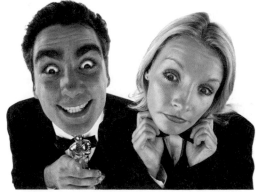

8 He stares in wonder at his trophy as if he can't believe he's really won it. She ponders the situation, wondering if next time the accolade will go to her instead.

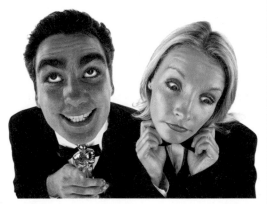

9 Now he's thanking heaven for the prize which has been awarded him – whereas she is wondering if she just saw a mouse scuttle across the floor.

5 Composing the scene

Game, test and match

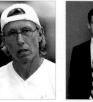
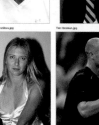
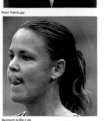
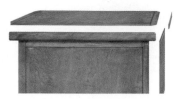

COMBINING PUBLICITY photographs of celebrities, politicians or sports stars is always a difficult business. Apart from the vagaries of color caused by pictures being taken in different locations, there's just too much grinning at the camera: it's hard to find pictures with any kind of emotion on display.

The commission for this montage, for tennis magazine Ace, was to put six tennis stars together in a schoolroom setting. The hard part was getting the people involved to look as if they were interacting, or at least aware of each others' existence! New bodies, please.

1 The supplied mugshots of the six tennis players had little dynamism to them. Fortunately, I was able to get hold of a couple of profile shots, which makes all the difference: when you've got a profile, you can make one character look at another.

2 Building the first desk was a time-consuming process, especially as I knew I'd have to build it in such a way that it could be reassembled in a different perspective later. The front panel is a photograph of a real school desk; sections of this were copied to three new layers to make the lid, side and lid profile. By grouping all the elements into a layer set, I was able to duplicate the set for the other desks.

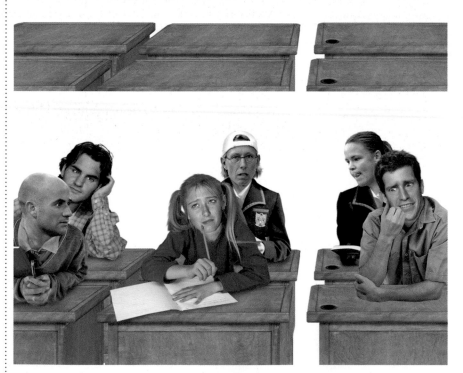

3 All the players needed new bodies, and I was able to raid my store of school uniforms to provide the necessary poses. Figure interaction is important, so I decided to place Sharapova center front as the focal point, picked out in bright red: all the male players could now be gazing at her with schoolboy adoration. I couldn't do much with Navratilova's vacant gaze (center back) but at least I could make Davenport lean over as if trying to copy her work. Keeping all the desks on separate layers made it possible to place the bodies in between them.

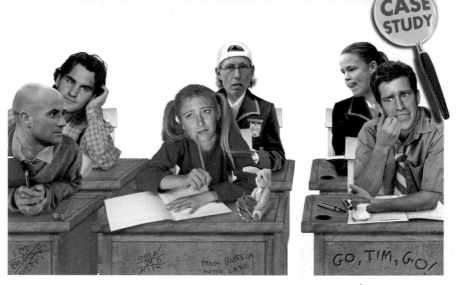

CASE STUDY

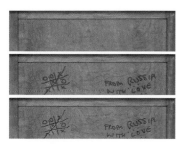

4 Those desks were just too clean (top) and needed some livening up. The graffiti and other scratches were drawn on a new layer (center), and then a slight bevel was applied to the graffiti layer to give it an incised look (bottom). It's a surprisingly simple technique that nevertheless produces acceptable results.

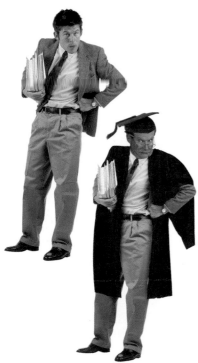

5 The graffiti helped the desks to look more like they were part of a schoolroom, but the overall effect was just too neat and tidy. Since this was an examination setting, it seemed appropriate to add typical exam paraphernalia: the lucky rabbit, the chocolate bar, the half eaten apple, the fountain pen. And the shirt on Henman (front right) was turned into a school uniform by the simple addition of a striped tie.

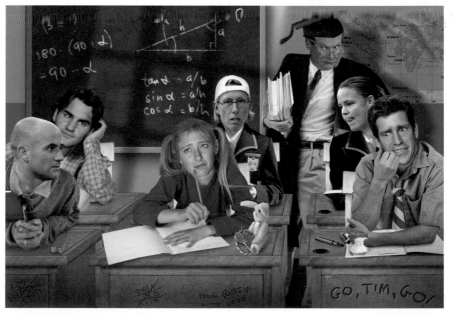

6 The teacher's body came from a Stockbyte collection, and was in exactly the right pose. But this teacher wasn't old-fashioned enough for the scene: so a new hat and gown were added from a different image and shaped to fit and a new spectacled head grafted on.

7 The back wall was pitted using the Alien Skin plug-in Splat!, which creates great realistic textures. The board comes from a photograph of a real blackboard – simply filling a rectangle with black doesn't look convincing. The chalk was drawn directly onto the board. The shadows, both front and back, help to complete the illusion. Of course, this schoolroom is a nonsense: who ever heard of a school setting in which the board is at the back of the class? But this is a mere technicality. It's unlikely many tennis fans, reading the magazine, would have picked up on the error.

HOT TIP

Don't panic when starting a job like this. One layer at a time!

101

Back to the foreground

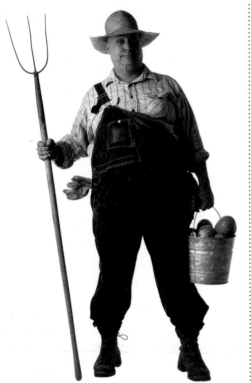

PLACING PEOPLE within a scene is rarely a matter of sticking them on top – because they rarely look like they belong there. To make the image more convincing, the people need to interact with the background to some degree. The easiest way to do this is to take a background element and bring it to the front: it's often a simple task, but it makes all the difference, as we'll see with this illustration of an urban farmer swamped by his modern-day environment.

1 When the farmer is pasted on top of the background, he looks like he doesn't belong there. Well, he doesn't – this patch of grass is really waste ground in the middle of a road junction. To make the scene work more convincingly, we need to make the farmer become part of the background rather than simply standing in front of it as he does at the moment.

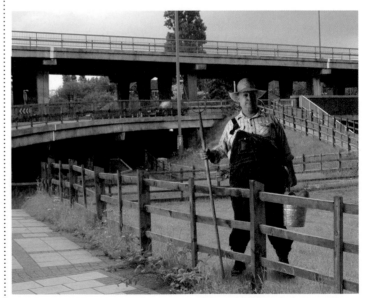

4 With the pitchfork now in front of the fence, which in turn is in front of the farmer, he looks fully integrated into the scene. A shadow of the pitchfork is painted on the fence, and another shadow created beneath the farmer; finally, small wisps are masked around his feet to make it look like blades of grass are growing up in front of them.

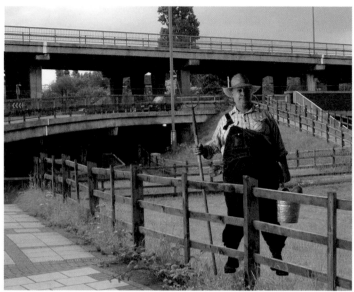

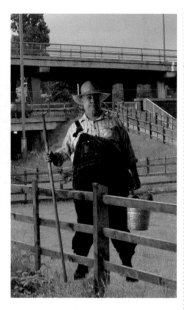

2 The fence is made up of straight lines, so it's a simple matter to select the front half of it using the Pen tool, make a new layer and bring it to the front. If you really can't get on with the Pen tool, use the Lasso instead – hold down ⌥ alt to constrain the tool to creating straight lines between pairs of click points. Now, the farmer is far more integrated.

3 This is a simple trick: we can just select the bottom half of his pitchfork, make a new layer out of it using ⌘⇧J ⌃⇧U and bring it to the front.

The final step requires that the background be selectively blurred – more at the back, less at the front. Go into QuickMask mode and, using the Gradient tool set to black–white, drag from top to bottom. This creates an area that's 100% selected at the top and 0% selected at the bottom: when you exit QuickMask and apply the blur, the image will be affected more at the top than at the bottom.

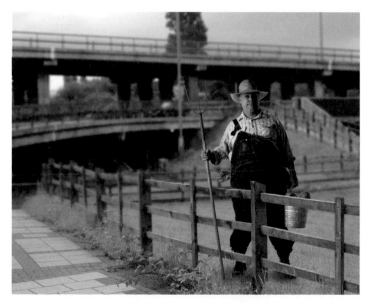

5 The background in the original image is busy, as befits an urban road system – but so busy that it's distracting attention. So the top half of the background was selected and blurred using Gaussian Blur, to knock it slightly out of focus. To make the fence section fit, the left edge of that layer was also blurred to blend into the background.

Composition tips and tricks

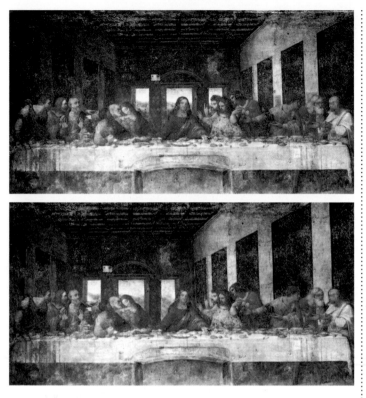

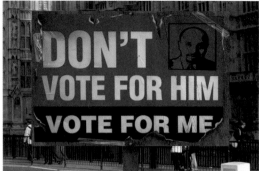

1 We'll learn how to create torn posters like this one in Chapter 11. In the meantime, let's just look at the placement of the image. When it's positioned dead center, it's so in-your-face that it loses all subtlety. Da Vinci aside, the center is rarely the best place for a focal point.

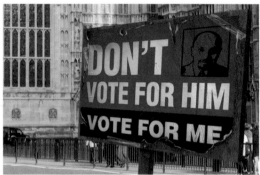

4 The placement may have been better at the end of the previous step, but there was a busyness to the background that made it hard to focus on the poster: the tones of the building were too similar to the wood tones in the board. Brightening the background overcomes this.

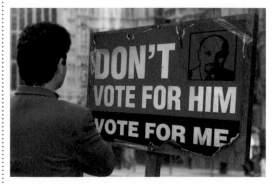

7 In the previous step, the figure in the foreground added a much-needed human element. But the distance between the figure and the poster, although tiny, made the two elements look disconnected. By overlapping the figure with the poster we unify the two.

D A VINCI'S LAST SUPPER is not only the painting that inspired the Da Vinci Code, it's also a masterpiece of classical composition.

Jesus sits right in the center, surrounded by his apostles – who form four distinct groups of three, each of which would be a perfectly composed painting in its own right if taken in isolation.

But what really makes this picture work is the background: in the original version (top) all the diagonals in the walls and that carefully painted lattice ceiling are balanced, and point directly to the central figure. Wherever we look, our eye is drawn back to him. When we shift the background (bottom) the integrity of the whole image falls apart. That Leonardo certainly knew a thing or two about composition.

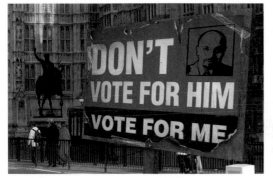

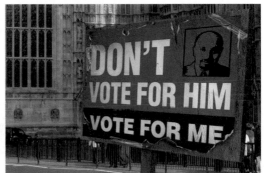

2 Adding a little perspective to the object greatly increases the sense of it existing in real space. Of course, it's necessary to add a side edge to the wooden board and the post, to complete the new viewpoint. The trouble now is that the perspective of the poster points to that horse statue.

3 Objects in the background can distract the eye and lose the central focus. The statue pulled our eye away; and that traffic bollard in the bottom right was an unnecessary intrusion. By sliding the whole background to the right we create a less distracting, more harmonious image.

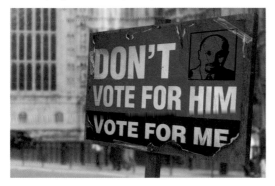

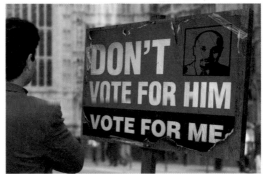

It's often hard to judge whether a composition is working as a whole, especially when there are strong foreground elements that shout for attention. One trick used by both artists and graphic designers is to turn the image upside down: that way, none of the image elements make much sense on their own, and we're free to concentrate on the way they fit together.

5 We can make the background recede still further by giving the impression of it being out of focus, using the Gaussian Blur filter. This sort of depth-of-field effect makes it impossible for the eye to focus on the background, bringing our attention back to the poster.

6 As every cartoonist knows, a block of text on its own is meaningless without a figure looking at it. Build up a stock of photographs of people from the back – they'll always prove useful. This is one of a series I took of myself for just this purpose.

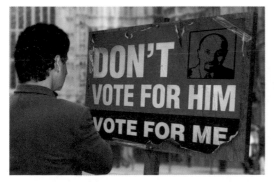

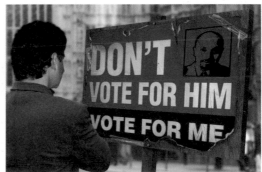

8 Make sure your figure is looking at the poster, and not off into the distance! Here, replacing the original head with one taken from a more appropriate angle leaves us in no doubt that he's really looking at the poster, drawing the viewer's eye back to the main focus.

9 It's important to make sure any foreground elements really do their job of drawing the eye in, and don't distract from the image. The jacket on our rear-view figure was far too stong a color: we can use the Hue/Saturation adjustment to make it blend in with the background tones.

People and cars

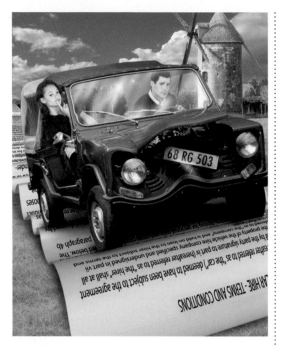

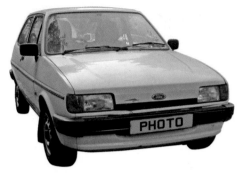

1 Our original photograph of this car was shot in an ordinary street, some of which can still be glimpsed through the windows. The first job was to cut out the background, leaving just the car. (The number plate has, of course, been changed to protect the car's owner.)

PLACING PEOPLE IN CARS SHOULD BE A relatively straightforward task. But cars always have windscreens, which reflect light and muddy the issue. To make the job work effectively takes some care, involving several steps which are outlined here.

The illustration above was for a feature in the Daily Telegraph newspaper about the draconian contracts car hire companies impose on their customers. The idea of the contract as a bumpy road, causing damage to the car, was easy to come up with; the execution was slightly harder. The road itself was drawn using the 3D Extrude functionality of Adobe Illustrator CS, which was able to map the dummy text onto a bumpy surface made from extruding a wavy line. It's the kind of job that would have been much harder without Illustrator; and if I'd been asked to do it two weeks earlier I wouldn't have had the latest version. Roll on upgrades!

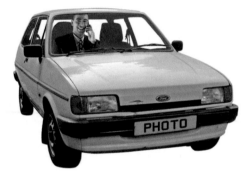

4 Now for the driver. Let's have him talking on his cellphone, for the simple reason that it's illegal. You'll find this man as separate layer in the Photoshop file. Remember that in England we drive on the left!

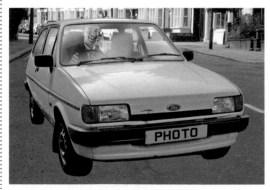

7 Now for the windscreen. Make sure the car body is at the top of the layer stack, and make a selection with the Lasso tool that includes all the window area. Make a new layer, behind the car body, and paint the glass with diagonal white strokes using a soft-edged brush set to a low opacity.

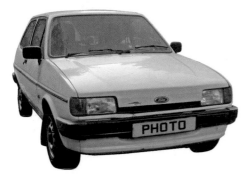

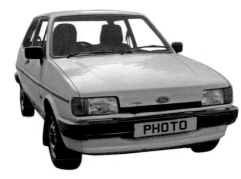

2 Now to remove the windscreen. The area highlighted is shown in red: we've left the windscreen wipers in place, as they belong in front of the glass. I've already saved the path for you as Front Windows, so load that and cut the selection to a new layer using `⌘` `Shift` `J` `ctrl` `Shift` `J`.

3 We now need to erase the windows on the side and the back of the car. Load the path Rear Windows, and delete; then we need to darken the car interior on the new layer, since it was photographed through reflecting glass – but we're going to add our own glass later.

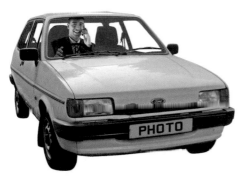

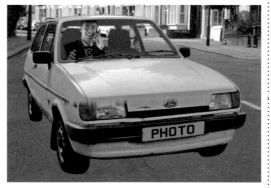

5 A new steering wheel needs to be placed in front of the driver, and to make it look convincing we'll stick in a hand holding it. Again, you'll find this hand/steering wheel assembly as a separate layer in the Photoshop file.

6 At this point, we should add a background to see how the final composition will look. Again, it's critical to the success of the project to find one that matches the perspective of the car. Try the one in the Photoshop file first.

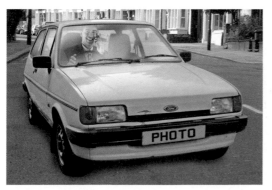

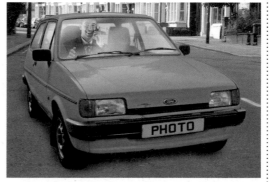

8 The rear windows also need some treatment. With the same area selected, make another layer behind all the car elements and this time paint with a light gray: these windows will appear darker since they reflect some of the inside of the car. A shadow beneath the car also helps.

9 Coloring the car is all a matter of selection. The easiest way is to make a new layer that uses the car as a clipping mask, set to either Hard Light or Multiply. Fill this with the color of your choice, and erase those parts that shouldn't be colored, such as the lights, bumper and wheels.

HOT TIP

When you cut the interior of the car from the body, as in steps 2 and 3, you may find a fine white line around the car's interior edge. One solution is to use the Defringe command (Layer menu) to remove it; alternatively, apply a fine stroke to the inside of the car to get rid of it.

Digital cameras

WHEN I FIRST wrote this interlude, back in 2001, digital cameras were still an optional accessory. In the first edition of this book, my job was to try to persuade you that these glittering gadgets would be able to make your Photoshop work easier and more productive.

In 2005, a digital camera is not so much a luxury as an essential and expected piece of equipment: there can be few readers of this book who don't

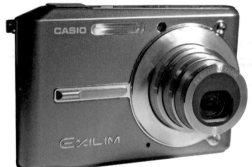

have one. I don't need to extol the benefits of instant capture, or digital printing. So this time around, I don't need to talk you into buying a digital camera. I'm going to try to persuade you that you need two.

First off, you need a heavy duty camera for serious image capture. The price of digital SLRs has dropped tremendously in the last four years. In 2001 you'd need to pay around $4000 for a

reasonable quality 3 Megapixel SLR – and that's without a lens attached. Now, you can pick up a high quality device for under $800.

At the time of writing, there are two serious contenders in the affordable digital SLR camp: the Canon EOS 400-D, and the Nikon D80. They're both chunky, traditionally shaped machines that look and feel just like film SLR cameras. Both will take superb photographs, either in fully automatic mode or using a variety of manual override settings. I use a rather elderly Canon 300-D, but there's little to choose between the two makes.

Because both these cameras are SLRs – which stands for Single Lens Reflex – you use the viewfinder for taking pictures, instead of peering at an LCD screen as you do with lower-end cameras. This has two consequences: firstly, it's a lot easier to get an image in sharp focus when you're looking directly through the lens, rather than at a pixellated screen. And secondly, because the LCD screen is only in use for playback, the batteries last forever. On my Canon, I get an average of 400 shots between charges; with a spare battery, this means I can go out for a day's shoot and can be certain I'll have enough battery power to last me out.

Memory has also plummeted in price. It used to be a deciding factor when a camera came with no memory card: but now that you can buy a 2Gb Secure Digital or Compact Flash card for under $30, which will hold several hundred images, it's hardly an issue.

The only drawback with these powerful SLRs is their sheer bulk. It's fine if you go out with the express purpose of taking pictures, but it's not the sort of thing you're going to have with you all the time. And that's the problem. Even more important than a camera that takes perfect pictures is a camera you've got with you. Which means having a camera that's small enough to fit in your pocket without bulging.

I've been through several of these tiny devices, and my current compact is the Casio Exilim X-S600. It's a 6 Megapixel camera, and has a zoom lens and a flash. It takes pretty good pictures, has a fantastically capable and well thought-out operating system, and costs around $300. Most importantly of all, though: I've always got it with me.

That's the secret to building up a successful image library of your own: keep taking pictures. Although there are dozens of image libraries on the internet, the everyday, commonplace items are the hardest things to find.

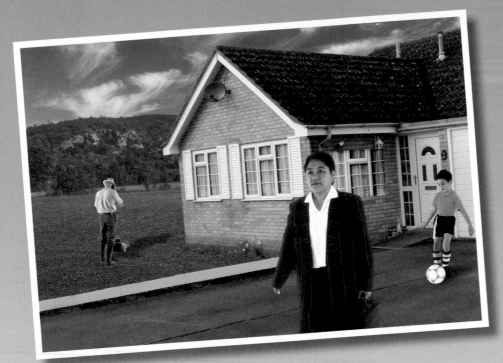

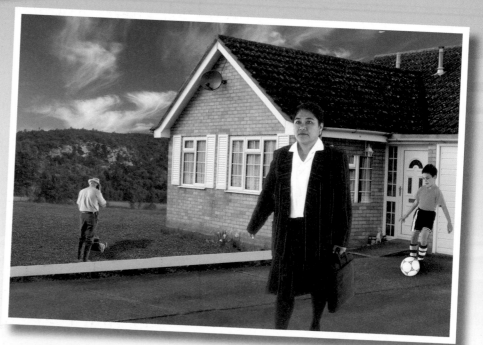

■ A woman leaves her house to go to work: her son is playing football, while the gardener mows the grass. The top picture looks realistic; the lower one looks somehow wrong. Why do we feel that she's floating, when we can't see her feet? Why does the gardener look like a midget? What makes the boy look overgrown? Perspective has all the answers.

6 Getting into perspective

PERSPECTIVE IS PROBABLY one of the most puzzling aspects of photomontage work. It's certainly the aspect of the job that seems to perplex users the most: the intricacies of how it works and how it's applied can seem like a mass of confusing jargon.

In fact, perspective is easy to master: it's simply a question of understanding the key facts. Some of these are those blindingly simple statements that sound obvious when you've heard them, but which can be near-impossible to work out for yourself.

One of the big new features in Photoshop CS2 was the Vanishing Point filter, which does a truly extraordinary job of making perspective child's play. We'll look at this later on in this chapter.

Establishing the horizon

THE HORIZON LINE IS THE defining point in any drawing, painting or montage. It determines the shape of the entire scene, and establishes the position of the viewer within that scene.

The horizon line is easily established using a simple, but absolute rule:

The horizon is always at the same height as the eyeline of the viewer.

It sometimes seems incredible that the key to a successful montage can be expressed in terms as simple as that: but this is the one area most people get wrong.

In practice, this means that the head height of all the adult figures in an illustration should be on the same level as each other, except for special purposes, such as when you want to give the impression that your viewer is sitting down, or looking from a child's perspective.

We'll demonstrate this principle on these pages, using a foreground figure to show how the horizon line varies with the height of the viewer.

IMAGES: HEMERA PHOTO-OBJECTS

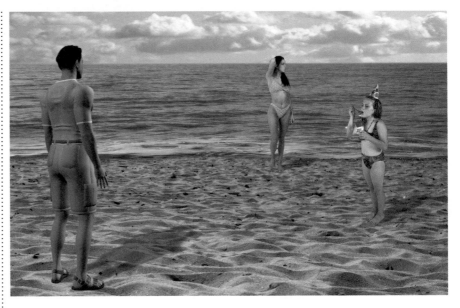

1 For most purposes, we can assume our viewer to be standing up. In these examples, the viewer is shown by the figure on the far left, and our viewpoint is taken to be the same as his. The horizon line, clearly seen in this seascape, is on the same eyeline; and so any adults in the scene have their eyes on the same line, since they're roughly the same height as us. Smaller figures, such as children, will appear below the horizon line to indicate their lesser size.

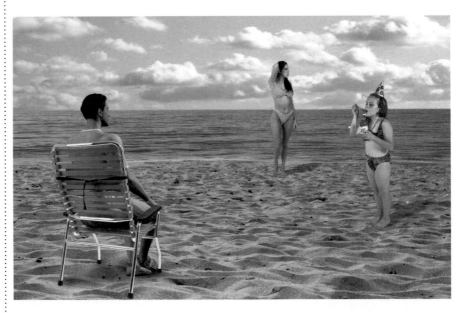

2 When the viewer is sitting down, the horizon is lowered so that it remains on his eyeline. In these cases, adult figures will appear with their heads some distance above the horizon, as we're now looking up at them. Children will now show their eyelines to be lined up with the horizon. Nearby figures, such as the child in this example, will appear correspondingly larger as the perspective of the scene changes to match the angle of view.

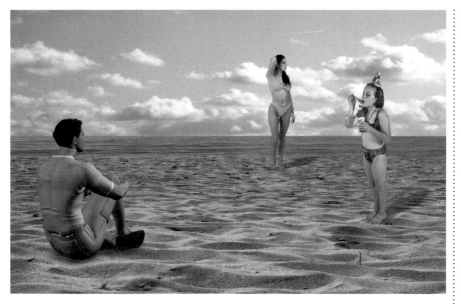

3 When our viewer is even closer to the ground, the view to the horizon is further compressed so that it remains precisely on his eyeline. Now, the adults in the scene are significantly higher than us – our head is on a level with this woman's knees – and even children appear to tower over us. Because of the reduced eye height, children will once again appear to be proportionately larger. We can now see much more sky, and much less sea.

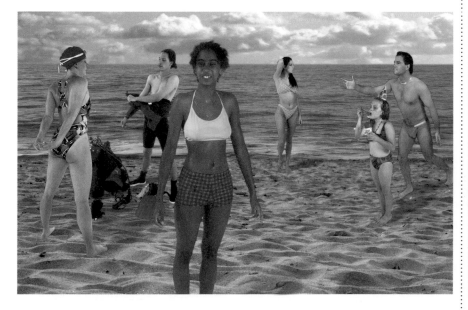

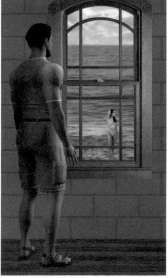

4 As a general rule, we can expect the viewer to be standing at standard head height. This means that all adults in the scene will have their heads on the same line, which will once again correspond exactly with the horizon (give or take the usual slight variations in adult height). This simple rule makes it easy to position a large number of people, at different distances from us, so that they all look as if they truly belong in the same visual space.

It doesn't matter if we're lying down, or standing at the top of a tall building: the horizon is always at the height of our eyes. Look out of the window and try it for yourself!

Introducing vanishing points

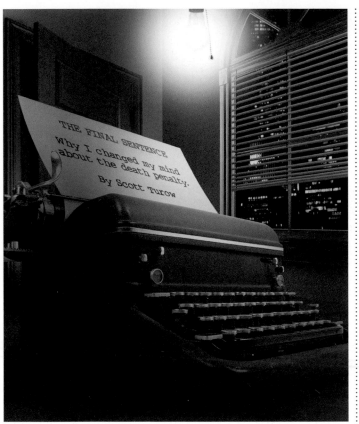

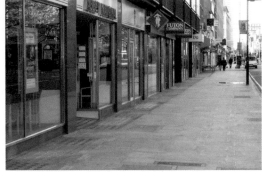

1 This straightforward street scene includes strong diagonal lines – the tops and bottoms of the shop fronts. We know that, in reality, these lines will be absolutely horizontal: and so we can use them to calculate the horizon line for this image.

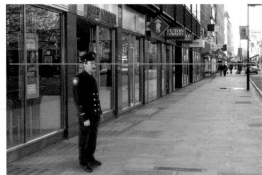

4 Now let's bring in a security guard to stand outside the first shop. We position him, naturally, so that his eyeline is exactly on the horizon. (We've assumed him to be the same height that we are.) I've added a bit of shadow below and behind him to make him look more part of the image.

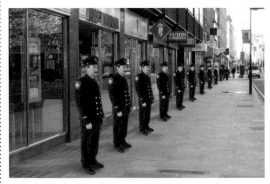

7 Here's a good trick: pressing `ctrl` `Shift` `T` `⌘` `Shift` `T` will repeat the last transformation. But pressing `ctrl` `Shift` `alt` `T` `⌘` `Shift` `⌥` `T` will *duplicate* the last transformation. By pressing it several times, we can build an entire row of security guards.

GETTING PERSPECTIVE RIGHT is the key to an illustration succeeding or failing. In the cover montage for The Guardian, above, I chose a low viewpoint to increase the drama of the scene. With this extreme perspective, the sheet of paper, the text and the door frame all had to fit in with the typewriter's perspective or it would have made no sense to the reader.

In this section we'll look at vanishing points, and how they can be used to enable us to create convincing three-dimensional images. There's also a fantastic time-saving technique that will enable you to make rows of people or objects in seconds!

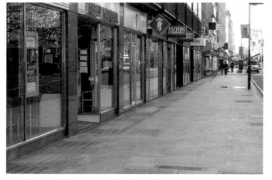

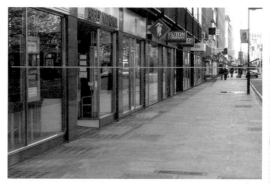

2 Use the Line tool, set to Shape Layers mode, to draw two lines along these diagonals. (The Line tool is one of the Shapes tools.) Where they cross is the vanishing point, towards which all perspective lines in the image will tend.

3 Now draw a horizon line: a horizontal, again drawn with the Shapes tool, that intersects the vanishing point. Note how this horizon passes through the heads of the distant pedestrains, as predicted by the previous lesson. See! It really is true!

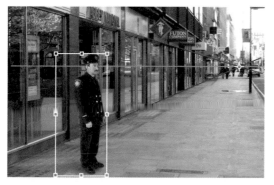

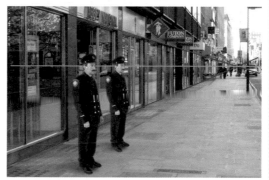

5 Next, duplicate the guard layer. Enter Free Transform mode (*ctrl* *T* *⌘* *T*) and drag the center point marker out so it sits directly on top of the vanishing point. Now grab the bottom left corner handle and, while holding *alt* *Shift* *⌥* *Shift*, drag the cursor towards the vanishing point.

6 The *alt* *⌥* key scales from the 'center' – in this case, the vanishing point; adding *Shift* keeps the transformation in proportion. The result is an identical guard, positioned further down the street – but in exactly the correct perspective for this view, eyeline on the horizon.

This Repeat Transformation operation can be used for horizontal elements as well. It's great for duplicating railway sleepers, for example, as well as tiled floors, cattle grids and so on. Scaling or shearing towards the vanishing point will always produce precise perspective distortions.

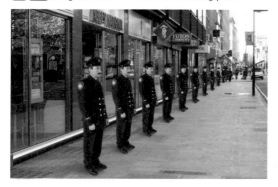

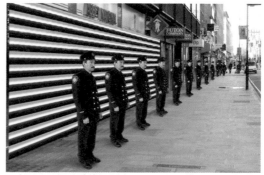

8 We'll use a similar technique to build shutters. The first shutter is drawn in perspective by adding lines from the vanishing point: in addition, we need to paint a tiny circle on the vanishing point itself as part of the shutter layer. That's because we can't move the center marker for this operation.

9 Duplicate the layer again, but this time shear the layer instead of scaling it. Enter Free Transform, and hold *ctrl* *Shift* *⌘* *Shift* while dragging the centre left handle vertically. Again, *ctrl* *Shift* *alt* *T* *⌘* *Shift* *⌥* *T* will repeat the transformation to make this row of shutters.

SHORTCUTS
MAC | WIN | BOTH

Two point perspective

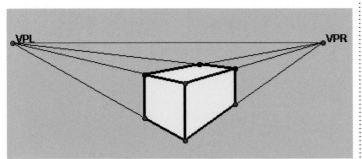

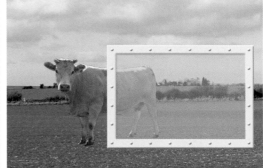

1 Here's our task: we've got a field with a clear, visible horizon in it, and a cow gazing out at us. Fortunately, the cow's on a separate layer so we can hide it easily. Our job is to put the cow in a glass tank, Damien Hirst style: and there's a panel of framed glass there waiting for us.

O N THE PREVIOUS PAGE we looked at setting the vanishing point. When you're looking at the inside of things – boxes, rooms, streets – there's just a single vanishing point: this is one point perspective. When you're looking at the outside corners of objects you need to use not one, but two vanishing points, at the far left (VPL) and far right (VPR) of the field of view. All planes in the image will tend to one or other of these vanishing points.

Deciding where to place the VPL and VPR is a tricky matter, since it affects the perspective of the image in the same way as when you switch between a wide angle and a telephoto lens.

Fortunately, technology has come to our rescue. The screen shot above is from a java applet written by the talented programmer Cathi Sanders, which she has kindly agreed to let me include with this book. It shows how the perspective process works: you can move either the VPL or the VPR along the horizon line, and change the dimensions and position of the yellow box by dragging any of the red dots, to see exactly how altering the vanishing points affects the perspective of the scene. You'll find this java applet on the CD-ROM, and it can be opened in any standard browser.

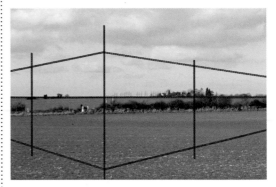

3 Now draw two more verticals, again with the Shapes tool, at the left and right corners of the tank. So far, we've drawn in the two sides facing us: but because this is a glass tank, we'll need to draw in the back panels as well, which we'll do next.

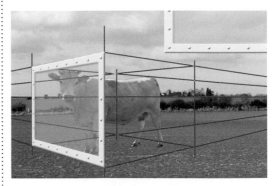

6 Move the original panel well out of the way, then take a copy of it (hold *alt* ⌥ and drag with the Move tool) and enter Free Transform mode. Now hold *ctrl* ⌘ as you move each corner handle to distort the panel to fit the guide lines: hold *Shift* as you drag to keep the verticals straight!

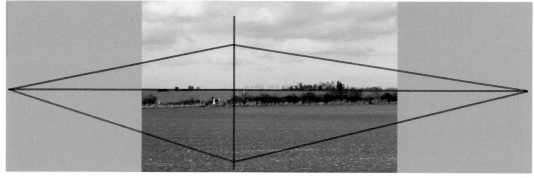

2 The trouble is, the image isn't nearly wide enough to draw our vanishing point lines. There's a simple solution: we'll draw them using pen paths. First, zoom out until your image has plenty of spare window space around it (hide the panel and cow layers, so you can see what's going on). Now,

using the Line tool set to Path mode, draw in the horizon line on the visible horizon. Draw a vertical for the nearest corner, then add perspective lines to arbitrary left and right vanishing points. The position of these points is largely up to you.

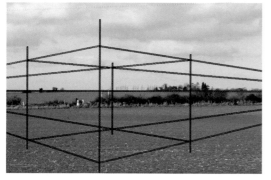

4 Starting at the four back corners, draw lines from each to the opposite vanishing points. All the lines drawn will now be perfectly in perspective: just for good measure, we can add a final vertical in the far corner to aid us in positioning the back panels.

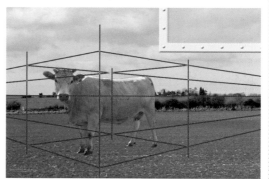

5 We now want to distort those panels to fit the space. But you can't use Free Transform when a path is visible, or the path will be distorted instead; so make a new layer, turn the path into a selection, and fill the perspective lines with a color. Time to show that cow and panel again!

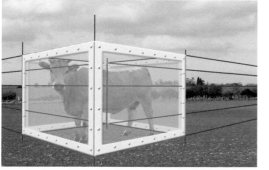

7 Repeat this procedure with three more copies of the original panel to make the other front side and the two back sides. Remember to move the back side layers behind the cow! As long as you make the panels fit the guide lines, the perspective should work perfectly.

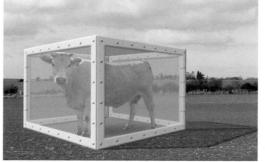

8 As a final step, I've darkened the right-hand panel and added a lid and base to the tank. The shadow is easily made by desaturating a further copy of the panel (using `ctrl Shift U` `⌘ Shift U`), setting its layer mode to Multiply, and then distorting it so it lies along the ground.

HOT TIP

You'll get the most successful results when you balance the left and right vanishing points so that they're at equal distances each side of the center of your artwork. The closer together they are, the more extreme the perspective of the scene will be, just as if you were using a wide angle lens. Oh, and for those of you who don't know: Damien Hirst is a contemporary British artist renowned for cutting animals in half and pickling them in clear tanks of formaldehyde.

SHORTCUTS
MAC WIN BOTH

117

Three point perspective

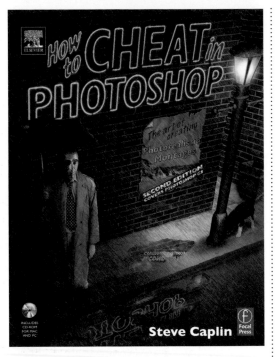

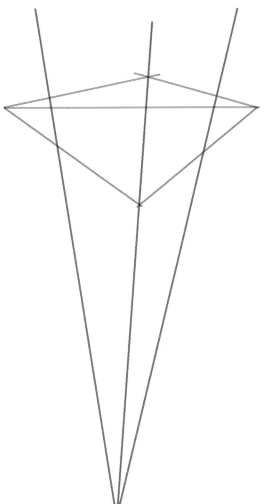

ONE AND TWO POINT PERSPECTIVES may work for most tasks, but they both assume that verticals in the image are truly vertical. This isn't always the case: the cover of the second edition of this book featured a top-down view that used a more complex system.

The further you are from the subject, the less important perspective becomes. I made the panorama of London below by stitching together a dozen photographs: each had its own vanishing points, so the result shouldn't make sense. But so great is the distance that the eye ignores the discrepancies.

1 When we're looking at a scene from an angle off the horizontal, the verticals will no longer be straight up and down. A third perspective vanishing point needs to be created – either below the object, if we're looking down on it, or above it if we're looking up.

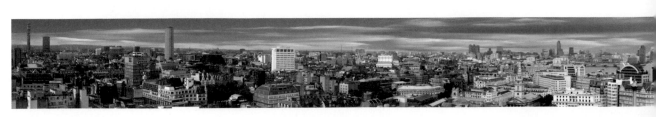

3 The same panels we used in the previous example have been distorted using Free Transform once again, to fit the perspective lines. But we could just as well have used brick walls to build a view of a house.

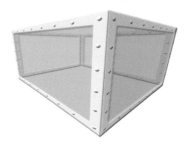

HOT TIP

The lower the third vanishing point is, the less extreme the perspective viewpoint will be. Even with it way down, as it is in this example, there's still a strong distortion on those verticals: for a less exaggerated effect, you need to zoom out a long way and place the third vanishing point at a great distance from the artwork.

2 The perspective lines can get very hard to interpret, so it can be worth creating them in two batches. Here, Shapes paths making up the front edges and the horizon have been made into a selection and filled with red; the rear edges have been filled with green on a new layer.

4 With all the perpsective lines removed, and some shading added, the box looks convincing enough. It would have been almost impossible to draw this view without using vanishing lines. Trying to find a cow to fit this extreme view would be another matter entirely!

Correcting perspective

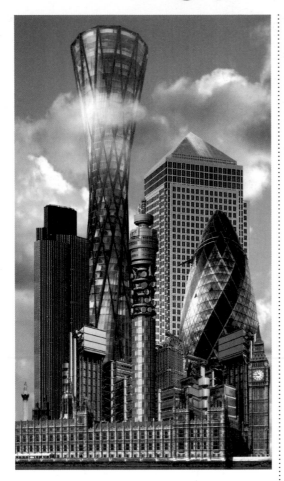

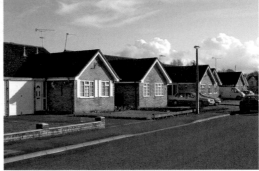

1 A typical suburban street scene. I photographed this with plenty of spare road in front, so it would be easy to add in extra vehicles, pedestrians or galumphing space monsters as required. No nearby corners – so one-point perspective.

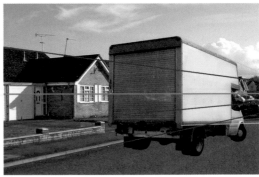

4 Let's bring the truck back, and draw some perspective lines (in yellow) on a new layer attached to it. Right away, we can see the problem: the bottom line should be going upwards, not crossing the red perspective line.

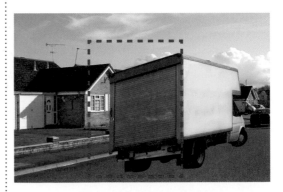

7 Well, the front may look OK, but the back end's all over the place. Unlink the layers, then draw a marquee selection around the back end of the truck. Be sure to place the right edge of the marquee so it aligns precisely with the corner of the truck nearest to us.

OBJECTS DON'T ALWAYS FIT into the scene as neatly as we'd like them to: frequently, the perspective needs to be adjusted to fit in with the background.

The montage above was for the front page of The Guardian, and was to illustrate the relative heights of London buildings (the big colorful one at the back is the proposed Vortex skyscraper). The rest of the buildings came from a variety of sources, and had to be adapted to make them look as if they all belonged in the same visual space. There was a lot of dividing up into planes and shearing involved, exactly as described here.

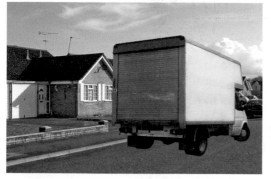

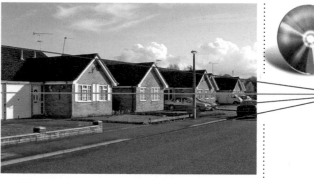

2 When this dirty white truck is placed in the scene, we can see that something's not quite right. It's hard to pin it down, but there's a feeling of unease about the composition. Let's hide the van and find out why.

3 With the truck hidden, we can now draw in perspective lines using the Line tool, following the angles of the road and the roof line. Where they meet is the horizon, here drawn in green. Note that it's at head height on the doors!

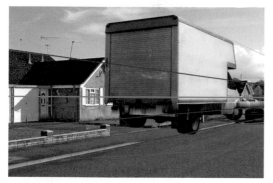

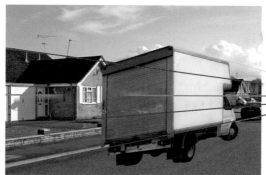

5 In fact, this is how we'd position this truck in order for it to be in the correct perspective for the street. I'd obviously photographed it from a low viewpoint, which is why it's now floating in the air! Let's see how to fix it.

6 Link the truck and its perspective line layers together. Now enter Free Transform, and move the center marker on top of the vanishing point: then grab the middle handle on the left side and shear it downwards.

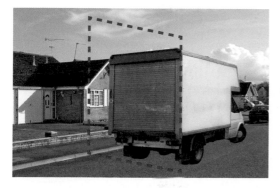

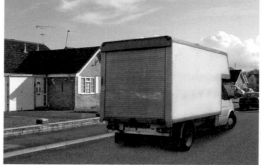

8 Now enter Free Transform once more, grab the center handle on the left side and drag it upwards. The top edge of this side should be aligned with the angle of the roof of the house directly behind it – another clue to drawing this scene in perspective.

9 The truck itself may be a convenient rectangular box, but the same can't be said for the wheels. There's almost always a litte tidying-up to be done in cases like this; here, a simple brush with a hard-edged eraser can fix the wheel. And a well-placed shadow can hide a number of errors!

HOT TIP

With practice, you don't need to draw in the perspective lines at all: after a while you get to the stage where you can imagine where they are without having to see them exactly. Looking at step 2, it's possible to see at a glance that the bottom edge of the truck side is at a contrary angle to the low wall behind it, and to the edge of the road; correcting the perspective can be done purely visually.

121

Using existing perspective

HORIZONS AND VANISHING POINTS are able to give you accurate guidelines for drawing scenes in perspective. But if you can't see the horizon – as is usually the case – how are you to tell what point perspective lines should tend towards?

The answer is to read perspective lines out of clues already present in the image. Although it may not look like it, even a simple picture such as the one shown here contains many perspective hints.

This example was first posted as a Friday Challenge on the Reader Forum section of the website that accompanies this book, and some of the entries are shown below. The Challenge was simply entitled Open the Door: it was up to the readers to make what use they chose of the view beyond.

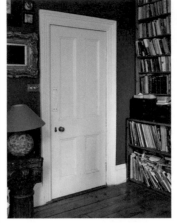

1 Here's our starting point: the corner of an ordinary room, showing the door closed. The object of the exercise is to open the door.

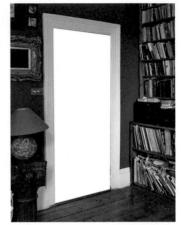

2 The door itself is easily removed: selected with the Pen or Lasso tools, it's cut to a new layer for safe keeping. I've hidden the layer for now.

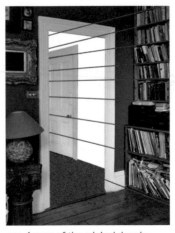

6 A copy of the original door is flipped horizontally, and distorted using Free Transform to follow the perspective lines once again.

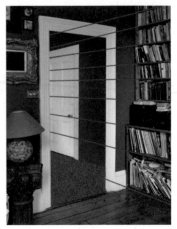

7 The back wall is simply a flat layer behind both the door and carpet layers: a little shading helps it to blend in better.

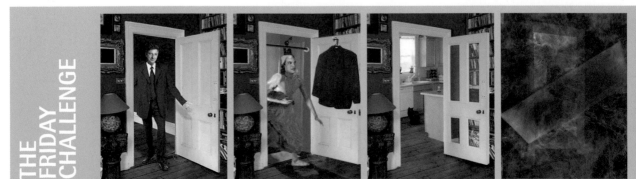

maiden   raymardo   Russ Davey   atomicfog

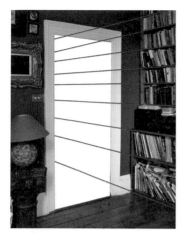

3 We can use the horizontals on those bookshelves to project perspective lines through the open door. Use the Line tool for this!

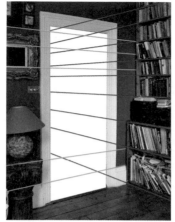

4 We can also show the perspective on the left wall (although it's not needed here): the frames, lamp stand and skirting board all give us clues.

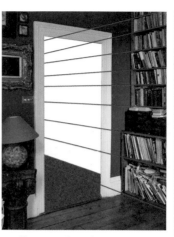

5 The carpet is made on a new layer behind the open doorway, following the perspective lines to get the angle right.

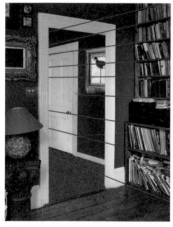

8 Other elements can be added using these perspective lines: the picture and the skirting board are easy to place in this image.

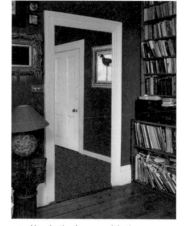

9 Here's the image with the perspective lines hidden. All the elements seen through the door now conform to the scene's perspective.

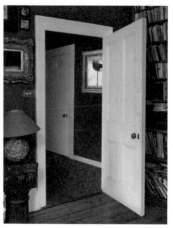

10 Finally, the original door is opened (see Chapter 12) and shading added to make the scene more realistic.

HOT TIP

Partly hiding some elements helps to make the scene more realistic. Because both the far door and the picture are cut off by the door frame, our sense of the view continuing is accentuated. If we'd been able to see the second door in its entirety, the image would have been far less convincing as a montage. Try it for yourself on the CD image, and you'll see what I mean.

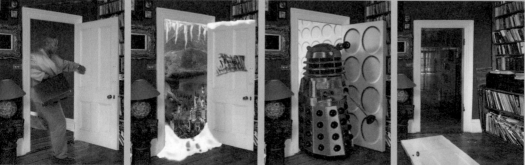

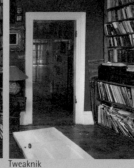

droo31k   tabitha   David Asch   Tweaknik

Boxing clever: doubling up

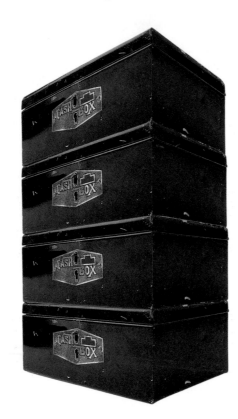

BUILDING TOWERS OF OBJECTS is not a difficult task. We don't even need to worry about vanishing points, or locating horizons: we can rely on the perspective that's already built into the starting object, and trust that perspective to be carried through when we apply our distortions.

The technique is used here to distort boxes piled on top of each other. The text here deals with distorting just one box, but it's easy to follow through and build a stack of them like the one above.

Of course, this isn't a technique reserved for the somewhat occasional need to pile cash boxes on top of each other. The principle also applies to making office blocks twice as high, or any application which requires doubling up.

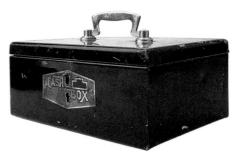

1 Here's our original box. We can see the lid, which means we're viewing it from above: in other words, the entire box sits below the horizon line (although the handle may stick up above that line). When another box is added on top, however, we'll no longer be able to see that lid, although we may be able to catch sight of the handle poking up.

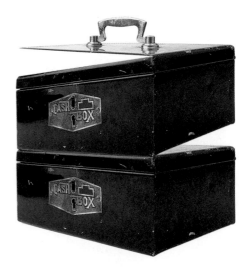

4 Select the first side, and use Free Transform (*ctrl* **T** **⌘ T**) to shear it. Grab the left center handle (not a corner!) and drag straight down, adding *Shift* to keep the movement vertical: this will move the whole side in the correct perspective.

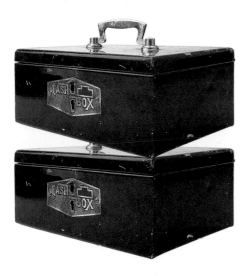

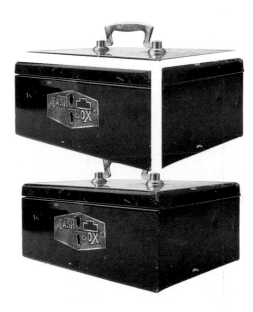

2 The first step is to duplicate the box and drag the copy directly above it. Clearly, this isn't enough: the perspective error is glaringly obvious. In order to distort the box we need to split it into its constituent parts. To do this, use the Lasso tool to first select one of the sides, and cut it to a new layer using `ctrl` `Shift` `J` `⌘` `Shift` `J`.

3 Once you've made the new layer, you'll need to go back down to the duplicate layer (using `alt` `[` `⌥` `[`) and cut the other side into a new layer as well. Don't drag the layers apart or them above – I've only done that here to show you how the box has been split up into its three visible faces.

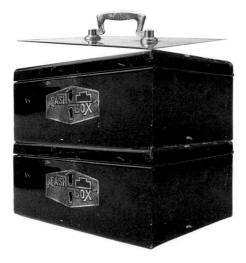

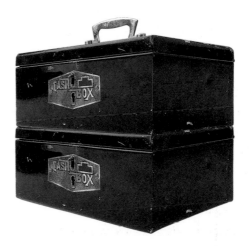

5 Now repeat the process with the opposite side. Once again, a simple shear moves the side in correct perspective. There may be a small gap at the top corner nearest us, which can easily be fixed using a hard-edged Smudge tool.

6 All that's left now is the lid. Make sure it's behind the two side layers, and shear it using Free Transform once more to follow the angle of the front edge of the lid. It may be necessary to erase some stray bits of lid that project out of the top, but that's the only adjustment required.

Vanishing Point filter 1

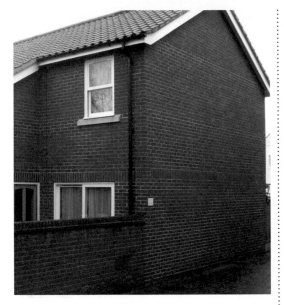

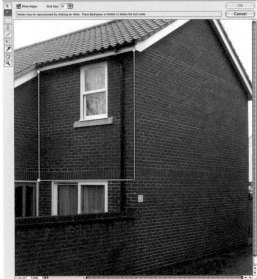

THE VANISHING POINT FILTER is one of those tour-de-force extras that astonishes anyone to whom it's demonstrated. No-one expected Adobe to come up with this one, and it's unique in computer software: this is the first time a two-dimensional illustration program has addressed the third dimension in this way.

Simply put, the Vanishing Point filter allows you to move, copy and clone in perspective, dragging objects around corners with a freedom that's hard to comprehend even when you've seen it done. This, together with the new Image Warp feature, are the two best reasons to upgrade to Photoshop CS2.

We'll begin by showing the basics of this filter, and continue over the next few pages to give just an idea of how impressive this revolutionary tool really is. To demonstrate its capabilities, we'll be using this photograph of an urban dwelling that's sorely in need of refurbishment.

1 Enter the Vanishing Point filter by pressing `ctrl` `alt` `V` `⌘` `⌥` `V`, or choose it from the Filter menu. You begin by placing four points at the corners of any element in the scene that is truly rectangular: here, we can follow the lines of the bricks and the corners of the building.

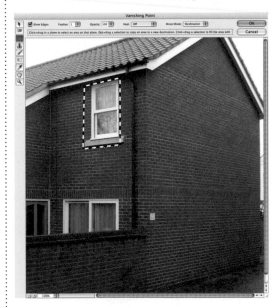

4 Now switch to the Marquee tool within the Vanishing Point filter (**M**), and make a selection of the upstairs window, as shown here. Even though we're drawing a rectangular selection, notice how it's being drawn in perspective: the marquee is following our perspective grid.

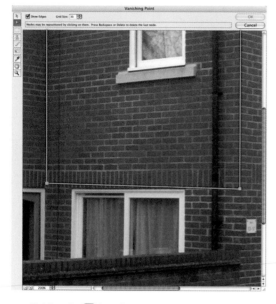

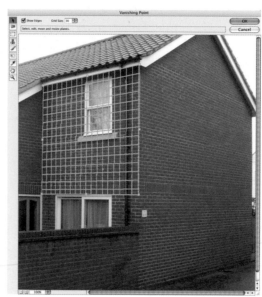

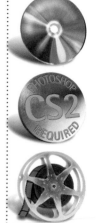

2 Holding the **X** key allows you to zoom in for more accurate placement of these corner points: here, we're a little high. The aim at the bottom here is to follow the line of the vertically-arranged bricks, to guarantee that the bottom of our box is parallel to the world in this image

3 When all four points have been placed, a grid will appear showing perspective lines that fill the space we've defined. There's still the chance, at this stage, to adjust the corners if they don't match the perspective of the building perfectly.

HOT TIP

If you don't want to see the selection outlines when you're moving elements around, press *ctrl* H ⌘ H and they'll be hidden. That's how we're able to check how well the window blends in with the wall around it in steps 5 and 6 here.

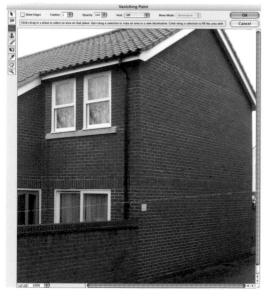

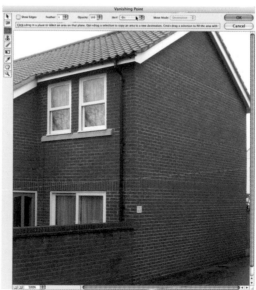

5 Let's make a copy of that window. Hold *alt* ⌥ and drag the window to the left to make a duplicate: it will move in true perspective. Add the *Shift* key and it will stay in the line. But note how the window is now getting smaller, as it moves further away from us!

6 At the end of the last step, the window fitted perfectly, but the shading was wrong: the left edge of the brickwork was too bright to match the corner. At the top of this window, check the Heal pop-up: Healing automatically blends the selection in with its surroundings.

SHORTCUTS
MAC **WIN** **BOTH**

Vanishing Point filter 2

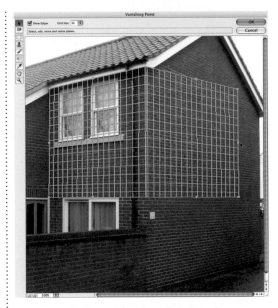

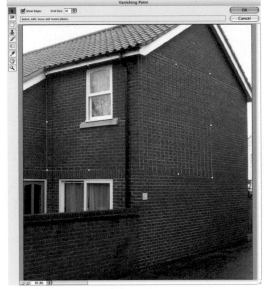

1 On the previous page we looked at how to create and use the basic 3D grid. Now let's take it into another dimension. Switch to the Arrow tool to show the grid, then hold the **ctrl** **⌘** key and grab the center right-hand handle. Drag the handle to 'tear off' the grid around the corner.

2 It's likely that the grid won't match the side wall perspective perfectly: the top and bottom points on the right will need adjusting. (You can't alter the left-hand corners because they belong to the original grid.) If the whole grid goes red, it indicates an 'illegal' perspective.

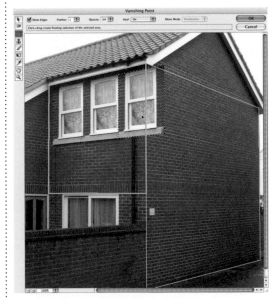

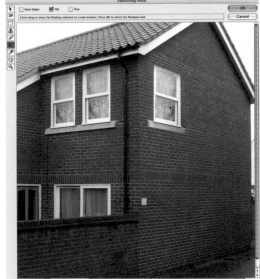

5 Now select that original window again, and start to drag it towards the corner – again, holding **alt** **⌐** to move a copy, and **Shift** to keep it in on a horizontal. It will move out of the grid on the wall to which it belongs, until it's more than half way around over the boundary...

6 ...and then it will snap around the corner, to follow the new perspective. Here, I've used the Vanishing Point filter's Free Transform mode (**ctrl** **T** **⌘** **T**) to flip the window horizontally, and make it a little wider. Notice how the bricks line up, because we held the **Shift** key.

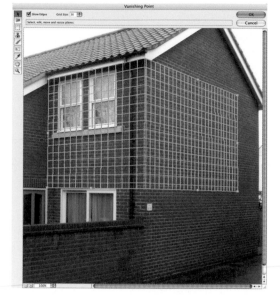

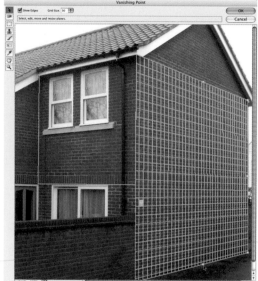

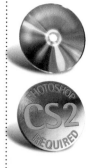

3 With a bit of fiddling, you should be able to get the side wall grid to match the perspective of the wall perfectly: follow the lines of the bricks, and trust that the original bricklayer used a spirit level to make sure they were truly horizontal.

4 We can now drag the center handles on the right and bottom, to extend the grid to the end of the wall and to the floor. Note how it still follows the wall's perspective! Once again, adjust the corners it if doesn't appear to be precisely in the right position.

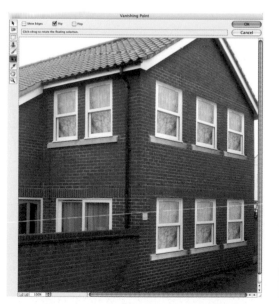

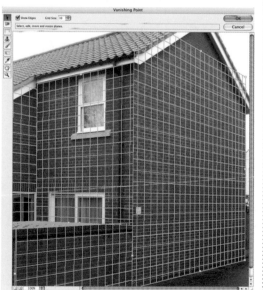

7 Keep dragging, while holding *alt* *Shift* ⌥ *Shift*, to make two more windows on the upper storey of the house. Then move one down to the bottom, and make another row of windows on the ground floor: again, they're perfectly in perspective.

8 With a bit of patience, you can extend the grids and 'tear off' new ones at right angles, to fill all the planes in the image. Try placing windows on side walls, or sideways and upside down using the Free Transform mode of this filter!

HOT TIP

The grid goes red or yellow to indicate an illegal perspective. Usually, it takes only a small amount of adjustment to get the grid to snap back to blue again, which indicates a perspective view that's consistent. It's worth taking the trouble to get it right on the first two walls, as things get more complex when the grid extends to a third!

SHORTCUTS
MAC **WIN** **BOTH**

Vanishing Point filter 3

THE SOPHISTICATION of the Vanishing
Point filter goes further than we might
suspect at first glance. Some tools work in
a more advanced way inside the filter than
they do outside: the Clone tool, for example,
shows a feathered preview of its effect, and the
feathering on the Marquee tool can be adjusted
after the selection has been made and moved.

Best of all, you can choose to work on a new
layer and still have access to the objects and
perspectives of the base layer – so that any
alterations you make can be kept separate from
the main artwork.

On these pages we'll look at a few of the
more advanced capabilities of this truly
astonishing filter.

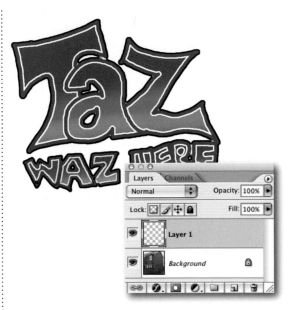

1 Begin by opening the file VP Graffiti.psd: Select All and
copy, then close the file. Back on our house, create a
new, empty layer. We'll work entirely within this layer so we
don't damage the underlying building. We could have used
this method for the windows on the previous pages, too.

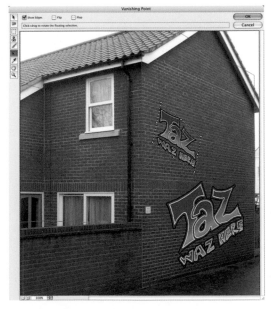

4 The graffiti can be moved around, scaled and even
rotated using Free Transform within the filter. By
holding *alt* ⌥ as you drag, it's even possible to make
perspective copies of it at different locations around the
artwork.

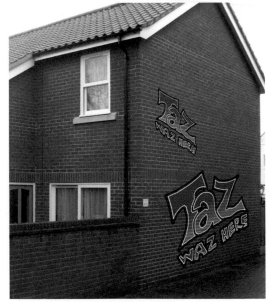

5 The trouble with the last step was that the graffiti
didn't look part of the wall. Since it's a separate layer,
though, we can exit Vanishing Point and change the layer
mode to Hard Light to enable us to see the texture of the
wall through it.

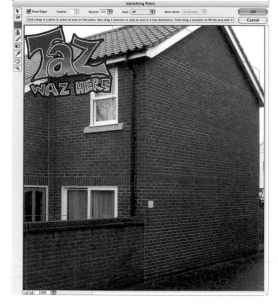

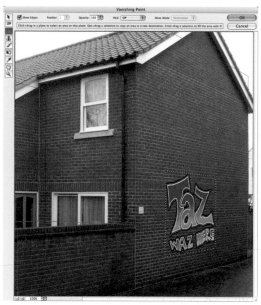

2 Open the Vanishing Point filter again, and draw in the grids if they're not already there. You'll need to revert to the version on the CD if your wall is full of windows! Now choose Paste, and the copied graffiti will appear up in the top left corner.

3 As we move the graffiti onto a perspective plane, it will flatten itself onto that wall and move in perspective as we drag. Drag it onto the blank side wall, and it will glide smoothly around the plane of that wall. Any object can be included by copying and pasting: it's like an Import function.

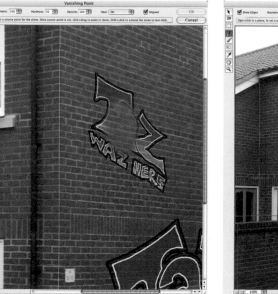

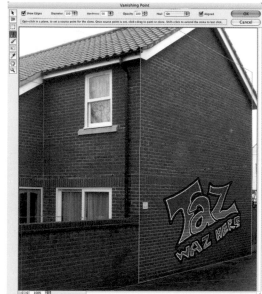

6 Let's imagine that graffiti was painted directly onto the wall, and we want to erase it. Open Vanishing Point again, and choose the Clone tool. Hold *alt* ⌥ and click to define a source point: now notice how, rather than a crosshair, we see the area to be cloned in preview.

7 Here, we've managed to clone out the whole of that upper graffiti by cloning in perspective, with the Heal option chosen for a perfect blend. By being able to see the Clone preview, we can line up the bricks exactly with the existing ones.

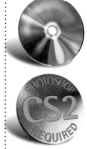

SHORTCUTS
MAC WIN BOTH

131

Cropping in perspective

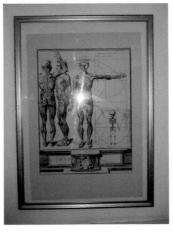

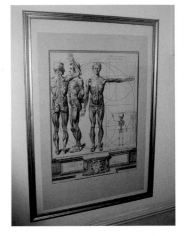

SO FAR IN THIS CHAPTER, we've been looking at how to create perspective effects, and how to use and match existing perspective to make montages look more realistic.

But there are times when you simply want to get rid of the perspective that's already in a photographed scene, as is the case with the picture used here. The Perspective Crop feature is the perfect tool for straightening out skewed images: rather like a Free Transform in reverse, it will take images photographed at an angle and square them up.

The technique is not one reserved for archivists designing museum catalogs. It's also a great tool for changing the perspective of, say, a building or box: by dividing the object into its constituent faces and squaring them up, it's frequently much easier to then reassemble the parts in any perspective view you want.

We'll also look, briefly, at the Lens Correction filter introduced in Photoshop CS2. This powerful tool is able to correct barreling and fisheye distortion with a greater ease than was previously possible, and is a tremendous addition to the Photoshop toolbox.

1 Here's the problem: a framed engraving hanging in a dark alcove on a stairway. There's no natural light, so we need to use a flash; but when we stand directly in front of the picture the flash glares off it, making it impossible to see the center of the image. We can't use imported lighting, and we can't get further away from the picture itself.

2 The only solution is to stand halfway up the stairs and photograph the picture from an angle. That way, we can be certain to avoid the issue of the flash reflecting directly off the glass.

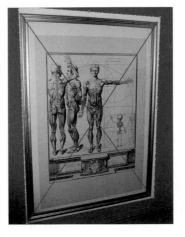

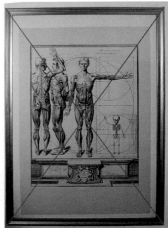

6 The crop cuts off the borders of the frame: this is because the frame bulges slightly due to the wide-angle lens. Hold `alt` `Shift` `⌥` `Shift` and drag two opposite corners apart a little way to enlarge the crop.

7 Now hit `Return`, and the picture will be cropped and squared up. You can now delete those diagonals, since they're no longer required. (You did remember to make a new layer before drawing them, right?)

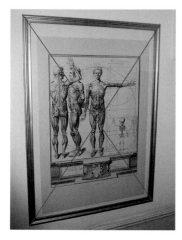

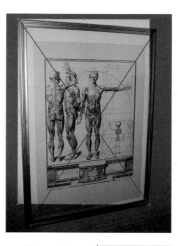

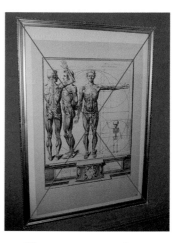

3 Before we attempt to crop the image, there's one step we need to add. On a new layer, draw two diagonals that run from opposite corners of the picture. This is best done using the Shapes tool, set to Line mode. The reason is that in a moment, we'll need to find the center point of the image, which is easily found where the diagonals cross.

4 Now switch to the Crop tool, and drag from the top left corner to the bottom right. The area outside the crop boundary is overlaid with gray. Check the Perspective box on the Crop tool's Options bar to enter the perspective mode for this tool.

5 When you now drag the corners, they'll move independently of each other rather than constraining the crop to a rectangle, as they did before. Move the corner handles so they line up precisely with the corners of the picture. The next step is to drag the center marker to the intersection of the two diagonals. It will try to snap to the 'center' of the image: but, due to a programming error, this is set to the intersection of the midpoints on each side, which gives a false perspective.

HOT TIP

If you don't have Photoshop CS2, you won't be able to use the Lens Correction method described in step 8. Instead, open the Spherize filter, and apply a very small negative amount to the image: this should be able to help with most kinds of fisheye distortion.

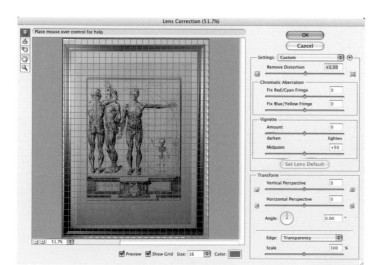

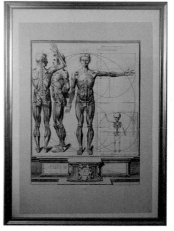

8 If you have Photoshop CS2, you can use the Lens Correction filter. By raising the Remove Distortion value, it's possible to correct even the most distorted of fisheye views. In addition, this filter allows you to correct color fringing, rotate angled images, and tweak both vertical and horizontal perspectives to remove the keystoning effect which sometimes results from holding the camera at an angle.

9 Here's the finished image, corrected both for perspective angle and for lens distortion. All we need to do now is remove the dark shadows at the bottom...

SHORTCUTS
MAC WIN BOTH

133

Photomontage ethics

A FEW YEARS AGO the issue of photomontage was brought into question when a photograph of a prominent left-wing politician, on a night out with his wife, appeared in a London newspaper. In front of him on the table were a couple of bottles of beer, the kind that has a foil-wrapped cap. Someone at the newspaper had enlarged one of the beer bottles so that it looked like a bottle of champagne – a deception magnified by the headline 'Champagne Socialist' that proclaimed his decadence.

As distortion of the truth goes, it seemed like a minor infraction. But the issue made national news. I was interviewed about it on a national radio station, and asked whether I condoned this sort of underhand trickery. I pointed out that, had the photographer merely rearranged the scene, moving one of the bottles to the foreground so that it obscured less of the politician in question, there would have been no debate; yet the results would have been identical. It's only because the change was made in the cold light of the newspaper offices that it caused an outrage. That's all very well, opined the interviewer, but how would I feel if he took the interview he'd just done with me and rearranged it back at the studio to suit his own purposes? But that, I pointed out, was exactly his intention: he was going to boil down 40 minutes of interview into a five minute segment, choosing the parts that told the story he wanted to tell. My comment never made it into the final broadcast.

There's a lot of confusion about photomontage, much of it stemming from the misconception that photographs somehow tell the truth, as if there's an absolute truth out there that can be captured in one-sixtieth of a second; any tinkering with that truth must be a lie.

But photographs don't tell the truth any more than words. The photographer may take several rolls of film, each frame capturing a slice of time; the photo editor will then choose the picture that tells the story his newspaper wants told. The sub-editor may then crop the picture to fit the space available, and in doing so will again retell the story.

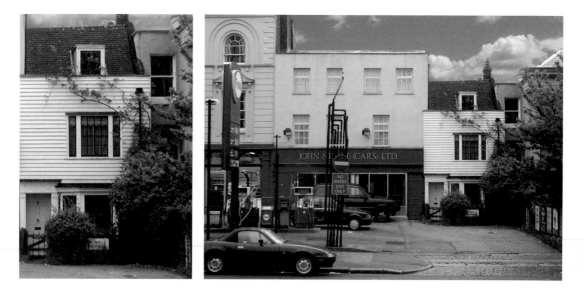

The photograph above left shows an idyllic view of a small cottage, set amid verdant foliage. But it's a lie: the picture has been cropped from the original image, above right, which tells a very different story. Anyone who had rented this as a holiday home after seeing it on a website would have every right to feel cheated by the reality: and yet there's been no Photoshop trickery involved, simply a selective decision about how much of the 'truth' to tell.

We may take a roll of film on holiday, from which we choose half a dozen to go in the album. The rest are discarded – one person has their eyes closed, the expression isn't so appealing, a tourist got into shot in the background. Yet we are just as guilty of editing the truth as if we'd montaged the elements together in Photoshop: we're telling the story we want told.

Is deliberate manipulation of photographs a new occurrence? Not at all. The creator of Sherlock Holmes, Sir Arthur Conan Doyle, was fooled in 1912 by the Cottingly Fairies, a set of photographs of paper sprites faked by two young girls in their suburban garden. During the American Civil War, photographer Alex Gardener produced a best-selling book of images, *Gardner's Photographic Sketch Book of the War*. He didn't mention the fact that he had hauled a cart load of dead bodies between locations, dressing them up in appropriate uniforms and posing them in each place.

I'm not saying there aren't limits to what should be done with photomontage. But if obvious montages make more people realize that the camera nearly always lies, then the world will be a better place.

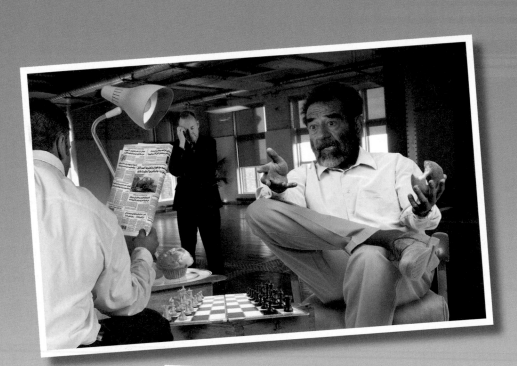

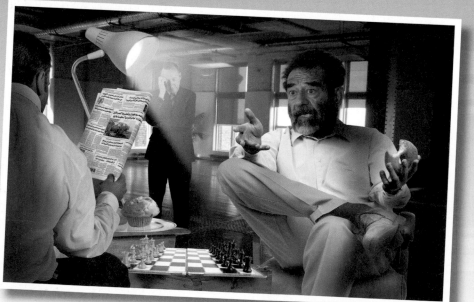

■ Saddam Hussein under interrogation: a montage for The Independent newspaper. In the version above, all the elements are crisp and well lit; but everything's clamoring for attention, and there's little focus to the piece. The addition of some visible light and shadows, right, makes the picture come to life.

7 Light and shade

SHADOWS ARE THE KEY to placing people and objects within the scene. Without shadows, images can look dull and unconvincing; even the hint of a shadow can make a montage come to life. First, we'll look at some of the ways of creating and using shadows to your advantage.

Light is another matter. Whether it's the beam from a table lamp or the glow around a candle, or the suggestion of sunlight across a scene, visible light can add interest and mystery to a montage. It's easier to create than you might think, although such elements as the flame of a candle can take a little effort to get right.

We'll also look at how to make a neon sign that looks like the real thing, and how to simulate an image on a screen.

Shadows on the ground

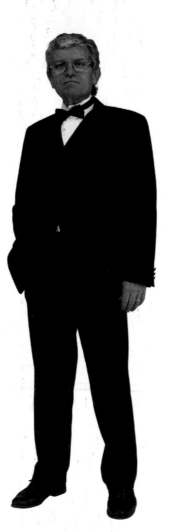

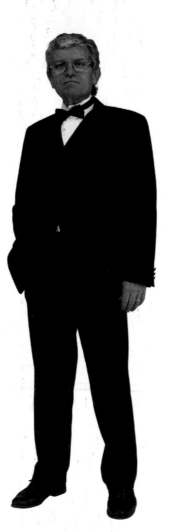

1 Duplicate the figure layer, lock the transparency (using the checkbox on the Layers palette, or the shortcut **/**) and fill the layer with black – use **⌥⌫** **alt⌫** to fill with the foreground color.

GROUND SHADOWS are among the easiest types of shadow to create in Photoshop. To make them convincing, you'll need to put in a small amount of extra effort: here, we'll look at how to graduate the blurring effect so that the shadow appears to lie in a true perspective plane as it fades away from the viewer, rather than just darkening the background.

Creating shadows directly from existing objects is always easier than trying to paint them to match. They're also more convincing, as they correspond precisely to the object or person being shadowed.

5 The shadow needs to be more blurred at the back to look convincing. But simply blurring the whole shadow, as shown here, makes it far too indistinct at the front, and the man looks like he's floating.

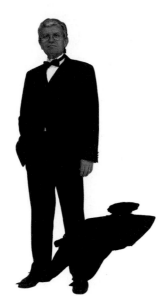

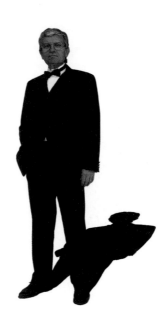

2 Now uncheck the Lock Transparency box (or use [icon] again) and then use Free Transform to distort the shadow so that it lies along the ground.

3 The bottom of the shadow, where it meets the object, almost certainly won't conform to it – so just use the Eraser and the Brush tool to paint it where it should go.

4 The shadow will need some softening so it doesn't look too harsh. Use Gaussian Blur to add a small degree of blurring: here, a radius of 2 pixels has been applied.

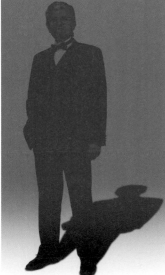

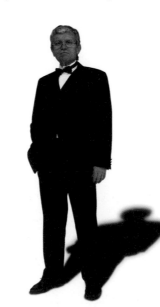

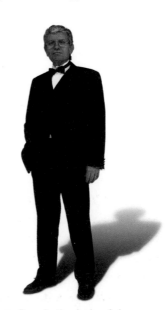

6 The solution is to go into QuickMask mode (press [Q]) and then use the Gradient tool to drag from the top of the shadow (not the top of the image) to the bottom. This will create a graduated selection.

7 Now, when you exit QuickMask (use [Q] again), the shadow will be fully selected at the top, and not selected at the bottom. Apply a Gaussian Blur again (8 pixels used here) to see the graduated blurring effect.

8 To make the shadow fade away, make a layer mask for the shadow layer and use the Gradient tool once again, dragging from top to bottom. The higher you start, the more opaque the top of the shadow will be.

HOT TIP

If you're using a layer mask to selectively fade the shadow, as detailed in the final step here, you could spend hours with the Gradient tool trying to get the fade just right. But there's an easier way: after the first application of the tool, you can use Brightness and Contrast on the layer mask to change its balance and opacity – and it will work without changing the underlying layer.

SHORTCUTS
MAC WIN BOTH

Shadows on the wall

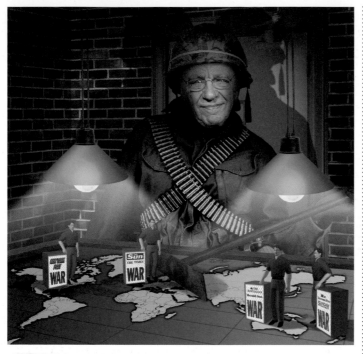

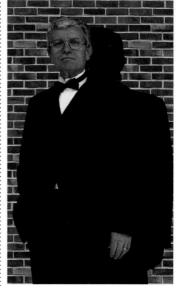

1 To create the shadow, duplicate the layer and fill it with black in the same manner as shown on the previous page.

SHADOWS ON WALLS are also easy to create – but you have to think about the relationship between the figure and the surface the shadow is cast upon. The closer the shadow is to the figure, the closer the figure will appear to be to the wall.

Under normal lighting conditions, the shadow will be placed slightly below the figure to give the impression of natural daylight illumination. But raised shadows can have a different effect: the immediate impression is to make the figure look more sinister, as if lit from below (which is why the baddies in horror movies often carry candles just below their faces).

The illustration above was for The Guardian, and illustrated how Rupert Murdoch's newspaper empire was covering the war in Iraq. I'd finished the illustration, or so I thought, but something was missing: it wasn't until I added the two lamps over the table, with the resulting shadows behind, that the image really came to life. The lamps helped distinguish between the map and items on the table – the focal point of the montage – and the figure of Murdoch behind, pushing him further into the background for a sinister, shadowy look.

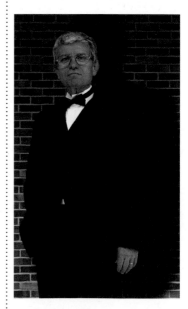

5 When the shadow is enlarged, the light source looks closer to the figure: when it's raised up, the light source is low down, making the figure look more sinister.

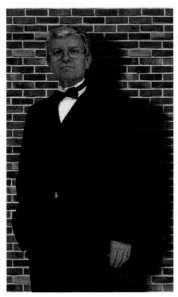

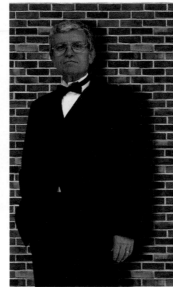

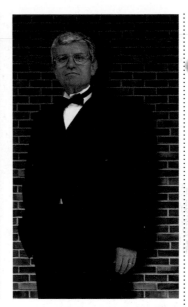

2 Because the surface is flat, an even blur can be applied to the whole shadow. Reducing the transparency of the layer allows the wall to show through behind it.

3 Moving the shadow closer to the figure positions him closer to the wall: here, he's standing with his shoulder almost leaning against the surface.

4 Darkening the wall itself helps to make the shadow look real. A simple black-to-transparent gradient created on a new layer makes the wall look more convincing.

HOT TIP

Create shadows on their own layer, filling them with solid black. Then reduce the transparency of the whole layer until you get the effect you want. This is far more reliable than filling the layer with a low opacity first, as It's easier to change when the illustration is complete.

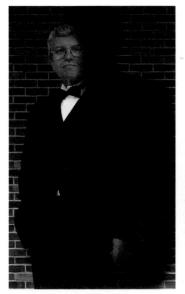

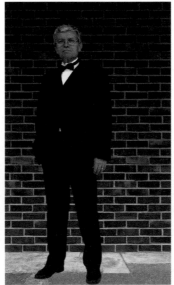

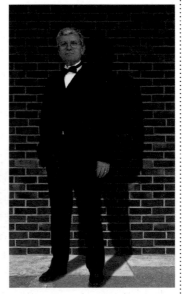

6 With a light source this close, we need some shading on the figure itself. This shadow is simply painted on a new layer, which is grouped with the figure layer so it only intersects it.

7 When the background shows the ground as well as a wall, we need to combine both shadow techniques detailed so far: the shadow must run along the ground, then up the wall.

8 Easily done: the shadow is offset, then the bottom (where it overlaps the wall) is distorted to join the feet. Some extra painting and erasing is needed to complete the effect.

Creating complex shadows

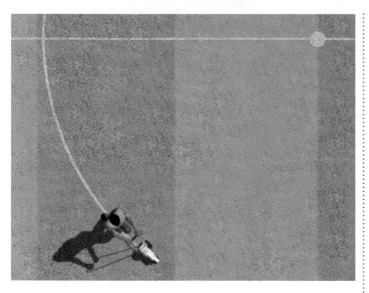

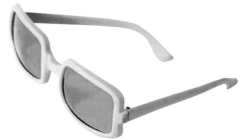

1 Before we begin to create our shadow, it's important to check the light direction. The near side of the arm is darker than the front: the light's coming from the top left.

ARLIER IN THIS CHAPTER we've been looking at how to create shadows from figures. It's not always that straightforward: in the illustration for The Guardian, above, the shadow had to be created from scratch – there was no way it could be interpolated from the vertical view of the line marker.

Sometimes we can use the existing data, but have to split it up into its constituent parts in order to distort each one individually. The task of creating a shadow for these sunglasses was originally set as a Friday Challenge on the How to Cheat Reader forum – results below.

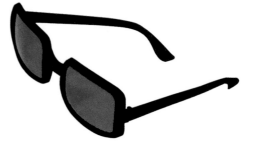

4 Now inverse the selection , and then hold ⌘ ⌥ *Shift* *ctrl* *alt* *Shift* as you click on the glasses thumbnail to limit the selection to that area. Fill with black.

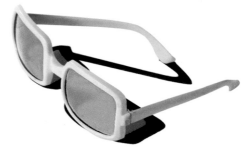

7 Bring in the far leg shadow, flip it vertically and rotate and scale it. Remember the light position: the shadow needs to fall on this side of the arm in order to look right.

THE FRIDAY CHALLENGE
www.howtocheatinphotoshop.com

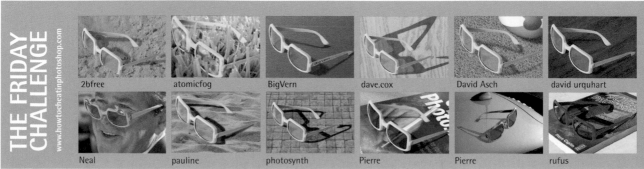

2bfree   atomicfog   BigVern   dave.cox   David Asch   david urquhart

Neal   pauline   photosynth   Pierre   Pierre   rufus

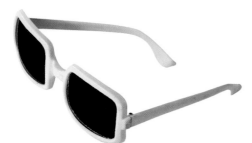

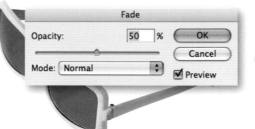

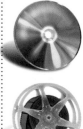

2 To begin, select the lens area of the sunglasses with the Magic Wand tool. Make a new layer for the shadow, and fill this selection with black.

3 Immediately press ⌘ Shift F ctrl Shift F to open the Fade dialog. Here, we can reduce the opacity of that fill to 50%, so that the lens area is partially transparent.

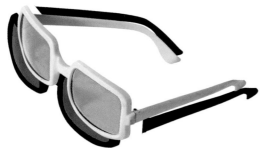

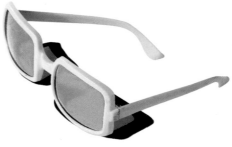

5 In order to make this shadow work, we're going to have to split it up into separate layers for the front, and the two arms, and move it behind the glasses.

6 Begin by distorting the front of the shadow, using Free Transform, so the bottom touches the bottom of the glasses, and the top falls away along the ground plane.

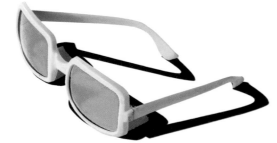

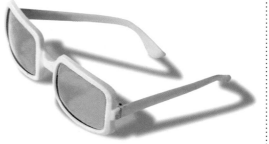

8 Even though we're viewing the near arm from above, its shadow will still be cast from the side. Duplicate the previous arm's shadow, and use that instead.

9 Now merge all the shadow layers, and apply Gaussian Blur to the whole shadow. Reduce the opacity to around 50% (darker if it's on a dark background), and we're done.

SHORTCUTS
MAC WIN BOTH

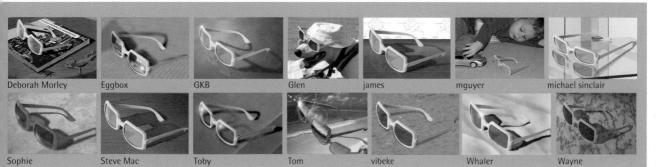

Deborah Morley   Eggbox   GKB   Glen   james   mguyer   michael sinclair

Sophie   Steve Mac   Toby   Tom   vibeke   Whaler   Wayne

Light from windows

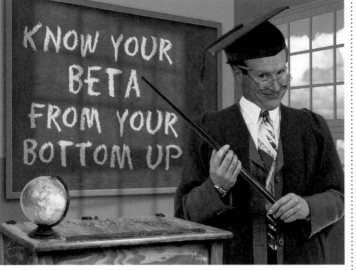

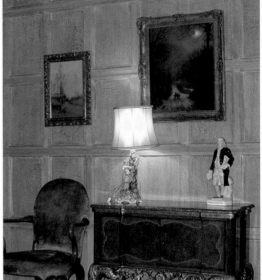

T HE ROOM ABOVE WAS BUILT from scratch, and needed the feeling of a light source to make sense of it. A financial illustration for the Sunday Telegraph, it may be cartoony in its appearance – that was the intention – but it still needed to have that extra element of realism if it was going to look good on the page.

Adding the effect of late afternoon light streaming through a window helps to add interest and warmth to a picture. It's a relatively easy technique to master, and can be used to great effect.

1 A pleasant enough scene: attractive wood paneling, an Atkinson Grimshaw oil painting, and even a bust of Benjamin Franklin to keep an eye on things. But the scene is still a bit flat; it could do with some more interesting lighting.

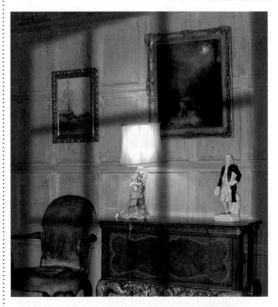

4 Select the pixels in this layer by holding ⌘ *ctrl* as you click on the layer's icon in the Layers palette. Now inverse the selection (⌘ *Shift* *I* *ctrl Shift I*), then feather it (Select>Modify>Feather) by about 8 pixels. Make a new layer, and fill the selection with black; then lower its opacity to around 50%, and hide the white layer.

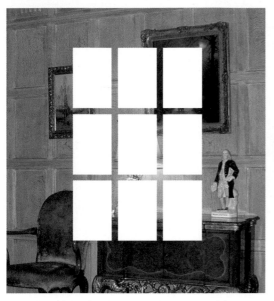

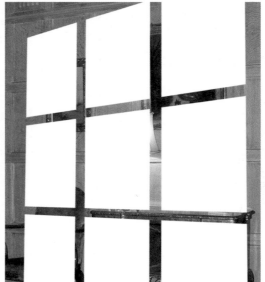

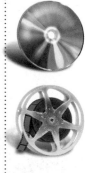

2 On a new layer, make a grid of white rectangles in the shape of your chosen window. The size isn't important: although we're going to enlarge this quite a lot, we'll end up by blurring the edges so any pixellation that may creep in will be lost.

3 Distort the array of panes using Free Transform, so that they fall at an angle across the image. Keep the top edge more or less in a line with a horizontal line in your photograph for a more realistic effect.

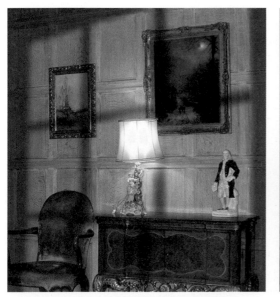

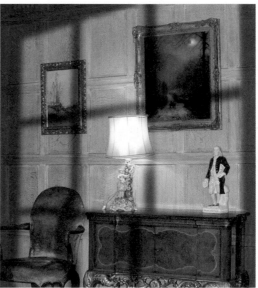

5 You can choose to bend the shadows around any protruding objects with the Smudge tool or Liquify filter; here I've moved the shadow to the left where it falls on the front of the cupboard, and bent it slightly over the chair. Be sure, though, to erase the shadows where they fall on any light sources, such as the table lamp shown here.

6 Now for the rosy glow from the window light. Load up the pixels in the shadow layer, and inverse the selection so that only the soft-edged panes are selected. From the Adjustment Layer icon at the bottom of the Layers palette, make a new Curves adjustment: add some red and a little green to the Curve to complete the effect.

Mood, light and emphasis

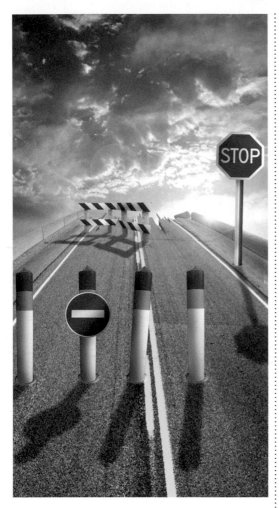

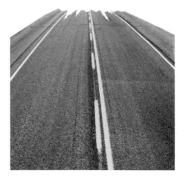

1 The road image was taken from a stock library shot. Although the original road wound over a hill, I chopped it off short to make it come to a sudden end.

2 The end of the road was easily fragmented by making jagged selections with the Lasso tool, and deleting. I used a Layer Mask so I could undo it if I needed to.

THIS ILLUSTRATION, commissioned by The Independent on Sunday, was to accompany a story on the lack of funding for building new roads. Drawing 'the end of the road' could have resulted in a dull image; but by adding a visible light source – through setting the scene at dusk – we're able to bring drama to the image.

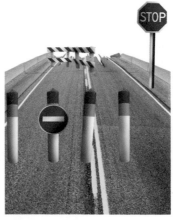

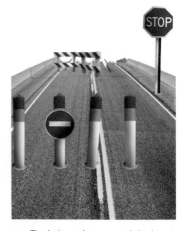

6 The Stop and No Entry signs were easier to draw than to source. Again, a little shading using Dodge and Burn makes them look that much more realistic.

7 The indentations around the bases of poles were made by making elliptical selections of the road surface into a new layer, and applying Bevel and Emboss layer effects.

146

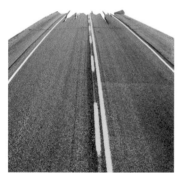

3 The broken road end was given depth, and the suggestion of the concrete reinforcement, using the techniques described in Chapter 13 – Smashing Things Up.

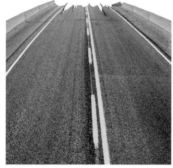

4 The two side walls were originally stretches of pavement, elongated and then curved using the Shear filter to make them fit the perspective of the road.

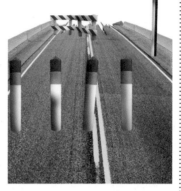

5 The poles and barriers came from the Hemera Photo-Objects collection. After positioning them, shading was added to make them look less new and less uniform.

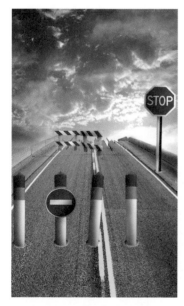

8 Once a suitable sky was found (and I tried several), the only change to the main image was to darken the retaining wall on the sun's side, to put it into shadow.

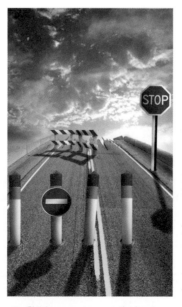

9 Shadows, as ever, are the key to making montages look alive. The only constraint here was to make sure they all pointed towards the sun, the obvious light source.

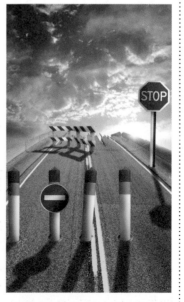

10 The final step was to add a Lens Flare on top of the sun, to make it burst over the retaining wall. The Lens Flare filter is easy to overuse, but applied with subtlety it works well.

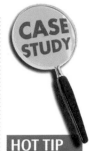

HOT TIP

Lens Flare can be a difficult filter to position accurately. The trick is to make a new layer, filled with black, and apply the filter to that. Set the new layer's mode to Screen, and all the black will disappear, leaving the flare alone. Now you'll be able to position it where you like within the montage.

147

Multiple shadowed objects

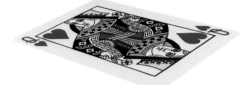

1 This photograph of a playing card has been distorted using Free Transform to make it appear as if it's lying on a horizontal surface.

THROUGHOUT THIS CHAPTER I've recommended always creating shadows on a separate layer. But there are times when a shadow should be part of the layer to which it belongs, as in the example shown here.

It would have been possible to create this stack of cards using a separate layer for each card, and then simply flattening all the layers at the end. But since a pack like this could include up to 52 layers (54 if you include jokers), we'd be talking about a document that's unnecessarily unwieldy for the effect we're trying to create. This way, we can draw an entire pack of cards in a single layer.

The technique used to get rid of the overhanging shadows in steps 9 to 11 is a little tricky. Here's how it works: when we go into QuickMask mode, the solid cards are shown as solid red; the partly transparent shadows are a paler pink. Using the Levels control, we can work on the mask as if it were a normal layer. So we adjust the mask so that the pale pink disappears, leaving just the solid red – the fully selected area. When we then exit QuickMask, our selection will be constrained to just the area that was fully opaque initially, so inversing and deleting the rest will get rid of the unwanted shadows.

4 Select the card pixels again. Then use ⌥⌘D *alt ctrl D* to feather the selection: with the Marquee tool selected, nudge the selection area down a couple of pixels, set the foreground color to black, and use Fill (Edit menu) to fill *behind* at an opacity of 50%.

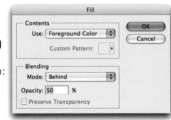

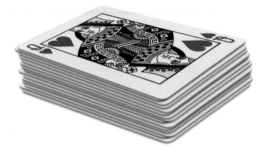

7 Any number of cards can be stacked up in this way: as long as you keep the ⌥ *alt* key held down, you'll keep moving copies. Don't make the offsets too regular!

10 Now we can 'tighten up' that shadow using the Levels control. Drag the white arrow slider to the right, and the partly selected (lighter red) area will vanish.

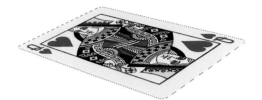

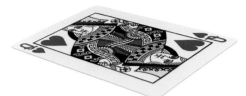

2 The first step is to give some depth to the card. Begin by 'loading up' the pixels in its layer – hold ⌘ `ctrl` and click on the thumbnail in the Layers palette.

3 Now hold ⌥ `alt` and nudge the card up a couple of pixels: then inverse the selection using `Shift` ⌘ `I` `Shift` `ctrl` `I` and darken up the edge you've just created.

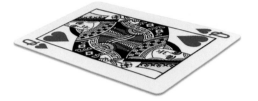

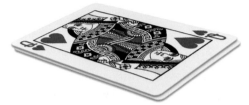

5 This creates a soft shadow beneath the card – but on the same layer as the card. Make a duplicate of this layer to work on, as we'll need the original later.

6 Now Select All using ⌘ `A` `ctrl` `A`. Holding down the ⌥ `alt` key with the Move tool selected, move the card to create a copy on top – and the shadow moves with it.

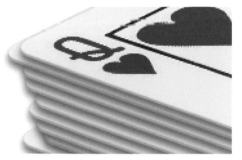

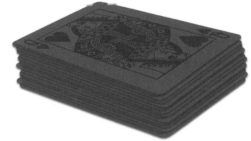

8 But there's a problem here: if we zoom in, we can see that there are shadows beneath the overhang of the cards where there's nothing for them to sit on.

9 To get rid of the excess shadows, select the card layers by ⌘ `ctrl` clicking on the layer name, and go into QuickMask mode by pressing `Q`.

The nudge keys will behave differently depending on which tool is currently active. If the Move tool is selected, as in step 3, the selected pixels within the layer will be moved: if another selection tool (the Marquee or Lasso, for instance) is active, the selection area will move but not the pixels themselves. You can always hold ⌘ `ctrl` to access the Move tool temporarily while a selection or painting tool is active.

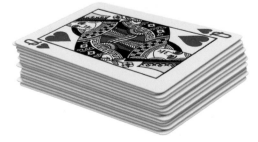

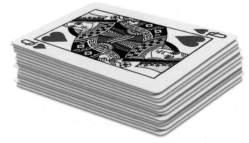

11 All we need to do now is to exit QuickMask and inverse the selection, then press Delete: those extraneous shadows will simply disappear.

12 The last step is to bring back that original card that we duplicated, so we return the shadow beneath the bottom card in the stack.

Shading on Hard Light layers

ON THE PREVIOUS PAGES we looked at adding shadows to multiple objects. But to preserve editability, it's a good idea to keep all your shadows on a separate layer. There were a lot of shadows required in this illustration for The Independent, above; by keeping them separate from their layers I knew I'd be able to make any changes asked for.

We'll use a Hard Light layer to add shadows to the elements within this box. We'll also show how to remove selected areas from the Hard Light layer, so we can paint the shadow of one object cast upon another.

The first three steps involve loading up selections, making a Hard Light layer, filling it with mid tone gray, deleting the region outside the selection, and locking its transparency. This sequence is an obvious candidate for a Photoshop Action: being able to perform all the operations with a single keystroke can be a huge time-saver.

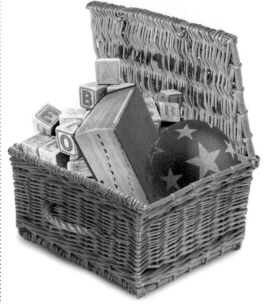

1 To make the shading layer, hold ⌘ *ctrl* and click on the thumbnail for the Blocks layer. Then hold ⌘ *Shift* *ctrl* *Shift* and click on the Book and Ball thumbnails to add them to the selection.

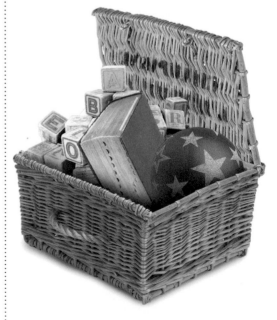

4 We can use the Burn tool, set to Highlights, to paint shadows onto the new layer. But this isn't enough: we also want shadows cast from each object onto those behind it. We can do this on the Hard Light layer as well.

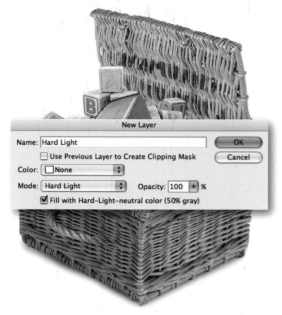

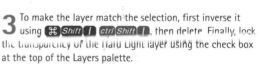

2 Now make a new layer above these three: set its mode to Hard Light, and check Fill with Hard Light neutral color. The entire layer will be filled with gray – but we can't see it, as gray is invisible in Hard Light mode.

3 To make the layer match the selection, first inverse it using ⌘ Shift I ctrl Shift I, then delete. Finally, lock the transparency of the Hard Light layer using the check box at the top of the Layers palette.

HOT TIP

In step 3, we locked the transparency of the Hard Light layer. This prevents the Burn tool from affecting areas outside the original selection, even when the area is deselected. It also means we can paint in color on the Hard Light layer for special effects.

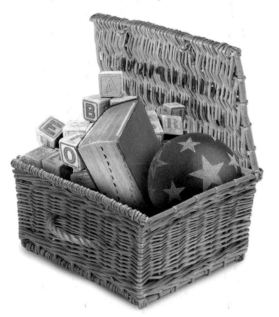

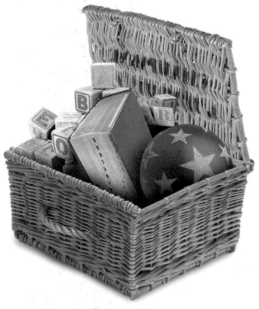

5 Load up the Hard Light layer's pixels by ⌘ ctrl clicking on its thumbnail. Hold ⌥ ⌘ alt ctrl and click on the Ball layer's thumbnail to remove that area. Still on the Hard Light layer, paint the ball's shadow onto the book.

6 Now remove the book's area in the same way – by holding ⌘ ⌥ ctrl alt and clicking on its thumbnail in the Layers palette. We can now paint the shadow of the book onto the blocks.

151

Visible light sources

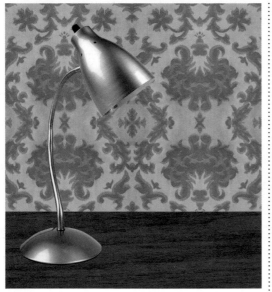

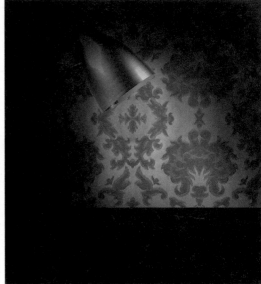

1 Begin by adding a shadow to the scene. This is simply painted on a new layer, using a large soft-edged brush. Setting the brush to a low opacity allows us to paint the shadow on in small stages, being careful to leave an unshaded area where the light will eventually be cast.

SO FAR THIS CHAPTER has dealt with shadows cast by far-off light sources. When the light itself is in the frame, we obviously need to show it. In this workthrough, we're straying into the realms of hyper-realism: by deliberately over-emphasizing the visible light, the montage becomes more appealing than if we simply tried to reproduce reality. In real life, a light source wouldn't cast a visible beam unless the room were full of smoke; but then real life is often far duller than fiction.

Shadows are still important, for two reasons: first, because they add life to the image; and second, because a dark background will make the light itself stand out better. Here, we'll take the simple montage shown above and add both lighting and shadow to make it into a far more entertaining image.

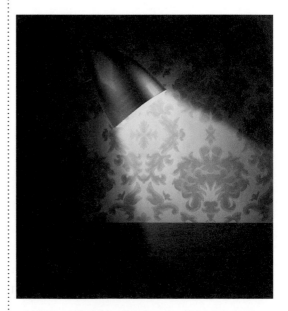

4 Now exit QuickMask and, on a new layer, pick a pale yellow color (about 20% Yellow should do the trick) and then use the Gradient tool, set to Foreground to Transparent. Drag it from within the shade perpendicular to the shade edge, away from the lamp.

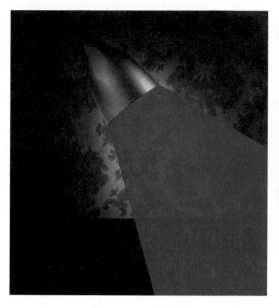

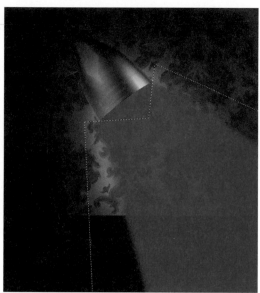

2 Next, we need to define the light. This is best drawn with the Pen tool, following the contour of the edge of the lamp shade and radiating outwards from the light source. Turn the path into a selection using ⌘ Enter ctrl Enter, then go into QuickMask to adjust the selection area.

3 In QuickMask, trace around the edges of the light area with the Lasso tool, omitting the edge around the shade. Then use Gaussian Blur to soften the edge – here, an 8-pixel radius blur was applied. Because the edge by the lamp shade was not selected, that part remains crisp and unblurred.

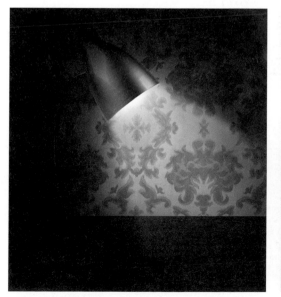

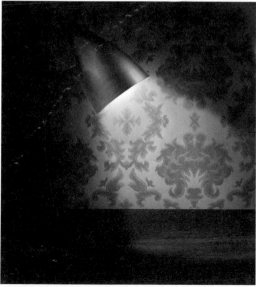

5 We now need an extra glow around the bulb itself. With the light area still selected, use a soft-edged brush to paint a spot of white at the focal point. Don't use a hard-edged brush: although bulbs are solid, you can't look at them when lit without seeing a haze around them.

6 Now we need to show the light acting upon the table surface. Using the Elliptical Marquee tool, draw an ellipse on the table. Feather the selection (an 8-pixel radius was used here), and delete that area from the shadow to return the table to its previous brightness.

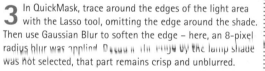

SHORTCUTS

153

The romance of candlelight

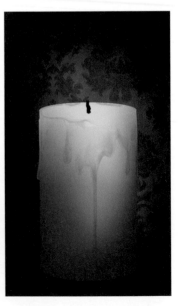

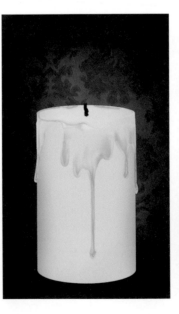

CANDLES ARE UNIQUE light sources in that the light they cast is fully visible: you can stare straight at a candle without hurting your eyes. Because they shed so little light around them your eyes remain accustomed to the darkened environment, so when you do gaze at a candle's flame, you see a hazy glow around it.

Unlike metal lamp shades, candles are translucent objects. The light travels down through the candle and exits through the side, as well as radiating from the flame.

It would have been possible to begin this workthrough with a photograph of a candle. But I thought it would be more fun (and possibly more instructive) to draw our candle from scratch.

1 I drew this candle by drawing an elliptical marquee for the base, then duplicating it to create the top. I flattened the top ellipse to create a sense of perspective: the greater the difference between the two, the nearer the viewer is to the scene.

2 To join the two ellipses together, a rectangular selection was made between the half-way lines on each ellipse, and simply filled with the same color.

6 Before we create the flame, we need a background in order to see it. The shadows were added to this table and wall with a soft brush, leaving a fairly blank area where the flame would eventually appear.

7 For the shading on the candle itself, a new layer was created on top with its mode set to Multiply. This is because I used dark brown rather than black to shade it, which matches the candle color better.

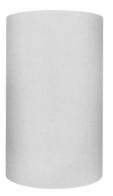

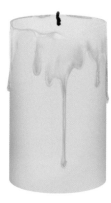

3 The shading on the candle was added using the Burn tool set to Midtones: if it had been set to Highlights, it would have created a grayish shadow. The Dodge tool provided the highlight.

4 The dripping wax was drawn as a path with the Pen tool and then filled with yellow, although it would be possible to draw it directly with a hard-edged brush if you really can't get on with Bézier curves.

5 The shading on the drips was added using the Plastic Wrap filter – see Chapter 9, Shiny Surfaces, for more about this technique. The wick was simply drawn with the Brush, set to Dissolve to make a ragged outline.

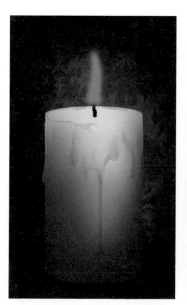

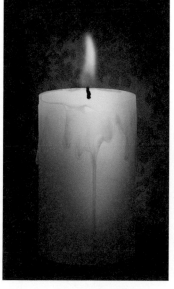

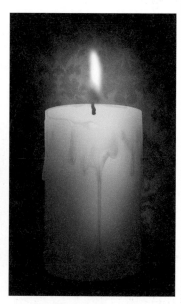

8 The flame outline was drawn with the Pen tool, then the selection was feathered (a 4-pixel radius here) and filled with a mid orange hue.

9 With the Lock Transparency box checked, the white parts of the flame were painted on with a soft brush. In addition, a tiny blue patch was painted at the base of the flame for added realism.

10 Finally, a new layer was created behind the flame, and a glow added by painting a spot of yellow using a large, soft-edged brush set to a low opacity.

HOT TIP

The Plastic Wrap technique used for creating the drips of wax produced a grayish result that looked out of place. By locking the layer's transparency and using a brush set to Color mode, I was able to sample a color from the candle and paint that over the gray to return it to its true waxen hue.

Turn the lamp on

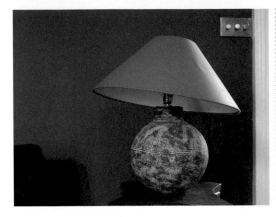

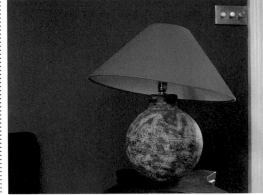

1 The first task is to even out the shading already present in the scene. The most obvious offender is the lampshade, which has strong side lighting coming from the window to the right of it. This is best outlined with the pen tool and copied to a new layer, where the right side can easily be cloned out. And don't forget to remove that hard shadow at the bottom left!

MORE LIGHTING UP: but this version offers a rather different sort of problem. The main difference is that we're working with a single composite image, rather than a montage composed of several separate parts. When you don't have the luxury of being able to arrange the elements within your scene to suit your whim, you need to approach the problem from a different angle.

This was set as a Friday Challenge on the website that accompanies this book, and some of the readers' entries are shown below. There was a variety of different approaches, but all managed to convey the impression of a hidden, yet still visible, light source within the shade.

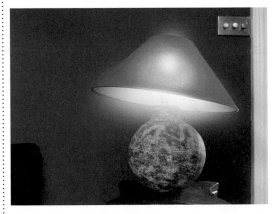

4 The next step is a subtle one, but it makes a big difference. At the end of the previous stage, we had the glow in place behind the lampshade: but the hard edge of the shade looked unnatural against the bright glow. Make a layer mask for the shade layer, and paint out the very bottom of the shade so we can see the glow through it.

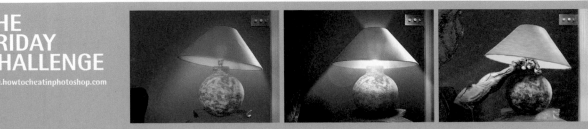

atomicfog   maiden   raymardo

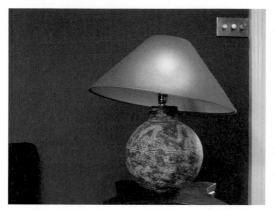

2 Since we made a new layer from the lampshade, we can work on it independently – which makes adding the glow within a piece of cake. Use the Dodge tool, set to highlights, and simply build up the glow in brief strokes: the result can be extremely convincing. The white spot that shows where the bulb is can be painted in with the Brush tool afterwards.

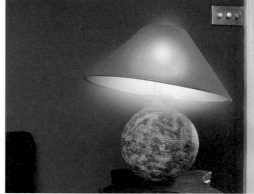

3 Now for the glow outside the shade. Make a new layer and move it behind the lampshade layer – another good reason for having copied the shade to its own layer. The glow is painted in using a soft, low opacity brush, and a pale yellow foreground color; this is followed by a small amount of painting in white closest to the shade.

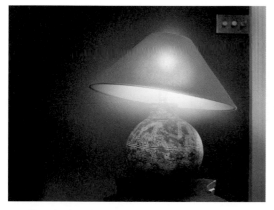

5 Now for the rest of the scene. On a new layer, paint a shadow on the bottom half of the lamp base, and on the table beneath it. Then, on another layer, use a large, soft brush set to a low opacity to add shadows in the corners of the scene, stronger the further they get from the lamp source.

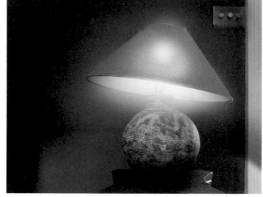

6 Finally, the *pièce de resistance* that makes the whole scene come to life. Make an elliptical selection within that last shadow layer, feather the edges slightly, and delete (or make a layer mask and fill with black). The lamp now casts a convincing light beneath it on the wall, greatly adding to the overall realism.

HOT TIP

When in doubt, make a new layer. Here, I copied the lamp base to a new layer before adding shading beneath it; and I duplicated the background layer before cloning out the shadow in the bottom left. By making new layers each time you're going to make a big change you keep your options open, so you can always retrieve the original in case the effect looks wrong later.

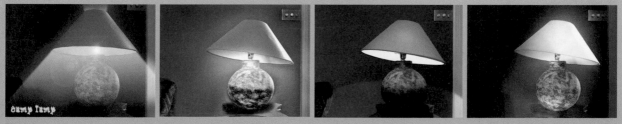

Russ Davey   tabitha   Tweaknik   Uk2usadaz

Shading using Dodge and Burn

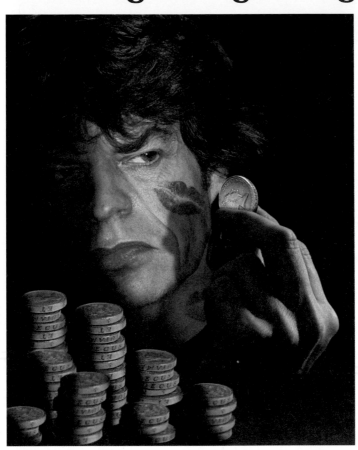

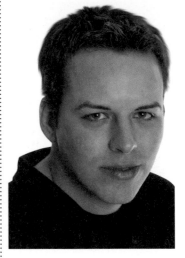

1 This man has been photographed with even, direct lighting that's perfect for the photomontage artist: it's far better to start with flat lighting and add shading where you want it, than to have to make the whole illustration conform to one original.

PAINTING ON A SEPARATE LAYER is a good technique when adding shadows to walls, floors and many other kinds of inanimate objects, but the technique works badly when you're working with skintones: black shadows, even applied at a low opacity, can easily just turn to gray.

When working on the image of Mick Jagger above for the Sunday Times Magazine, I knew the direction the lighting was coming from – and it wouldn't change. If the positions of elements in a montage are known, then there's nothing to be lost by using the Dodge and Burn tools to add light and shade directly onto the image. But Dodge and Burn have three operating modes – Highlights, Midtones and Shadows; they each affect the image in different ways.

To be safe, work on a copy of the original layer: that way, if things go wrong, you can always get back to where you started.

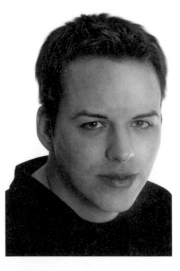

5 The Dodge tool, set to Midtones, brightens up the other side of the face without destroying the original coloring. This is far more convincing for subtle tones, such as skin, than setting the tool's mode to Highlights: but we lose some definition this way.

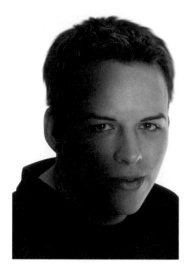

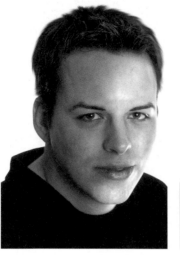

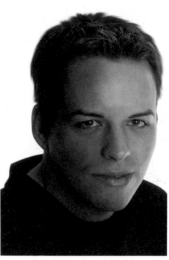

2 Using the Burn tool to darken the side of the face, set to Highlights, results in a grayish tinge that's unappealing and unconvincing: it darkens the image, but also has a muting effect on the original skintones.

3 The Dodge tool, also set to Highlights, has a rather different effect: it brightens up the image, but leaves a drastic impression on the colors. Those soft pinks and browns have become far too intense.

4 When set to Midtones, the Burn tool no longer loses color as it darkens the skin. Rather, the opposite is true: the shaded area becomes more saturated as the shading is piled on.

To avoid having to reach for the toolbox to switch between Dodge and Burn, there's a useful keyboard shortcut. When either of the tools is selected, holding down ⌥ _alt_ will temporarily select the other tool. I've mentioned this tip elsewhere in this book, and will continue to do so every time the Dodge and Burn tools crop up: it's an essential shortcut.

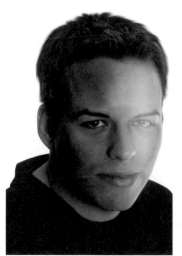

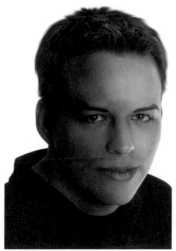

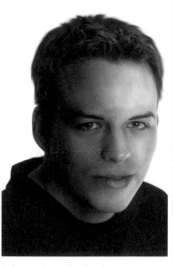

6 Set to Shadows, both tools have an unfortunate effect on skin. The Dodge tool (right) makes the shadows look like they've been doused in talcum powder, while the Burn tool (left) turns the subject into a vision of the red death. Neither effect is what we want here.

7 The best technique is to use a combination of the two. Using a low opacity, use the tools set to Midtones first to retain the color; this achieves the light/dark effect we want, while retaining the color of the skin.

8 Now change the mode of the Burn tools to Highlights, and paint at an even lower opacity to add depth to the shadows. The Dodge tool, also set to Highlights, adds interest to the right side of the face, bringing back the contrast that we lost earlier.

Shading using light modes

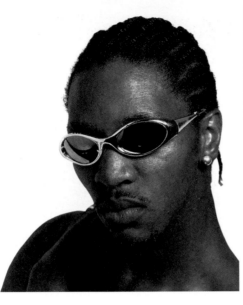

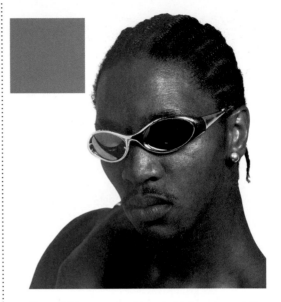

SHADING USING THE THREE LIGHT MODES – Hard Light, Soft Light and Overlay – can have a far more cinematic effect than shading using the Dodge and Burn tools. But if Dodge and Burn are Nosferatu, then Hard Light is more Saturday Night Fever: shadows can take on a strong hue of their own. There are, of course, more than three light modes, especially in Photoshop 7; here are the main ones.

Rather than painting directly onto the layer, create a new layer and set it to Hard Light mode. You then have the option of filling the layer with 50% gray: this makes a good background when applying the shading to multiple layers. By filling your selection area with 50% gray and then locking the transparency, you can be sure that the light you paint will only be applied within the area where you want it.

If you must paint directly onto the layer, you can set the brush mode to Hard Light (or any of the other Light modes) to get the same results.

1 Be careful to use reasonably muted colors when painting shadows, or the effect will be too bright and unrealistic. This light blue is too bright for use either as shading or as a light reflection: it merely swamps the image with its color.

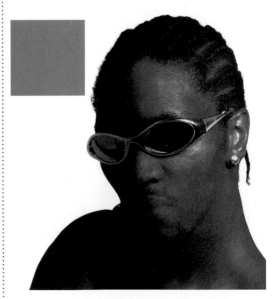

4 Now for the spotlight effect. Too bright a shade would have the unfortunate results shown in step 1 above; a muted brown gives us a color that lets the original skin texture show through, while adding a good amount of extra color to it.

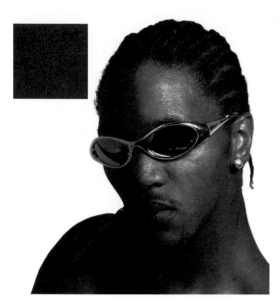

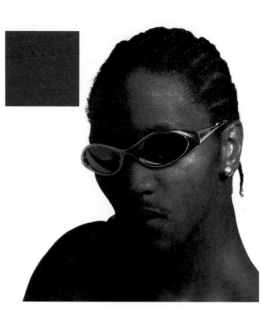

2 Using a darker blue allows us to paint a shadow that's far more moody and evocative. This is the kind of shading that's often seen in films, where day-for-night shooting produces shadows that have a strong blue cast to them.

3 Switching to a strong pink gives us a good color with which to paint a transition on the face, between the shaded and the brightly lit areas. It's the effect produced by theatrical lighting, where colored gels are used instead of plain white lights to add emphasis to the actors' faces.

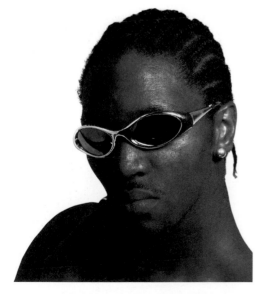

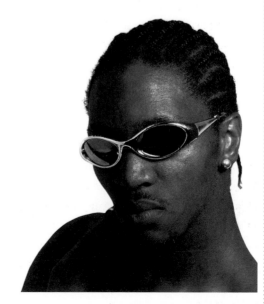

5 Here's the same effect set to Overlay mode instead. This is rather softer: the colors still have their effect on the image, but obscure the shading and texture of the original to a lesser degree.

6 More muted still is Soft Light mode, which produces an altogether subtler result. The three modes are variants of each other, and can be used in combination on different layers to build up the overall lighting effect.

HOT TIP

If you're using multiple colors when painting with Hard Light, as we are here, it's easy to apply the wrong color by accident – there's some trial and error involved in choosing shades that work. To prevent the possibility of losing a good effect, you can work on multiple Hard Light layers so that the effect is produced by the combination of all of them.

161

Extreme shading

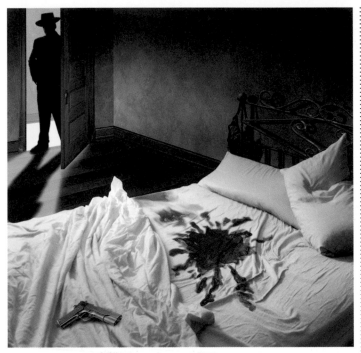

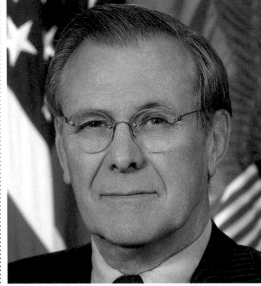

1 This official portrait of US Secretary of Defense Donald Rumsfeld shows him brightly lit, set against a strong American background. But this doesn't represent the shadowy figure we've come to recognize: let's add some strong shading to make him altogether more sinister.

PAINTING SHADOWS DEMANDS SUBTLETY, and the more extreme the shadow, the harder it is to make it look convincing.

Here's a different approach. This time, we'll use an Adjustment Layer to create an overall shadow, and then paint the shadow out on the Layer Mask that comes with the Adjustment Layer. The shading that results from this method is more subtle, and more controllable; because we're working on a mask, it's easy to keep on adjusting the shadow until it's perfect.

This technique was used to produce the very faint highlight in the image above, produced for The Guardian.

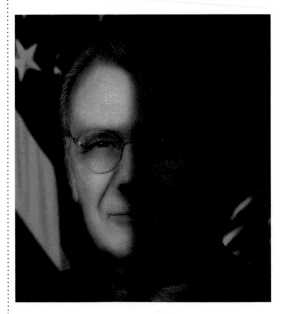

4 With the initial highlights in place, we can now double-click the Adjustment Layer's main icon to edit its contents. Now we can reduce the amount of green and red to make a more convincing shadow tone. Play around with this one, until you get exactly the effect you want.

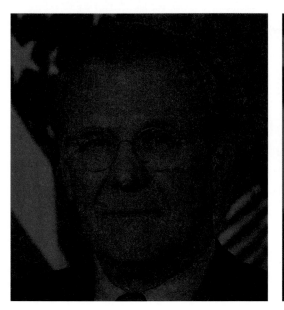

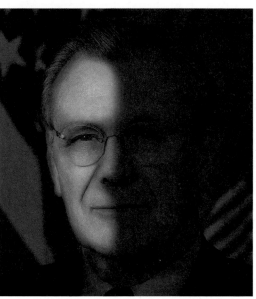

2 Begin by making a new Curves adjustment layer (choose Curves from the pop-up menu at the bottom of the Layers palette). To begin with, simply darken the entire image; at this stage, we only want to see where to begin painting the shadows.

3 Every new Adjustment Layer automatically opens with its own Layer Mask. We can paint on that layer mask, using a soft-edged brush with black paint, to selectively hide parts of the Adjustment Layer. Effectively, we're starting with an image in total shadow, and painting in the highlights.

The advantage of this method is that we can change the overall effect of the Adjustment Layer without changing the mask we've painted in. This means that we can change the tone of the shadow to suit any purpose: if we suddenly decide we want our figure outdoors, for example, all we have to do is replace the background and then add more blue to the shadow layer.

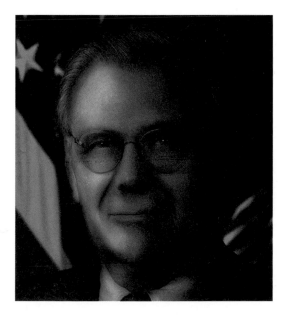

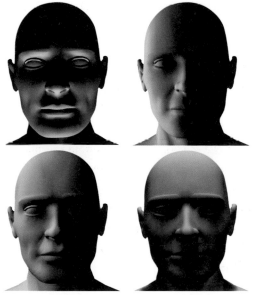

5 Now that the shadow has the correct tone, it's time to refine its visibility. Use a soft brush, set to around 30% opacity, and paint the highlights back into the picture on the mask. The key here is subtle blending; avoid harsh edges. I've also added a slight shadow of the glasses for completeness.

6 It can be tricky to get the shading right in these circumstances, so here's a visual aid. Clockwise, from top left: bottom lighting; side lighting; high side lighting; top down lighting. Use these models as a guide to placing shadows on your own figures.

Making smoke without fire

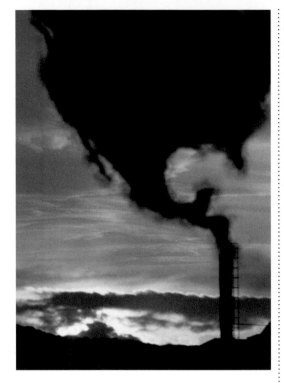

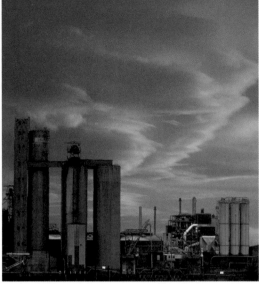

1 Here's our starting image: an apparently dead oil refinery. It's our task to bring it back to life. Here, the refinery and the background clouds are on two different layers; this will make it much easier to place the smoke behind the refinery, which will blend it into the scene better.

THIS IMAGE OF SMOKE FROM AN OIL refinery, for The Independent, tells its own story: industrial pollution in America. This is an extreme example – but every Photoshop artist needs to know how to create convincing smoke for any purpose.

It's not a difficult technique, as long as you take it slowly and build up the initial smoke pattern in small stages. This isn't the kind of effect that will happen instantly!

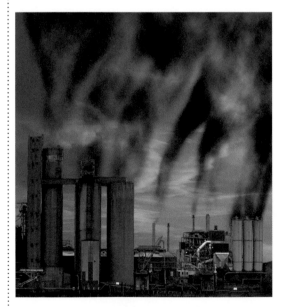

4 The texture we created in the previous step looked far too hard for realistic smoke. But that was just the beginning: by changing the mode of this layer, we can change the appearance. Here, we've changed the mode to Multiply for a dirty look.

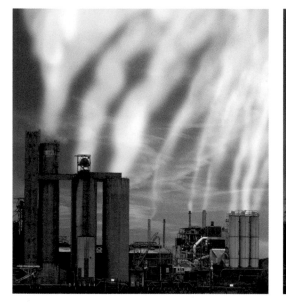

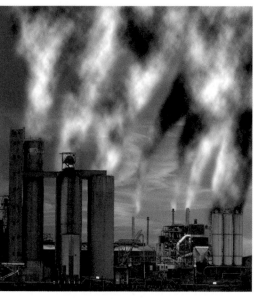

2 On a new layer, use a soft-edged brush with a white foreground color to paint the smoke. Use a low opacity – if you have a graphics tablet, you'll find the job easier. Paint in small strokes, building up a convincing shape. It's worth taking the time at this stage to get it right.

3 Now for the texture. Lock the transparency of the layer by pressing the / key. Set the foreground and background colors to their default black and white (press D to do this), and choose Filter > Render > Clouds. This fills the smoke area with a random marbled texture.

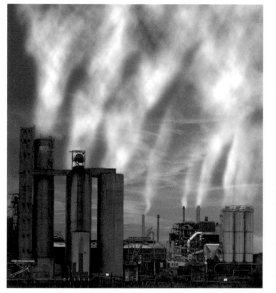

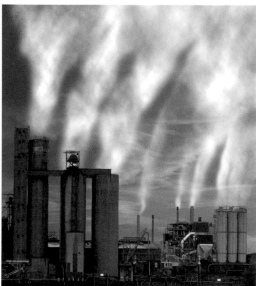

5 Just as we used Multiply mode in the previous step to make dirty smoke, so we can change the mode to Screen – the opposite of Multiply – for a bright, clean white smoke effect.

6 To make the smoke blend in better with the surroundings, make a new layer and set it to Hard Light mode; then press ⌥⌘G alt ctrl G to make a clipping layer with the smoke. Sample colors from the background, and paint with a large, soft brush to blend the smoke.

HOT TIP

The fact that we've used the Clouds filter in step 3 has nothing to do with smoke and clouds being similar substances! This filter simply creates random textures, and can be used for any purpose where natural texture is required. Hold ⌥ alt as you choose the filter for a tighter, smaller pattern effect.

SHORTCUTS

Making fire without smoke

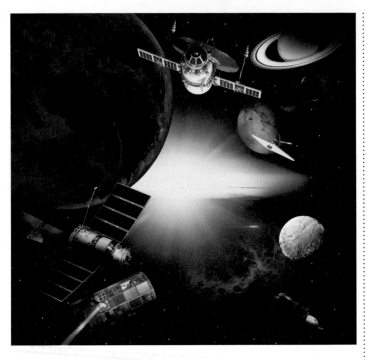

T HERE ARE MANY WAYS TO MAKE
explosions in Photoshop: the controlled
example in this illustration for the magazine PC
Pro, above, uses a variety of techniques.

Elsewhere, we've looked at using fireworks to
give the impression of a destructive explosion.
Here's another method, which is good for
making fireballs: it's easy to create, and is a
curious process which doesn't really make sense
until the final step of the operation.

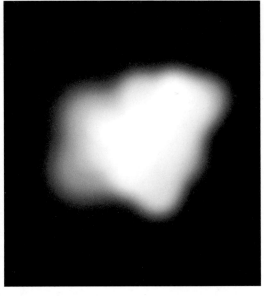

1 Begin by making a new layer. Paint a random shape
in white, using a soft-edged brush. All we're after at
this stage is a shape with some slight variation in density.
Because we're painting with white, it helps to have a black
background so we can see it more clearly.

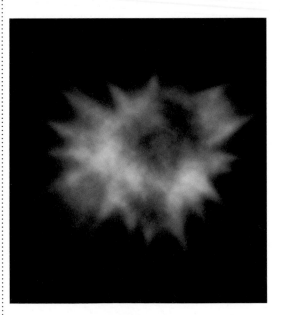

4 Now, with the transparency still locked, set the
foreground and background colors to the default black
and white (use the **D** key to do this). Apply the Clouds filter
again. All the color will have been lost: but we'll get that
back in the next step.

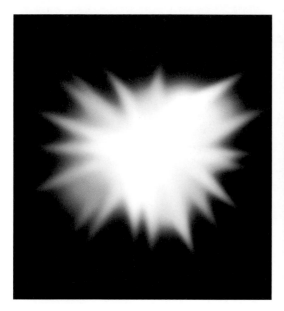

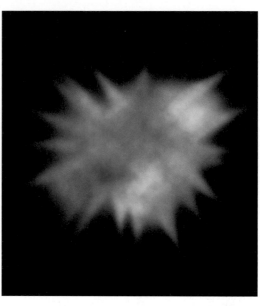

2 Use the Smudge tool, set to a soft brush at about 70% opacity, to streak out the mass of white from the center. Try not to let the streaks waver too much: each one should look as if it's radiating directly from the middle of the object.

3 Now lock the transparency of the layer, by pressing `/`. Set the foreground color to yellow, and the background color to red. Now choose Filter > Render > Clouds, which will add a random texture of red and yellow in our object. Repeat the filter, if you like, until you achieve a pleasing effect.

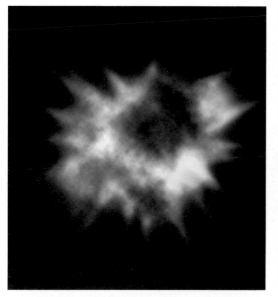

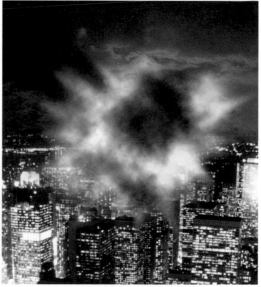

5 Before you do anything else, apply the Fade command to that last filter by pressing *Shift* ⌘ *F* *Shift* *ctrl* *F*. From the resulting dialog, choose Linear Light. This is a layer mode we haven't looked at before: it produces a harsher version of the Hard Light mode.

6 On its own, the explosion works well enough; but it really comes into its own when we place it on a suitable background. Here, we have the effect of a powerful airburst exploding over a nighttime city.

167

Lighting up: perfect neon

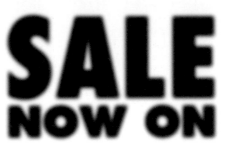

1 To begin with, create a new white layer beneath the basic lettering, and then merge the two. Then apply a Gaussian Blur until the hard corners are smoothed away. The actual amount will vary with the size and font chosen; I've used a blur radius of 4 pixels.

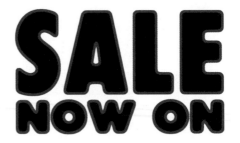

3 Select the pixels in the text layer using the Magic Wand tool and then, on a new layer, create a stroke outline using the Edit/Stroke menu. Don't use Layer Effects to make the stroke, or you won't be able to edit the outlines afterwards.

NEON LETTERING is one of those effects you can knock up in a few moments: simply create the outlines and add a glow to them. But to do it properly takes rather more time and patience.

The simplest way to create the smooth outlines for the lettering is to use the Round Corners feature in a program such as Illustrator. But since we're trying to work entirely in Photoshop, the technique described here – that of blurring and applying Levels – works just as well, and has the advantage that no additional software is required.

6 Now's a good time to add a background, with shadows as appropriate. I've also changed the color of the bottom row of text for the sake of interest, using Hue/Saturation. The next step is to make the outline look like tubing: this is achieved by darkening it with the Burn tool (set to Midtones) at the points where it's been strongly bent.

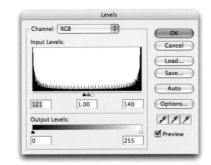

2 Now we can apply the Levels control to tighten up that blur. Open Levels and drag the small white and the small black triangles towards the center, and all the blurred area will turn to either pure white or pure black (see the screen grab, shown above right). If the whole group, including the

gray triangle, is dragged to the left the outlines will thicken up; dragged to the right, they'll thin out. Note that this effect only works when the text has been merged into a white layer: if the text had simply been blurred on its own, the Levels control would have had no effect.

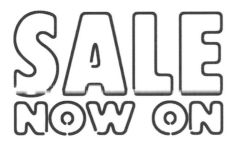

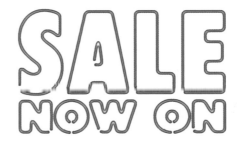

4 Now hide the original text layer, and erase portions of the stroke to simulate the way neon lettering is constructed in the real world. Since all the lettering is made from a single bent glass tube, it needs to break within each letter where it turns to join the next letter.

5 To create the inner glow, select the layer's pixels by holding ⌘ ctrl and clicking on the thumbnail in the Layers palette. Use Select/Modify/Contract to reduce the selection size by, say, 3 pixels; then apply a 3-pixel Gaussian Blur to it. Now turn on the Lock Transparency checkbox, and fill the selected area with white.

HOT TIP

The technique used here to soften the edges of lettering is one that was devised by Photoshop guru Kai Krause, before he went on to create the Kai's Power Tools range of plug-ins. He invented it as a way of cleaning up ragged artwork, such as faxed logos; but it's also perfect for rounding off text, and can even be used to apply rounded corners to a hard-edged outline.

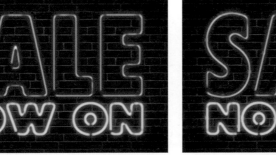

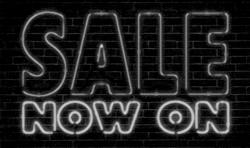

7 The glow is created on a new layer, behind the tubing layer. First load up the pixels as outlined in step 5, then hold Shift ⌥ Shift alt as you enclose it with the Marquee tool to limit the selection to just the top word. Feather the selection (8 pixels used here), and fill with the same color as the tubing; then repeat with the bottom line of text.

8 The last step is to add the details. The wires are drawn on a new layer, shaded and shadowed using the Pipes and Cables technique shown in Chapter 12. One clip, which holds the lettering to the wall, is created on a separate layer; this clip is then copied around each letter in turn, rotated as appropriate so it appears to grip the neon tubing.

169

Day for night

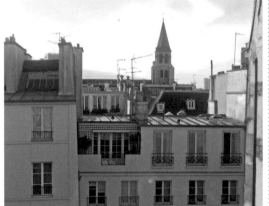

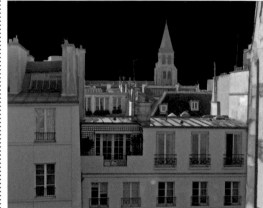

MOVIES SET AT NIGHT are generally filmed during the day, using special filters to simulate the effect. In Photoshop, turning a day scene into a night one is not difficult – and it turns out to be one of the more enjoyable photomontage jobs, particularly since the results can be spectacular.

We'll look at how to turn this view of Paris rooftops into a night scene, with remarkably few steps. The technique makes extensive use of Adjustment Layers, to preserve editability.

This task set as a Friday Challenge on the How to Cheat website, and produced many striking images, reproduced below.

1 Begin by removing the existing sky. The Background Eraser Tool (see page 184) proves invaluable for this task, easily cutting all the bright sky away for us. A dark background layer helps us to see the result as we erase.

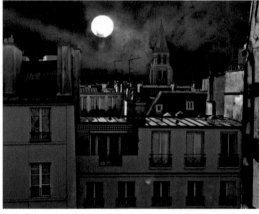

4 Select each of the windows you want illuminated with the Lasso tool (holding ⌥ *alt* to create straight line joins), and copy them to their own layer.

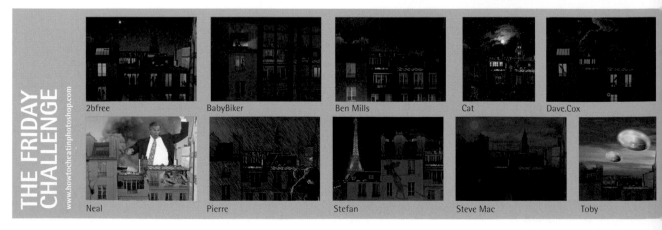

2bfree

BabyBiker

Ben Mills

Cat

Dave.Cox

Neal

Pierre

Stefan

Steve Mac

Toby

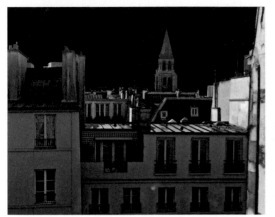

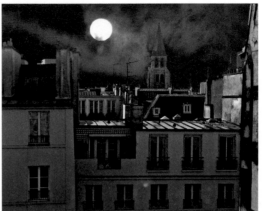

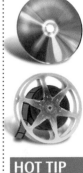

2 We can use a new Curves Adjustment Layer, using the background as a Clipping Mask, to lower the brightness of the scene. As well as reducing the RGB curve, lower the red and green channels for a blue cast.

3 The building on the far right remained too bright. Select it with the Lasso tool: a second Curves Adjustment Layer can be used to reduce the brightness of this layer, and will automatically be masked by the selection. Note the new sky!

HOT TIP

It's important that the Adjustment Layers should affect only the layer directly beneath. To do this, hold ⌥ *alt* as you choose ⌐▯▯▯▯▯ ▯▯▯▯ the Adjustment Layer menu at the bottom of the Layers palette; a dialog will pop up, where you can check "Use previous layer as clipping mask".

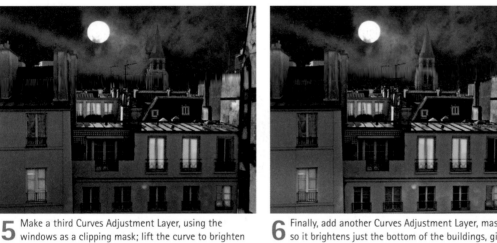

5 Make a third Curves Adjustment Layer, using the windows as a clipping mask; lift the curve to brighten the windows, adding red and green for a yellow glow.

6 Finally, add another Curves Adjustment Layer, masked so it brightens just the bottom of the buildings, giving a sense of street-level glow.

SHORTCUTS
MAC WIN BOTH

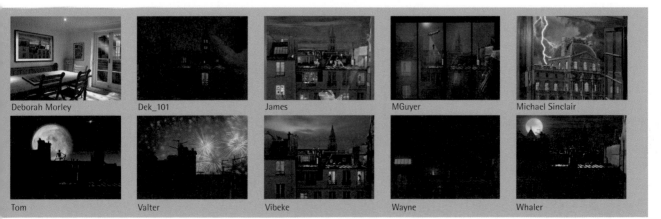

Deborah Morley

Dek_101

James

MGuyer

Michael Sinclair

Tom

Valter

Vibeke

Wayne

Whaler

Sourcing images

DIGITAL CAMERAS have provided Photoshop artists with the single most useful tool since Photoshop itself. But there are some objects that aren't readily available to be photographed. Such items as space shuttles, polar bears and plates of roast turkey are notoriously hard to lay your hands on in a hurry. Fortunately, there's a solution: there's a huge amount of readily available imagery out there in the form of royalty-free photographic collections.

The 'original' distribution method for royalty-free images was CD-ROMs: a disk costing an average of $400 contains around 100 images at high resolution, which you're free to use as many times as you like, for just about any purpose that isn't obviously illegal. The quality of royalty-free images is almost uniformly high, but the type of material on offer is generally more suited to the designer than to the photomontage artist. You'll find dozens of CDs of stressed businessmen in high-tech offices and glamorous couples on tropical beaches; there are far fewer collections of cutout people and objects that can be used to form the basis of an original photomontage.

Among the best sets of images on CD are those from **Stockbyte** (*www.stockbyte.com*) and **PhotoDisc** (*www.photodisc.com*). The PhotoDisc images tend to feature glossy models who look like they've just walked out of a hairspray commercial, with the exception of one or two discs – their In Character CD, for example, is a collection of 100 people in a variety of costumes from medieval wizards to lion tamers.

Stockbyte, on the other hand, have a range of a dozen CDs in their Busy People series that feature everyday people in a huge variety of poses. The people here are often old, ugly and badly dressed – in other words, just the sort of people you see on the streets. I've used these throughout this book. Two other CD-ROM collections worth mentioning are Faces 2 from **Rubber Ball** (*www.rubberball.com*), which contains 100 images of everyday people, and Bodyshots from **Digital Wisdom** (*www.digiwis.com*), which includes over 300 images of businessmen and women in a variety of poses.

Now that more people have broadband, there's a better way of getting images: direct download from royalty-free websites. Many of these sites offer a subscription deal, whereby a monthly or annual payment grants you a license to download a fixed number of images per day.

By far the best of these sites is **Photos.com** (*www.photos.com*), which offers a vast range of images, both cutouts and traditional photography, on a subscription basis. Photos.com have kindly agreed to give readers of this book 100 free, high resolution images so you can see their quality and which you're free to use in your own work: see pages 404 to 407 for full listings of the images, on the DVD that accompanies this book.

If you only want cutout images of people and things, try the excellent **PhotoObjects** (*www.photoobjects.net*), which is an offshoot of Photos.com that offers only images with clipping paths, at a lower subscription rate.

Many of the PhotoObjects.net images appear in much lower resolution on the three sets of CDs that make up the **Hemera Photo–Objects** collection. The 50,000 images in each set cost $99 per volume, and are now available from *www.encoreusa.com*. The images here are of uniformly low resolution, supplied up to around 900 x 900 pixels, but are immediately available: I use these images constantly, and many feature in tutorials in this book.

Other websites worth investigating are *www.istockphoto.com*, an ever-growing image exchange that holds a vast number of images, available from just a couple of dollars depending on the size; and *www.absolutvision.com*, which offers low-cost subscriptions and has a good range of both cutout and background images.

A good collection of images of people comes in the form of a book entitled **500 Model Poses**, published by Ilex Press and available through photolibra.com. Five hundred high resolution images all come with alpha channel masks rather than clipping paths, allowing for better cutouts of hair and other translucent areas; it's available at the bargain price of just $31.95.

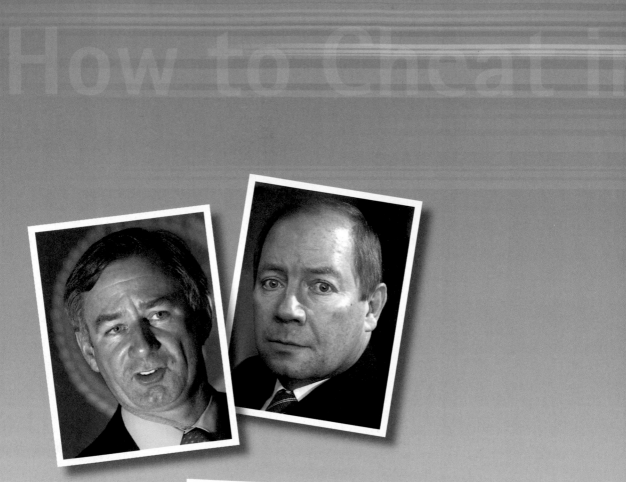

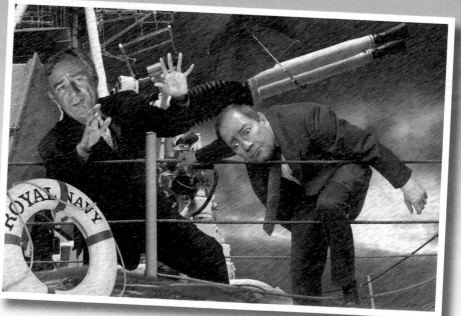

■ The photographs of UK Defence Minister Geoff Hoon and BaE CEO Mike Turner, above, are standard publicity shots. But even these dull images could be cutout, distorted, shaded and placed onto new bodies for this illustration for the Sunday Telegraph about naval defense contracts. Given a clear starting image, anything is possible.

8

Heads and bodies

PHOTOMONTAGE ARTISTS are frequently asked to put one person's head on another person's body. In this chapter, we'll look at how to make heads and bodies join seamlessly together. Eye contact, as we discussed in Chapter 5, is crucial to making characters relate to one another. So here's a technique for changing the direction your subject is looking in.

Hair has always been a problem in montage creation. We can't always work with Telly Savalas or Yul Brynner; those flyaway strands always seem to get in the way. In this chapter we'll look at how to ease the pain of cutting hair from its background.

Making the head fit

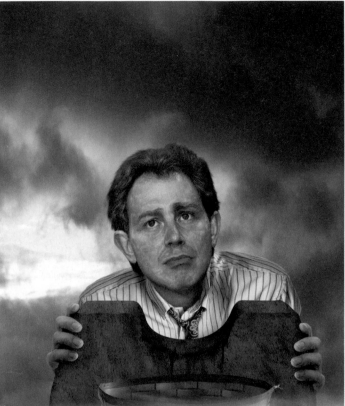

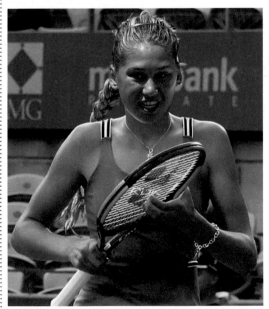

1 Here's our base image: the tennis player Nicole Vaidisova. We're going to place the head of another tennis player, Anna Kournikova, on top of this one to achieve a perfect fit.

P UBLICITY PHOTOGRAPHS of celebrities and politicians tend to be either highly staged or snatched papparazzi images. Taking the head from one body and placing it on another, as in the illustration of Tony Blair above for The Guardian newspaper, is an essential skill.

When the head you want to use already has a similar color and shading to the body on which you're fitting it, it's a relatively easy job to graft the new head in place. Overleaf, we'll see how to work with more difficult bodies, with very different lighting conditions.

4 With the head in place, make a new Layer Mask and, using a small, soft brush, paint out the neck and T-shirt – see Chapter 3 for more on Layer Masks. It's a neat touch to have the hair hanging down behind her: use a hard edged brush to hide it behind the shoulder.

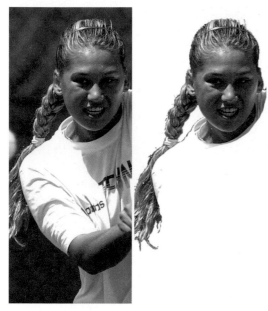

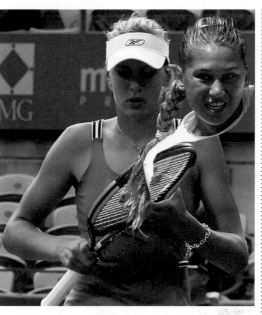

2 We first need to cut Kournikova's head from the background. The tricky part is the hair, which is most easily lifted from the background using the Magic Eraser tool (see *The Perfect Haircut* later in this chapter); we don't need to worry about the neck and shirt much at this stage.

3 With the basic cutout done, place the new head next to the old one. Don't put it on top at this stage: we want to scale it using Free Transform so it looks the right size, and it's easiest to judge this when we can see the two together. Once the scale is right, move it in place.

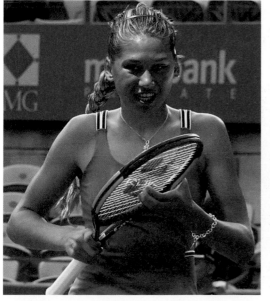

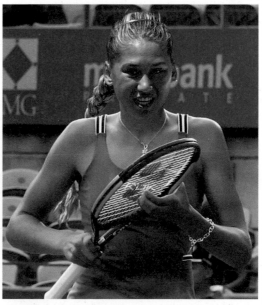

HOT TIP

When matching bodies to heads, try to choose combinations that have been photographed from as similar an angle as possible. While you can place just about any head on just about any body, the more extreme differences of view will make the montage less plausible.

5 Kournikova's chin had a white highlight on it, caused by reflection from her dazzling white shirt. We need to lose that glare. Switch from the mask to the main layer, lock the transparency with 🔲 and, with a small soft brush, paint over the highlight in a color sampled from her chin.

6 Finally, we need to remove those pieces of Vaidisova just visible on the background. Use the Clone tool to sample and paint out those stray pieces of hair that are still visible. The skin tones are a good fit between these two images: this simple montage is now complete.

SHORTCUTS
MAC WIN BOTH

Complex head fitting

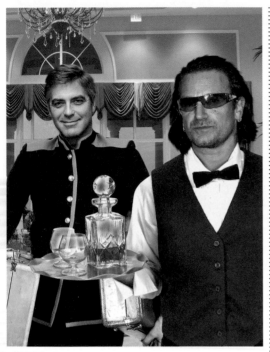

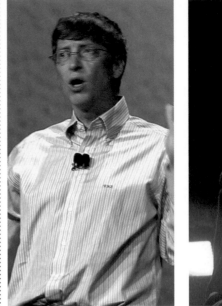

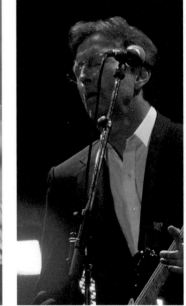

1 Here's an unlikely pairing: Bill Gates, promoting the latest version of Windows, and Eric Clapton, showing a few of the moves that has made ol' Slowhand a guitar legend. They're both performing; they're viewed from a similar angle; so let's see if we can put the two together.

PLACING HEADS on bodies involves matching the color and tone of the two. In the illustration above, for The Caterer magazine, George Clooney and Bono had to look as realistic as possible.

There are several potential dangers. There may be objects in the background photo that fall in front of the face; the head and body could be of radically different colors; there could be peculiar lighting on the original; and the grain of the two images may not match perfectly. We'll look at all those issues here.

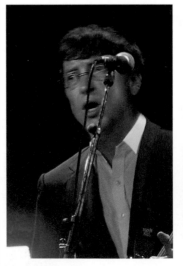

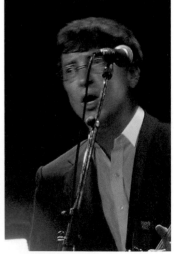

5 With the head the right color, we can add a layer mask and, using a soft edged brush, paint out the bottom of Gates' neck so it blends in smoothly. We can also soften around the edge of his face and hair with the mask. Now's also a good time to clone Clapton's head from the background.

6 We need to capture some of that stage lighting effect. Make a new layer, set to Hard Light mode. Make a Clipping Group with the head layer using ⌘ ⌥ G ctrl alt G, and paint around the top of the hair with a soft brush, using colors sampled from the blue highlight on the shoulder.

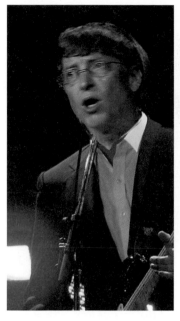

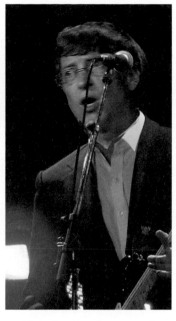

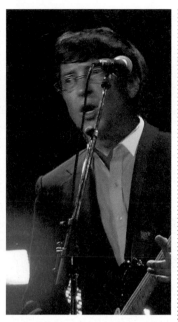

2 Begin by cutting out Gates' head and neck. Place and scale it over Clapton's body, using the techniques described in the previous pages.

3 That microphone has to come in front of Gates. Hide his layer, draw a Pen path to select the microphone, and bring it to the front on a new layer.

4 Use Curves (see page 78) to make Gates' face match Clapton's body. Here we need to lower the blue and green, and raise the red amount.

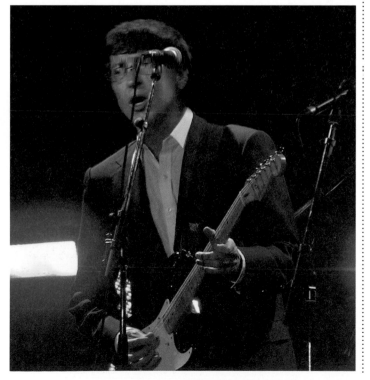

7 There's a graininess on the Clapton photo: we need to add this to the Gates layer. Make a new layer from a clear area of background, and lighten it with Curves; move it on top of Gates. When the mode of this layer is set to Hard light, it will result in a grain that closely matches the original (right).

SHORTCUTS
MAC WIN BOTH

Combining body parts

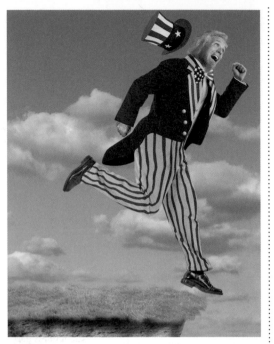

COMPLEX MONTAGES FREQUENTLY require several bodies to be combined to produce the finished character. The image above, for the Daily Telegraph, was composed of a large number of separate limbs; the coloring and patterns helped to unify the coat and trousers.

Here, we'll look at a more straightforward problem: combining a man removing his shirt with a woman's body for comic effect. The key lies in choosing images photographed from similar angles: once you've found the right pictures to work with, it's a straightforward montage.

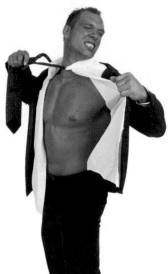

1 Here's our starting image: a man ripping off his shirt. If he had a costume underneath, he could be a superhero; I reckon he's just a sloppy dresser.

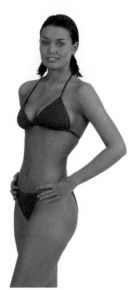

2 This woman has been photographed from a similar angle, and we can use her to replace his exposed body. Never mind the position of the arms: we won't be using them.

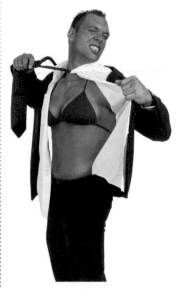

6 We can blend the body in more easily by painting a little of the man back in on the layer mask, using a soft edged brush, around the neck and above the belt. This helps to follow the original through to the new body.

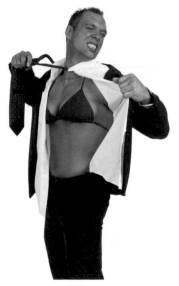

7 There's still a gap behind the shirt on the left. Make a new layer, filled with mid gray, behind the whole assembly, that covers this region.

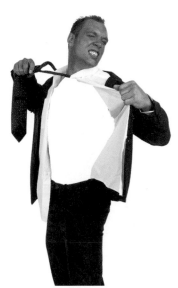

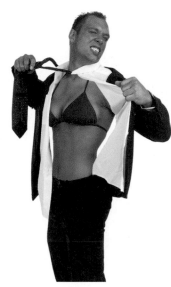

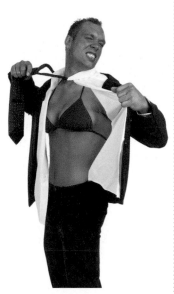

3 First, make a layer mask for the man and paint out his chest. The tie gives us a neat line to work to at the top, so there are no blending issues to worry about.

4 A section of the woman's chest, placed behind the male figure, needs to be rotated slightly to fit: the belly button and the neck need to line up with the belt and neck of the man.

5 The more slender back of the woman doesn't fill out the shirt enough. Copy a portion of the back to a new layer, and stretch it so it fills that white space behind the shirt.

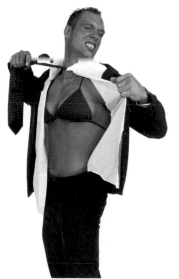

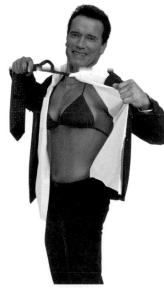

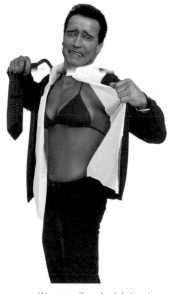

8 Adding a little shading to the woman's chest, on a new layer, helps to make it look more like it's slightly in the shadow of the shirt. It's a subtle difference!

9 Now that we've got the body finished, let's give him/her a new head. This shot of Arnold Schwarzenegger seems the ideal candidate – but his head is the wrong color.

10 We can adjust Arnie's head with Curves to brighten it and add some red to match the body. While we're at it, let's distort the features, add some new eyes and recolor that tie to a more fetching shade.

HOT TIP

The hardest part about choosing pieces from multiple bodies is not matching the skintones, but the clothing. You'd think it a simple matter to combine a jacket with a pair of trousers (sorry, I can't bring myself to call them pants) but matching the weave of the fabrics is harder than matching contrasting faces and bodies. Research the images available carefully before you begin the montage!

Changing history

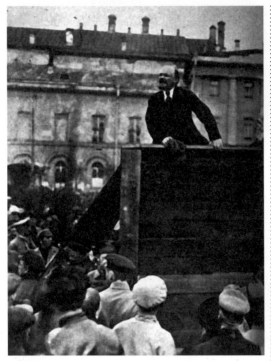

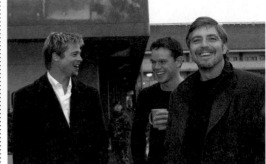

1 Here are our three film stars – and an awkwardly placed soldier in the background. Let's close up this grouping.

S O FAR IN THIS BOOK, WE'VE LOOKED at montage in terms of assembling images from a variety of sources. Here, we'll see how to adjust a single image to remove one of the characters. In this case, we'll take Matt Damon out of a photograph showing him with Brad Pitt and George Clooney.

Removing people from photographs is the sort of practice that has given photomontage a bad name ever since the days following the Russian revolution, when protagonists were taken out of the frame to suit political ends.

The image above shows Lenin addressing a crowd in 1920: the figure of Trotsky, originally on the right of the frame, has been airbrushed out of the picture.

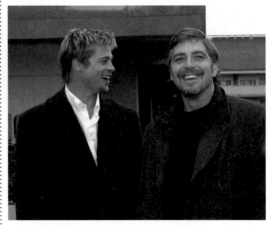

4 Scaling Clooney down so that Pitt is now looking at his eyeline helps; but he still seems too big in comparison. This is a good time to crop the image, too.

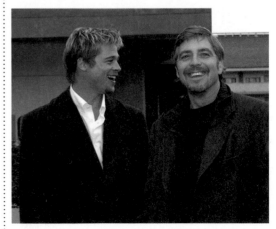

7 Now we can simply stretch the bottom half of his body down to fill the frame. With clothing like this, it's impossible to see that it's been stretched.

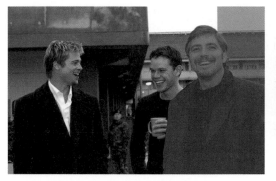

2 Make a selection of George Clooney, including some sky and background, as in this QuickMask representation.

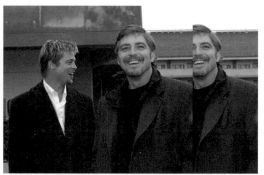

3 When we move Clooney over to the left, we can see a scale problem: Pitt's looking at someone behind him.

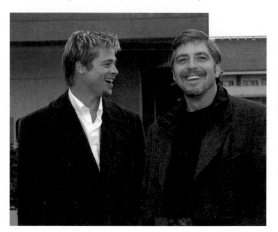

5 There's a problem here. When we make Clooney the right size – keeping his eyes on a line with Pitt – his body is now too short to reach the bottom of the frame.

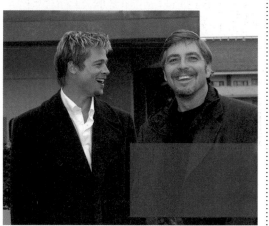

6 The best solution is to scale the bottom half of his body. Make a rectangular selection of Clooney, shown here in QuickMask mode to show the selected area.

HOT TIP

The technique used in steps 6 and 7, to extend Clooney's clothing to reach the bottom of the frame, can be applied to many purposes. In general, we are able to spot when a person's head has been distorted; but bodies – particularly in loose clothing – can be stretched by a surprising amount before we notice something amiss.

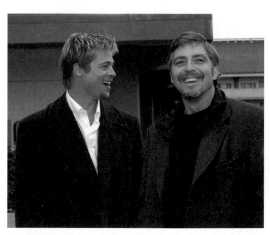

8 There's still a hard edge where the sky behind Clooney's head cuts into the building immediately behind. Add a Layer Mask and paint it out where it overlaps the building.

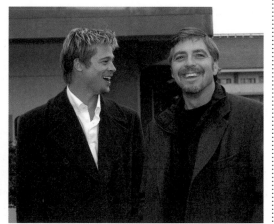

9 So far, so good: but Clooney's edge is still too hard and crisp. Using the technique described in *Losing the Edges*, page 26, we can soften his layer to complete the picture.

183

The perfect haircut

CUTTING OUT HAIR has always been a tricky task for the Photoshop user. Several third-party plug-ins, such as Extensis Mask Pro and Corel Knockout, have attempted to make the job easier; Knockout comes closer than most, although it still isn't an easy tool to use.

The introduction of the Background Eraser tool in Photoshop made the complex removal of backgrounds easier than it had ever been before. It's a tool that works best with hair and other loose objects photographed against a plain, preferably white background; even then, it can be a fiddly activity, and its success depends in large part upon the kind of background the image will eventually have. Users who find the prospect daunting should skip to the next section, where I'll explain how to cheat with hair.

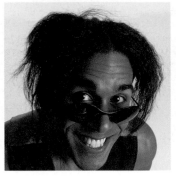

1 This stock image has been photographed against a plain, near-white background. It's the ideal candidate for cutting the hair using the Background Eraser tool.

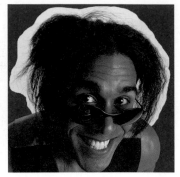

2 First cut out the image loosely, leaving a margin around the hair. I find it useful to make a new layer filled with a solid color, so you can see more clearly what's being erased.

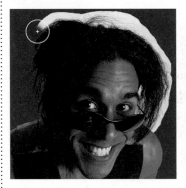

4 Start working your way around the head. The crosshairs in the center of the tool pick up the color that will be erased; everything within the circle radius is removed.

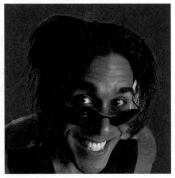

5 Sometimes, the tool will erase areas you wanted to keep – such as the highlights within the shoulder at the right of this figure. That's where Protect Foreground Color comes in.

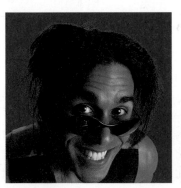

9 With all the background erased, you'll probably be left with a figure whose hair has a definite bright tinge to it. It was, after all, photographed against white.

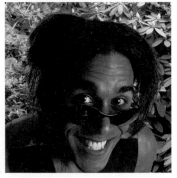

10 If you're going to end up with your figure on a light or complex background, this may be sufficient: you won't notice that the edges are brighter than the middle.

Brush size: Don't use too large a brush, or you'll erase white areas such as the eyes and teeth.

Sampling: Stick to Once when working with a plain background, Continuous if the background is varied.

Limits: Set to Discontiguous to erase background areas surrounded by hair.

Tolerance: Set too low, the brush won't erase the background; too high and you'll lose too much hair.

Protect Foreground Color: Use this to sample skin tones as you work around the head.

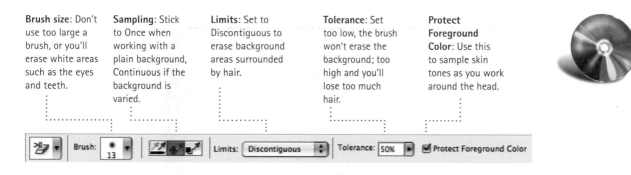

Brush: 13 | Limits: Discontiguous | Tolerance: 50% | ☑ Protect Foreground Color

3 Access the Background Eraser tool by choosing it from the pop-up menu that appears when you hold the mouse button down on the Eraser tool in the toolbar. There are several parameters that need to be considered. We'll use the Discontiguous setting, which allows the tool to erase background areas that are totally enclosed by other colors; and we'll set the sampling to Once, since the background is a single flat color. The Tolerance depends on the contrast between the hair and the background: experiment to get the best setting.

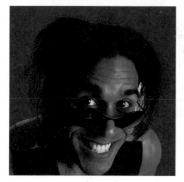

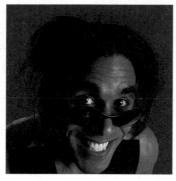

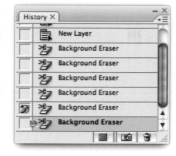

History

New Layer
Background Eraser
Background Eraser
Background Eraser
Background Eraser
Background Eraser
Background Eraser

6 Hold down ⌥ *alt* and click on the shoulder color: it will become the foreground color, and will not be erased. You'll need to keep resampling as you work round the head.

7 Sometimes, even protecting a foreground color can't stop some bright areas from being erased – such as the highlights around the eyebrow seen here.

8 The solution is to use the History palette. Choose the History brush, and click next to the step immediately before: you can now paint the erased areas back in again.

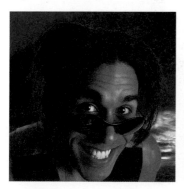

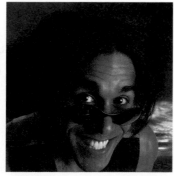

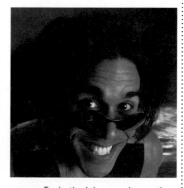

11 If your background is dark, however, the bright hair fringe will look awkward and out of place. There are two ways of solving this, depending on your patience.

12 The easiest way is simply to use the Burn tool set to Highlights, and darken the edges of the hair. With luck, no-one will notice that it doesn't really look like hair.

13 To do the job properly, use the Clone tool. Check the Lock Transparency box and work your way around, cloning hair texture from within the hair to cover the edges.

HOT TIP

Using the Clone tool to copy hair texture from one area to another is a fiddly job, because you need to make sure the strands of hair you're copying from lle In the same orientation as those you're copying to. For some tasks, it may be simpler to copy locks of hair to a new layer, group them with the base layer and twist them to make the hair fall the right way.

SHORTCUTS
MAC WIN BOTH

185

Heads and bodies

The solution for flyaway hair

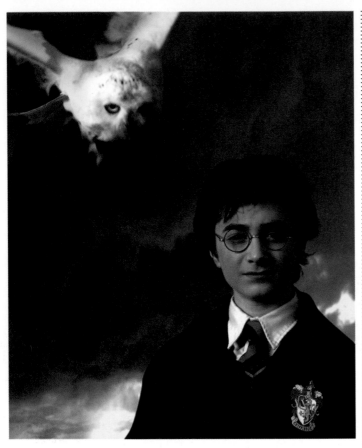

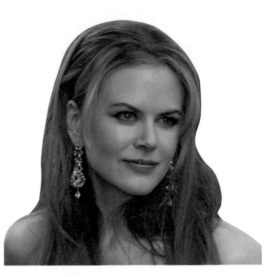

1 Start by creating a smooth cutout of the hair, being careful not to include any of the background. If you use images from royalty-free libraries or CD collections, you'll find that in most cases the clipping path will cut just inside the hair edge, making them perfect for this technique.

THIS COVER FOR THE SUNDAY TIMES magazine was a surprisingly complex montage – the owl and background were two separate layers, and no less than four images were comped together to make Harry Potter. His original hair was cut out using the techniques shown on the previous pages; but to make it more windswept, I added stray strands using the Smudge tool, as shown here.

The Smudge tool is by far the quickest way of creating a soft hair effect. Here we'll take this photograph of Nicole Kidman and place her on a background.

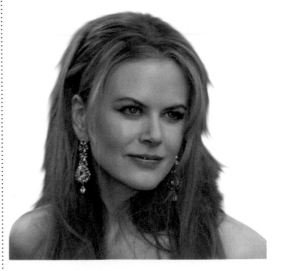

4 For the bottom right section of hair, it looks more convincing to work the other way: starting outside the image with the Smudge tool, and brushing into the hair. This approach works better when the hair is in clumps, rather than flowing directly from the head.

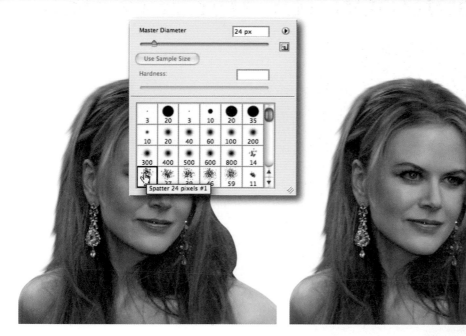

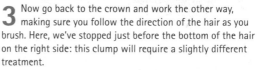

2 Use the Smudge tool, and choose a small Spatter brush with an opacity of around 70%. Begin at the crown and work down one side of the head, smudging from the hair outwards, tweaking out strands as you go. A pressure sensitive graphics tablet is very helpful here.

3 Now go back to the crown and work the other way, making sure you follow the direction of the hair as you brush. Here, we've stopped just before the bottom of the hair on the right side: this clump will require a slightly different treatment.

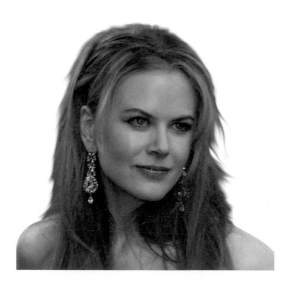

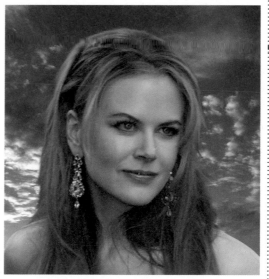

5 Using the Spatter brush with the Smudge tool is a quick method of moving several strands of hair at once. For greater realism, though, switch to a small soft round brush and pull out one strand at a time. You may need to increase the pressure to 80% or even up to 95% for this.

6 When viewed against a white background, hair treated in this way will always tend to look a little fabricated. But when placed against any texture or image, it will blend in perfectly: the translucence of the hair strands will pick up any background it's positioned on.

HOT TIP

If you don't have a graphics tablet, you'll need to constantly adjust the pressure of the Smudge tool to get the right effect. Remember you can always change the pressure from the keyboard: press 7 for 70%, 8 for 80%, and so on. For intermediate values, press two numbers in rapid succession: so pressing 8 then 5 will give you 85%, for example.

187

The problem of hair loss

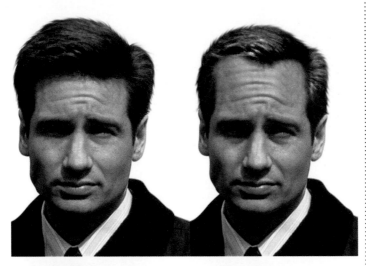

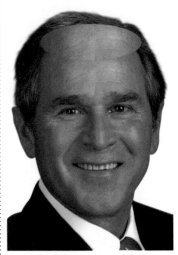

1 Begin by making an elliptical selection from whatever forehead is visible. Make the selection as large as you can without going into the hair line, then turn it into a new layer using ⌘ J *ctrl* J and place it roughly in position.

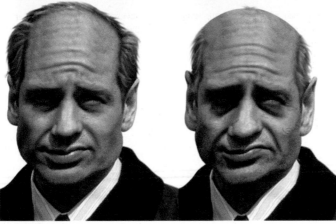

DAVID DUCHOVNY growing older, in stages: the image above, for Focus magazine, was always intended to be more cartoony than realistic.

We'll look at how to achieve an ageing effect in a more authentic and plausible manner on the following pages. For now, though, let's just see how easy it is to turn a full head of hair into a shining bald pate, using our customary model. When you're ready, Mr President.

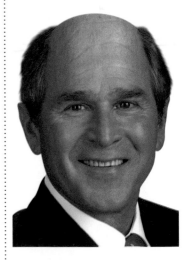

5 Next, we can turn that smoothed-out hair into more realistic strands using the Smudge tool, as described on the previous pages. The difference here is that rather than smudging the hair itself, we're smudging the mask: we're not creating new strands, but revealing those we'd painted out.

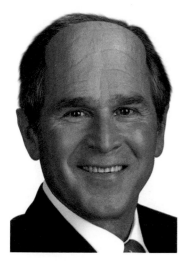

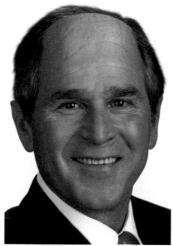

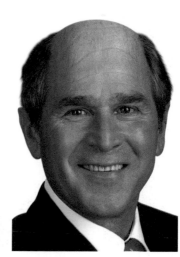

2 Stretch the ellipse to form the shape of the dome of the head. Because we copied the original forehead, we can be sure that the skin tones, textures and lighting will match perfectly.

3 Now make a layer mask and, using a soft-edged brush, paint out along the bottom of the layer so that it blends smoothly into the original forehead. For more on layer masks, see Chapter 3, hiding and showing.

4 Now for the hair. Make a layer mask for the Bush layer, and paint out the hair behind the bald dome so that it recedes in a natural manner. It's easy to paint back areas that were erased accidentally.

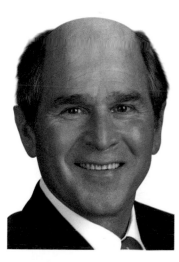

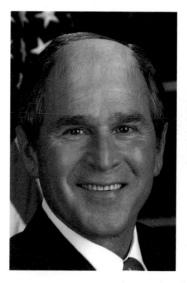

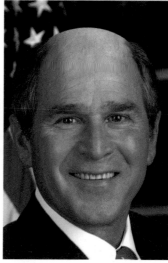

6 The bald dome needs a little work with the Clone tool to remove the obviously stretched forehead lines. Now is also a good time to add a slight shine to the top of the head, using the Dodge tool set to Midtones to avoid changing the colors.

7 We can now put the newly bald Bush back on his original background. The trouble is, the hair on the original still shows through; but it's easy enough to get rid of, as we'll see in the next step.

8 Even with a complex background such as this, we can use the Clone tool to replicate stars and paneling from one area and place them behind the head. Back on his original background, George W looks more at home than ever.

8

Beards and stubble

DESIGNER STUBBLE has always been a matter of some consternation for me. How do rugged actors like Bruce Willis and George Clooney always manage to be interviewed sporting just a couple of days' worth of growth? Do they only use blunt razors? Or do they shave with hair clippers?

Fortunately, we don't need to concern ourselves too much with the vanities of Hollywood's finest. We can draw exactly the level of stubble we want, from a simple five o'clock shadow to a neatly trimmed goatee, using a few simple steps.

Here, we'll add some facial fuzz to our own tough guy, and look at how to achieve a more carefully coiffured appearance as well.

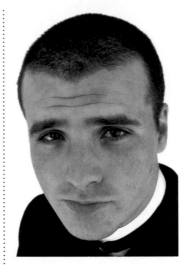

1 Our original figure is gazing moodily into the camera, with just the hint of a bow tie suggesting his status as a club bouncer. But he doesn't look tough enough yet; a bit of designer stubble will help.

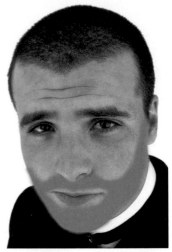

2 On a new layer, paint the beard area using a midtone gray and a soft-edged brush. Accuracy isn't that important at this stage, as we can always mask out any stray areas later, but try to avoid the nose and mouth.

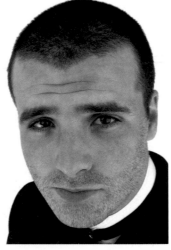

6 We now need to make that stubble more transparent – and we do this by changing the layer mode to Hard Light, which causes all the midtone gray to disappear.

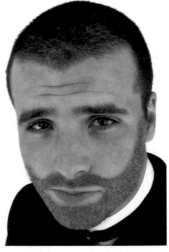

7 Turning the layer to Hard Light mode allows us to see through to the skin beneath. This level of stubble is OK for a day's growth, but let's see if we can beef it up. Make a new Curves Adjustment Layer, grouping it with the beard layer, and lower the brightness of the beard to bring some more strength back into it.

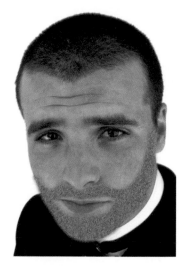

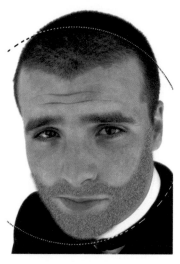

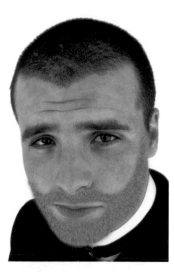

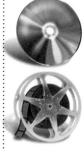

3 Add some Gaussian Noise to the gray you've just painted. I've used about 30% Noise here, but the precise amount you use will depend on the size of the image you're working on.

4 Next, we're going to use Radial Blur to make the stubble; but first, we need to set the midpoint for the blur to act on. Hold ⌥ *alt* as you draw an elliptical marquee from the center out, starting from the bridge of the nose and enclosing the whole beard area.

5 Now use the Zoom setting in the Radial Blur filter at a low setting: around 5% will be appropriate for this length of stubble. (Higher settings will result in facial fur that looks like it belongs on a dog.) Radiating from the bridge of the nose makes the stubble lie in the right direction.

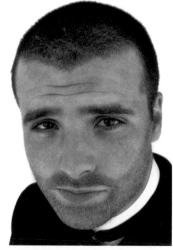

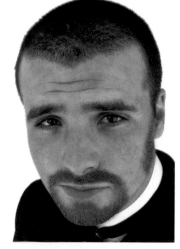

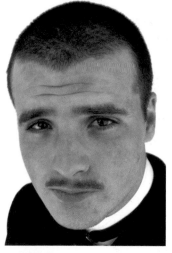

8 The result so far is a beard that looks far too neat. So create a Layer Mask for the beard layer, and paint out some of the harder edges. Painting inside the beard with a low opacity brush also helps the stubble to look more varied in depth, which adds to its realism.

9 As well as creating convincing stubble, we can also modify what we've drawn to make a stronger beard. The effect here is achieved by changing the Curve in the Adjustment Layer to darken the beard further; more sections are painted out on the beard's Layer Mask to give it a more tailored shape.

10 If all you want is to draw a mustache, there's a simple solution: use an eyebrow. QuickMask was used here to make a soft-edged selection of one of the eyebrows, which was then duplicated and distorted to sit on the upper lip. Using the eyebrow ensured that it matched the original.

HOT TIP

When painting the layer mask on a 'real' beard (as opposed to stubble) as in step 9, remember that you can use any of the painting tools on the mask – not just the brush. Added realism can be achieved by using the Smudge tool set to a scatter brush to push hairs into the skin.

SHORTCUTS
MAC WIN BOTH

A fuzzy hairbrush

ON THE PREVIOUS PAGES we created a neat, controlled beard from scratch. Here's how to make an altogether wilder, more shaggy affair: it's the type of beard Saddam Hussein was seen with after his capture. And who better to model it for us than the man responsible for apprehending him, former Defense Secretary Donald Rumsfeld.

The technique involves creating a custom brush to do the deed for us. Making your own brushes in Photoshop can be a tricky affair: this relatively simple example will give you an idea of how it's done, so you can go on to create your own brushes later.

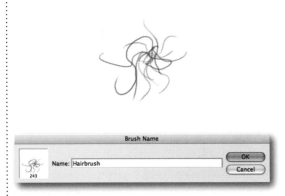

1 Begin by making a new, empty layer in a Photoshop document. With a small, soft brush, draw some random squiggles like those above. It helps to vary the opacity as you paint, for a less uniform effect – most easily done with a graphics tablet. Then choose Define Brush Preset from the Edit menu to make a brush from the squiggles.

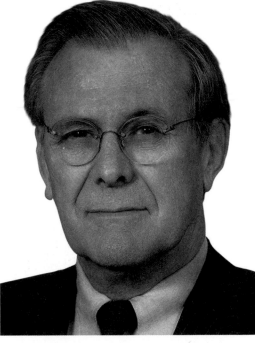

5 Rumsfeld's wide expanse of clean, bare jaw is precisely the canvas we need to begin experimenting with our new brush. Sample the darkest point in the hair with the Eyedropper tool; switch the foreground and background colors (using **X**) and sample a lighter part of the hair.

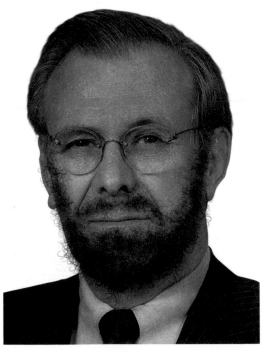

6 Switch to the Brush tool, and start to paint in the beard. You'll probably have to reduce the size of the brush (using the **[** key); it will take several brushstrokes to create this much beard. Note how the color matches the colors in Rumsfeld's hair.

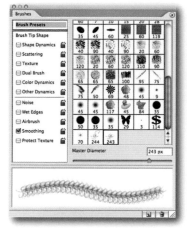

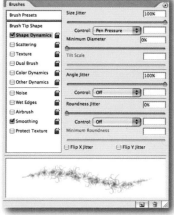

2 Open the Brush Presets palette, and our newly created brush appears right at the bottom. As the preview shows, at present it's set to paint a steady stream; we'll change this in the following steps.

3 Switch to the Shape Dynamics section and set both the Size and Angle Jitter to 100%. This will make each brush stroke rotate and scale randomly as you paint with it, as the preview at the bottom now shows.

4 Now change to the Color Dynamics section, and set the Foreground/Background Jitter to 100% as well. This will bring variation into the color of the brush, which will help it to match the hair in the photograph.

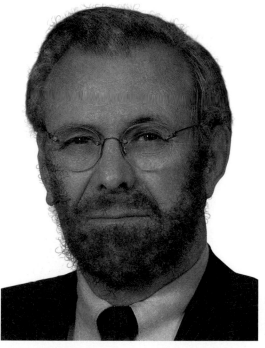

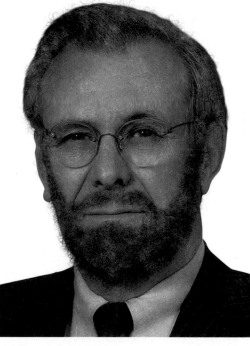

7 So far, so good: but he's grayer than that. So set your foreground and background colors to the default black and white (press **D**) and paint some more: this will add some good gray highlights to the beard. We've also painted a little on his hair, just for fun.

8 If you don't want such a ragged appearance, add a Layer Mask to the beard layer and paint out the more ragged extremes with a soft-edged (regular) brush. And there you have it: one Defense Secretary who's now badly in need of a visit to the barber shop.

The ageing process

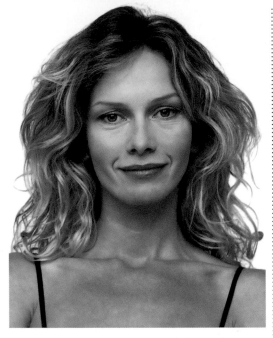

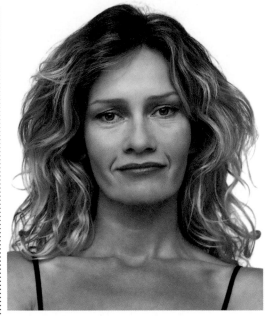

1 The Liquify filter is the obvious choice to distort the shape of the face, as it allows us to push and pull the outlines: here, we've sagged the jaw line, thickened the nose slightly and made the eyes a little more doleful.

Adding a few years to a face is an enjoyable process: you can keep working on the image until you get exactly the state of decrepitude you need. Graying up the hair is an obvious starting point; but there are other, more subtle indications of advancing years. The most noticeable change is not so much the hair or even the wrinkles, but the way a face changes shape with advancing years.

This pair of illustrations was a commission for *People* magazine, who wanted to show the effects of age on a young model. The original photograph, above, was the starting point; to make the difference between young and old more pronounced, I made the starting image more youthful, as we'll see in the final step.

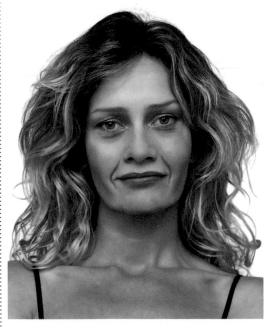

4 We need to remove some of that healthy glow from the skin. The simplest method is to make a new Hue/Saturation Adjustment layer and lower the saturation: paint out the areas where you don't want it applied on the mask.

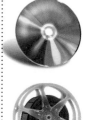

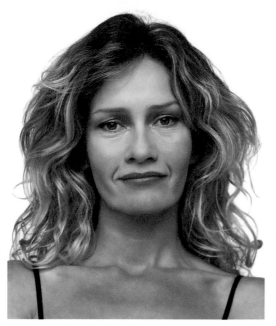

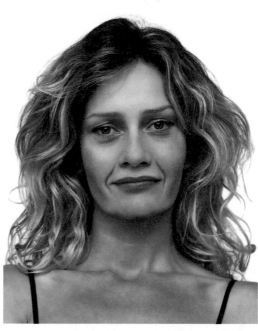

2 To make the hair more gray, first make a new layer and set its mode to Color. Now, using a soft edged brush, paint in either black or white (it makes no difference) to knock the color out of the hair.

3 Make another new layer, set to Hard Light mode. With a low opacity brush, sample colors from the darker parts of the face and build up shadows around the cheeks and under the eyes, and paint in darker lines around the mouth.

HOT TIP

The techniques shown here apply equally to ageing pictures of men and women. But when working with male faces, it's a good idea to add some stubble as well, as this really completes the effect. Use the technique described in Beards and Stubble, on page 190.

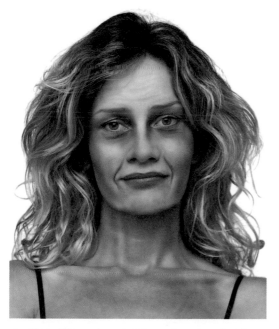

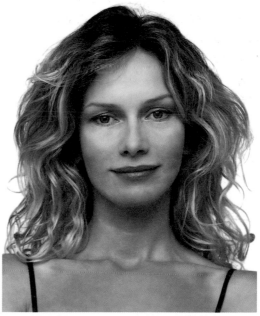

5 We could have stopped at the previous stage, but the client wanted a more pronounced effect. So we can continue to accentuate the lines in the neck and the bags – again, painting on a Hard Light layer.

6 To make the difference between the before and after images clearer, I made the original photo a little more youthful. Using the Healing Tool to sample clear areas of skin, it was easy to paint out the mouth lines and eye bags.

Reversing the ageing process

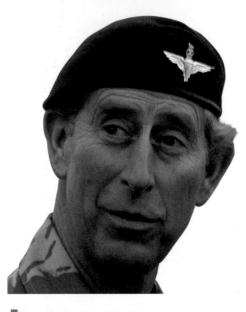

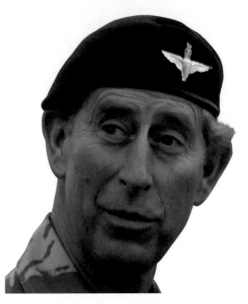

IN THE PREVIOUS EDITION of this book we looked at how to add age to a youthful Prince Charles (you'll find that tutorial on the DVD-ROM if you want to compare the two).

Here, we'll perform the operation in reverse: starting with a photograph of Prince Charles as he is today, we'll look at how to remove the wrinkles and restore some of his erstwhile youthful vigor.

It's an extreme version of the sort of retouching that's standard practice among glossy magazine publishers: models are routinely retouched to remove blemishes, wrinkles and other signs of age.

1 Before we get down to details, we need to smooth out that craggy skin. Here's a good technique: use the Median filter (under 'Noise') – I've used a setting of 3 – to smooth the entire image. If anything, it's too effective: look at the cap badge to see how much detail we've lost.

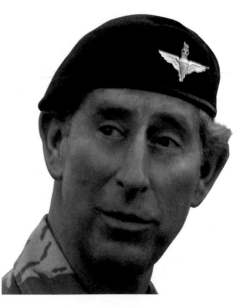

4 As we grow older the five o'clock shadow remains more visible throughout the day. Sample the color from a clear area of skin before selecting a soft brush, set to Color mode; paint out the dark area around the chin. It doesn't hurt to lose some of that redness in the cheeks, as well.

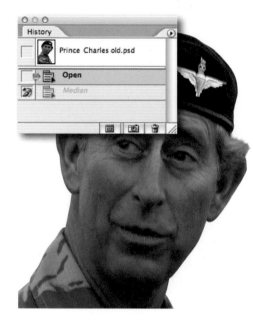

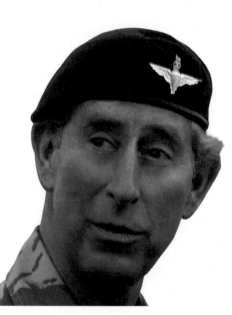

2 As soon as you perform the Median filter, open the History palette. Click the space next to the Median line to mark it; then click the previous step to undo the operation. Use the History Brush to paint the Median filter back in where we want it – around the large areas of skin.

3 The next step is to remove all those wrinkles. This is best done using the Healing brush: ⬚ *alt*-click to set a source point in the middle of the cheek, then paint over each wrinkle, eye bag and blemish in turn. Already, this makes him look very much younger.

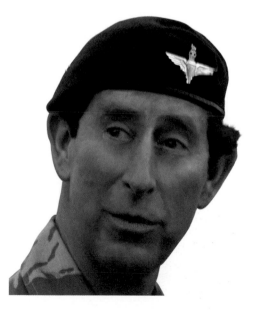

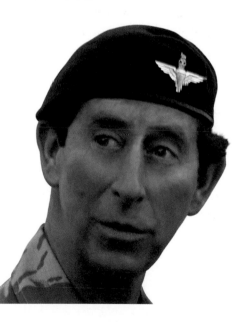

5 The hair is a simple task: select it using QuickMask, and then use Curves to lower the brightness. It's remarkably effective: we can get rid of all that gray in seconds by simply taking all the brightness out of it. The process would be exactly the same even if he weren't wearing a cap!

6 Finally, we need to address how faces sag when they age. Here, I've used the Liquify filter to make the chin tighter and the cheeks a little less saggy. I've also enlarged the eyes very slightly, as eyes tend to close up as we become older; and brightened them a little with the Dodge tool.

HOT TIP

The technique introduced in step 2 is a new one, but has many applications. By applying a filter – and it could be any filter – then pinning it in the History palette and undoing it immediately, we can paint the effect of that filter selectively, exactly where we want it. The possibilities are endless!

SHORTCUTS
MAC WIN BOTH

A change of clothing

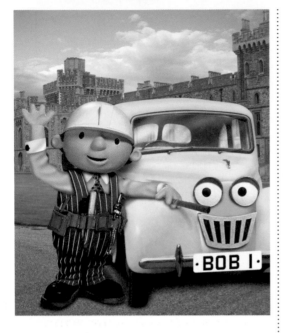

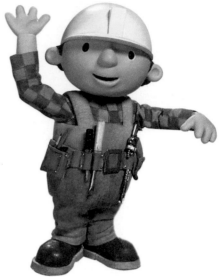

WHEN THE GUARDIAN NEWSPAPER ran a cover story for its magazine section on how the British animation series Bob the Builder was making a fortune through worldwide sales, they wanted an image to demonstrate his success.

The car was colored yellow to match his truck, and the headlights and smiling radiator copied from there onto a more sedate vehicle. What concerns us here is the clothing: turning the denim overalls into something akin to a pinstripe suit, complete with club tie, cuff links and shiny black shoes.

In the end, this illustration never appeared. The reason? I did the artwork on the morning of September 11th 2001 – and by the afternoon newspaper editors had more important matters to talk about.

1 The original figure of Bob was cut out from a standard publicity shot. I had several images to choose from, and chose this one so I could drape the arm over the car. Cutting the image from its background was a simple task using the Pen tool to create smooth curves.

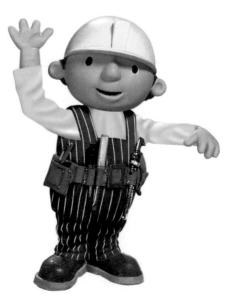

4 It would have been impossible to rescue any shading from the original checked shirt, so the only solution was to trace its outline and draw a new one. The new shirt was filled with a light gray, and shading was added using the Dodge and Burn tools – see Folds and wrinkles in Chapter 11.

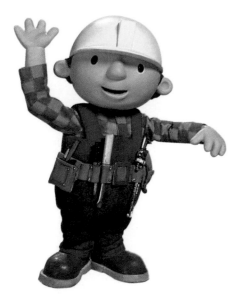

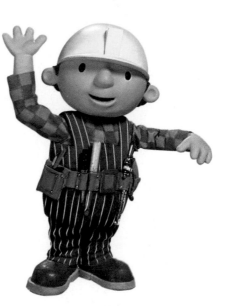

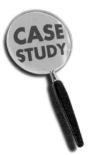

2 The existing overalls were selected, tracing carefully around the tools, and made into a new layer. Turning that bright denim into dark blue serge was a piece of cake using the Curves dialog.

3 It's the pinstripes that make sense of the new clothing, and they took some time to draw. Each stripe was drawn as a path using the Pen tool, being careful to trace bumps over the contours of the folds in the clothing; the path was then stroked with the Brush tool and shaded.

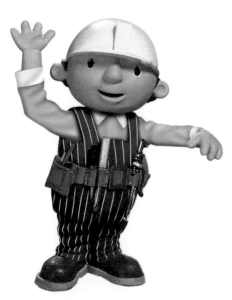

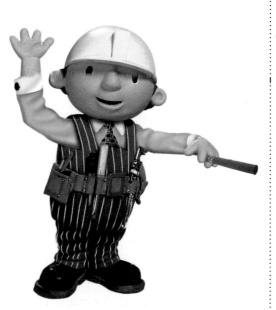

5 The shaded shirt was colored pink using the Hue/Saturation dialog, which can be simpler than Curves for a colorizing job like this. The collar and cuffs were then brightened to make them stand out, and shading added beneath the straps of the overalls.

6 The final elements were all added separately: the cigar, cuff link, and the tie were pinched from other photographs. While it would have been possible to draw a tie, using a real one adds to the realism of the image. The shoes were also desaturated and darkened.

HOT TIP

Drawing the stripes on the overalls was the hardest part of this job. The trick is to keep their spacing as even as possible, and to accentuate the folds in the clothing by making the stripes wrap around them – it's this that makes them look convincing. Shading, using the Burn tool, made them appear to belong to the clothing.

199

It's all in the eyes

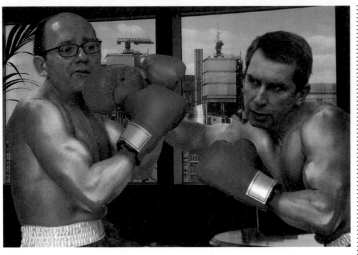

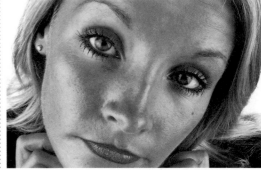

THIS ILLUSTRATION for the Sunday
Telegraph shows two captains of industry
slugging it out in the boardroom. Both images
were standard publicity shots, with the central
figures gazing directly at the camera. But by
moving the eyes of both so that they stared
at each other, it was possible to create some
emotional interaction between them that would
have been lacking if they'd remained gazing at
the viewer.

In Chapter 5 we looked at how important eye
contact is – which means having the ability to
move eyes at will. Here, we'll take one of the
figures used in that chapter and show how to
prepare the eyes so that people can be made to
look in any direction you choose.

1 This figure has eyes that are wide enough for us to be
able to position the eyeballs wherever we choose. More
importantly, there's enough of the pupil visible to allow us
to use it later. Begin by making a circular selection that
encompasses the iris.

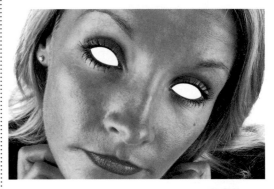

4 Turn the path into a selection by pressing ⌘ Enter
ctrl Enter, then make a new layer named Eyeball and fill
the selected area with white. This will form the basis for our
new eyeball.

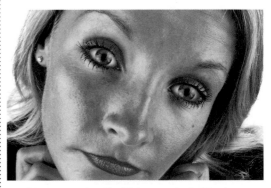

7 We can now show the iris layer again. Position it
above the Eyeball layer and make a Clipping Mask
using ⌘ ⌥ G ctrl alt G, so that we only see it where
it overlaps the eyeball. Select the iris and drag a copy until
both are looking in the same direction.

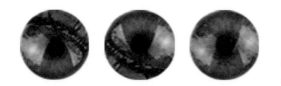

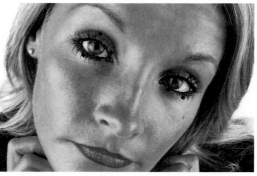

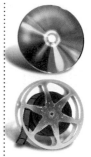

2 Make a new layer from the selection using ⌘ J / ctrl J, then duplicate the layer and rotate it 180°. Now erase the eyelid showing on the new layer, and continue erasing until the two halves of the iris become one. When the eyeball looks convincing, merge the two layers.

3 Hide the new iris – we'll come back to it later. Now, using the Pen tool, draw a Bézier path around each eyeball. Use as few points as possible for a smooth outline: I try to use anchor points just in the corners of each eye, making the path handles do all the work.

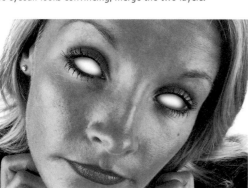

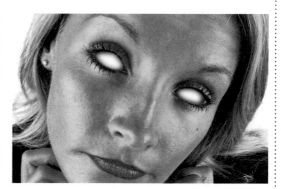

5 Add shading around the color of the eyeball using the Burn tool set to Highlights, using a low opacity. Build up the shading slowly, so that it doesn't appear too harsh.

6 The original shading will appear to have a bluish tint, although in fact it is purely gray. Use Color Balance to add a little red and a little yellow to the eyeball, then soften the edges using the Blur tool.

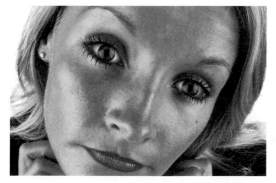

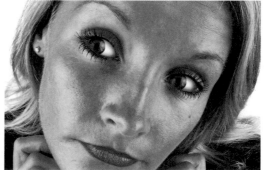

8 So far, so good: but the eyes still don't look real. The solution is to change the layer mode of the irises from Normal to Multiply, so that the shading we applied to the eyeballs shows through onto the irises. It's a subtle difference, but it completes the effect.

9 With both eyes now complete, we can move the irises independently of the eyeballs to make them look in any direction we choose. Because the two layers are grouped together, the irises always appear to move within the range of the eyeballs.

SHORTCUTS

201

A change of expression

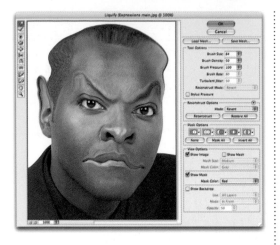

T HE LIQUIFY FILTER is a powerful tool for distorting images – far stronger than the Smudge tool in its effects, and much more controllable.

Liquify is a great filter for creating massive distortions and twists in images. Here, however, we'll look at its more restrained application: that of changing the expression on a face.

The key to getting this technique to work is subtlety. Small distortions can create the effect of different expressions without giving the game away; it's easy to get carried away, and one or two of the examples here verge on the cartoony. Use a large brush at a fairly low pressure for best results.

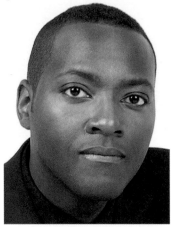

1 Here's our original image – a bland, expressionless gaze directly into the camera. Yet from this vapid starting point we can create a huge range of emotions. All the effects here are created using just the first tool in the Liquify toolbox.

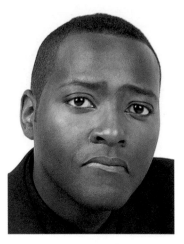

2 SCEPTICAL: a downturn on the corners of the mouth, with a slight wrinkle on the lower lip. The eyebrows are pushed down in the middle, and one is raised slightly at the corner to complete the effect.

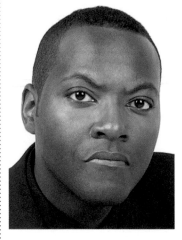

6 PEEVED: a slightly cross look, achieved by turning the corners of the mouth down slightly and curving the eyebrows so that they're raised in the center but both corners are dragged down.

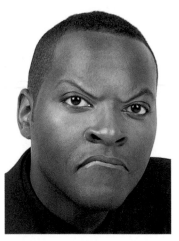

7 ANGRY: a stronger version of the previous effect. The eyebrows are curved in a more pronounced manner, and the mouth has a much more definite downwards curl. The effect is strengthened here by stretching each nostril up and outwards to give them that furiously flared look.

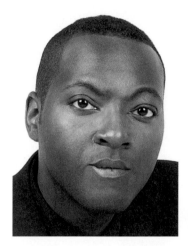

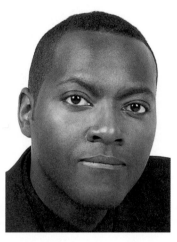

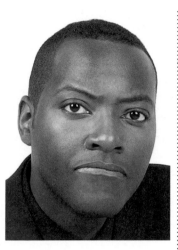

3 QUIZZICAL: one eyebrow pushed down in the corner, the other raised in the middle for an asymmetric look. The mouth is narrowed to give a pursed appearance, and one nostril is pushed up slightly.

4 SINCERE: a face you can trust. This subtle effect is achieved by thinning the line of the mouth to make it more hard-set, and pushing the corners of both eyebrows down in an expression nearing a frown.

5 RESOLUTE: an effect that differs in technique only slightly from the previous example, but which results in a more determined appearance. The eyebrows are made thinner, and the mouth is widened with a slight downturn.

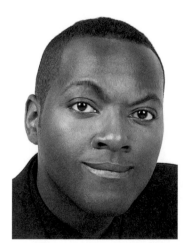

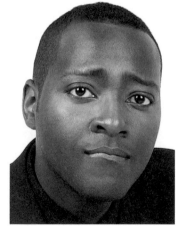

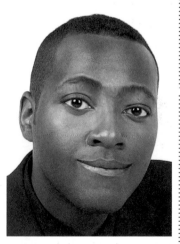

8 SMUG: this man knows something you don't, and it isn't to your advantage. It's similar to the Quizzical look, above, with one eyebrow raised dramatically; but the smile, created by raising both corners of the mouth, makes this figure look more in control of the situation.

9 ANXIOUS: this worried expression is produced by raising the corners of both eyebrows and lowering the midpoints of the eyebrows. The mouth is raised slightly on one side, and the nostril above it is also raised to reflect the way the musculature works beneath the skin.

10 HAPPY: the hardest expression to create using a closed mouth. Since we can't make him grin, we have to rely on a broad closed-mouth smile made by widening and raising the corners of the mouth. Both eyebrows are raised significantly to complete the effect.

HOT TIP

In all these examples, we've distorted the mouth and eyebrows but left the eyes largely intact. This is because any distortion on the pupils would make the whole face look false and unconvincing. More powerful results can be obtained by distorting the eyes as well, and then replacing the pupils using the technique described on the previous tutorial.

Liquify: Turning heads

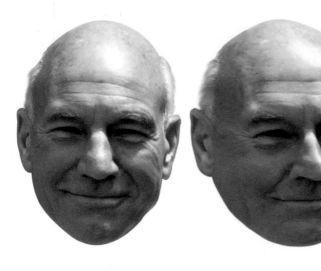

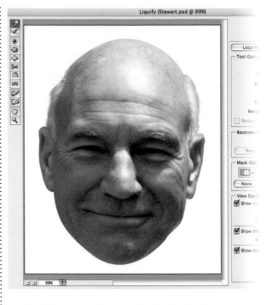

O N THE PREVIOUS PAGES WE LOOKED at ways of using the Liquify filter to change the expression on a character's face. Now we'll use this powerful filter to turn an entire head, to make it look as if it's pointing in a different direction.

This is a tricky manoeuver, which takes both skill and patience to complete successfully. It helps greatly to arrange your monitor so that you can see the original head while working in the Liquify dialog: it's easy to lose track of the character's original appearance, and it's important to remember what he really looked like before you started.

Because there are so many small brushstrokes in this tutorial, it isn't possible to show every tiny step on these pages: check out the QuickTime movie on the DVD to see the full transformation in real time.

We'll use everyone's favorite starship captain, Jean-Luc Picard – as played by actor Patrick Stewart – as our guinea pig for this experiment. The Borg was never this terrifying.

1 Begin by opening the head in the Liquify filter. I've isolated this head from its background, as it's hard enough to distort just the head without worrying about the neck as well; we can always find a suitable body later.

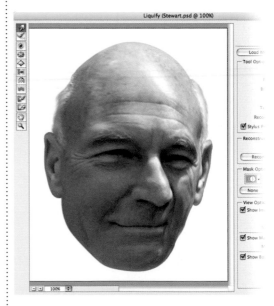

4 It's important to remember that while the nose was photographed head-on, in the three-quarter view we're aiming for it's going to have a lot more apparent depth. Using a smaller brush, drag the tip and the left nostril (as we're looking at it) apart to give the impression of scale.

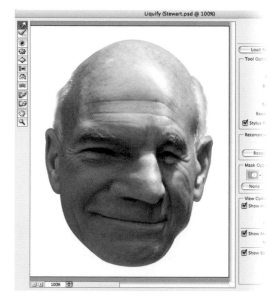

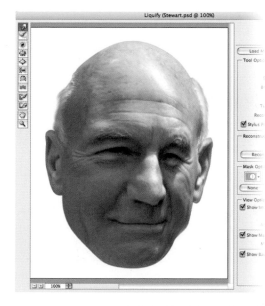

2 With the Warp tool (**W**) on a large brush size, move all the center line elements – the nose, the middle of the mouth, the middle of the forehead – to the right, in the direction we want the head to point. So far, it will look fairly awful, so don't worry about details yet!

3 Now follow on behind with the same brush, moving all the elements to the left of that center line: the eye, the cheek, the bone in the temple, and so on. The left side of the face is starting to look more plausible now.

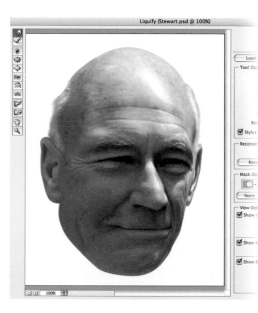

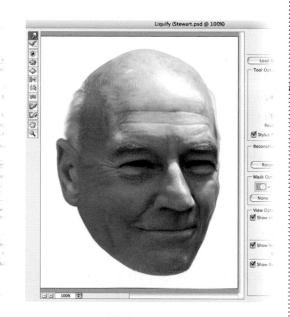

5 The philtrum – that indent in the upper lip directly beneath the nose – needs to be vertical, not slanted. At this point we can also stretch the right eye into shape, and move the line of the mouth so that it more closely resembles the original.

6 A lot more tweaking and pulling gives us the result we want. Note the newly pointed chin, the line of the left of the jaw, and the compressed right cheek. All that remains is to hide the right ear (as we see it) with a Layer Mask, and the transformation is complete.

HOT TIP

This technique is one of the more difficult in this book. It helps if you've seen images of the subject in profile. Because we're stretching the pixels on one side of the face to fill a much larger area of the image, it helps to begin with a high quality original photograph. Don't expect to complete the process within the Liquify dialog: here, we've erased the hidden ear afterwards.

Sleep and the art of healing

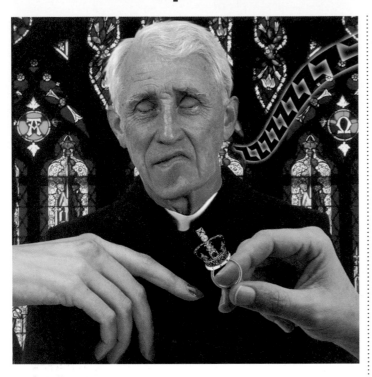

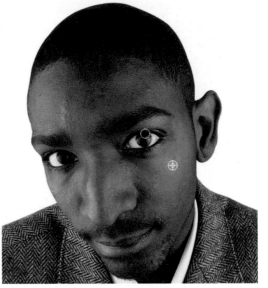

1 The first step in using the Healing tool is to specify the clone target. Hold the ⌥ *alt* key and click on the point you want to clone from. Choose an area of skin that's relatively free from wrinkles, lines and stubble, such as the cheek in this example.

ONE OF THE MAIN NEW FEATURES in Photoshop 7 was the Healing tool. Designed for the removal of noise and scratches from photographs, it can also be used for more wide-reaching applications: a prime example might be to remove the hole left by the earring in the model on the right.

Here, we're going to use the tool to make this figure look like he's sleeping. If I'd had Photoshop 7 when doing the illustration above for Time Out (about the tedium of royal weddings) I'd have made a far more convincing job of it. Now, in just a few steps, we can close our model's eyes far more easily.

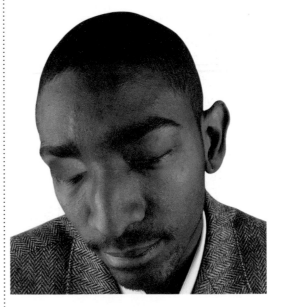

4 Repeat the process for the other eye. There's no need to specify the target point again, since this will be chosen automatically. Once again, the eyelid appears too bright while we're in the process of using the healing tool – but this will be corrected when the button is released.

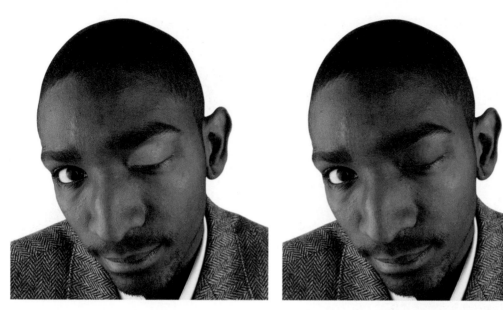

2 Now begin to paint over the area you want to heal. As you paint, the target area will be cloned directly, as shown here – and it will appear badly shaded as a result. Avoid healing over the bottom eyelashes, as they'll mark the closure of the eye.

3 Once you release the mouse button, the cloned area will take on the light and shade characteristics of the area you healed into. Note how the eyelid, previously far too bright, has now toned in well with the area of skin that lies around it.

HOT TIP

Because you don't see the full effect of the Healing tool until after you've finished painting (and after Photoshop has processed the result), you can't always see what you're doing as you go along. It's often best taken in short steps, alternating between large and small brushes as you go, so you can watch the result build up in stages.

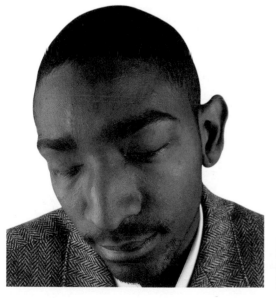

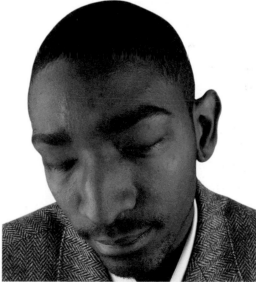

5 With both eyelids now fully healed, we can see how the shading closely matches the surrounding skin. The problem now is that the eyelids have taken on the color values of the open eyes, resulting in a grayish hue that looks a little artificial.

6 This is easily fixed by using a soft-edged paint brush set to Color mode, and painting over the eyelids with a color sampled from nearby. Now, our previously wide-awake figure looks like he's sleeping peacefully.

SHORTCUTS
MAC WIN BOTH

Coloring black+white images

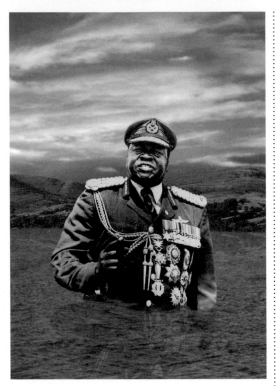

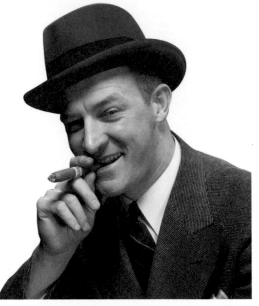

1 Our starting image is a great retro photograph taken from a royalty-free collection. Since the original image is, naturally, grayscale, we need to make sure we convert it to RGB before continuing. Even in RGB, it's always worth keeping your swatches in CMYK so they'll work in print.

ALTHOUGH PHOTO LIBRARIES SUPPLY many thousands of color images, there are times when the Photoshop artist needs to color up black and white photographs. It may be to repurpose a historical figure, such as the image of Idi Amin, above, for the cover of Giles Foden's novel The Last King of Scotland.

The more usual scenario is those cases where only a genuine 1950s photograph will supply that retro look. Coloring monochrome images is fiddly, but not difficult; the secret lies in choosing the right colors to work with.

Because painting with color can produce dramatic changes in an image, it's worth always working with a very low opacity brush when painting in color mode: I frequently use just 5% opacity when painting the beard area.

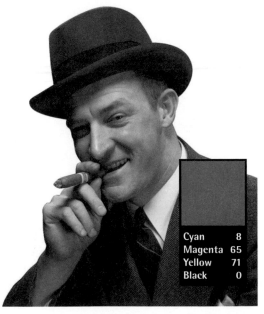

Cyan	8
Magenta	65
Yellow	71
Black	0

4 Now for the blush color. Set the foreground color as shown above and, using the same brush opacity, paint dabs of color on the cheeks, nose, ears and forehead. With a much smaller brush, set the opacity to around 30% and paint the color on the lips.

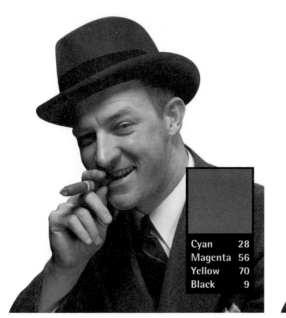

Cyan	28
Magenta	56
Yellow	70
Black	9

2 We'll start by applying a general flesh-colored wash to the whole image. After setting your foreground color according to the swatch above, choose Fill from the Edit menu and select Color Fill with Preserve Transparency: this will flood the image with our skintone color.

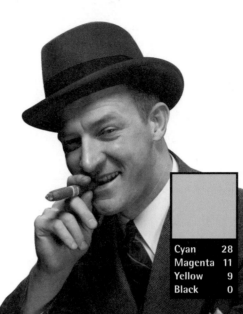

Cyan	28
Magenta	11
Yellow	9
Black	0

3 The next step is to paint the beard area. Set the foreground color as shown, and use a soft-edged brush set to Color mode: make sure the transparency of the layer is locked in the Layers palette. Set the brush to a very low opacity – 10% or less – and paint the beard area.

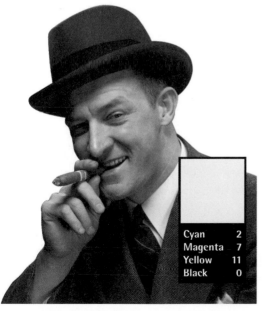

Cyan	2
Magenta	7
Yellow	11
Black	0

5 We need to color the eyes and teeth as well, but painting with pure white will make them look blue (try it). Set the color as above and use a very small brush, still set to Color mode, to paint those areas. Use the Dodge tool here as well to bring some sparkle into the teeth and eyes.

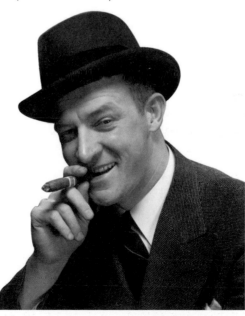

6 To color the clothing, select all but the skin areas and make a new layer from it using ⌘ J *ctrl* J. Then use Curves, Color Balance or Hue and Saturation to recolor those areas, making additional selections as necessary. You can still use the brush set to Color for details such as the tie.

SHORTCUTS
MAC WIN BOTH

A change of skin

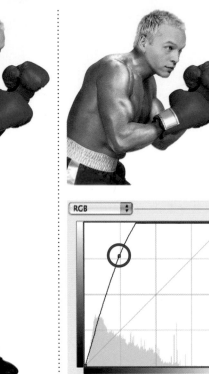

IMAGES: PHOTOOBJECTS.NET/DIGITAL STOCK

POLITICAL SENSITIVITY aside, there are times when we need to change a figure's skin color to match the head we've placed on it.

It's most urgent when using images which show a lot of flesh, such as the sporting pictures used here: we very often find ourselves with a body that's in exactly the right pose, but of a skin tone that doesn't match our brief.

This was an issue with the cover of this book: the body was in a perfect position, but didn't fit Humphrey Bogart's head.

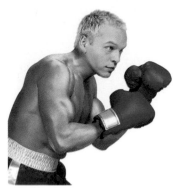

1 Begin by copying the skin to a new layer. Hold ⌥ *alt* as you choose a Curves Adjustment Layer, and check 'Use Previous Layer to Create Clipping Mask'; then grab the center of the curve and drag up and to the right.

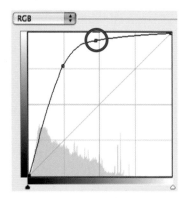

2 The previous step produced some rather hard highlights, which we can address next. Grab the middle of the curve, right at the top, and drag down a short way. This reduces the glare to some degree.

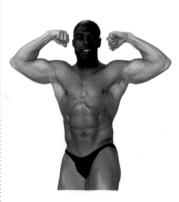

1 Here's the same problem in reverse: we want to darken this body to match the head. It's a similar process, but one or two steps work differently here.

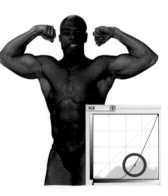

2 Make a new Curves Adjustment Layer, as before, and drag the center point of the curve down to darken up all the skintones. Don't worry about the color yet!

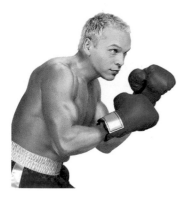

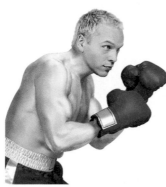

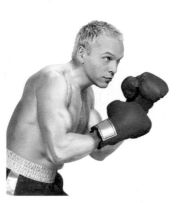

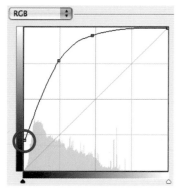

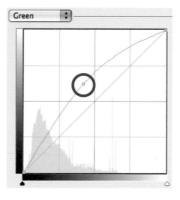

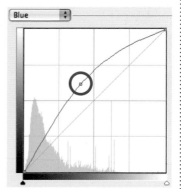

3 So far, so good: but there's too much contrast here. The shadows are darker than we need. So grab the bottom left point on the curve and drag it up around a quarter of the way towards the top.

4 With the tonal range more or less right, we can address the color. Our head is extremely pale; so let's first switch to the Green channel (⌘ 2 ctrl 2) and raise the center point on the curve slightly.

5 Finally, we need to boost the Blue channel as well. Switch to it using ⌘ 3 ctrl 3, and raise the midpoint of the curve here as well. you may need to apply further adjustment on the RGB Composite (⌘ ` ctrl `).

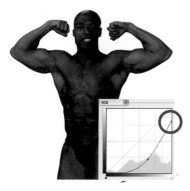

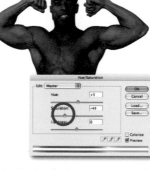

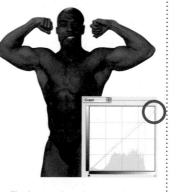

3 There's too much contrast here: the highlights are once again too strong. So grab the top right end of the curve. and drag this down a little way to reduce the effect.

4 It's hard to fix that over-saturated body in Curves; so add a new Hue/Saturation Adjustment Layer. Lower the saturation and, if you like, tweak the Hue setting slightly as well.

5 That's very close: but there's still too much green in the highlights. Open the Curves Adjustment Layer once more, and lower the bright point on the Green curve.

SHORTCUTS
MAC WIN BOTH

211

Sourcing images for free

IN THE PREVIOUS INTERLUDE we looked at photo libraries, both online and on CD, which offer royalty-free pictures for use by the Photoshop artist. But not everyone has the budget to invest in additional photography. Fortunately, the internet offers us an infinite library of photographs to use in our montages.

The best source of image is, of course, Google. Check the Image tab, and Google will search just for pictures: select the Large option and you'll find photographs that are generally of good enough quality to use. The images you find in this way will, however, all be subject to copyright, so while it's acceptable to use them for your own personal projects, don't be tempted to use them for any commercial work. Companies such as Disney, in particular, guard the use of their images with a ferocity matched only by the zeal of their lawyers. Seriously! This means you!

There are several websites that offer royalty-free images on a zero cost basis. Among the best are **stockxchng** (*www.sxc.hu*) and **MorgueFile** (*www.morguefile.com*), both of which take contributions from the public and make them available for public use. They both have good category and keyword search, and can be the perfect source for hard-to-locate shots of just about any subject you can imagine. The best place for textures of all kinds is **Mayang** (*www.mayang.com/textures*) which includes a huge range, freely downloadable.

Company logos can be particularly hard to track down. At the time of writing, there's a good Russian website – *www.logotypes.ru* – which holds around 5000 company logos from around the world. Whether this dubiously legal site will still be in existence when this book is published is anyone's guess, though; and the logos held here tend to be of a rather low resolution.

If you need a high res logo from a particular company, you're almost sure to find it on their website. Ignore the obvious masthead logos found on the front page: these are bound to be too small to be used, and will often be adaptations of the original logos that have been reworked to reflect the electronic nature of the web page. Instead, search for the company's annual reports, usually found in the Investor Relations section, which will almost always be in the form of downloadable PDF files. The great thing about these is that they're infinitely scalable: so while the photographic images will become badly bitmapped when you zoom in, the logos themselves are almost always embedded in the documents in their original EPS format. Zoom in as far as you can, and take a screenshot of the logo: it will be crisp and clear at any size.

Product photography, particularly from technology companies (computers, cell phones, consumer electronics) is usually available in high resolution on company websites, generally in the Press area. Normally, no registration is required: you can just go in and download the images you need. Again, though, you may need to be careful how you use them.

For free photographs of individual objects at a reasonable resolution, there's no better place to look than **eBay**. Everyone with something to sell will include decent photographs of their wares: I've used *www.ebay.com* to find garden gnomes, fireworks and antiques when all other sources have failed.

Finding useable images of people is very much harder. They're almost all protected by a variety of copyrights, and should be used with extreme caution: there have been a few occasions when photo libraries have contacted me after I've inadvertently used one of their images, and demanded payment. The same goes for famous paintings. The best place for celebs is **Wikipedia**, whose Creative Commons license permits use of images unless otherwise marked.

The US Government has a policy of putting images in the public domain, which means they're freely available for download and use. (That's the only reason why George W Bush appears in these pages!) Check out *www.nasa. gov* for space images, *www.photolib.noaa.gov* for skies and nature, and *www. defenselink.mil/photos/* for all things military – including past and current presidents and other world leaders.

The golden rule, however, is: be careful. If you're in any doubt as to the copyright status of an image, don't use it. It's not worth the repercussions.

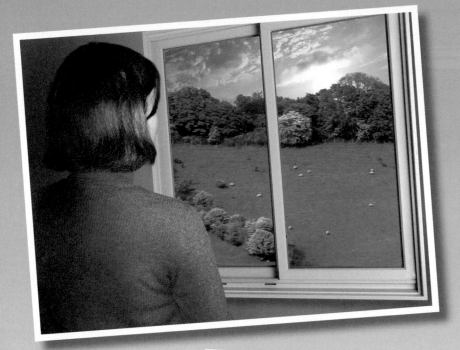

It's a fine summer's evening, and a girl gazes out of the window at the view beyond. Except that, in the top version, there's no sense of the window itself being present: sure, we can see the frame, but the glass is missing. In the second version, we've added a 'reflection' of the room onto the glass. In fact, this is just a photograph of a different room placed behind the window frame at an opacity of 20%. It gives the glass some substance, a sense of it existing in the real world.

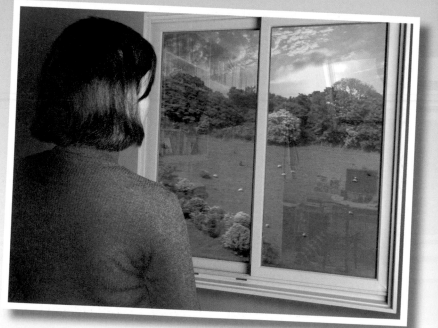

9

Shiny surfaces

GLASS, WE'RE TOLD, is really a liquid. Which is little
consolation when you're traversing a glass-floored
walkway, but the resemblance between the two can be a
great help when you're working in Photoshop.

Glass and liquids share many properties in common:
they both refract light, and they can both be drawn
more easily than you might have thought possible. In
this chapter we'll look at some of the different ways of
creating glazed objects, from bottles and windows to
brains in jars.

Shiny surfaces also reflect objects around them, so we'll
also look at the best way to get reflections to look right.

Introducing... Plastic Wrap

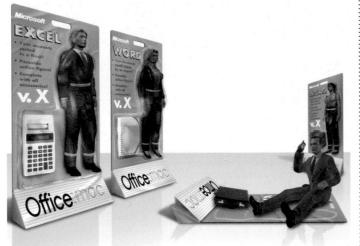

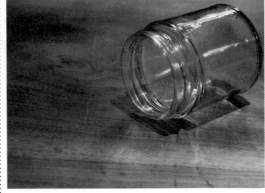

1 I photographed this jar sitting on a wooden surface. Just about any container would do: rotate a stock photo of a mug on its side for the same effect.

THE PLASTIC WRAP FILTER is one of the most useful special effects Photoshop has to offer. Use it to make anything glisten – from beads of sweat on a dancer's forehead to visceral internal organs (see the Case Study on the following pages). Oh, and if you really want to, you can also use it to draw plastic wrapping.

The illustration above, for MacUser magazine, needed the figures to look as if they were encased in plastic. And, of course, I used Plastic Wrap to do this. But I also used it on the sitting figure itself, to make him more shiny; all the figures were modeled in Poser, and needed to look more plastic-like.

In this workthrough, we're going to use Plastic Wrap to create a syrup spill out of a jar. Exactly the same technique could be used to draw coffee, blood or just about anything that dribbles.

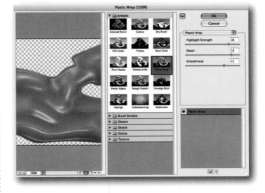

4 You'll find the Plastic Wrap filter under the Artistic section of the Filters menu. Drag the sliders until you get the effect you want.

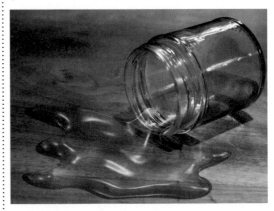

7 Changing the color of the water turns it into different liquids. Here, I've used Hue/Saturation to darken it and add an orange tint – just right for our spilled syrup.

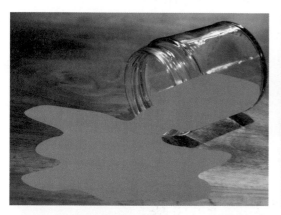

2 On a new layer, paint the spill in mid gray, with a hard edged brush. Try to imagine how the liquid would pour through the opening of the jar and lie on the table.

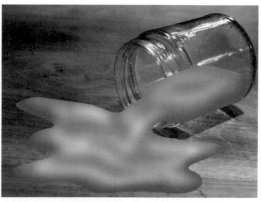

3 Use the Dodge and Burn tools to add some random shading to the layer. This is simply a matter of practise; you may have to adjust the shading and reapply the filter.

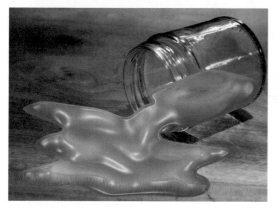

5 Here's the result of applying the filter. If it doesn't look right, Undo and then fiddle with the shading, then use ⌘ F ctrl F to apply the Plastic Wrap filter again.

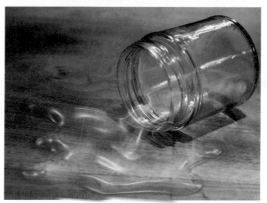

6 When we change the mode of the layer from Normal to Hard Light, all the gray disappears - leaving us with just the highlights and shadows. Perfect! Instant water!

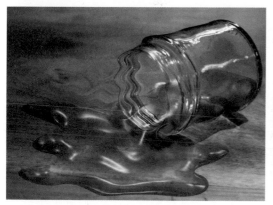

8 To complete the effect, let's add some refraction. I've taken a copy of the background image, and applied the Wave filter to it to create a slight rippling effect.

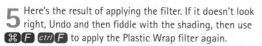

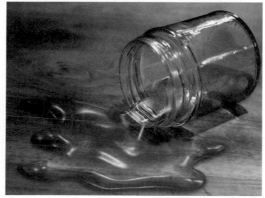

9 The distorted layer is masked out everywhere except where it overlaps the syrup: this givs us a convincing distortion of the neck of the jar, which adds to the effect.

SHORTCUTS

217

Blood and gore, no sweat

THE BRIEF for this illustration was to produce a realistic image of a heart, to be used on the front page of The Guardian. I was supplied with an image of a basic 3D model; it had everything in the right place, but looked like the model it was. I immediately asked if the illustration had to be accurate enough to fool heart surgeons: 'No,' came the reply, 'it only has to fool Guardian readers.' A much simpler proposition altogether.

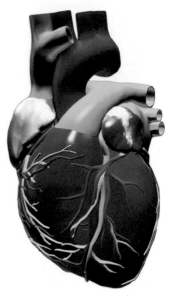

1 The original image, generated from a 3D model, may have been a useful teaching aid – but there was no way this would look like a convincing heart as it stood. As with most basic 3D modeling, this one looks like it's made of plastic rather than flesh and blood. This is the kind of application at which Plastic Wrap excels.

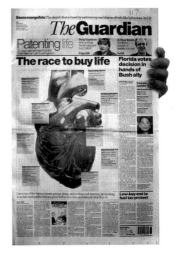

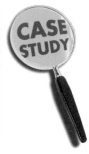

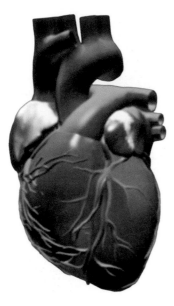

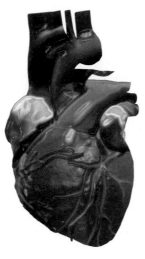

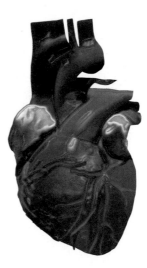

2 The first step was to desaturate the image. Then, after locking transparency (so the edges didn't fuzz up), I appled Gaussian Blur to smooth out the veins.

3 The first application of Plastic Wrap picked up the contours and added a shiny, glistening tone to the image – without a brushstroke having been added.

4 The image was colorized using Hue/Saturation to give it a base color on which to build. Already, it was starting to look far more real and organic.

HOT TIP

When working on an image like this, it helps to create multiple layers for coloring and tinting the different areas: that way, the strength of each layer can easily be reduced by simply lowering the opacity of the layer. Make a clipping mask of each new layer with the base layer to make sure no color leaks out around the edges.

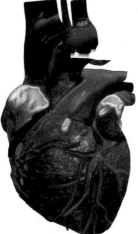

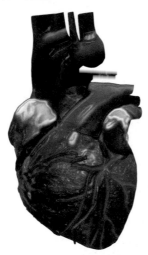

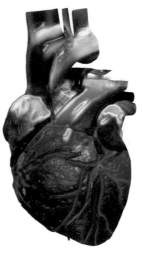

5 A second application of Plastic Wrap was added, which was then masked out selectively over areas where it seemed too strong – mainly the large expanses of flat aorta.

6 The veins were painted in on a new layer using Hard Light mode, which allowed the underlying texture to show through; the tubes and pipes at the top were painted on a layer set to Color mode.

7 Finally, the plumbing at the top was copied to a new layer (by using a soft brush in QuickMask to ensure smooth edges) and then brightened up and tinted to look convincing.

Getting hot and sticky

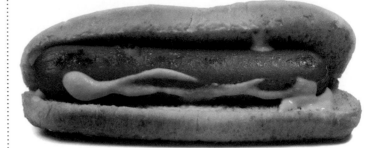

ADDING SHADING to any object will help to make it look more three-dimensional. But when the object is fiddly and intricate, painting in consistent shadows and highlights can be a really tricky process.

The solution is to let Photoshop do most of the hard work for you. This example was an illustration for The Independent, who wanted a hot dog to look as appealing as possible with the words 'Eat Me' written in mustard along the side.

The first step was to find an appealing hot dog image – which was not an easy task. I eventually found this one on iStockphoto.com, a website where photographers offer their work, royalty free, at very low cost. The creator of this hot dog, Dan Brandenburg, has kindly allowed me to include the image on the CD so you can all have a go at this one. Thanks, Dan.

1 Here's the original hot dog image. Although it was photographed against a light background, I cut this out using the Pen tool to make sure the background would be pure white. But I kept the original image just for the shadow: placed behind the cutout, and bleached out using Curves, it made a realistic shadow beneath the hot dog.

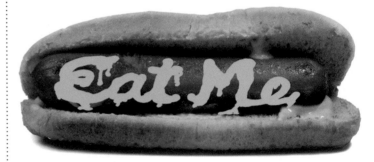

3 The lettering was painted in on a new layer, using a hard-edged brush. It's not difficult to do, but it takes a little patience: the trick is not to make it too even. The drips were painted in using the brush as well, and the edge roughened up slightly by painting over it with a much smaller brush. So far, it looks far too flat and dull: we'll fix that next.

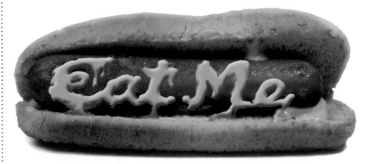

6 To turn the mustard into a more editable layer, I selected it by `ctrl` `⌘` clicking on the name in the Layers palette, then made a merged copy using `ctrl` `Shift` `C` `⌘` `Shift` `C`, followed by Paste. With the embossing now part of the layer proper, I could add a little Gaussian Noise, followed by a small amount of Gaussian Blur, to add a little texture.

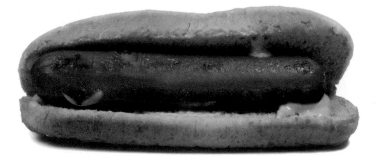

2 In order for the new lettering to show up, I had to remove most of the original mustard. Not that difficult a job: the top half of the sausage was duplicated to a new layer and rotated 180°, and a layer mask used to blend the two together. A little darkening using the Burn tool helped to add shading to the underside, to make it look more convincing.

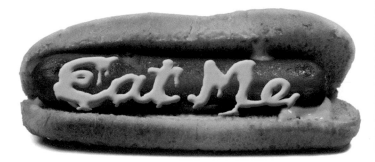

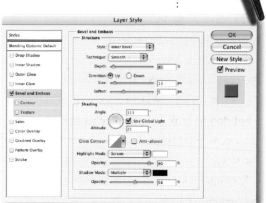

4 Rather than painting the shading on the mustard lettering by hand, it made much more sense to use the Emboss section of the Layer Style dialog to let Photoshop do this for me. After playing with the depth and size settings, I arrived at this version: increasing the highlight from the default 75% helped to make the shine stand out on the top edge.

5 Here's the final Emboss setting. There are no absolute values here: it's just a question of doing what looks right for the image you're working on. Each case is different.

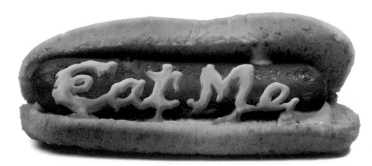

7 The mustard still wasn't shiny enough. You've guessed it – Plastic Wrap to the rescue. But to make it more controllable, I first duplicated the mustard layer, then desaturated the copy and set its mode to Hard Light, and then applied the Plastic Wrap filter to that layer. Keeping the two separate allows you to adjust the contrast of just the shininess, without affecting the shading on the original.

Shiny surfaces

I'm forever blowing bubbles

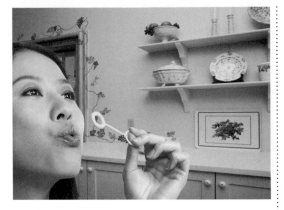

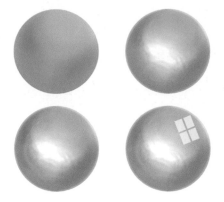

THERE ARE TWO TRICKS to making bubbles work. The first is to draw the bubble correctly in the first place; the second is to distort the view seen through them.

When bubbles touch, they form a flat disk at the plane of intersection. Tricky to draw, perhaps; but if you use the method shown here, this disk will appear automatically as you Spherize the view seen through them, also turning the flat window into a rounded view.

This was set as a Friday Challenge on the How to Cheat website, and produced some remarkable results. As always, several readers chose to take their bubble blowing in a different direction altogether...

1 Begin by drawing a circle on a new layer: fill it with a mid-tone gray. Use the Burn tool to add a little shading. Apply the Plastic Wrap filter; then paint on some color, and finally add the outline of a window.

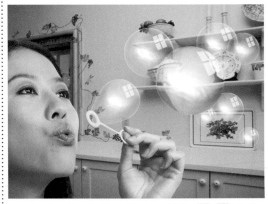

4 Load up the selection of one bubble by ⌘ ctrl clicking on its thumbnail (I've chosen the largest one), and press ⌘ Shift C ctrl Shift C to make a merged copy. With it still selected, Paste; the copy will appear in place. ⌘ ctrl click to select it again, and apply the Spherize filter at 100%.

THE FRIDAY CHALLENGE
www.howtocheatinphotoshop.com

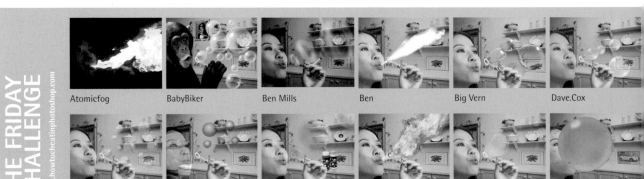

Atomicfog   BabyBiker   Ben Mills   Ben   Big Vern   Dave.Cox

James   maiden   mguyer   Neal   Pauline   Pierre

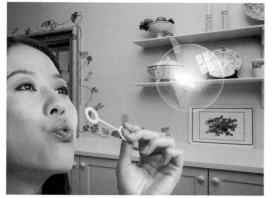

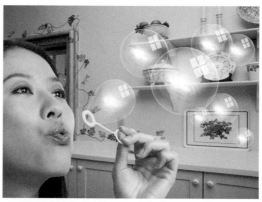

2 When the bubble is placed in the scene, change the mode of its layer to Hard Light. All the gray will disappear, leaving us just with the highlights. If you can't see it clearly, increase the brightness of the bubble slightly.

3 Duplicate the bubble around the image, scaling it as you go to create different sizes. If you make a couple of the bubbles overlap you'll increase the realism of the scene. Remember to include one bursting out of the wand!

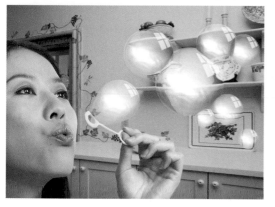

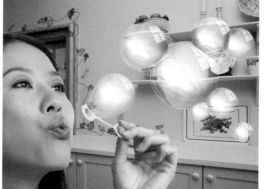

5 Repeat the process with each bubble in turn – load it as a selection, make a Merged Copy and then paste, load the selection once more, and use ⌘ F ctrl F to repeat the Spherize filter. Where they overlap, you'll get a convincing join – and the window will distort, too.

6 Let's add some more color. Load up one of the bubbles by holding ⌘ ctrl and clicking on its thumbnail; then hold ⌘ Shift ctrl Shift as you click on the other bubbles' thumbnails. Apply a Hue/Saturation Adjustment layer to the selection, and increase the saturation.

HOT TIP

In step 4, we distorted the bubble that's coming out of the wand to make it look as if it's being blown. If you have Photoshop CS2 or later, you can use Image Warp to do this easily; otherwise, distort it with the Liquify filter.

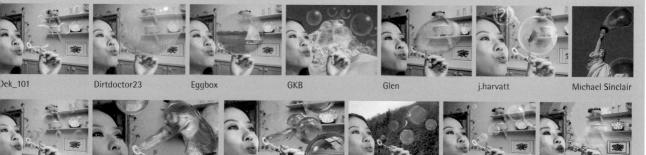

Dek_101   Dirtdoctor23   Eggbox   GKB   Glen   j.harvatt   Michael Sinclair

teve Mac   Chris Martin   Tom   Vicho   Wayne   Whaler

Water, water everywhere

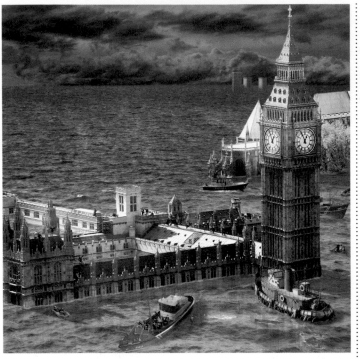

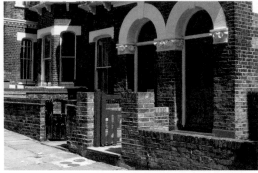

1 This straightforward suburban scene is about to be flooded by water. The differing angles across the image will involve treating both the water and the reflections to follow the perspectives of the original image, as we'll see over the next few steps.

ART EDITORS LOVE SUBMERGING THINGS. Whether it's a computer (Dotcom Firms Sink Without Trace), a confused businessman (Is Stress Swallowing You Up?) or an entire city (Global Warming: Life in 2050), they just can't get enough of floods.

The image above was for the Independent on Sunday, showing London after the waters have risen. The original photograph, incidentally, was taken from the London Eye – a boon to illustrators as well as to tourists!

In this section we'll look at flooding a single street, which involves reflections as well as submerging.

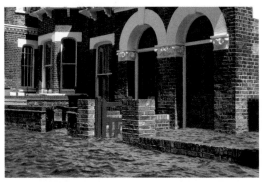

4 Now the water needs to run along the walls that sit perpendicular to the one at the front. Because we made a layer mask in the first instance, rather than simply deleting the water, it's easy enough to paint it back in again, following the contours of the bricks as a guide.

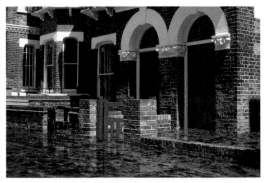

7 Next, the sections of wall that face away from us are copied and again distorted into place. This includes elements such as the pink gate, which clearly lies in a different plane to the front of the wall.

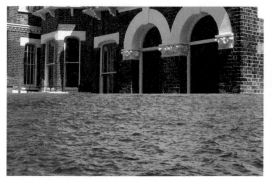

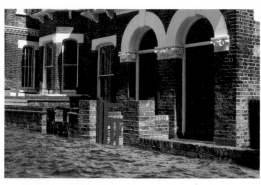

2 First, find yourself some water. This image was taken from a photograph of the sea, from which the sky has simply been deleted: water can be devilishly tricky stuff to draw, so it's worth finding a real picture if you can.

3 The first step in making the water fit the scene is to decide on the level at which it will sit. Make a new layer mask (Reveal All) for the water, and paint it out along an obvious perspective line: here, the brick wall at the front provides a useful horizontal to set the water on.

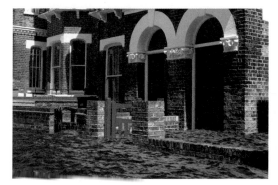

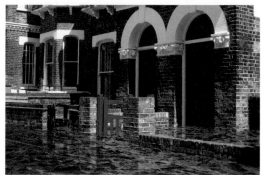

HOT TIP

Although we've added a rippled reflection in this instance, in many cases it's enough just to reduce the opacity of the water along the flood line. Lower the brush opacity to around 30% and paint it out on the layer mask for an instant transparent effect.

5 The original water was far too bright: it had been photographed on a sunny day, when there was plenty of blue sky for it to reflect. In this urban setting, the sky would be minimal, so its saturation needs to be reduced using the Hue/Saturation dialog.

6 The background is copied in sections, flipped vertically and grouped with the water, using the techniques described in Glass Reflections later in this chapter. First, the sides facing us – the front of the wall and the wall holding the door – are flipped and distorted into place.

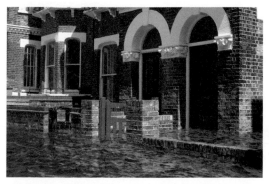

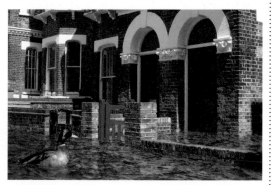

8 But the surface of the water is rippled, not flat; so the reflections need to be distorted as well. Here, the Wave filter (appropriately enough) has been used to add a small amount of rippling to the reflected image. I've also reduced the opacity of the ripples for a better effect.

9 As well as reflecting the scene above it, we need to make sense of the water as a dense medium. Simply placing this duck on the surface helps the eye to interpret the water for what it is, as well as adding visual interest to the scene.

Making water from thin air

I N THE PREVIOUS TUTORIAL WE LOOKED at how to flood a scene with water. Here, we'll take the process one step further: not only will we build the reflections in the pool, we'll also create the water surface from scratch.

The only difficult thing here is the complexity of the reflection: the image has to be broken into three parts for the reflected view to work correctly. Adding a ripple to the whole reflection, and creating the water surface, is easy in comparison.

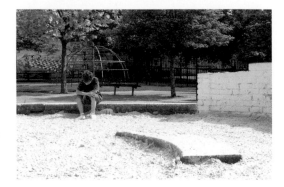

1 Here's our initial picture: a boy sitting on the edge of a sandpit. The walls of the sandpit provide the perfect setting for the paddling pool which could well have been placed there instead.

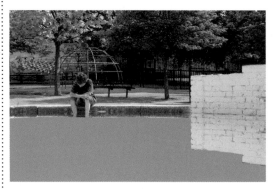

4 We'll use this initial reflection to make just the wall of the pool, so select and delete the rest. It's a close fit, but not perfect: you'll need to select chunks of the wall and shear them downwards to follow the angle of the original.

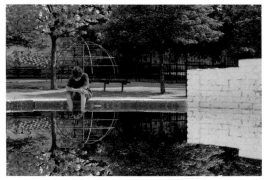

5 Now duplicate the background again, flip it and place it behind the reflected wall layer (again, using the water as a clipping mask). Now we can slide it vertically, so we no longer see the playground surface. Much more convincing!

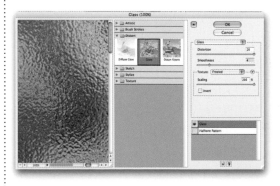

8 To create the water surface, first make a new document about twice the size of the one you're working on. Use the Clouds filter to fill it with random texture; then apply the Glass filter to make a detailed, rippled distortion that will simulate our water. Well, clouds are almost thin air.

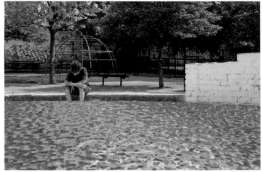

9 Duplicate the water mask layer from step 2, then drag the texture we just made into the document, using that layer as a clipping mask. Use the Perspective mode of Free Transform (hold ⌘ Shift ⌥ ctrl Shift alt as you drag a corner handle) to give the water surface a sense of depth.

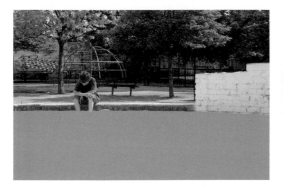

2 Make a new layer, and paint the area to be occupied by the water. After you're blocked in the basic shape, go round the edges with a hard brush to ripple them slightly – and don't forget to leave some space round the ankles.

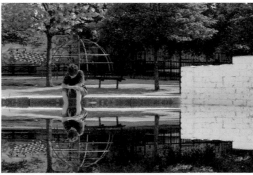

3 Now duplicate the background and flip it vertically; use the water layer as a clipping mask to limit its scope. The reflection as it stands is unconvincing: we shouldn't be able to see the surface of the playground from this angle.

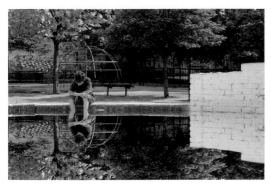

6 The boy now needs to be isolated from the original flipped vertically and placed on the reflected wall. You'll need a little masking to make him look as if he's actually sitting on the wall itself.

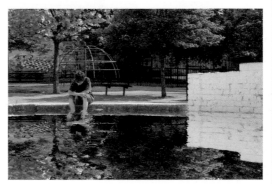

7 Make a new group (layer set) from all the reflected layers. Now duplicate the group, merge its contents into a single layer, and hide the original group. A small amount of the Ocean Ripple filter gives it the distortion we need.

Breaking the reflected view into its multiple planes can be a fiddly process, which is made more difficult with more complex views. I photographed this image with reflection in mind, knowing that the walls would provide a vertical element behind which I could hide the reflection of the view behind. It isn't always so easy! If you're going to attempt this technique with your own images, think about how the reflections will work while composing the scene in the camera.

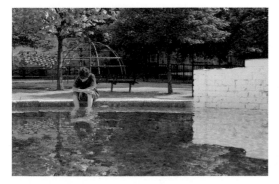

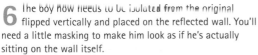

10 The water surface looked too strong in the previous step, so reduce its opacity to around 30%. Adding a slight blue tint, using Color Balance or any of the other adjustment dialogs, helps to give the impression that it's reflecting a blue sky.

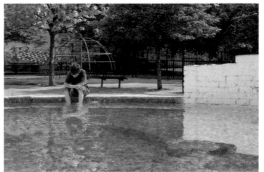

11 We could have stopped there – but let's take it one step further. Lowering the opacity of the merged reflection layer to 50% allows us to see through the reflection to the original sandpit below, adding an extra dimension of realism to the scene.

227

Snow and icicles

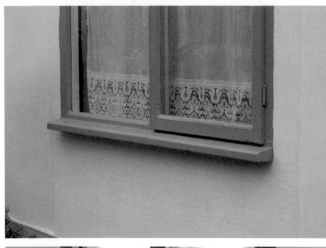

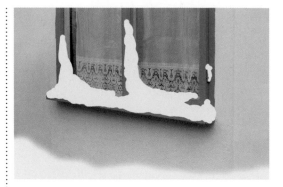

1 To get started, draw the snow shape on a new layer. Use a hard-edged brush where the snow sits on the windowsill, and switch to a large, soft brush to paint the area where it drifts up the side of the wall.

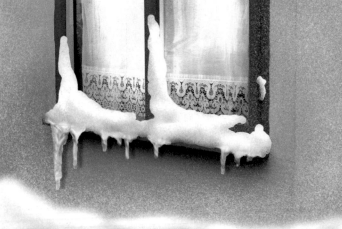

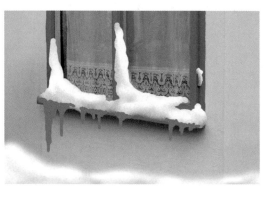

4 Make a new layer, and paint the icicles using a midtone gray and a small, hard-edged brush. Try to make them look as drippy and natural as possible, and don't add too many of them!

MAGAZINE DEADLINES BEING WHAT they are, people always want pictures of snow for their Christmas editions – but they need them in September. Every Photoshop artist should know how to add snow to a scene to give it that festive flavor; we'll see how to turn the rather dull photograph (top) into a yuletide experience. We're even going to throw in a few icicles for good measure.

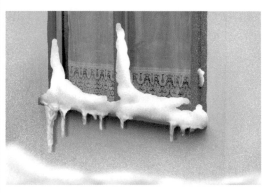

7 To add a sprinkling of snow to the walls, choose a large, soft brush and set its mode to Dissolve. With white paint, and the brush set to a very low opacity, it's easy to apply this speckled effect with just a few strokes.

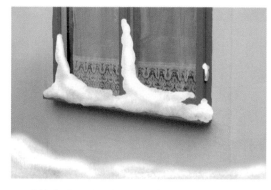

2 Add shading using Dodge and Burn, then add the texture. Begin with a little Gaussian Noise and then, to soften the effect, lock the transparency of the snow layer and use Gaussian Blur to smooth it slightly.

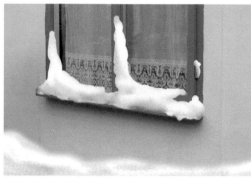

3 There are several ways of adding color: in this instance, it's probably easiest to use Color Balance to up the blue and cyan content slightly. Don't make it too strong – we only want a hint of the color effect.

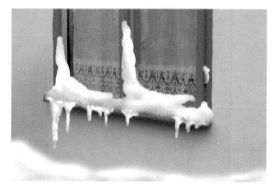

5 We're going to treat the icicles with Plastic Wrap (what else?), so first we need to add some shading using Dodge and Burn. This can be done in a fairly random way; there's no need to simulate accurate shadow placement.

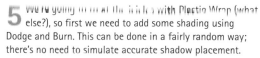

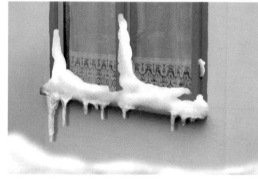

6 Apply the Plastic Wrap filter as before, erase the tops of the icicles so they merge into the snow. Add a little color, and change the layer mode to Hard Light for transparency, then duplicate to make the shadow behind it.

HOT TIP

It's easy to get carried away with too much Dodging and Burning, too strong a color and too much snow overall. The key to making this effect work is subtlety; always try to use the minimum possible to get the effect you want, and the result will be that much more convincing.

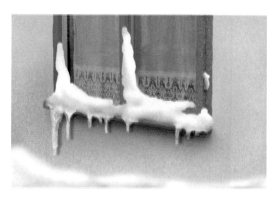

8 The snow we just drew looked rather harsh, so once again we can use Gaussian Blur to soften it. Don't check the Lock Transparency box this time, though, as we want to blur those edges slightly.

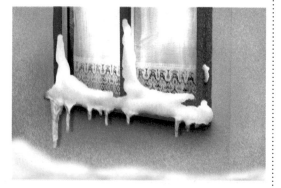

9 As a final step, add some color to the walls for a wintry feel. To get a good contrast inside the window, make a new layer from the window and increase the contrast, adding a yellowish hue for that warm interior glow.

229

Making it rain

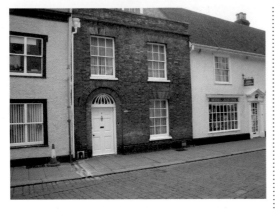

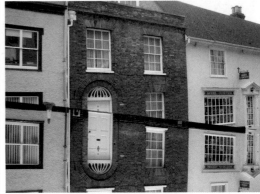

1 Begin by selecting just the buildings – including the base of that traffic cone. Make a new layer from the selection, and flip it vertically to make the basis of the reflection.

WATER TAKES MANY FORMS. We've looked at ice, snow and flooding; here we'll turn this scene into a rainy day, adding reflective puddles as well as the rain itself.

Whether or not you want to add rain to your images, creating reflections in surface water is a task that should be within the scope of any Photoshop artist.

This was originally a Friday Challenge on the How to Cheat website: there were so many good entries, it would do them an injustice to squeeze them into the tiny space available here. Go online and check them out for yourself – there are some especially good animations to look out for.

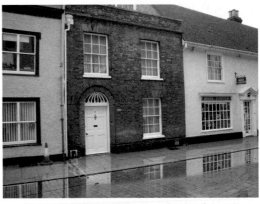

4 Now make a layer mask for the reflection. Select the sidewalk, and darken the mask to lower the opacity, making this surface look damp; then paint out the high points in the road, as these will be above the water surface.

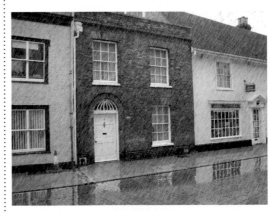

7 We need to make that noise look like rain, and to do this simply apply the Motion Blur filter to it. Increase the contrast, if you like, until it looks right.

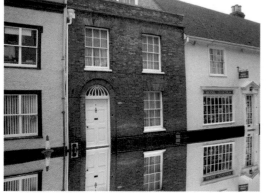

2 When we drag the reflection into place, we need to shear it to follow the base line of the buildings. Hold ⌘ *ctrl* as you drag a side handle in Free Transform mode.

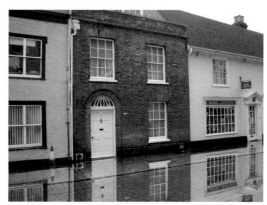

3 The reflection was leaning back slightly, so shear it horizontally a little to make the verticals line up. Lower the transparency of this layer to around 50%.

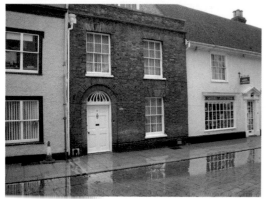

5 To add some rippling, first apply the Ocean Ripple filter to the entire reflection, using low settings. Then make a series of elliptical selections, applying the ZigZag filter to each one to make individual ripples.

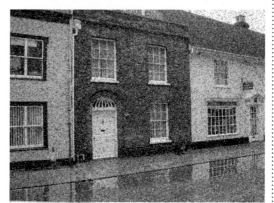

6 Now for the rain. We'll begin by making a new layer set to Hard Light mode, filled with mid gray. Use Gaussian Noise to make the texture; then enlarge a quarter of the image area so it fills the whole space with a bigger texture.

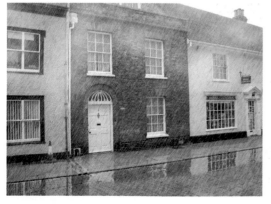

8 Let's add a little mist. On a new layer, run the Clouds filter; set the layer mode to Screen, and all the black will disappear. Paint out the bottom area on a layer mask.

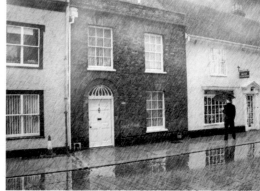

9 Finally, I've added a figure (with reflection) as well as a Curves adjustment layer to increase the contrast. And don't forget to turn a couple of lights on in those windows.

HOT TIP

There's a trick to getting the reflection right in step 3. We can assume that the walls and doors are exactly vertical, and that the water surface is horizontal. So the reflections will go directly down, following the line set by the vertical elements (the sides of the doors, the divides in the walls, and so on). Once the angles are right, the whole image will look more convincing.

A cool glass of water

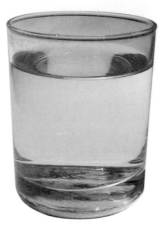

GLASS IS ONE OF THE hardest objects you can photograph, as any commercial photographer will tell you. Stylists will spend hours combining plastic ice cubes with piped-in carbon dioxide to get effects such as this – they can't use real ice, which would quickly melt under studio lighting conditions.

Fortunately, there is an easier way. We begin with a straightforward digital image of a glass of water, which was photographed on a curved sheet of white paper so there was no crease visible where the background joined the base.

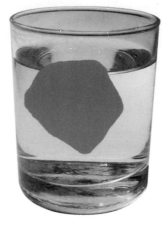

1 We begin by drawing the outline of our first ice cube on a new layer. Use a hard-edged brush and paint with a midtone gray (we'll need to use this color when we change the layer mode later). Aim for an approximation of a rough cube viewed from an angle.

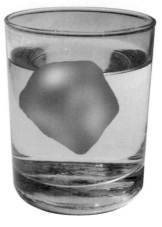

2 Now add a little light and shade using the Dodge and Burn tools. Aim to place a blob of light in the center of what will become each face of the cube. Subtlety is the keyword here: keep the strokes very pale and don't be tempted to overdo it.

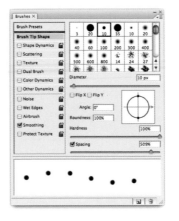

6 We could draw the bubbles one at a time, but it's a lot easier to let the brush do all the work. Select a hard-edged brush and open the Brushes palette: now set the spacing to a large figure – we've used 500%. Don't worry about 'corrupting' your brushes, since these settings will be forgotten when a different brush is selected from the palette.

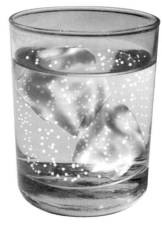

7 Using white paint, draw wiggly lines on a new layer to create the bubbles. The spacing we just set will create strings of dots, rather than solid lines. Now reduce the brush size using the **[** key, and paint smaller bubbles as well: these should be placed particularly at the edges of the glass, to give an impression of the bubbles falling away in perspective.

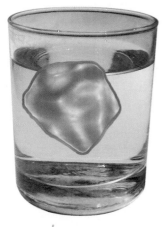

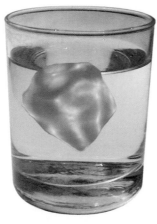

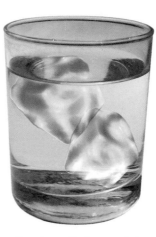

3 Now apply the Plastic Wrap filter, as described earlier in this chapter. If you've applied the Dodge and Burn correctly, the filter should now form the shape of three visible faces of our ice cube. If it doesn't look convincing, undo and adjust the shading before applying the filter again.

4 The Plastic Wrap filter can frequently leave an untreated edge around an object, as seen in the previous step. Rather than trying to correct it, it's far easier to delete that edge. Hold ⌘ *ctrl* and click on the ice cube layer's name, then contract the selection, inverse and delete.

5 Now change the layer mode to Hard Light to make the ice cube shiny and semi-transparent. Moved to the top of the glass, a layer mask can be used to hide the region on the surface where it isn't poking through. The second ice cube is simply a duplicate of the first.

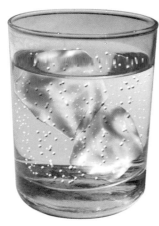

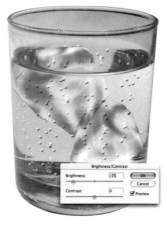

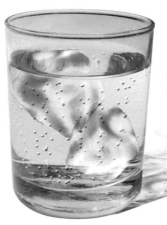

8 To make those strings of dots look three-dimensional, use the Emboss section of Layer Styles to give them some automatic roundness. (You didn't seriously think we were going to shade each bubble individually, did you?) You'll need to set a very small offset to avoid the bubbles looking too fuzzy, but experiment with the settings and you'll get a good result.

9 Now to give those bubbles some transparency. Begin by changing their layer mode to Hard Light once again. In this mode, midtones become invisible, while the highlights and shadows remain; so we need to lower the brightness of the bubbles so that the pure white we drew approaches a midtone gray. Any of the adjustment dialogs can be used to do this.

10 Finally, adjust the color of the glass to make it bluer, since the original indoor lighting looked far too brown. The shadow is created by hiding the background layer, performing Select All and taking a Merged Copy (*Shift* ⌘ *C* *Shift* *ctrl* *C*) of the image. This is then pasted behind the glass, desaturated, and knocked back using a gradient on a layer mask.

Getting the glazing bug

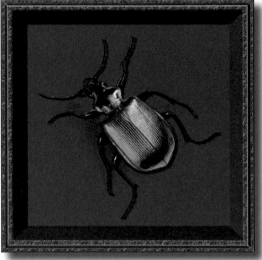

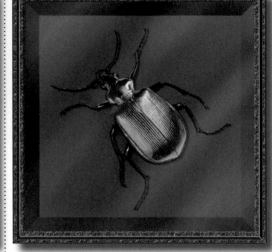

GLAZING EFFECTS are easy to create, and make the difference between an object looking like it's in a box and looking like it's inside a picture frame. The bug I've used here is in a three-dimensional box, but the technique works equally well for flat pictures in frames – or for windows, museum cases and other glazed surfaces.

Here, I've taken this bug box and added three different glazing effects to it, from simple glass to rippled plastic. The inset pictures show each effect in isolation against a black background, so it's easy to see how it works without the distraction of the main image getting in the way.

1 The simplest way to create a glass effect is simply to paint one on. Create a new layer behind the frame, and use a large soft-edged brush to add white bands. Set the opacity of the brush low – 10% or 20%

– and draw a series of diagonal white strokes. This can be a very subtle effect, and is most noticeable at the edges (where the glass meets the frame) rather than in the middle of the image. Build up the strokes as you go until the effect works. This is one of those occasions when a pressure-sensitive graphics tablet really comes into its own. The glass layer is shown here (inset), although obviously it makes more sense to draw it while viewing the full image.

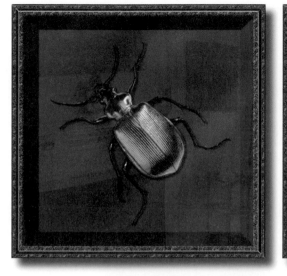

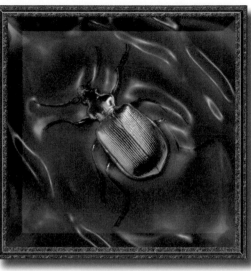

2 To make the glass more convincing, consider adding a background image. Here, this shot of a room (inset) has been distorted slightly using the Wave filter: without the distortion it would look too flat and

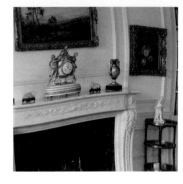

rigid. The opacity of this layer was then reduced to 10% so it was barely visible – after all, you don't want it to swamp the main image. The white bands used in the previous example were added over the top, their opacity reduced to 50%.

Any background image can be used; the choice depends largely on the supposed location of the object in question. For outdoor scenes, such as looking in through a window, a cloud reflection is particularly effective. Remember to keep the opacity low; if necessary, increase the contrast of the reflected image to make it more dramatic.

3 This version uses the Plastic Wrap filter to make the bug look like it's encased in polythene. First, a new layer was created and its mode set to Hard Light: this was filled with 50% gray, which is transparent in Hard Light mode. The brushstrokes (inset, top) were painted on using the Dodge and Burn tools to add highlight and shading to the image; the Plastic Wrap filter was applied (inset, bottom) to show the full effect. In

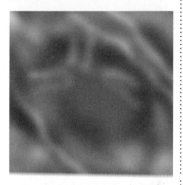

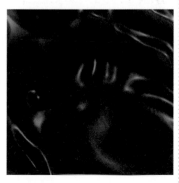

cases like this, it's worth applying the filter frequently as you paint to check the effect, which can be unpredictable; Undo after each time to carry on adjusting the background.

HOT TIP

Experiment with different layer mode settings – Hard Light, Screen and Overlay in particular – to see the different effects they have on reflected images. Often they can serve to reduce the clutter and intrusion of a reflection, while maintaining its strength.

Glass: refraction

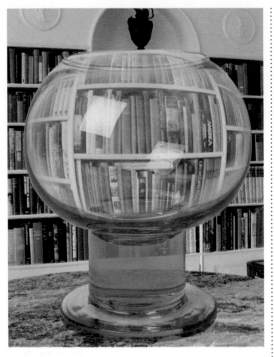

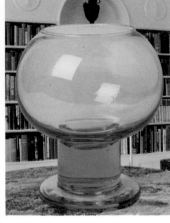

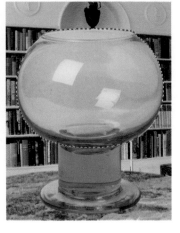

1 In this simple montage the glass vase, the table and the background are on three separate layers. The task is to make the background visible through the vase.

2 Begin by loading up the area taken up by the vase, by holding ⌘ *ctrl* and clicking on its thumbnail in the Layers palette. Then use the Elliptical Marquee tool, holding down ⌘ ⌥ *ctrl* *alt* to limit the area to just the bowl itself.

GLASS OBJECTS not only reflect what's around them, they also refract the view behind them. This refraction is easy to achieve; the trick to making the montage look real is to bring back the reflections in the original photograph so that they sit on top of the refracted image.

In this workthrough, we'll make this photograph of a glass vase look as if it's sitting within the scene, rather than simply stuck on top of it.

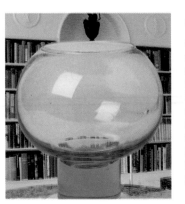

6 Now for the tricky bit – adding back the reflections from the original vase. Duplicate the vase layer, and delete the layer mask (without applying it). It will completely obscure the distorted background. Now choose Layer > Layer Style > Blending Options and drag the small black triangle under the This Layer slider (in the Blend If section) to the right. After a certain point, the vase will begin to turn transparent as all pixels darker than the position specified disappear.

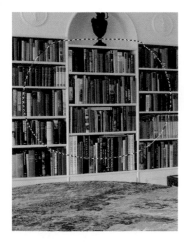 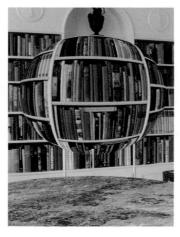 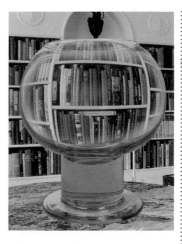

3 Now hide the bowl layer, switch to the background and make a new layer from the selection using ⌘ J ctrl J.

4 Reselect the new layer by ⌘ ctrl clicking on its thumbnail in the Layers palette, and use the Spherize filter to create the refracted view. (If the bowl had been full of water, you'd need to flip this vertically to simulate the solid lens refraction.)

5 Turn on the vase layer so it's visible again, and create a layer mask. Using a large soft-edged brush, paint out the interior of the bowl so that the background becomes visible.

HOT TIP

Spherizing works well with spherical objects, as you'd expect. But if you want to distort the view seen through a cylinder, such as a glass wine bottle, you can still use the Spherize filter; this time, though, change the mode of the filter from Normal to Horizontal Only in the filter's dialog box.

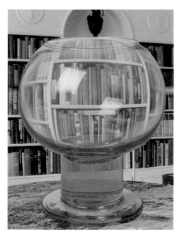

7 Dragging the slider produces a hard cutoff as pixels darker than (in this case) 173 are hidden. That black slider is actually two sliders pinned together: to split them, hold down ⌥ alt and drag on the right half of the slider. Having split it in two, with the left half still in place and the right half over to the right, any pixels whose brightness values are higher than 243 (in this instance) are fully visible; those pixels whose brightness values lie between the two sliders fade gradually from fully opaque to fully transparent.

Using Blending Options in this way to hide and show areas of a layer selectively is an extremely powerful tool: find out more about how it works in Chapter 3, Hiding and Showing.

As a final touch, the refracted background seen through the vase has been given a blue-green tint using the Color Balance dialog; I also painted out some of the stem on the layer mask to make it partially transparent.

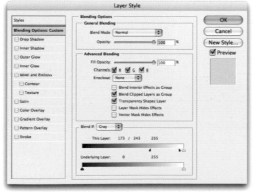

237

Glass: reflection

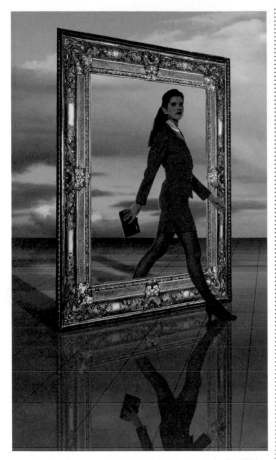

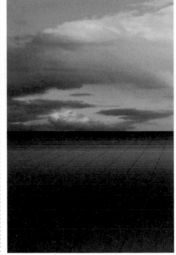
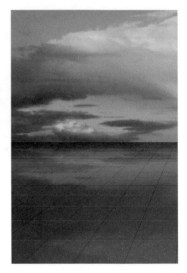

1 This montage consists of two elements so far: the clouds and the grid floor. The first step is to adjust the color of the floor so that it more closely matches the colors of the sky.

2 The reflection of the sky in the floor is made by duplicating the sky layer, flipping it vertically and grouping it with the floor. With its opacity set to 30%, we can see the floor through it – but it looks rather dull.

CREATING REFLECTIONS in floors is easy to do, and can – with a little care – result in the kind of shiny, perfect reflection that looks like it was created in a 3D modeling program.

Here, we'll look at how to turn the dull floor we started off with into a highly reflective, polished surface.

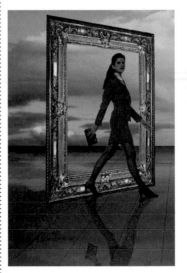
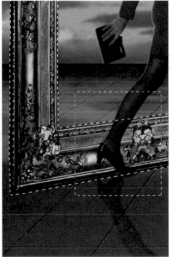

6 Adding this angled frame will present a different kind of reflection problem. First, though, we need to mask the woman's legs so that she's stepping through the frame.

7 Create a layer mask for the woman, and load the frame's area into it by holding ⌘ *ctrl* and clicking on the thumbnail; then hold ⌥ *Shift* *alt* *Shift* as you draw a marquee to limit the selection. Fill the mask selection with black to hide the leg.

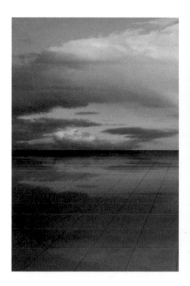

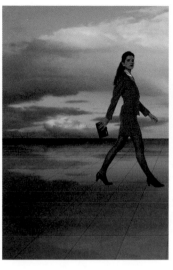

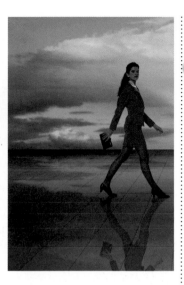

3 Changing the reflected sky's layer mode to Hard Light makes its reflection that much more punchy. This mode allows the light and dark in the underlying layer to show through, as in the highlights and shadows on the cracks.

4 This figure is walking parallel to the horizon, and so presents no problem when making the reflection. When the object to be reflected lies at an angle it gets more complicated, as we'll see later.

5 Once again, the reflected figure is lowered in opacity: this time, however, the reflection is set to Overlay mode, which produces a softer and less dramatic result.

HOT TIP

The technique shown here really only works for flat objects (such as the frame) or those parallel to the surface (the woman). To reflect more complex objects, you'll need to break them up into their component parts and distort each one individually. It can be done, but it's not a job for the faint-hearted.

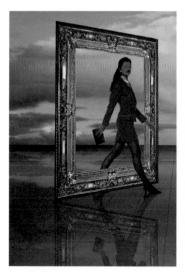

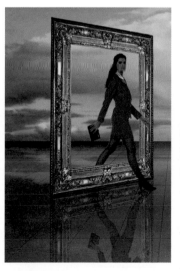

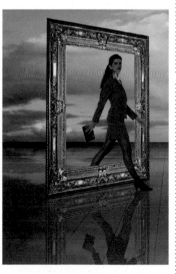

8 Simply flipping the frame to create its reflection clearly doesn't work: it ends up at completely the wrong angle. The solution is to use Free Transform to shear the reflection so that its top edge aligns with the bottom edge of the original frame.

9 To perform the shear, first use ⌘ T ctrl T to access Free Transform, then hold ⌘ Shift ctrl Shift while dragging a side handle (adding the Shift key constrains the movement to purely vertical).

10 Now we need to delete (or mask) those parts of the reflected frame and woman that intersect, in the same way as before. Also, the cloud reflection needs to be hidden behind the frame and woman reflections.

SHORTCUTS
MAC WIN BOTH

239

Complex reflections

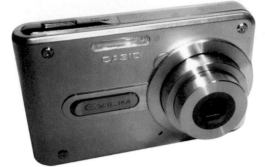

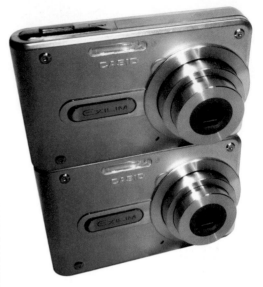

1 Begin by taking a copy of the camera, and moving the copied layer behind. Now use Free Transform to shrink the copy so that the sides form a continuous straight line down the original camera and through the copy. A small amount of distortion is needed to achieve this.

S OME REFLECTIONS ARE AS SIMPLE
as flipping an object vertically or
horizontally: a man's profile looking in a mirror,
for example, would suit this technique. Other
reflections don't fall into place so easily.

In this example, we're going to create
a reflection of the digital camera as if it's
standing on a somewhat reflective surface. The
procedure is made more complicated by the
fact that we're looking down on the camera,
resulting in a tricky three-point perspective
viewpoint: not only is it going away from us left
to right and front to back, it's also receding top
to bottom.

The technique we'll use is a little surprising,
because we're not going to flip the camera at
all to create the reflection: instead, we're going
to translate it down the lines of perspective,
through the imagined surface.

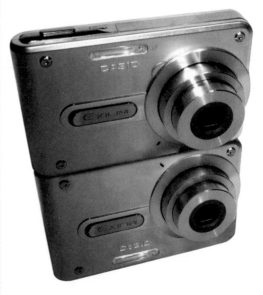

4 We now need to get rid of the original flash and other elements that shouldn't show up on the reflection. The easiest way to do this is to make a new 'patch' layer, and use the Clone tool set to Sample All Layers. This way, we can keep the cover-ups on their own layer for convenience.

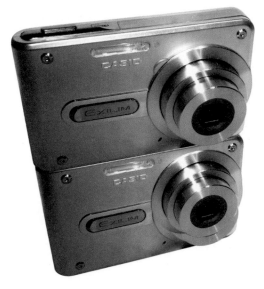

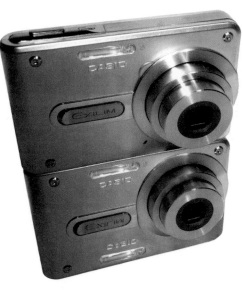

2 The lens is in the wrong place: it's sited lower than half way down the face of the camera, so in the 'reflection' it looks too high. Using the Pen tool, we can select just the lens in the reflection and copy it to a new layer. It then needs to be dragged up to the right optical placement.

3 The old lens on the reflection can be removed with the Clone tool and a little Dodge and Burn. The new lens also needs its highlights to be removed, by copying and rotating a section of it; and we can also copy and distort the reflected elements such as the flash and camera name.

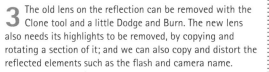

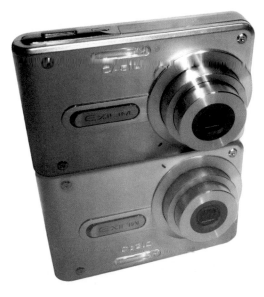

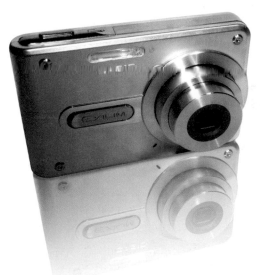

5 We need to lower the opacity of the reflections as a whole. The trick here is to make them into a new Layer Group, and then to lower the opacity of the group. Remember, you can change the opacity of a layer or group by pressing the number keys 1 to 0 for 10% increments.

6 The reflection looks more convincing if it fades away. Create a layer mask for the reflection set, and use the Gradient tool set to Black-White. Drag it along the central vertical axis of the camera; then adjust the resulting mask with Brightness & Contrast until the effect looks right.

241

Putting things in bottles

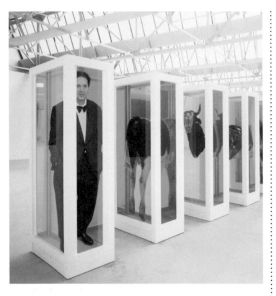

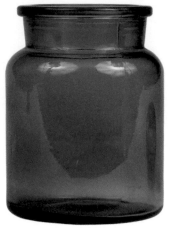

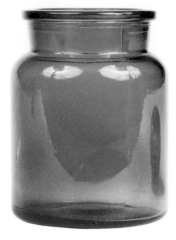

1 Our glass bottle was originally a much taller and thinner object. It was simply scaled using Free Transform to make it fit the shape of the object we want to place inside it. Most containers are as adaptable as this one: everything scales in proportion, so the end result still looks plausible.

2 Since the bottle was too dark for our purposes, it had to be brightened up – I used the Curves dialog, but Brightness/Contrast would have done the job as well. Some of that strong green hue was knocked out with Hue/Saturation.

T HE MONTAGE ABOVE shows noted art collector Charles Saatchi in one of the Damian Hirst boxes that make up part of his collection, and was commissioned by the Sunday Times magazine.

Putting things in glass boxes, jars and bottles is a fairly straightforward technique: the trick lies in reproducing the surface of the glass, complete with its reflections and refraction, to make it appear as if the object in question is really sitting inside it. Here, we'll look at the procedure involved.

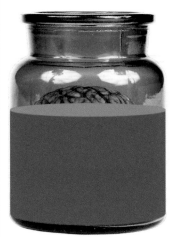

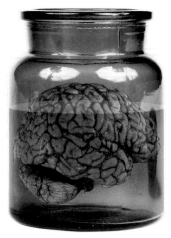

6 To make the brain look like it's floating, we need a medium for it to float in. On a new layer, draw a shape that fits the sides and bottom of the bottle, remembering to draw the surface in perspective, and fill with the color of your choice. The top surface is brightened with the Curves dialog.

7 Changing the mode of this layer, as well, to Hard Light not only makes it look as if it's inside the bottle, but makes the brain look much more like it's floating in a supportive liquid. I've chosen to leave part of the brain sticking out to accentuate the overall effect.

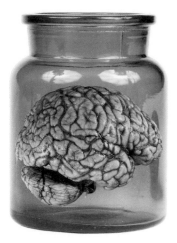

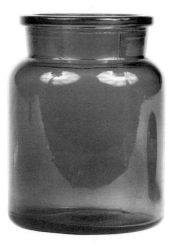

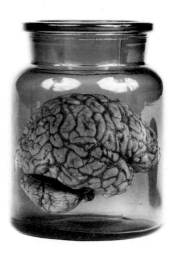

3 Now for our brain (well, what else would you expect me to stick in a bottle). Placed on top of the bottle, it looks totally unrealistic; there's no sense here that it lives inside the glass, and looks as if it's sitting in front of it (which it is).

4 To make the ensemble more convincing, we'll begin by duplicating the bottle. Bring this copy to the top of the layer stack, and knock all the color out by desaturating it using ⌘ Shift U ctrl Shift U. As it stands, we can't see through it.

5 Easily fixed: we simply change the mode of the layer from Normal to Hard Light, and we can see through it. Already, the brain is looking like it's inside. The new Hard Light layer has also affected the rest of the bottle, but we can sort that out later.

Step 10 involves matching a layer mask to fit two different layers. First, load up the distorted brain area by holding ⌘ ctrl and clicking on that layer's thumbnail in the Layers palette. We want to subtract the mask from the brain layer, so hold ⌘ Shift ctrl Shift and click on the brain layer's mask icon. Now, to add the area of the original brain, hold ⌘ ctrl again and click on that layer's icon. Now, on the Hard Light bottle layer, choose Add Layer Mask – Reveal Selection to see the result.

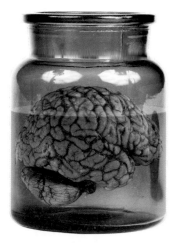

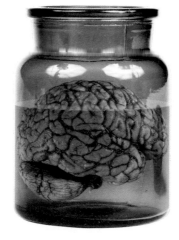

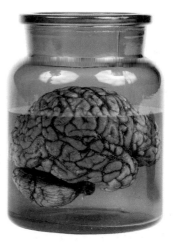

8 To make the surface of the brain stick out, add a new layer mask to the liquid layer and paint around the contours of the brain so it looks as though it's poking out through the surface. Use a fairly hard-edged brush to get the most realistic effect.

9 All very well so far - but we need to remember that the liquid will distort as well as color the object inside it. Here, I've duplicated the brain and applied a horizontal-only Spherize to it, then added a layer mask to the distorted version so that it only shows up where it's beneath the liquid.

10 Finally, we can apply the original Hard Light bottle layer just to the brain. But there are two versions of the brain, so we can't just group them; instead, we need to make a layer mask. See the Hot Tip for a good way of making a layer mask to match multiple layers.

SHORTCUTS
MAC WIN BOTH

243

Distortion with backgrounds

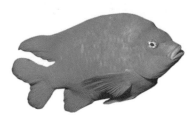

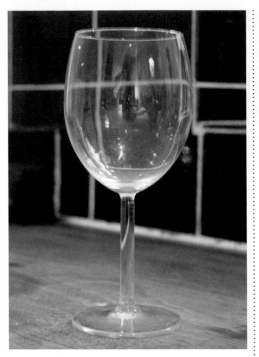

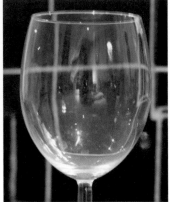

1 Begin by outlining the area to be taken up with the water, using the Pen tool. Stay just inside the glass perimeter for a better effect.

O N THE PREVIOUS PAGE, we looked at ways of fitting objects inside glass containers. Here's a similar, but different situation: in this case, our glass already has a background.

This was set as one of the first Friday Challenges on the Reader Forum that goes with this book's website. Readers' entries are shown below.

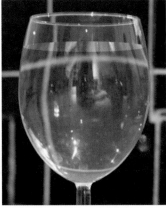

5 To complete the effect, make an elliptical selection on the surface (in this view, we're looking *up* at the surface) and brighten it.

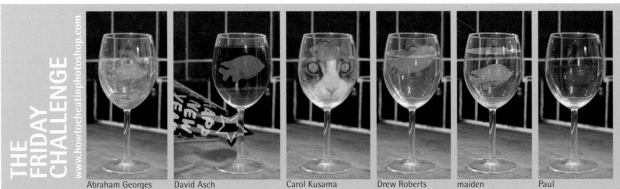

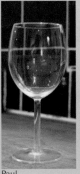

Abraham Georges   David Asch   Carol Kusama   Drew Roberts   maiden   Paul

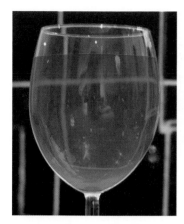

2 Here's that area shown in QuickMask form: notice the slight rim around the edge. Make a new layer from the selection, then duplicate it.

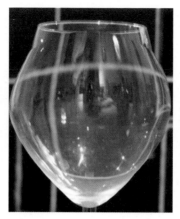

3 The duplicated version of the water area is here distorted using the Inflate mode of Warp Transform: but you could use Spherize instead.

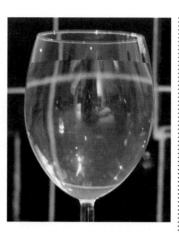

4 When the distorted view is clipped (pre-CS: grouped) with the first water layer, we get the sense of a magnified view seen through the glass.

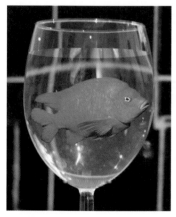

6 It's easy to make the fish fit inside the glass: scale it down so it sits comfortably inside. You may choose to add a small Spherize distortion as well.

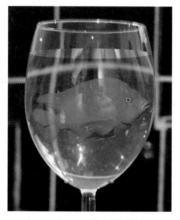

7 Lower the opacity of the fish – about 50% here – so we can see the shine on top. But we don't want to see the tiles through its tail!

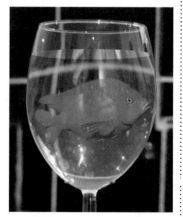

8 Load up the fish's transparency by *ctrl* ⌘-clicking on its thumbnail; switch to the distorted background and clone out that grout between the tiles.

HOT TIP

Working with glass objects on pre-existing backgrounds is a far more difficult proposition than creating a montage with separate elements. The background isn't usually as obliging as the one used here: a lot of complex cloning can be required to remove the background (but not the shine) from objects within a glass. In these circumstances, the best advice is to cheat: take out all the background, and then paint the shine on afterwards.

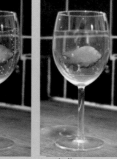

| itsjustaname | Russ Davey | Ryan | tabitha | tweaknik | Russ Davey |

SHORTCUTS
MAC WIN BOTH

Glass: putting it all together

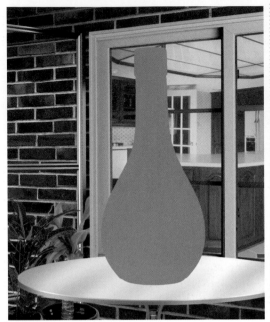

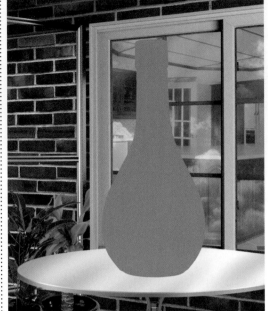

NOW THAT WE'VE LOOKED at different ways of rendering glass, let's finish off this chapter by putting several of those elements together. Starting off with the simple montage above, we'll use the techniques covered in this chapter to glaze everything in sight.

To begin with, the bottle is only a shaped outline: we'll create this (as well as the rest of the glass) directly in Photoshop. The end result, on the opposite page, shows off our glazing efforts to their best advantage.

1 The first step is to glaze the window. This is achieved using the techniques discussed in the section Getting the Glazing Bug: first, a cloudscape is placed behind the window frame and set to 40% opacity, then, on a new layer, diagonal white brushstrokes are added to brighten the edges of the glazing. This technique is clearly a lot simpler if the window frame and the room interior are on separate layers.

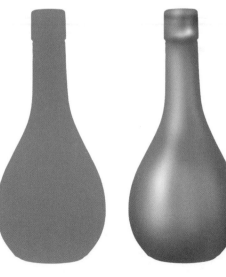

The outline of the bottle is drawn with the Pen tool, and filled with mid gray.

Shading is added using Dodge and Burn tools to simulate lighting.

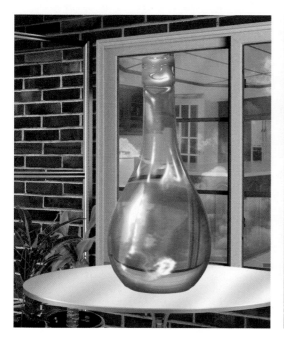

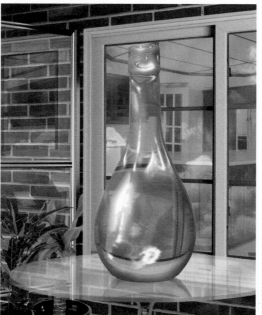

2 The bottle (below) was drawn using the Plastic Wrap technique explained at the beginning of this chapter; the refractive effect was created using the method shown in the section Glass Refraction. Because this bottle is not spherical, the Spherizing of the background was performed in two stages – one for the neck, and one for the bowl. The steps used to draw the bottle are outlined below.

3 The table was drawn directly in Photoshop, using the Dodge and Burn tools to create the highlights. To make the surface transparent, that section was cut to a new layer and its opacity reduced. The reflections of the bottle and window in the table used the techniques described in the section Glass Reflections; the reflection in the greenhouse needed perspective distortion to achieve the correct angles.

HOT TIP

You can always photograph a bottle or glass rather than drawing it from scratch. The choice of background is critical: you need something bright enough for the glass to be visible, but must make sure the lighting doesn't cast shadows on it. It's also important to avoid reflections in the surface, unless you want to end up in your own montages.

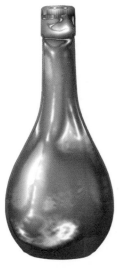

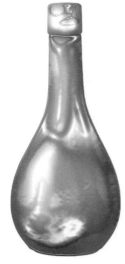

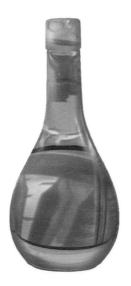

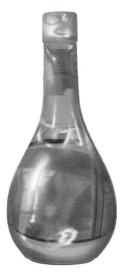

Plastic Wrap adds the glass effect; with nothing reflected, it's unconvincing.

Increasing the contrast helps; the green color is added afterwards.

With the layer mask painted in, the refracted background becomes visible.

The original bottle is copied over the top, and Blending Options applied.

247

9 Shiny surfaces

Through grimy windows

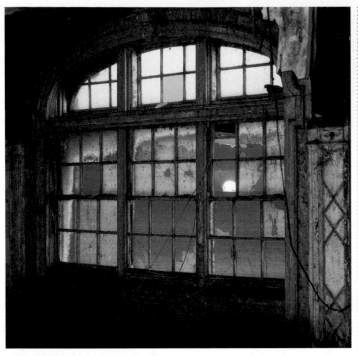

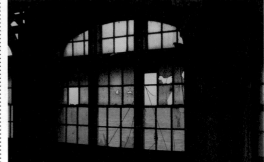

1 This photograph was taken with a digital camera through the window of a broken-down seaside theatre. I couldn't use a flash, or I would have lost the grime on the windows; so the rest of the walls were in darkness.

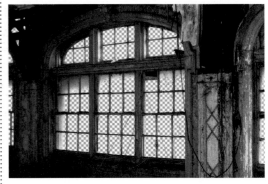

4 With all the transparent window selected, either delete it or make a layer mask and hide it. Note how the grime itself, not selected by the Select Color process, remains apparently hanging in mid-air.

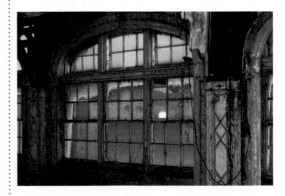

7 Before we address the opacity of the windows, we need to delete the broken panes. This is best done using the Lasso tool, with the [⌥] *alt* key held down to constrain it to drawing straight lines. Take out each pane in turn.

ALTHOUGH SO FAR IN THIS CHAPTER we've dealt mainly with the technique of creating windows from scratch, there are times when the texture of real broken glass is simply impossible to improve upon.

That said, photographing a scene through such a window presents a technical nightmare for the photographer. To attempt to light the interior of the building, the glass and the view beyond for a single shot would take photographic expertise beyond the reach of most of us. The solution? To cheat, of course. The only tricky part is to make the glass look as convincing as possible, which means treating it in a number of different ways and adding all the effects together to get a good result.

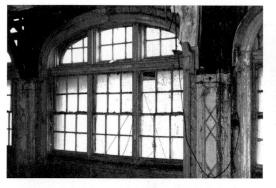

2 Before enhancing the image, duplicate the background layer - we'll need the original later on (but hide it for now). Adjust the brightness and contrast using the Curves diaog: a lot of the lost detail can be recovered.

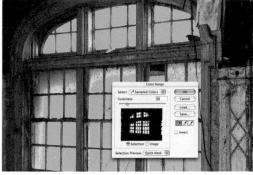

3 The easiest way to select the windows is to use the Color Range dialog, and click on a pure white area. This will select the totally transparent regions, leaving the grimy parts alone - and this is what we want.

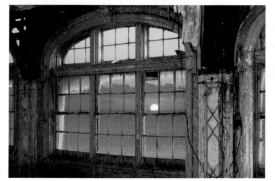

5 In order to work on the windows further, we need to add a new background. This sunset was, in fact, photographed further down the same beach, and so belongs properly to the scene.

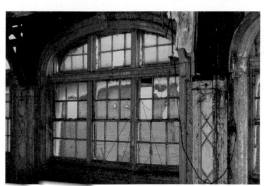

6 Now show the hidden, original background again, which should now be positioned behind the version we were working on. We can now see the original windows (and background) through the panes we deleted.

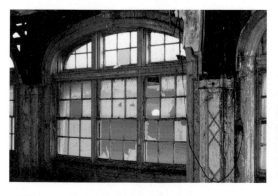

8 So that we can see through the new glass, we need to change its layer mode. Changing the mode to Screen is the obvious choice, as it makes the glass transparent; but the result is, overall, a little too subdued.

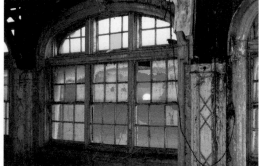

9 Duplicate the layer and change its mode to Hard Light, which adds detail and texture. You may find now that the overall effect is too bright; a simple solution is to reduce the strength of the Screen layer to 50% opacity.

SHORTCUTS
MAC WIN BOTH

The photographic studio

NOW THAT DIGITAL CAMERAS are commonplace, it's likely that most Photoshop users will be taking more of their own photographs and relying less on images found on the internet and elsewhere. When taking pictures of small, everyday objects, it really helps to have a miniature studio – a corner of a room somewhere that you can devote to this task.

Use two large sheets of white paper for your backdrop, one for the floor and one for the wall. It really helps if the join between the two can be a slight curve rather than a hard corner, as this will remove the need for you to paint out the corner later. Better still would be to use off-white card, which would glare less and will make selection easier later.

It's not really necessary to invest in heavy-duty professional lighting, either, unless you're fond of spending money. Ordinary household spotlights will do the job well: it's best to buy some that have easily adjustable heads, so

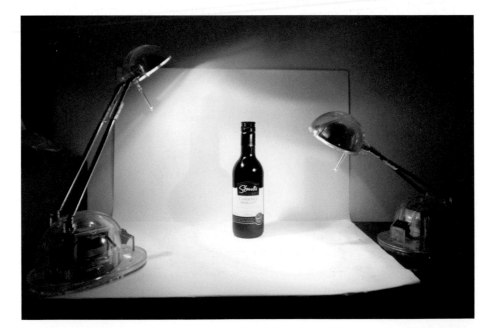

they can be positioned as you need them. True, the light from these sources will tend to have a strong yellow hue – but hey, this is Photoshop, right? We know how to fix that. And since the introduction of Photo Filter adjustments, the task is even easier.

The only thing you do have to watch out for is glare from the lamps, which can produce unwanted hot spots in the object you're photographing. There are several solutions to this: one is to place a sheet of tissue or tracing paper over the lamp head, to diffuse the lighting. I wouldn't want to be responsible for your house burning down, though, so I can't say I'd recommend this technique. A better method is to point the light away from the object and bounce it off a sheet of white card. This works well, but you do need a stronger light source with this method.

The best method of all is to invest in a light tent – a cube of translucent white material that you put your object inside, shining lights through from the outside. The results can be excellent, as a soft, diffused light is produced that's perfect for product photography and occasions when totally neutral lighting is required. They're available in a variety of sizes from around 12 inches square, and cost from around $25.

Before photographing any object, be sure to clean it thoroughly. I know this sounds absurd, but it's surprising how much dust can show up under strong lighting. I once spent 20 minutes painstakingly cloning and healing the years of accumulated dirt and grease on each key of a photograph I'd taken of a computer keyboard, before I realized that I could have cleaned the keyboard itself in half the time.

Finally, each time you photograph a new object – even if it's for a specific job – take a variety of shots from different angles, then save the files to disk somewhere and keep them. Disk space is cheap, and recordable CDs are virtually given away; but you'll be kicking yourself if you have to reshoot an object that you've already photographed once.

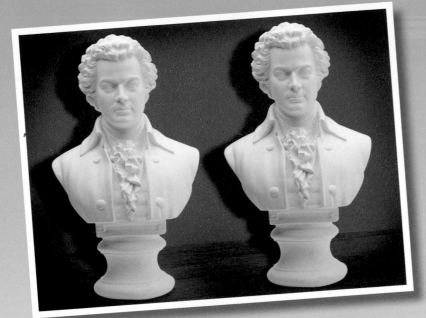

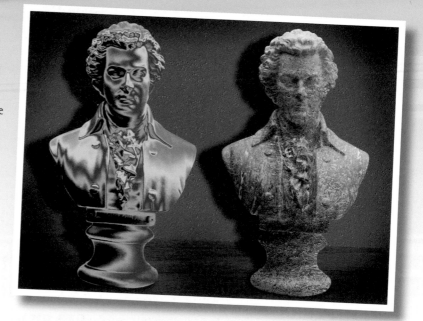

A couple of busts of Mozart, sitting on a shelf waiting to be sold (above). But who's going to go for plain plaster when they could have the same thing in gleaming chrome, or tactile marble? Changing the surface properties of even the most basic materials is a task that every Photoshop artist should be familiar with.

10
Metal, wood and stone

HARD SURFACES are generally easier to simulate in
Photoshop than those with transparency. Often, it's just
a case of grouping a surface texture with the object you
want to apply it to, and then adjusting the layer blending
method so that the contours of the underlying object
show through.

Reflective surfaces, such as metal, require special
treatment: unlike wood or stone, you can't simply place
a scan of a piece of metal on top. But the technique is
easy to grasp and, once you get the hang of it, easy to
reproduce.

In this chapter we'll also look at different ways of making
lettering appear to be cast in the surface of a variety of
materials.

Instant metal using Curves

1 Begin by opening the Curves dialog using ⌘ M *ctrl* M and click near the left-hand side of the diagonal line: drag vertically upwards

3 Now click again, further along the curve, and drag up again to make the high point for the next step. Once

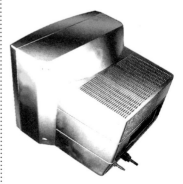

5 Click further along the curve once more, and drag upwards to make the high point for the final step. At this

THE SIMPLEST WAY to create an instant metallic effect is to use the Curves dialog. Metal differs from non-reflective surfaces in that it reflects the light in unpredictable ways: the light and shade aren't simply created by a single light source, but vary across the surface of the object.

We can simulate the effect of metal by drawing a stepped curve that reproduces the way metal reflects the light. On the following pages we'll look in more detail at how to get the best out of this technique; here, we'll simply turn this dull plastic monitor into a chrome-plated version.

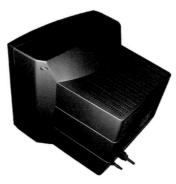

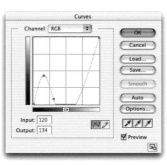

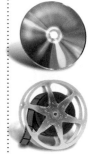

to make this steep curve. The image will appear very washed out at this stage, but it's just the initial step – it will all make sense later.

2 Now click a little further along the curve, and drag downwards as shown in the dialog. This will now make the image very much darker and

more contrasted. So far, we've created the first of what will become three peaks; we'll go on to build the other two to make the metallic effect work.

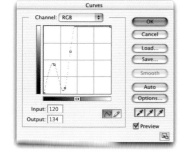

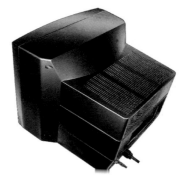

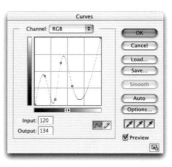

again the image will appear washed out: but the data is all still there, and we can continue to manipulate it.

4 Click further along, and drag down to complete the second step of our staircase. Now the image is beginning

to look far more shiny; but it still looks like it's made of plastic rather than metal.

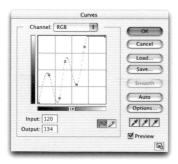

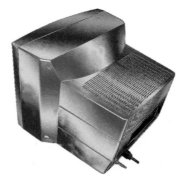

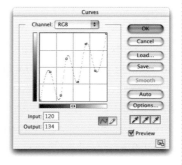

stage, we can begin to see the metallic effect taking shape, although the image still looks too bright.

6 Finally, click in the middle of the remaining part of the curve, and drag downwards. Now we've completed

the effect, and that dull metal monitor looks like it's made of gleaming chrome.

Metal with Adjustment Layers

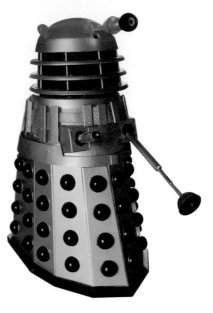

1 This original Dalek model has been painted using what the tin claimed was a metallic paint. But when it was photographed, the result looked dull and lifeless. We can use Curves again to bring the shininess back.

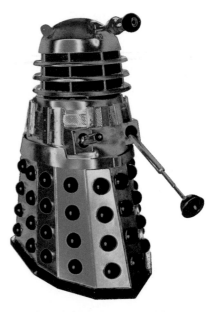

CREATING METALLIC EFFECTS using the Curves technique described on the previous pages works fine, but gives us little control over the result. It's far better to draw the Curves on an Adjustment Layer: not only can we mask and change the mode of the effect, we can always go back and change the shape of the curve at any time. Here, we'll use this system to make our plastic Dalek look more like the real thing.

4 As expected, the Curves effect has produced some harsh pixellation. But because we applied it on an Adjustment Layer, we can modify the target layer to fix the problem. After locking the transparency of the Dalek using ✓, apply a small amount of Gaussian Blur (a 1-pixel radius maximum).

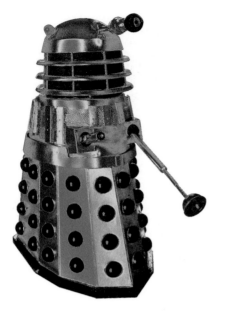

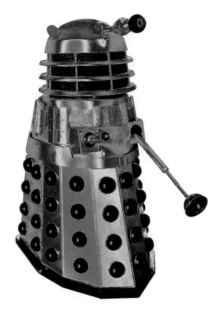

2 Create a new Curves Adjustment Layer by selecting it from the pop-up menu at the bottom of the Layers palette, and draw the same curve as we used on the previous pages. Here's the problem: the Curves effect has altered the color component as well, resulting in an ugly rainbow effect.

3 Because it's an Adjustment Layer, the problem is easily fixed. Simply change the layer mode (from the pop-up list at the top of the Layers palette) from Normal to Luminosity. Now, the Curves effect only affects the brightness and contrast of the underlying layer.

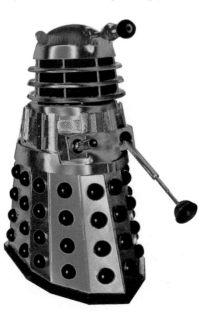

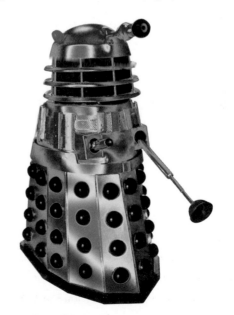

5 Each Adjustment Layer comes with its own mask, which works precisely like a standard layer mask. We can use this to paint out the Curves effect on unwanted areas – the end of the suction cup, the orange light and the highlights in the black hemispheres on the Dalek's body.

6 The skirt still looked rather dull and lifeless. Easily remedied: we simply use the Burn tool to add a little shading to that area. Because we're looking through the Adjustment Layer, we can see the effect of the Curves as we paint with this tool.

HOT TIP

The edges of layers can often look highly pixelated when a stepped Curves effect is applied. To get rid of this unwanted noise, simply group the Adjustment Layer with the target layer and most of the noise will disappear. Any extra noise can be painted out on the Adjustment Layer's mask.

SHORTCUTS

257

Metal with Layer Styles

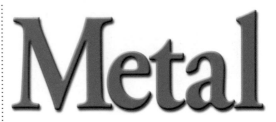

MAKING CONVINCING METAL TEXT IS often seen as a kind of Holy Grail among Photoshop artists. Here, we'll look at how to make metal with Layer Styles alone. The advantage of this method is that the text remains editable; and the style itself can easily be adapted to suit any purpose.

If this process seems a little long-winded, you can always cheat – after all, that's what this book is all about. I've included this style on the DVD that accompanies this book, so you can just load it up into your copy of Photoshop and start using it straight away.

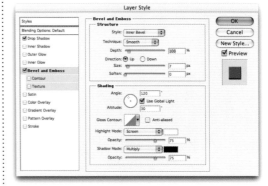

1 Begin by creating your base layer – in this case, it's live text. Open the Layer Style dialog and add an Inner Bevel, sized to suit your artwork. I've also added a drop shadow for a more three-dimensional effect.

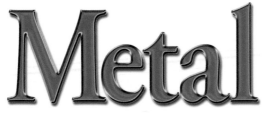

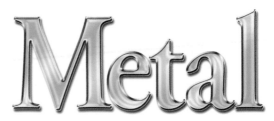

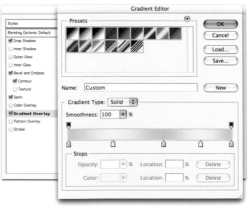

4 To give some sheen to the inside of the lettering, click the Satin tab and apply a bowl-like contour. You'll need to experiment with the distance and size to get the right combination, so just drag the sliders until it looks right.

5 To apply a gold color, we'll make a new gradient. Click on the Gradient Overlay section, and make a subtle gradient of alternating bars of light and dark yellow to complete our gold effect.

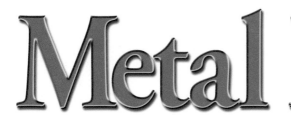

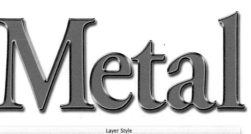

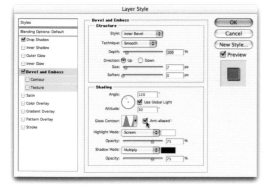

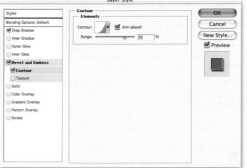

2 Now to liven it up. In the Shading section of Bevel and Emboss, click on the Gloss Contour icon and change it to a bumpy map such as this one, which adds sparkle to the lettering's bevel.

3 Next, we're going to add some reflection to those bevels. Click on the Contour section, and use the pop-up Contour icon to choose this sort of shape for our curve. That plastic image is beginning to look more like metal.

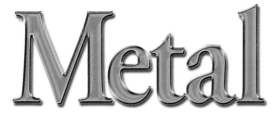

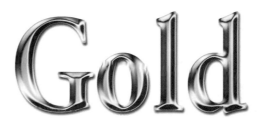

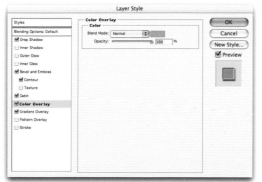

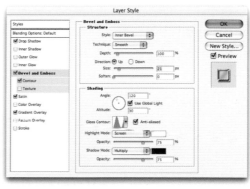

6 To turn the gold into silver, add a Color Overlay. Go to the blue section of the spectrum, and choose a gray with only the smallest hint of blue in it to avoid too much color creeping in.

7 Because we're working with live text, we can change the lettering or font as we need to. Here, I've also increased the size of the bevel to make the lettering look lumpier; the choice is up to you.

SHORTCUTS
MAC WIN BOTH

Turning silver into gold

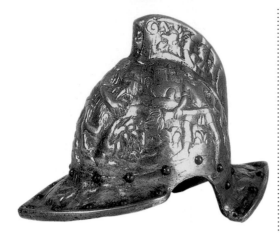
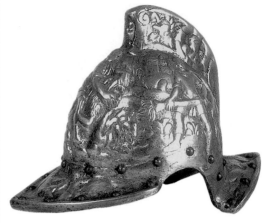

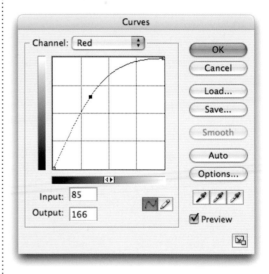

T URNING SILVER INTO GOLD may not be precisely the medieval alchemist's dream – they were, of course, more concerned with creating gold from base metals – but it's an easy technique that anyone can master.

If you were painting, you might expect to add red and yellow to achieve a golden hue. But in the Curves dialog, we only have access to each of the three RGB channels - red, green and blue. You might not think there's any green in gold, but it's surprising how this is the color that makes the effect work so well: just one more example of the need to think laterally when working in Photoshop.

1 Begin by opening the Curves dialog, using ⌘ M ctrl M. Switch to the Red channel, either by choosing it from the pop-up list at the top of the palette, or by using ⌘ 1 ctrl 1. Now grab the midpoint of the straight line, right in the dead center of the graph, and drag up and to the left. The distance you drag depends on your image, but you should aim for something like the curve shown here.

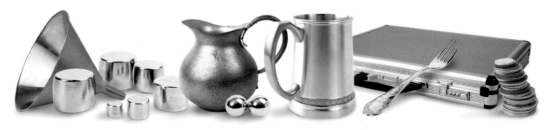

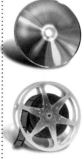

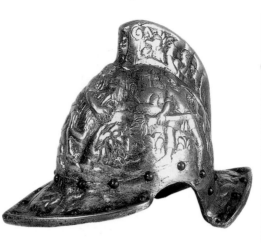

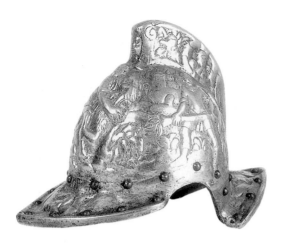

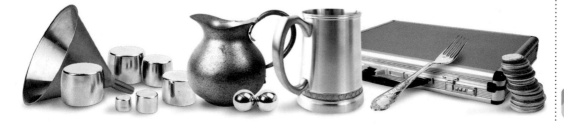

2 Now switch to the Green channel, either using the pop-up menu or with ⌘ 2 / ctrl 2 . Once again, grab the midpoint of the line and drag up and to the left, but not quite as far as with the Red channel. You'll be able to tell when the color looks right.

3 In the previous two steps, we brightened both the Red and Green channels – which meant brightening the image overall as well. Now we need to restore the depth of shading we had originally. Switch to the RGB (composite) view, using the menu or ⌘ ` / ctrl ` . Grab the midpoint again, and this time drag *down* and to the *right* to darken the whole image. And that's all there is to it!

Metal with Lighting Effects

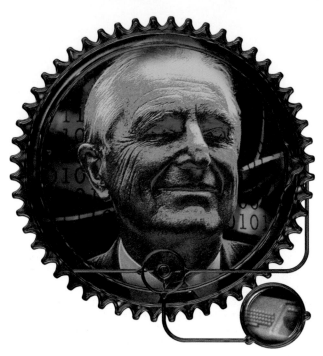

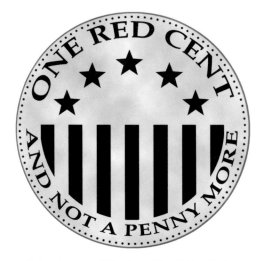

1 First make a new Alpha channel by clicking the icon at the bottom of the Channels palette. Since Lighting Effects only works in RGB, this will be Channel 4; its default name is Alpha 1. All the elements can be drawn directly on the channel, although you'd find it easier to create them as standard layers and then paste a merged copy into the channel afterwards. A faint application of the Clouds filter has been added to the background disc, as we'll see later.

THE LIGHTING EFFECTS FILTER is a useful tool for adding light and shade to an image: simply point the spotlights where you want them and adjust the settings. But the hidden function of Lighting Effects is its ability to use Alpha channels as bump maps to simulate three-dimensional images.

An Alpha channel is an additional channel (in addition to Red, Green and Blue) that Photoshop uses to store selection data. Some image libraries distribute CDs with their cutout information stored as Alpha channels rather than paths, because the channels can include transparency and fuzzy edges rather than just hard outlines.

The illustration above accompanied an article for PC Pro magazine about the man who invented the mouse: the graphic border was produced using the method shown here.

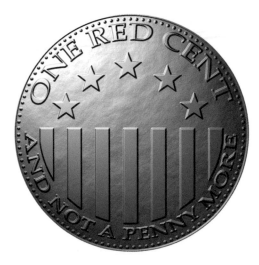

4 Here's the result of applying the filter to our Alpha channel: those simple shapes and letterforms now look convincingly three-dimensional. Notice the difference in texture between the flat vertical bars and the background of the coin, to which the Clouds filter had been applied: this filter prevents large flat areas from looking too shiny and synthetic.

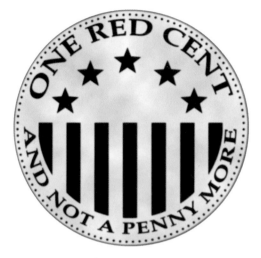

2 The next step is to blur the Alpha channel. This is necessary to prevent the final image showing hard edges around the contrasted elements; on the next page, we'll look in more detail at the effect of applying different amounts of blur to a bump map image. Now go back to the main RGB channels (you can use ⌘ ~ *ctrl* ~), create a new layer and fill the disc area with white – Lighting Effects won't work on an empty selection.

3 Open the Lighting Effects dialog, and specify the channel Alpha 1 from the Texture Channel pop-up list at the bottom of the dialog window. The default setting is White is High, which means that lighter areas will appear more raised than dark areas; I find it easier to work the other way around, so uncheck this box. Adjust the settings using the sliders until you get a clear effect with no burned-out hotspots.

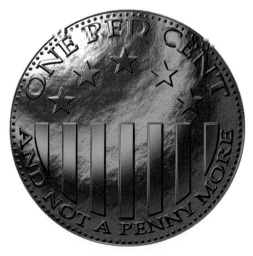

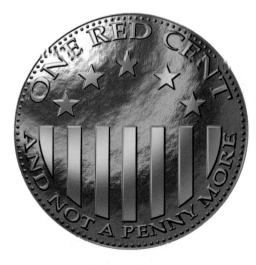

5 Applying the same Curves technique as described on the previous pages brings out the shininess in our coin, making it look less like plastic and more like metal. That Clouds texture is also accentuated by the Curves process, giving the coin a pleasing battered effect.

6 Since the elements were all created as separate layers, it's easy to select them by holding ⌘ *ctrl* and clicking on each layer thumbnail in the Layers palette, holding *Shift* as well to add new layer outlines to the selection. Now the selected areas can be recolored using Color Balance (or any of the other color tools) to make our coin come to life.

HOT TIP

Lighting Effects only works on RGB images, so if you're working in CMYK you'll need to convert to RGB first. Even if you're creating a black and white illustration, you'll have to change it to RGB to use the filter, then change back to grayscale afterwards.

SHORTCUTS

More on Lighting Effects

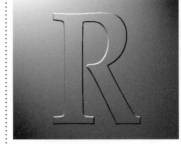

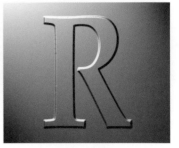

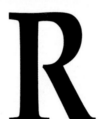

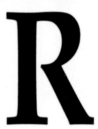

ALMOST ANY TEXTURE can be used as the basis for a Lighting Effects operation, as is shown here: Clouds and Noise are just two ways of generating natural-looking surfaces. Notice, as well, how the simple repeated screw heads shown in the final example produce an array of screws that are all lit slightly differently as their distance from the virtual light source varies.

The key to making artwork render well in Lighting Effects is to use just the right amount of blur on the Alpha channel that will be used as a texture map. So first, we'll look at how different amounts of blur affect the final appearance of the rendered artwork.

1 When no blur is added to the Alpha channel (above), the result after applying Lighting Effects (top) is harsh, with ragged, stepped edges.

2 Applying a 1-pixel radius Gaussian Blur to the Alpha channel softens the edges, and results in a far smoother image after Lighting Effects is applied.

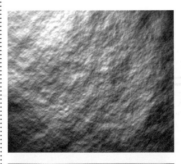

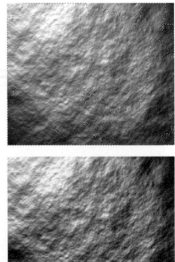

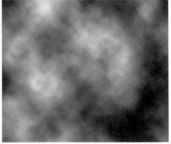

6 The Clouds filter (above) produces a pleasingly random surface (top) when used as the basis of a Lighting Effects channel. It's a useful way to create an instant stone effect, which can be easily modified until it produces exactly the result you want.

7 Because the Alpha channel stores selections, we can press ⌥⌘4 alt ctrl 4 to load up the lighter areas for us (top). We can now recolor them, then inverse the selection and recolor the rest to create a more dynamic effect (above).

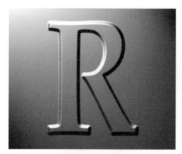

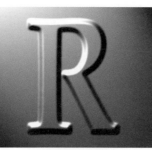

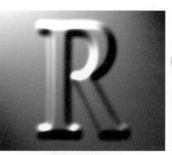

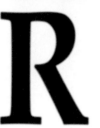

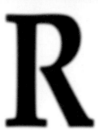

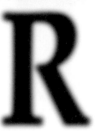

3 The greater the amount of blur, the more raised the result will be. Here, a 2-pixel blur results in a significantly taller object.

4 Increasing the blur to 4 pixels produces a result in which the edges thicken too much: this looks like it was cast from an old mold.

5 An 8-pixel blur is clearly a blur too far: Lighting Effects has trouble making sense of this, and the result is merely fuzzy.

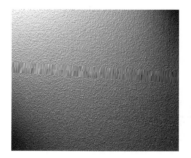

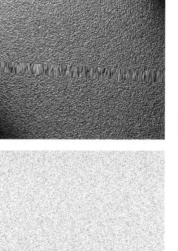

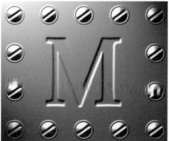

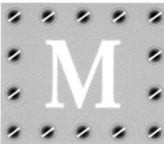

8 Even the tiniest variations in shade can have dramatic effects. The 2% Gaussian Noise (above) is too faint to be seen clearly here; but the result (top) is a grainy, textured surface.

9 Increasing the Gaussian Noise amount to 20% produces a far more striking result: here, we've produced a rough, stony surface in just a few seconds using this technique.

10 The screws around this perimeter were created by dabbing a soft brush once, then drawing a diagonal line across it. Because the letter M is brighter than the background, it appears to be recessed rather than raised.

SHORTCUTS
MAC | WIN | BOTH

Rust, grime and decay

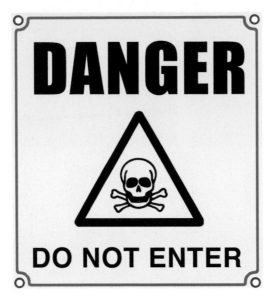

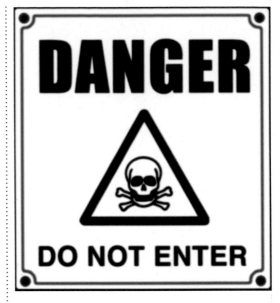

S O FAR, WE'VE LOOKED at ways of using Lighting Effects to make bright, shiny objects. But it can just as easily make metal surfaces that look as if they've been knocking around for a few years. Making objects appear to be old and used can greatly add to the realism of an illustration.

Starting with this simple sign, above, we'll run Lighting Effects a couple of times and hopefully end up with something that looks like it belongs in the real world.

1 The first step, as always, is to blur the artwork after it's made into a new channel. Because our sign is supposed to be pressed out of a sheet of metal, we don't want too much variation in height: there are basically just two shades here, black and white.

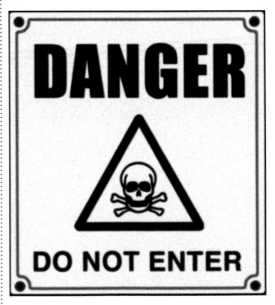

4 Now we'll return to our Alpha channel, and add some noise to it. This will form the basis for the rust, but we don't need a lot of noise: as ever, a small change in a channel makes a huge difference when Lighting Effects is applied. Here, a Gaussian Noise amount of 6 has been used.

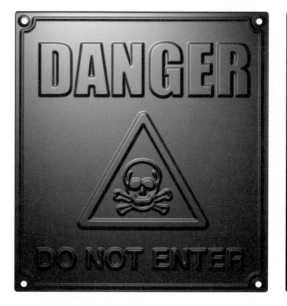

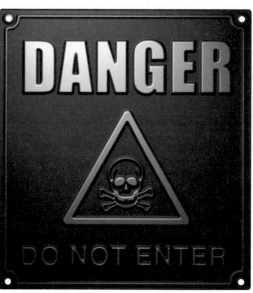

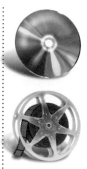

2 Here's the result of applying the Lighting Effects filter after the previous artwork was saved as a channel. So far, it looks more like plastic than metal; but since we want it to look painted rather than polished, we won't apply the Curves as in the previous examples.

3 Because the channel that Lighting Effects used can also store selections, we can press ⌥⌘4 alt ctrl 4 to load up the white areas as a selection. This is tinted using Hue/Saturation; the selection is then inversed using ⌘Shift I ctrl Shift I and the raised areas brightened up.

HOT TIP

If you don't want your rust to look as extreme as this example, stop after step 3 and create a new layer, set to Hard Light mode and grouped with the sign layer. You can now paint on this layer using oranges and browns to create rust-like shading on the layer beneath.

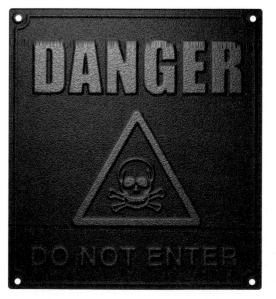

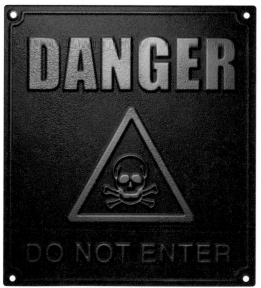

5 On a new layer, the Lighting Effects filter is applied again. This time the result is tinted brown, once again using the Hue/Saturation dialog. There's no need to load up specific areas using the channels: we want to tint the entire image.

6 Now it's just a matter of making a layer mask for the new brown layer, and painting it out selectively to reveal the original sign beneath. After using the Brush tool to paint out large areas, turn to the Smudge tool to fine-tune the result by smudging streaks of rust into the mask.

SHORTCUTS

MAC WIN BOTH

Reflection on a knife edge

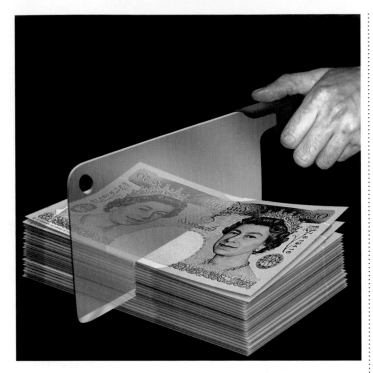

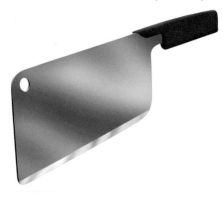

THE MOST ABSTRACT CONCEPTS are often the hardest ones to illustrate. This illustration for the Sunday Telegraph was commissioned to accompany a feature on how directors of top companies were facing pay cuts. Rather than going down the obvious, cartoony route of showing a miserable exec pulling out his empty pockets, the art editor came up with this idea of a sushi knife slicing through a pile of banknotes.

The property that makes flat metal look metallic is the reflections seen in it: but here, I didn't want any extraneous elements to confuse the issue. So the effect had to be created simply using light and shade, with only the copied banknotes making the reflection element.

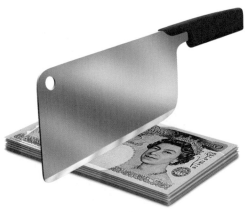

1 The knife blade and the handle were first drawn as two separate layers, using the Pen tool to create the outlines. The hole in the blade was made with the Elliptical Marquee.

4 After increasing the contrast on the blade, I selected a band at the bottom with the Lasso tool and added strong shading with Dodge and Burn to make the knife edge.

7 The banknotes were stacked up and shaded using the techniques shown in Multiple Shadowed Objects, page 148.

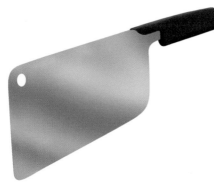

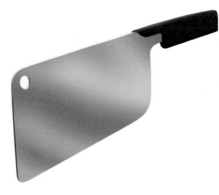

2 Basic shading was added using the Dodge and Burn tools; the strong diagonal slant gives the impression of light on a reflecting surface.

3 The blade selection was loaded up by ⌘ ctrl clicking on the layer name, and then nudged down and to the right; the inverse was shaded using Dodge and Burn again.

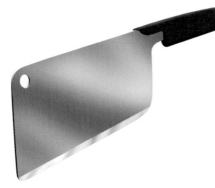

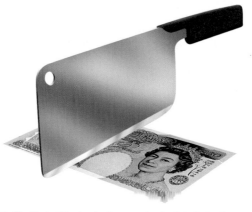

5 A new layer was filled with white, grouped with the blade and set to Multiply. The Noise filter was followed by vertical Motion Blur to make the brushed steel effect.

6 The first of the banknotes was simply distorted using Free Transform so that it lay in a convincing perspective across the knife blade.

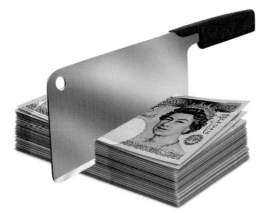

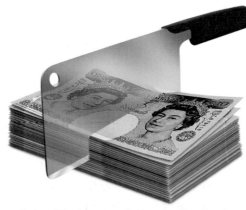

8 The top banknote was cut in half, stepped up, and the process repeated each side of the blade: an additional couple of notes were distorted to fly up from the pile.

9 Copies of the top note and sides were flipped and distorted and made into a clipping mask with the blade, their opacity lowered so that they looked like dull reflections.

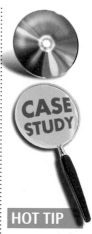

CASE STUDY

HOT TIP

The hardest part of creating this image was making the reflection of the topmost banknote marry correctly with the original: because the note had been distorted, it was difficult to handle the reflection. The solution was to ghost different sections of the reflection were distorted separately, so that the key elements matched those in the original note.

SHORTCUTS

269

Photographing shiny objects

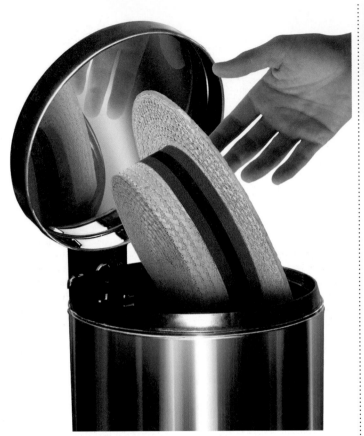

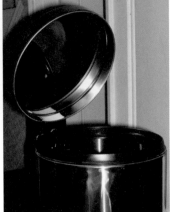

1 When you photograph a metallic or other shiny surface, the one thing you can't do is use a flash: the resulting glare would overwhelm the image. Instead, I dragged this trash can over to a window, holding the pedal down with my foot while I leant back and took the picture (memo: must invest in a decent house brick).

WHEN THE GUARDIAN RAN A FEATURE about a lifelong socialist taking the decision to send their child to a private school, the cover image was a simple cutout of a boater – the kind of hat traditionally worn in selective girls' schools. The following week, they countered with a story by a journalist who had recently taken his child out of the private sector, and decided to illustrate it with an image of the same boater being tossed into a trash can.

Although this was in many ways an easy montage to create, the texture of the trash can was the hardest element to reproduce. Photographing shiny objects can be a test for even the most hardened photographers; there is a simpler method.

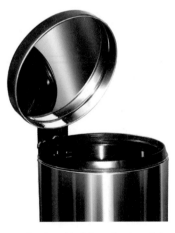

5 Getting rid of the reflection of the carpet in the lid involved a couple of stages. First, a new 'mask' layer was made, drawn with the Pen tool to fit exactly the shape of the inside of the lid (minus the reflection of the can itself). A copy of the blurred front was then clipped with this mask layer, and some Gaussian Blur applied to make the reflection less sharp.

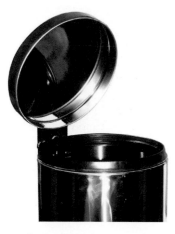

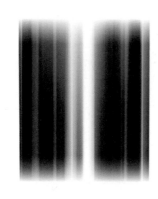

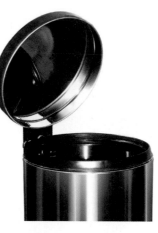

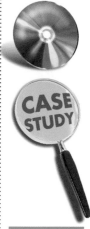

2 Cutting the background out was an easy enough process using the Pen tool to draw a smooth path, and the image needed just a little brightening with Curves to lighten it up. But the reflection remained smeary, and showed my hallway and carpet all too clearly. For a perfect image, it was necessary to clean up all those distracting elements.

3 The solution was to take a section of the front of the can and make a new layer from it, and then apply Motion Blur to it. I then stretched the result until it was tall enough to cover the whole front of the can. By using the original as the basis for the blur, it was possible to keep the same color range as appeared in the rest of the object, so it would blend in well.

4 The blurred texture was moved into position, and a layer mask made so that it exactly fitted the front curve of the trash can. Because the can had been photographed slightly from above, it was necessary to apply a slight perspective transformation on the blur to make it taper towards the bottom. The result is a convincing brushed metal effect.

HOT TIP

Rather than using Motion Blur to create the brushed metal effect, it would have been possible to either draw the surface from scratch, or use a photographed section of a shiny pole. But although the can's surface is, in theory, just black and white, there's actually a huge range of colors that define it. Using a blurred copy of the original is the best way to ensure that the color range matches the rest of the can.

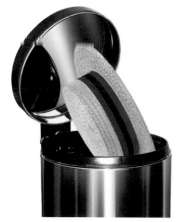

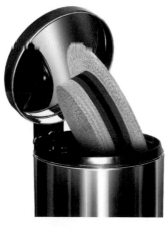

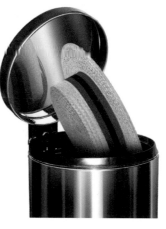

6 Placing the hat in the trash can was achieved by drawing a layer mask that exactly fitted the front of the can, up to the plastic rim. By clicking on the link between the hat and its mask in the Layers palette, the hat was separated from the mask, and so could be moved around independently.

7 Because the original hat had been photographed the right way up, the light naturally fell on it from above. Turned upside down, the top – previously the brightest part – now had to be darkened up. Rather than using the Burn tool, I made an elliptical selection of the top and used Curves to darken just this section until it looked convincing.

8 The reflection of the hat was added on top of a new mask, this time a copy of the entire inside of the lid. The hat was then masked where it would be hidden by the rim of the lid, and shading applied to it with the Burn tool. Finally, a third copy of the blurred front was placed above the reflected hat and grouped with the lid mask to dim the reflection slightly.

SHORTCUTS
MAC WIN BOTH

The art of woodturning

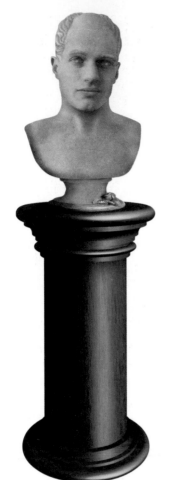

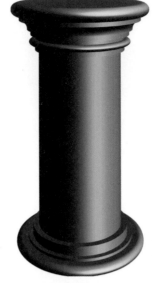

1 This plinth was created using Adobe Dimensions, and imported into Photoshop. It could also have been made in Adobe Illustrator.

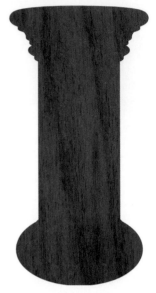

2 A scan of a piece of wood is placed on top of the plinth layer, and grouped with it by pressing ⌘ G *ctrl* G or by clicking the line between the layers in the Layers palette.

ALMOST ANY OBJECT can be turned into wood simply by wrapping a piece of wood around it and changing the layer mode so the original object shows through. Unlike other textures, though, wood has a grain which needs to follow the contours of the base object. To see how the bust was made, see The Philosopher's Stone later in this chapter.

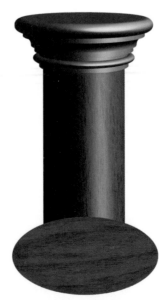

6 A new section of wood is taken using a circular selection, which is then rotated 90° and Spherized to make it wrap around the base better. The circle is then squeezed to make this ellipse, which fits the base dimensions.

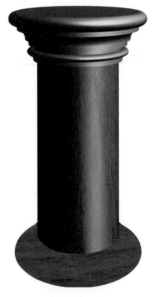

7 This base section of wood is then grouped with the plinth layer, and a new layer mask is added. We don't need to draw the mask again: simply duplicate and invert the mask that was created for the column layer.

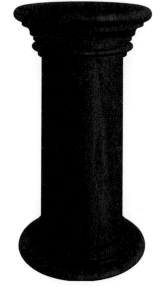

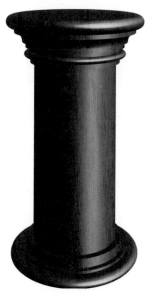

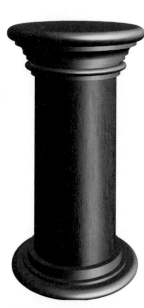

3 Now we need to make the base layer show through, by changing the layer mode using the pop-up menu at the top of the Layers palette. This is Multiply: it's far too dark.

4 Changing the layer mode to Overlay produces a far better result. We can clearly see all the contours of the underlying object, while maintaining the wood texture.

5 Having the wood grain running vertically is fine for the column, but looks wrong on the capital and base. Using the Pen tool, I've created a layer mask to hide the top and bottom.

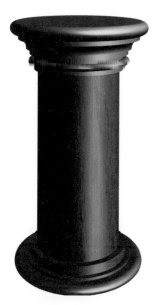

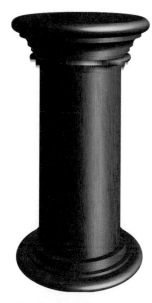

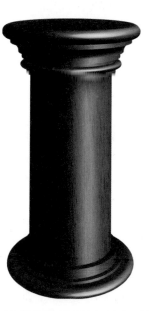

8 Once again, we set the mode of this layer to Overlay. The Spherized wood now fits the shape of the base perfectly; and because we inverted the column's layer mask, the two match together without a visible join.

9 To make the capital, we simply duplicate the base layer and then unchain the link between the layer and its mask. We can then drag the wood ellipse up into place, and the layer mask is already there for us.

10 All that's needed now is to add a little extra shading beneath the capital, and around the far side of the base of the plinth. This is painted directly onto the underlying plinth layer using the Burn tool.

HOT TIP

Although we set the layer mode of the wood layer to Overlay in this instance, it won't suit all purposes; it all depends on the characteristics of the base layer, and the texture and grain of the wood you're using. Try Hard Light and Soft Light, as well as Multiply, to see which produces the best effect for your artwork.

SHORTCUTS

273

Making a better impression

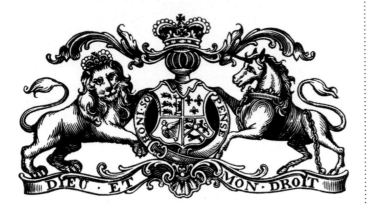

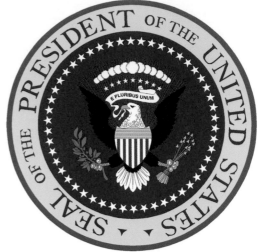

1 This may be an accurate representation of the Presidential Seal, but as it stands it's hardly a beautiful object in its own right. Let's take this flat artwork and make it a little more attractive by embossing it.

WE CAN USE THE TEXTURE of a wooden surface as the base for any artwork, turning a two-dimensional design into one that looks as if it's been carved in wood. In the example above, I've used the complex outlines of this coat of arms to create a solid-looking object. The original design for this crest was in black and white, so the embossing has to do all the work.

The Seal of the President of the United States, by contrast, has no interest in its outline – it's simply a round disk. Unlike the crest, it does have the advantage of color to create more interest, and we can make use of this.

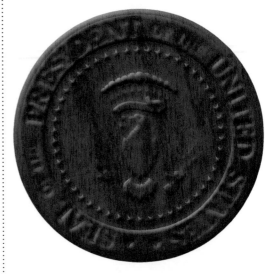

4 Now that the seal detail is in our Alpha channel, we can load it as a selection using ⌘ ⌥ 4 *ctrl* *alt* 4 ; the brighter areas will be more fully selected than the dark areas. Returning to the wooden disk, we can now make a new layer from that selection using ⌘ J *ctrl* J . This layer will appear with the bevel from the disk applied: as it stands, it's far too blobby.

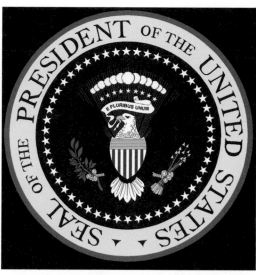

2 To begin, we'll take the same piece of wood as we used in the previous example. After stretching it so it covers the seal, hold ⌘ ctrl and click on the seal's name in the Layers palette to load up its selection; then inverse the selection using ⌘ Shift I ctrl Shift I and delete the outside. The bevel is applied using Layer Effects, with a 15-pixel bevel to give the disk a sense of three-dimensionality.

3 Now we're going to turn the original seal into a selection. Copy it, then make a new Alpha channel by clicking on the New icon at the bottom of the Channels palette; then paste the copy in place, where it will appear in grayscale. This can now be used as a workable selection.

HOT TIP

When copying a layer into a new Alpha channel, it's important to make sure the copied version appears in exactly the same position as the original. The easiest way is to hold ⌘ and then click on the layer's name to select its outlines; then copy, and with the outlines still selected, paste onto a new channel. This method will ensure the positioning is precise.

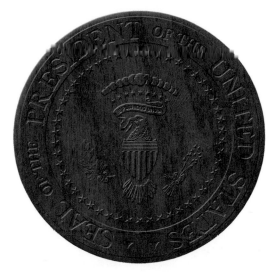

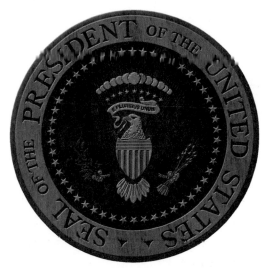

5 Double-click the layer effect in the Layers palette to open the dialog, and change the numbers. Here I've increased the depth from the default 100% to 200% to make it stronger; but I've also reduced the bevel size to just three pixels, so that the detail remains crisp. Some of the detail has failed to appear after the selection process, such as the wings of the eagle; but the next step will fix that.

6 Finally, move the original seal layer to the top. We need to change its layer mode so that the wood and beveling show through. Once again, we have a choice of layer modes open to us: although Overlay worked on the example on the previous page, it's too strong here. Instead, I've opted for Soft Light, which brings back much of the original color while retaining the subdued sense of stained wood.

SHORTCUTS
MAC WIN BOTH

Timber floors with varnish

1 To turn this piece of wood into a floor, the first step is to mark out the planks. It's easiest to draw a rectangular selection in QuickMask and fill it, then copy it across: that way you can be sure they're all the same size.

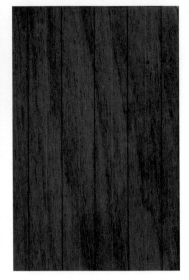

2 Make a new layer from the selection. I've used the Bevel and Emboss section of Layer Styles to add the shading lines. Be sure to keep the Highlight value fairly low, or you'll find it too glaring when the floor is finished.

I HAVE A CONFESSION to make: I only have one piece of wood. At least, there's only one piece I tend to use for all my wooden needs: it's this image of the back of an old pencil box I scanned in 1989. You can still see the screw holes that held the base to the sides – it wasn't even a particularly sophisticated pencil box. The point is, though, that you really don't need a lumber yard full of different types of wood; as long as the piece you're using has a strong enough grain, it can be put to most purposes fairly well.

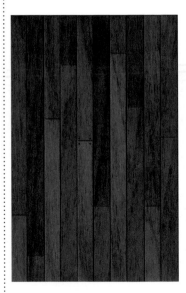

6 Adding the nails is optional, but can help with the sense of flooring. On a new layer, make a small circular selection, fill with a mid gray and add a little shading to it; then duplicate three times (you can see the nails on the fifth plank from the left).

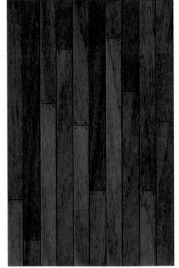

7 Copy that group of nails to all the other wood joins by holding ⌥ *alt* as you drag with the Move tool. Be sure to hold the mouse down within the nail area before dragging, or you'll create a new layer each time you drag. Finally, merge all the layers.

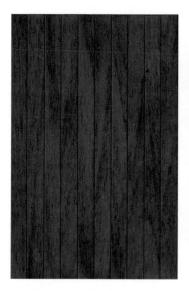

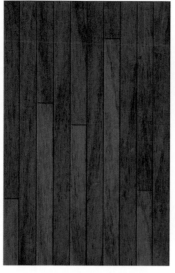

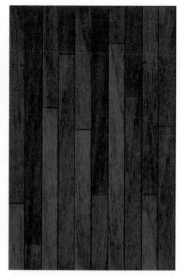

3 Now inverse the selection, and make a new layer from the wood base: apply the same beveling by dragging the layer effect from the previous layer onto this one. Finally, flip the new layer vertically so the grain lines don't match up.

4 Split one set of floorboards into irregular lengths by making rectangular selections, and make another new layer using ⌘ J ctrl J; the bevel will automatically be applied to the new layer.

5 Repeat the process for the other set of planks, and adjust the brightness of both to make more irregularity in the planks.

HOT TIP

Applying a perspective distortion to the wood necessarily makes it narrower at the top than at the bottom. If your target image is wider than the original wood flooring, duplicate the layer and move it horizontally so the two overlap by about an inch; then make a layer mask to blur the join lines and merge the two layers to make a floor that's nearly twice as wide.

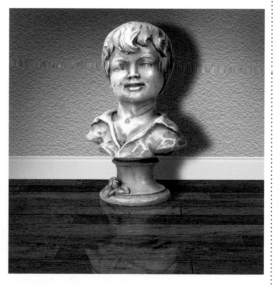

8 Your floor is now ready to be inserted in whatever document you want. Use Free Transform to make it fit the space: hold down ⌘ ⌥ Shift ctrl alt Shift while dragging one of the top corner handles to create the perspective distortion. A floor like this can be made to fit in just about any space you want to fill. This wall, incidentally, was easily made using the Texturizer filter.

9 With the shading in place, the floor looks very much more realistic. Applying the varnish is far less messy than working with the real thing: simply make a reflected copy of whatever object you're placing on the floor, and set its Layer mode to Soft Light for that glossy appearance. For more on how to achieve this effect, see the reflection sections in Chapter 9, Shiny surfaces.

SHORTCUTS
MAC WIN BOTH

277

The philosopher's stone

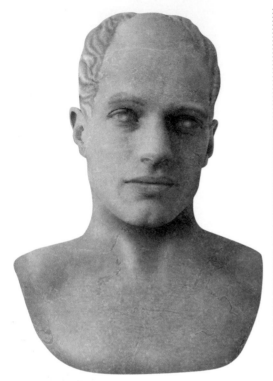

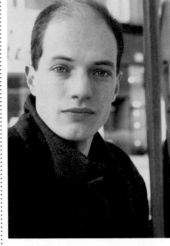

1 Choosing the original photograph was the key to the success of this project. I immediately rejected one that showed the philosopher smiling: the ancient Greeks never bared their teeth. This image showed the right sort of side lighting, without any strong shadows.

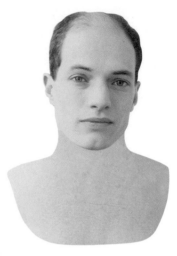

2 The first step was to cut out the head, and knock out the color using the Desaturate command ⌘ *Shift* **U** *ctrl* *Shift* **U**. I then copied a section of his forehead to get a suitable shade and texture, stretched it and cut it to the shape of his neck and shoulders.

WHEN THE INDEPENDENT newspaper wanted to run an article comparing ancient and modern philosphers, they had busts of the ancient Greeks – but only a photograph of contemporary philosopher Alain de Boton. It seemed like a good idea to turn him into stone to match his predecessors, and achieving the task in Photoshop was obviously going to be quicker and cheaper than finding a sculptor who could reproduce his likeness in marble in time for a 5pm deadline.

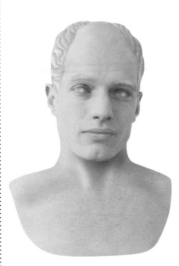

6 The pupils were painted in by making elliptical selections within the eyes, and using the Dodge and Burn tools once again to make them look recessed. Care was taken here to make the shading match the surrounding area as closely as possible – the shading had to be kept subtle.

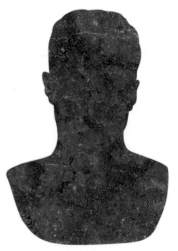

7 This scan of a chunk of marble would add both texture and color to our bust. Because the head and shoulders are two layers, I couldn't simply group the marble with the base; instead, I made a layer mask encompassing both the underlying layers.

278

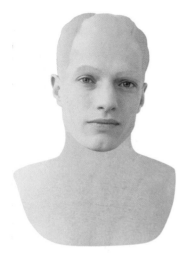

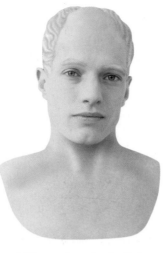

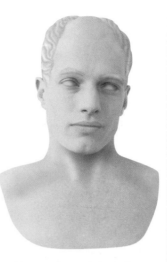

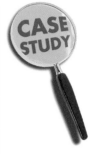

3 Carved hair is very different from the real thing, so I took another section of forehead and this time shaped it to cover the hair and eyebrows of the original. I also patched the forehead using the Clone tool to hide the stray hairs there.

4 Adding shading using the Dodge and Burn tools made the hair look carved in stone: I also added muscle lines to the neck. Remember you can temporarily access the Dodge tool while using Burn by holding ⌥ alt as you paint.

5 The eyes also needed painting out, again by cloning texture from the forehead; shading was added afterwards to make them look more three-dimensional. I also cloned over the lips at a low opacity to tone them down slightly.

HOT TIP

Figures carved in stone show light and dark areas only where these are caused by direct light and shadow: unlike real faces, there's no variation in skin tone or hair color. Highly contrasted original photographs don't work well; you should choose a fairly evenly lit image if possible, adding extra shading where you want it later.

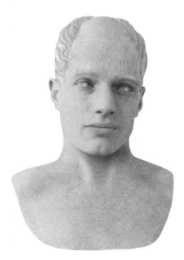

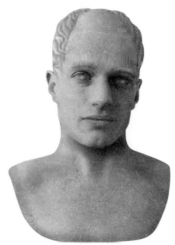

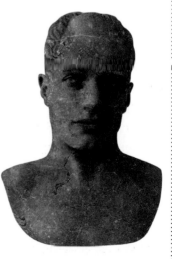

8 Multiply, Hard Light, Overlay and Soft Light modes would all have allowed the image to show through the marble. The choice is determined by each instance; in the end I chose Soft Light, reducing the opacity to 70% so that the strong texture in the marble didn't swamp the image.

9 To strengthen the whole image, I made a new Adjustment Layer and increased the Contrast while reducing the Brightness. Adjustment Layers have the advantage of being editable later, which meant I could always remove it if it needed altering or wasn't working.

10 Although I wanted the bust to look like pale marble, it's just as easy to make it appear to be modeled out of granite or any darker material. Here, I've taken the same piece of marble and changed its mode to Multiply to get an altogether stronger effect.

SHORTCUTS
MAC WIN BOTH

Bringing statues to life

O N THE PREVIOUS PAGES we looked at how to turn a photograph into a statue. Here, we'll reverse that process: starting with a stone model, we'll look at how to bring it to life.

The technique is similar in many ways to that used to color black and white photographs. But because the stone original is smooth, we'll also need to add some of those blemishes that make people human.

This was originally posted as a Friday Challenge on the How to Cheat website: the results are shown below.

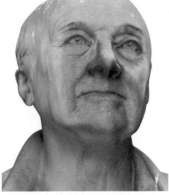

1 Our statue is of an unknown benefactor outside a church. He's been a perch for pigeons for too long: let's bring back some of his dignity.

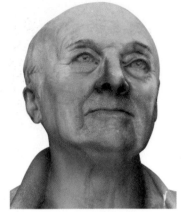

2 The first step is to add some basic color to the model, using the swatch we implemented in *Coloring Black & White Images*, page 208.

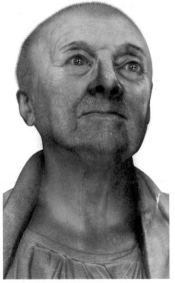

6 Another application of the *Beards and Stubble* technique, this time very subtly – to add some slight stubble beneath the chin. It's barely perceptible, but makes a difference.

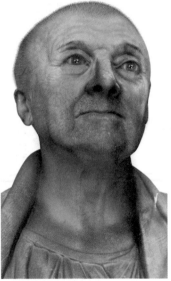

7 More shading: on a new layer, we add liver spots to the temples, wrinkles on the forehead and some extra shading beneath the chin and on the chest hair area.

THE FRIDAY CHALLENGE

  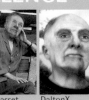 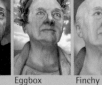

| atomicfog | BobbyJo | Chris | CWBasset | DaltonX | Dek_101 | Eggbox | Finchy | G.E.Sutton | jwhite | Kenney |

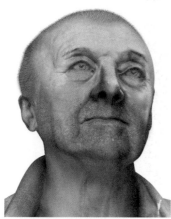

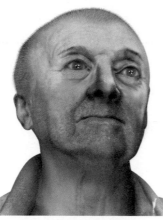

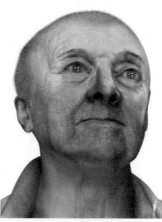

3 The hair and beard are both added using the *Beards and Stubble* technique described on page 190. The beard itself is given a very low opacity.

4 The eyes are added using the technique in *All in the Eyes*, page 200. The edges of the irises have been softened slightly with Gaussian Blur.

5 Fine lines are drawn on the cheeks and nose on a new layer using a tiny brush at a very low opacity, to simulate the effect of broken veins.

HOT TIP

Subtlety is a key element here: it's easy to go too far when adding veins, liver spots, stubble and so on. The trick is to work on a new layer for each element, painting the features in harder than you'd like them; the layers can then be reduced in opacity, and in some instances blurred, to make the overall effect more convincing.

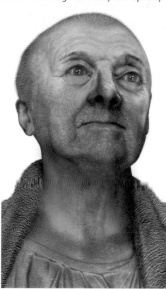

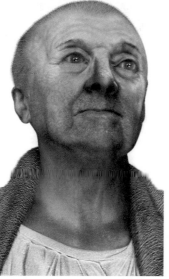

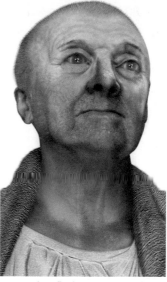

8 On a new layer, make a rectangular selection and fill it, then apply the Texturizer filter to it with Burlap. This is duplicated, and distorted to make the clothing.

9 The shirt is selected, copied to a new layer and desaturated and brightened. It's not bad – but it's lacking in texture, and looks too artificial.

10 As a final step, we can take another copy of the texture we created in step 8, and add it to the shirt layer on Multiply mode at a very low opacity.

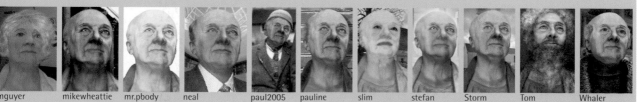

mguyer   mikewheattie   mr.pbody   neal   paul2005   pauline   slim   stefan   Storm   Tom   Whaler

Carving words in stone

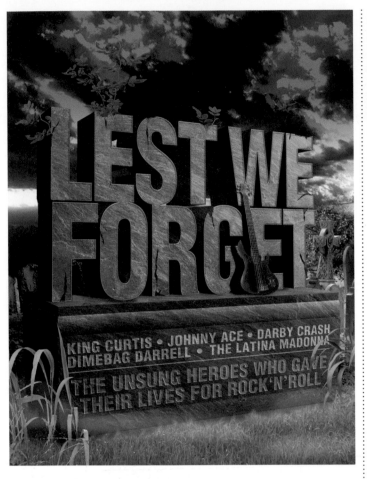

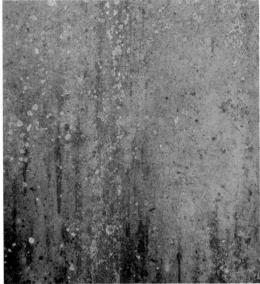

1 This piece of stone is nicely mossy at the bottom, and will do perfectly as the basis for our grave. I tend to carry my digital camera with me whenever I'm likely to stumble upon an interesting building or texture.

THIS ILLUSTRATION WAS FOR THE COVER of the Independent. The shape of the plinth and the cutout text were modeled in Adobe Illustrator (see Chapter 12), and the stone texture wrapped around both.

Carving text in stone is now easier than ever, thanks to the Emboss feature in Layer Styles. Here, we'll look at how to make a gravestone from scratch, in just a few simple steps.

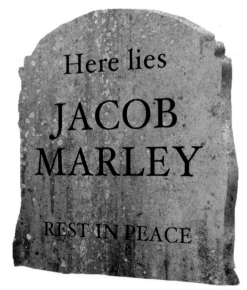

4 After creating your text, render it into a layer and then distort it using Free Transform to match the perspective of the tombstone. This text is loaded as a selection by ⌘ ctrl clicking on its name in the Layers palette, and the selection made into a new layer from the stone layer.

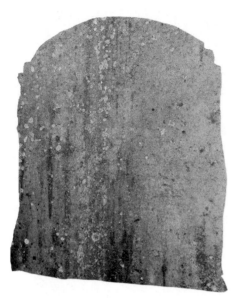

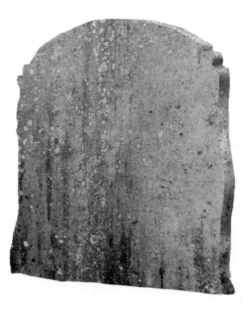

2 Because we want this grave to be somewhat rough around the edges, draw the outline using the Lasso tool to get the unevenness that couldn't be achieved with the Pen tool. This selection can then be made into a new layer using ⌘ J ctrl J.

3 The same selection is copied from a different part of the original stone material, and offset to make the edge. Shading can be added using the Dodge and Burn tools, making it darker on the undersides of the edge, and lighter on the upper faces.

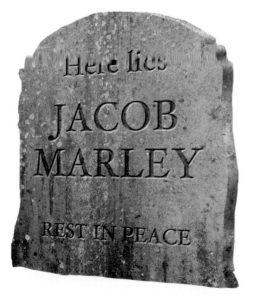

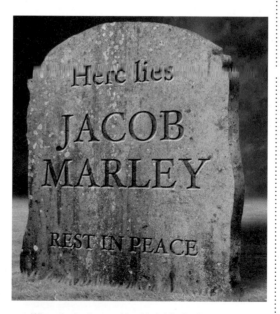

5 After darkening the stone lettering slightly to make it stand out better, use Layer Styles to create the carved effect. Use Emboss rather than Bevel for this, as it makes a more convincing carved effect; remember to set the position to be Down rather than Up, so it's lit from above.

6 When the background is added, it's simply a matter of blending the stone into its surroundings. Darken the edge slightly, and add a shadow on the grass behind it; the grass is brought in front of the base of the stone using the technique described in the Chapter 3, Hiding and showing.

A grave business

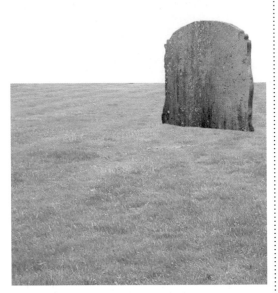

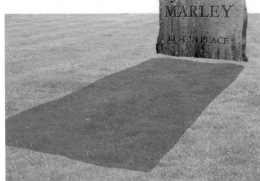

1 The first step is to draw the grave. I find it easiest to paint it in using QuickMask, to avoid straight lines at the edges. The perspective is tricky; it's just a question of doing what looks right. Make a new layer from the selection.

A READER POSED THIS QUESTION on the Reader's Forum section of the website: How do I dig a hole in the ground that looks convincing? Never one to pass up a good idea, especially if it's handed to me on a plate, I made it into the following week's Friday Challenge, the results of which are shown below.

It's not a difficult task, but there are some useful tips that will help you to make the effect more convincing. This is the image contestants were given to start with – it's the same gravestone we carved on the previous page. Here's how it's done.

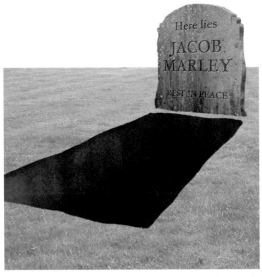

4 The shading makes all the difference. Use the Burn tool to darken the bottom of the hole; some vertical streaks make it look more dug. Finally, darken a thin rim around the top, beneath the lip of the grass.

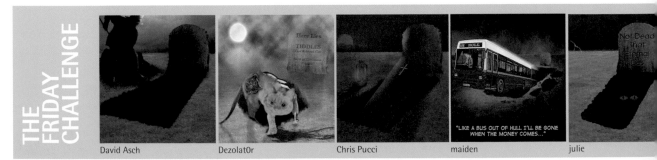

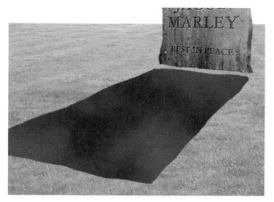

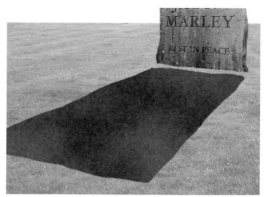

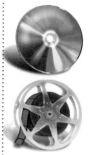

2 Lock the transparency and then choose two different browns for the foreground and background colors. Now apply the Clouds filter, holding *alt* ⌥ to produce a tighter effect: keep pressing *ctrl* *F* ⌘ *F* until it looks good.

3 The Clouds filter gave us some useful lumpiness, but not enough detail. To add an earthy appearance, add some monochrome Gaussian Noise, then blur it slightly with the Gaussian Blur filter.

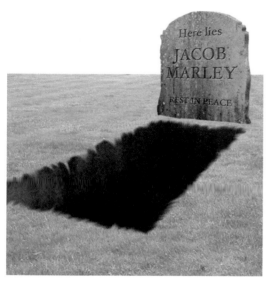

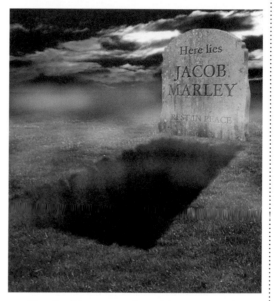

5 The real key to making this effect work is making the grass overhang the edge of the grave. This is easy: it's done in exactly the same way as we brought the grass over the couple in Layer Masks 3, in Chapter 3.

6 After that, it's up to you. For a night setting, choose a suitable sky and darken the grass using Curves – add a touch of blue for a night-lit effect. The mist here is simply painted on at low opacity using a soft-edged brush.

HOT TIP

In step 5, we made a layer mask to bring the grass over the edge of the grave. The front two edges of that layer mask can be applied to any other layers for objects you want coming out of the grave: it's better than simply using the grave itself as a clipping mask, since we want any skeletons, ghouls (or even buses) to be able to stick out over the top.

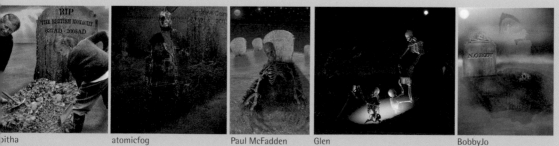

pitha   atomicfog   Paul McFadden   Glen   BobbyJo

SHORTCUTS
MAC **WIN** **BOTH**

The point of illustration

BRIEFS FOR ILLUSTRATIONS come in three basic varieties. There are those who will send you the copy for the article in question, and wait for you to come up with a visual idea to accompany it. There are art editors who will work out the idea on their own, get it passed by the editor, and sometimes even supply a rough sketch of what they want. And finally there are editors themselves, who will insist on the first idea that pops into their heads and expect it to be turned into a work of art.

I have nothing against newspaper editors. Many of them are charming individuals who are great conversationalists and probably make outstanding contributions to society. But they frequently lack the ability to think in visual terms. One of the illustrations I'm frequently asked to create is a montage showing a politician taking money out of someone's pocket (this usually happens around budget time). I pause, take a deep breath and explain patiently that the problem is that newsprint technology has yet to embrace animation. There's no difference, in a still image, between a politician taking money out of someone's pocket and putting money into it. This has to be explained with great tact, of course, since ultimately these are the people who pay for my children's overpriced trainers.

It comes down to a question of what's desirable, what's visually interesting and what's humanly possible. The purpose of an illustration in a magazine or newspaper is to draw the reader into the piece and to make them want to read the article to which it's attached. It should express the sense of the article without giving away the punchline, and without prejudging the issue (that's best left to the journalist who wrote the story). An illustration in a printed publication is not a work of art; it's an advertisement for the story, and its job is to sell the story to the reader. Sometimes – at the best of times – it can be a work overflowing with artistic integrity and perfect composition. But if it doesn't relate to the story in question (and make that story seem interesting) then it's failed to do its job.

Those taking up photomontage for the first time frequently fall into the trap of piling on evocative imagery in the hope that the result will be poignant. I've seen student artwork that incorporates a baby, a flaming pile of dollar bills, a nuclear explosion and a McDonald's wrapper within one image. Look, they say, all human life is here: it must mean something. But this is the visual equivalent of Tchaikovsky's 1812 overture with added reverb and a drum'n'bass backing: the cacophony simply prevents us from seeing the meaning.

Labeling, above all, is to be avoided at all costs. The days when you could depict Uncle Sam wearing a hat with Government printed on it rowing a boat labeled Economy while tipping out a handful of urchins labeled Unemployed rightfully died out in the early nineteenth century – and yet illustrators are still asked to label their artwork today. I nearly always refuse, unless the wording can be incorporated into the image in a meaningful way. The destruction of a building bearing the sign Internet Hotel seems, to me, to be a reasonable request; the sinking of a boat labeled Fair Deal does not.

When you execute an original idea successfully, you can confidently expect to be asked to reproduce it within a few months. I've drawn cakes for the 20th birthday of Channel 4, the 10th birthday of Sky television, the carving up of Channel 4, the first birthday of satellite channel E4, and the 50th birthday of ITV – all for the same newspaper. I've blown up computers, telephones, televisions and video recorders, and I've tattered the flags of at least half a dozen of the world's top blue-chip companies. And I've completely lost count of the number of company logos I've pasted onto the backs of poker cards.

The hard part is keeping each new version as fresh as the first. I've often made the mistake of assuming that readers will find the repetition of the same idea tedious: but it is a folly, for the stark truth is that readers of publications cast barely a glance at the image that an illustrator has sweated blood over. Illustration, for the most part, is simply the ephemeral wrapping that's discarded once it's done its job.

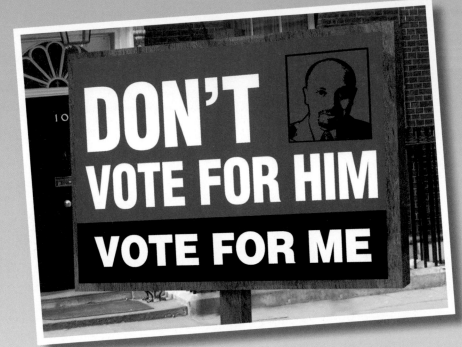

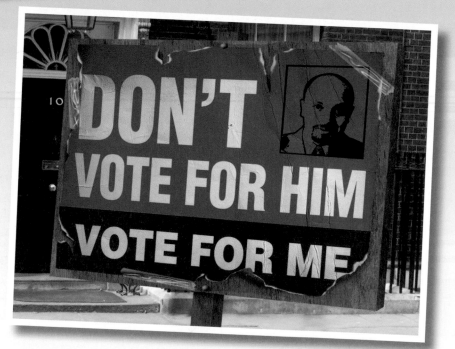

■ Two political posters, both pushing the same message. The top one looks artificial and unconvincing: it's too clean, too crisp, and too new. It doesn't take much work to turn this dull poster into something altogether more weatherbeaten and lived-in, giving it the air of having been left out on the street for a few weeks.

11

Paper and fabric

IN THE LAST CHAPTER we looked at hard surfaces – metal, wood and stone. Paper and fabric, by contrast, are floppy, malleable substances that bend, crease and crumple. It's getting these creases and wrinkles right that's the key to making paper look like it's really made of paper, and that includes banknotes as well as letters and documents.

The fabric section of this chapter covers clothes, flags and banners; all the objects that hang or flutter in an irregular manner. We'll examine the easiest way to make a flat drawing of a flag look like the real thing fluttering in the breeze, using simple shading techniques combined with distortion filters.

How to make a load of money

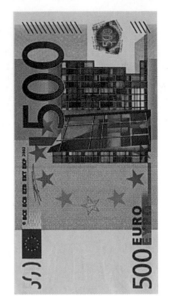

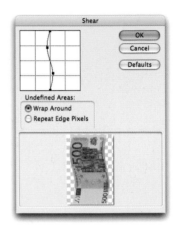

SCANNING BANKNOTES used to be easy: you just laid them on a flatbed scanner. These days, Photoshop will recognize a banknote and may well refuse to open it – even if it's been photographed with a digital camera, rather than a scanner. So much for progress.

To add more interest and realism to banknotes, we can use the Shear filter to give them a bit of a twist. If you've upgraded to Photoshop CS2, of course, you can use the Image Warp feature of Free Transform instead of the Shear filter; I've shown both methods here for the benefit of those who haven't upgraded (yet).

1 The Shear filter only works horizontally, so before you apply it you need to rotate the artwork by 90°. Increase the Canvas Size, if necessary, to allow extra space at the sides for the image to distort into.

2 When you first open the Shear dialog, you'll see a straight line. Click in the middle of this line and you'll create an anchor point: drag this point, and you'll make a smooth curve that precisely bends the artwork.

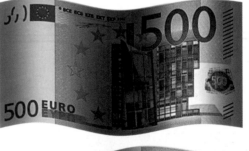

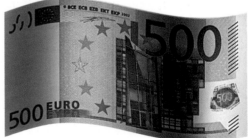

5 Repeating the Shear filter with different settings can make the banknote ripple in different ways. Here, two different applications of the filter show how the same bill can be distorted into different forms. Again, Photoshop CS2 users can use their own custom distortions to create different waving effects without having to rotate the artwork first.

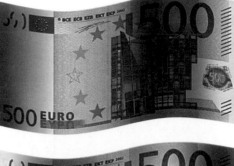

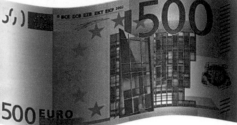

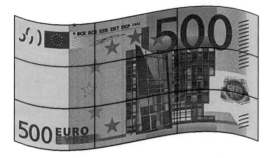

3 If you have Photoshop CS2 or higher, skip the previous two steps and use the Image Warp feature of Free Transform instead. Choose the Flag distortion from the preset menu, and drag the handle up and down to change the waviness of the image.

4 Shading added to the result, using the Burn tool, gives the sense of the note being three-dimensional. Rather like those gestalt optical illusions, you can choose to see the image in one of two ways. The eye will interpret shaded areas as being recessed, and unshaded areas raised: so in the top example above, the raised ripple is on the left; in the lower example, it appears to be on the right.

HOT TIP

You don't need to apply the Shear tool separately for every banknote in a pile: three or four sheared versions are usually sufficient. Distorting the notes using Free Transform will be enough to make them all look different. When you combine several notes in one montage, add shading using the Burn tool to enhance the effect.

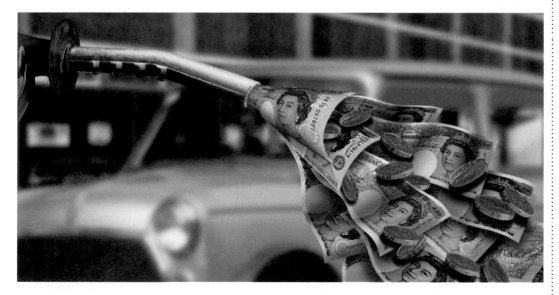

6 This illustration for the Sunday Telegraph was to accompany an article about the increased cost of motoring following a rise in the price of crude oil. The banknotes were all distorted using the Shear tool, as described here: those coming directly out of the pump's spout were also sheared horizontally. Each note was then distorted using Free Transform to achieve a sense of perspective, and shading was added beneath each note to make it stand out from the note below. Adding the coins simply made the result look more dynamic.

SHORTCUTS
MAC WIN BOTH

Judging a book by its cover

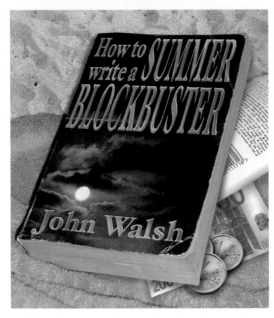

I F YOU WANT YOUR BOOK COVERS to look old and tattered, as in the illustration for The Independent, above, then your best bet is to take an old paperback and photograph it. For this image, I ripped off the cover, leaving just the blank flyleaf: that way, I was able to place my new cover on top while allowing the creasing of the flyleaf to add texture to it.

Clean, pristine hardback books, on the other hand, are hard objects to photograph. Apart from the problem of getting the right angle, the close trimming of the paper makes it look like a solid block rather than individual pages: it's a lot easier just to draw the whole thing from scratch.

1 The paper is created in the same way as the cards were stacked up in Multiple Shadowed Objects in Chapter 7. The difference here, of course, is that the pages are stacked neatly rather than randomly: select a shadowed page and then nudge it up and left a couple of times with the cursor keys, holding ⌘ alt to make the copies.

4 A copy of the cover is made, moved down one layer and filled with a dark blue. This is the edge of the board beneath the paper wrapper: it's only just visible, but it makes the difference between a paperback and a hardback. We'll use a similar technique for creating the back cover.

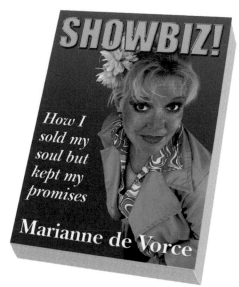

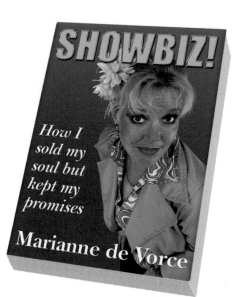

2 The cover is assembled using as many layers as required; these are linked and made into a new layer group. Duplicate this group and merge its contents; then distort the resulting composite layer to fit the shape of the book cover. The reason for this seemingly tortuous route is that the original cover is kept intact, so changes can be made later.

3 Shading on the edges of the cover helps to make it look as if it wraps around the hard boards. Using the Burn tool, click just above a corner, then hold **Shift** and click at the bottom of the same edge. A burn line will be drawn as a straight line between the two click points.

HOT TIP

If you have Photoshop CS2, then rather than making all the cover layers into a new group, make them into a new Smart Object. That way, you can always return to the original if you need to make any changes: it will open, flat, in a new window, and will be rendered back into perspective when you close the window. See page 374 for more on Smart Objects.

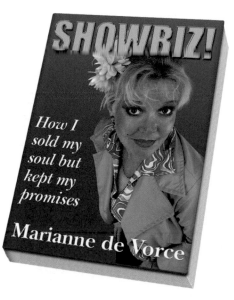

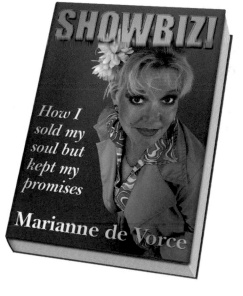

5 Now for the shadow of the cover cast on the pages. It's worth creating this as a separate layer, grouped with the paper layer: paint straight lines with the Brush tool, set to a low opacity, in the same manner as outlined for the Burn tool in step 3 above.

6 The final elements are added to complete the book: the back cover, the spine, and the flaps that tuck beneath the board covers. I've also added some general shading to the cover using the Dodge and Burn tools to prevent it looking too flat and two-dimensional.

SHORTCUTS
MAC WIN BOTH

Paper: folding and crumpling

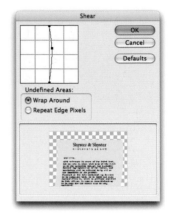

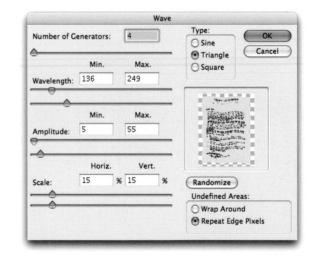

W HEN ART EDITORS are stuck for a visual idea, they fall back on a piece of paper with the concept written on it. An executive might hold a paper entitled Restructuring Proposal; a real estate agent might wield one with the word Contract emblazoned on it in red ink.

Whatever the wording on the paper, the last thing you want to do is to leave it as a flat sheet. Simply distorting it into perspective is rarely sufficient: this is paper, after all, and not a sheet of plastic; it bends, creases and deforms as it's handled.

Here, we'll look at a couple of different paper treatments: a simple fold, and the crumpled effect seen on a piece of paper that's been stuffed in a back pocket for too long.

1 Here's the business letter we'll use in both our examples. If you're going to use a letter, you'll obviously need some text on it. It doesn't usually matter what this is, as long as it doesn't begin Lorem Ipsum: readers may not recognize the fake Latin text, but the person who commissioned you certainly will.

2 Select just the top half of the letter and apply the Shear filter to it, using the technique described earlier in this chapter. When working on the top half of the paper, be sure not to move the anchor point at the bottom of the dialog box or the two halves will no longer match up. If you have CS2, you can use Image Warp instead.

6 To begin the Crumple effect, we'll use the Wave filter to distort the basic letter. This can be a confusing filter at first glance, because there appear to be so many variables: but it's quite controllable. The number of Generators determines the different number of waves; set to 1, the effect will be too regular and phoney. Because

we want long, sweeping curves, raise the Wavelength levels: the higher the levels, the greater the length of each wave. You can use the Amplitude sliders to determine the wave height, but you'll get far more control by simply lowering the horizontal and vertical scale to make the wave effect less extreme.

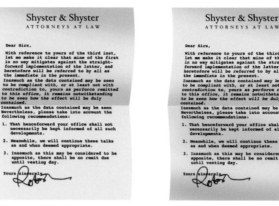

3 After applying the filter, leave the top half of the paper selected and use the Burn tool with a large, soft-edged brush to add gentle shading above the crease line. Add a little more where the paper turns away at the top to give the impression of it bending over away from us.

4 Now select the bottom half of the paper, and apply the Shear filter again. You'll need to click the Defaults button to reset the tool to a vertical line; you can then add whatever distortions you want.

5 Now, with the bottom half distorted as well, add some shading to that half of the paper, again without deselecting it. You can also add a little shading elsewhere on the paper to give the sense of a gentle ripple.

7 Now use the Lasso tool to make irregular vertical selections. Don't make the lines dead straight: hold the `⌥` `alt` key and click points at intervals along the letter to make the tool draw straight selection lines between each point you click.

8 Now use a large, soft brush with the Burn tool to add the shading. Keep the brush on the deselected side of the selection line, so that only the edge of the brush has an effect on the paper. Don't paint exactly along the lines, but fade off away from the edges for an altogether more realistic appearance.

9 Now deselect, and use the Lasso tool once more to make a series of horizontal selections. Use the Burn tool once more to add the new shading within the selected area, once again being careful not to overdo the effect.

HOT TIP

Although real paper tends to be white, you'll have a hard time working on it if you leave it pure white. Lower the white point of your paper using Curves or Levels to just take the edge off the brightness and you'll find it far easier to see what you're doing. You can always paint highlights back in later if you need to.

SHORTCUTS
MAC WIN BOTH

Folds and wrinkles

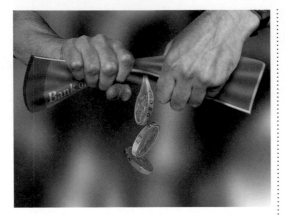

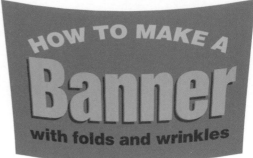

FABRIC NEVER HANGS STRAIGHT. It's the folds, creases and wrinkles that give it its distinctive quality. But it's an appearance that's surprisingly easy to reproduce in Photoshop.

Glancing at the composite image above, commissioned by the Sunday Telegraph, you might think that the lettering had been distorted using some complex system to make it follow the fold lines in the checkbook. In fact, the illusion of creased text and a crumpled book is created entirely by the play of light and shade across it.

Here, we'll look at how to paint folds and creases into fabric to make it look like it's hanging down, using just the Dodge and Burn tools to create the effect.

1 The lettering was created on a rectangular banner, and the text layers were merged into it. This banner can be curved slightly either using the Shear filter, or with Image Warp if you have Photoshop CS2. The version on the CD is already curved into this shape for you.

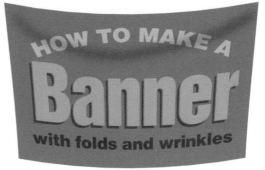

4 Now for the shading. Use the Burn tool, and choose a medium sized, soft-edged brush. Lower the opacity to between 20% and 40% so the effect isn't too strong, and paint a shallow curve running from corner to corner, dipping into the banner.

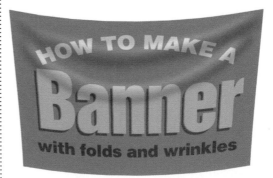

7 Hold the ⌥ alt key again to use the Dodge tool, and paint another highlight above that second shadow. It may take a few attempts before you're able to paint the Dodge strokes in the right way; if you make a mistake, just Undo and try it again.

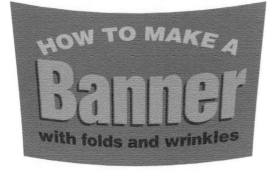

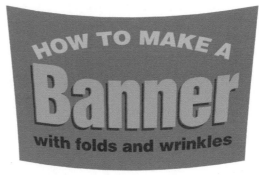

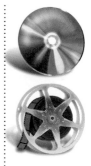

2 To add the texture, use the Texturizer filter with the Canvas setting. It's a simple way to make smooth, flat artwork look more natural. Any grayscale document can be used to generate the textures used by this filter, so you can define your own easily.

3 The result of the Texturizer filter is too strong, so we'll reduce it. Rather than going through the dialog again, there's a simpler way: after applying this filter, use the Fade command (⌘ Shift F ctrl Shift F) to reduce the opacity. Here, it's been taken down to 30% of its original strength.

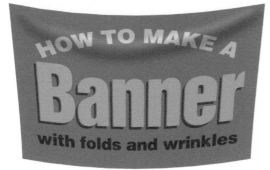

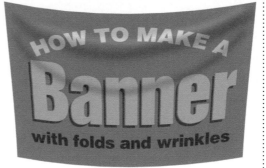

5 Now hold the ⌥ alt key to get the Dodge tool and paint a parallel curve directly above the one you just drew. This will brighten the artwork, where the Burn tool darkened it: used together, the effect will be of a highlight above and a shadow below the fold.

6 Using the Burn tool again, paint a second curve below the first, again running roughly from corner to corner. It helps to use a pressure-sensitive graphics tablet for a job like this, but it can be done with the mouse – just use a lower opacity and build up each shadow and highlight in stages.

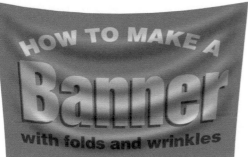

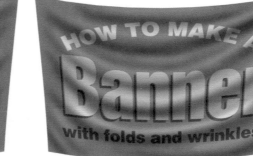

8 Continue in the same fashion until you've made a series of curves running right to the bottom of the banner. The flat artwork we started with now looks more like a piece of fabric that's hanging from its corners.

9 To finish off, add more folds in the corners of the banner. These won't reach right to the corners, but follow the same lines to make the edges of the banner look more realistic. Now's also a good time to strengthen those highlights and shadows that don't show up well enough.

HOT TIP

Using the Texturizer filter to add the canvas texture to fabric can result in a blocky, repetitive tiled pattern. If you have a digital camera it's worth instead photographing a piece of real canvas (the back of an oil painting works well) and then simply overlay that on top of your artwork using Hard Light or Multiply mode, at a low opacity.

SHORTCUTS
MAC WIN BOTH

297

Ripping and tearing

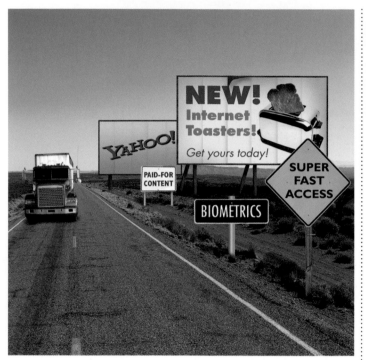

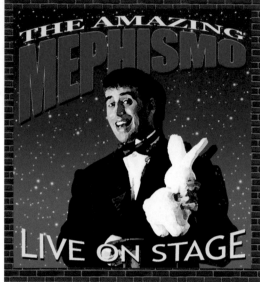

1 The initial poster was created using text distortion to bend the lettering; the figure was stylized using the Watercolor filter. As it stands, it's a brash image that looks nothing like a real poster.

THE POSTERS IN THE ILLUSTRATION ABOVE, created for .net magazine, needed just a little distressing to make them look more realistic. Here, we'll take the process several steps further to turn this flat, artificial poster into something that looks as if it's been hanging around on the wall for a long time.

In most cases, you wouldn't want to add this much destruction to a single poster – I've gone to rather extreme lengths to illustrate the techniques involved. Often, only the smallest amount of shading is required to make a poster convincing: in the illustration above, the Internet Toasters billboard has been shaded in vertical strips to make it look as if it has been pieced together from multiple sheets. Only one tiny corner turned down gives any hint of destruction.

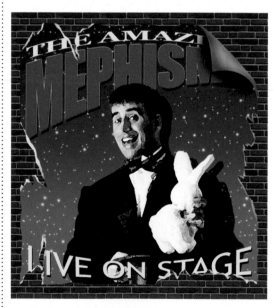

4 The corner is folded down by first masking the corner of the poster – a layer clipping path does the job without interfering with the layer mask. Now, on a new layer, draw the outline of the fold. Fill with a neutral color, and add a little shading with Dodge and Burn; then apply the Plastic Wrap filter to give the impression of sticky glue.

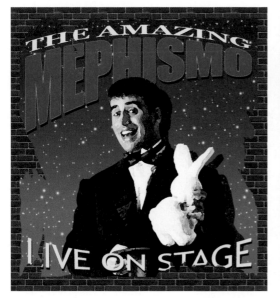

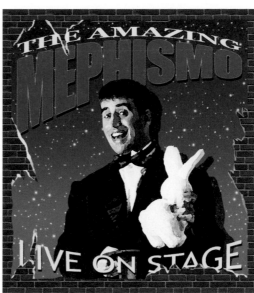

2 The first step is to create the tears. Make a layer mask for the poster layer, and make ragged selection using the Lasso tool. If you set the background color to black, you'll be able to remove chunks of poster simply by pressing `Backspace`. Because we're working on a mask, we can always undo any deletions that seem inappropriate later.

3 Simply removing pieces of poster isn't enough. We need to show the torn paper around each rip. Make a new layer, grouped with the poster layer, and paint on it using a small, hard-edged brush to trace roughly around each tear. It's important not to try to be too precise here: the rougher the painting, the more convincing the effect.

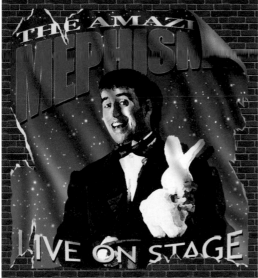

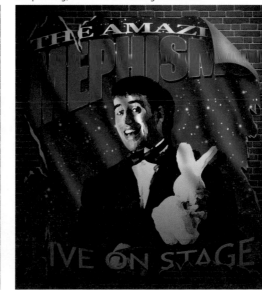

5 The folds and creases are added using Dodge and Burn, using the same technique outlined on the previous pages: first add a dark shadow using the Burn tool, then hold the ⌥ `alt` key (to temporarily access the Dodge tool) and paint above it to add the highlight. The lettering, which previously appeared flat, now looks rippled.

6 The lighting is added by making a new layer set to Hard Light mode, and filled with a neutral gray (it's an option when creating a Hard Light layer). Lighting Effects then adds both light and shade transparently through the layer. The drop shadow and the slight remains of old glue on the wall are both added as separate layers.

HOT TIP

Using a layer mask to create the tears, rather than simply deleting holes from the poster, meant it was always possible to reconstitute the original at a later time. This is a key principle: try not to make irrevocable changes to your artwork unless you're sure you want them. Before adding the folds and creases in step 5, I duplicated the poster layer so I'd have an earlier version to return to.

SHORTCUTS

MAC WIN BOTH

Simulating old photographs

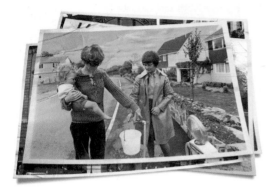

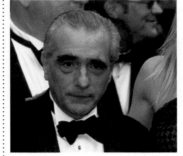

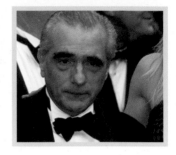

1 This photograph of film director Martin Scorsese is an ideal candidate for being turned into a snapshot. But we need to make it a more photo-like shape first.

2 Delete all but a photo-shaped portion of the layer. Then select a smaller rectangle within that – our image area; inverse the selection, and fill the area outside it with light gray.

T HE STACK OF PHOTOGRAPHS ABOVE was for a feature in The Guardian about life 20 years ago. The main image was originally in black and white, and needed recoloring.

Creating the effect of a stack of snapshots involved two processes: adding creases and wrinkles to the images, to make them look as if they'd been lying around in someone's attic for years; and adding shadows, to give the impression of a pile of curled photos.

These are two separate techniques, and they're both detailed here. First, we'll look at how to create a snapshot effect from a flat image; then we'll see how to add folds and wrinkles to make a photograph look very much older.

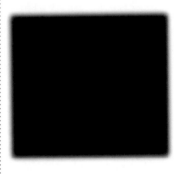

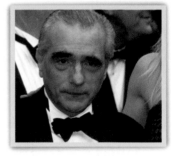

3 Load up the selection of the photo layer, and apply some feathering to it – around 8 pixels or so. Now make a new layer, and fill this selection with black to make the shadow.

4 Move the shadow layer beneath the photo layer, and lower its opacity to around 60%. If you're placing it on a dark background, you may want a stronger shadow.

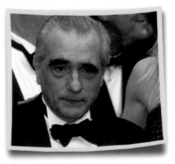

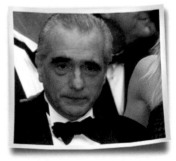

5 Now use Image Warp (CS2 and above only) to curl the corners of the photo up slightly. Because we created the shadow based on the flat photo, it remains straight – and this is what makes this technique convincing.

6 Finally, use Dodge and Burn to add a little highlight and shadow to the frame. Because we initially filled the frame with light gray, rather than white, we can be sure it will show up against a white background.

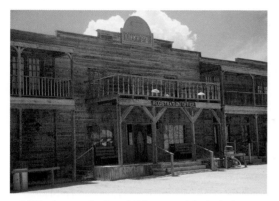

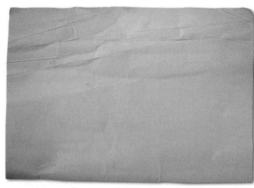

1 This photograph of an old Western saloon looks far too crisp. We can age it by a hundred years by adding some texture on top.

2 This texture is the inside cover of an old paperback book, which has yellowed naturally with age; some of the creases are natural wear and tear, and some were added.

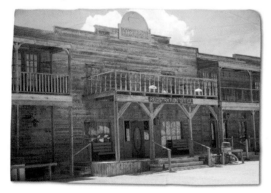

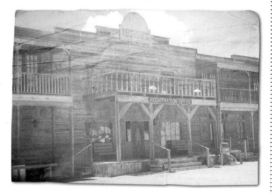

The inside cover of a book is a good starting point for our texture since it contains no text or pictures. Similarly, if you want to photograph a book to mock up a cover on it, take the existing cover (as long as it's a hardback) and simply turn it around so that the white side faces outwards.

3 The building is made into a clipping mask with the texture layer, so that it only shows up where the two coincide. The mode is then set to Hard Light, which allows a little of the texture and color to show through.

4 Now to add some more texture. Duplicate the original texture layer and bring it to the front. Set the mode of this new texture layer to Hard Light as well, so we can see through it to the photograph beneath.

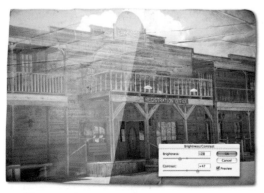

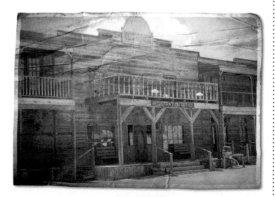

5 All we want from this second texture layer is the folds and wrinkles, and none of the color. So begin by desaturating it using ⌘ Shift U ctrl Shift U, which knocks all the color out of it. Now use Brightness and Contrast to boost its strength.

6 Now for the border. Hold ⌘ ctrl and click on the texture layer's thumbnail to load it as a selection. Contract that selection by say, 16 pixels, inverse the selection and make a new layer above the texture; fill this with white, and set its layer mode to Hard Light.

Waving the flag

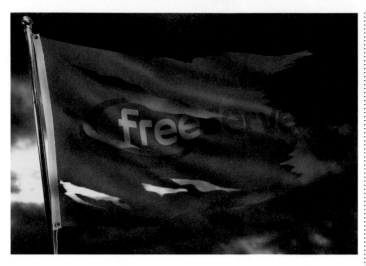

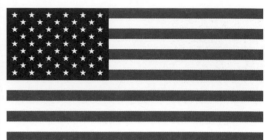

T HE ILLUSTRATION ABOVE was commissioned by the Sunday Telegraph to accompany a story about the tribulations of Freeserve, the internet service provider. The holes in the flag were made by selecting ragged areas on a layer mask with the Lasso tool and filling with black; the rough strands at the edges of the holes were created by smudging with the Smudge tool on the mask itself.

Any flag, banner or flat artwork can be made to ripple convincingly in the breeze using the technique outlined here. I've started with a PostScript flag, but it's easy enough to apply any company logo instead.

1 PostScript flags, banners and crests of all kinds are widely available, both on the internet and as part of clip art collections. Photographs of real flags are harder to come by, especially as cutout objects; but it's relatively easy to make our own.

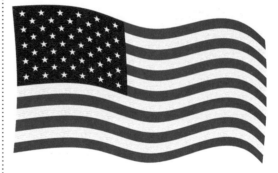

4 The Shear filter is applied once again, this time horizontally. This makes the left edge of the flag look as if it's being held by the top and bottom on a flagpole; it also prevents the edge of the star panel from looking too rectilinear.

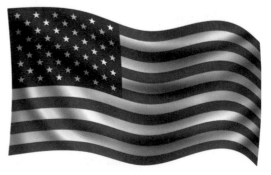

7 Now we can add the intricate creases and folds to the flag, following the Dodge and Burn technique described earlier in this chapter. Because we lowered the brightness in step 6, the Dodge tool still has its effect: if we hadn't done so, it would have made no difference to the white stripes.

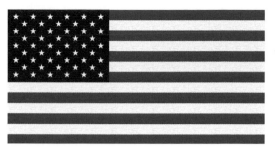

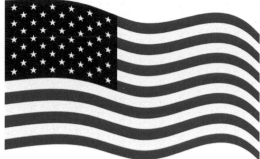

2 As a first step, we'll apply some texture to the flag using the Texturizer filter. On the previous page we used the Canvas effect; here, though, we'll use the looser weave of Burlap instead, set to a small size and applied at a fairly low opacity.

3 The flag is rotated 90° and waved using the Shear filter. It's also distorted using Free Transform to make the right edge smaller than the left, giving it a better sense of perspective. If you have Photoshop CS2, you can do this and the following step in one go with Image Warp.

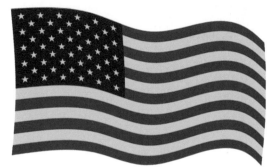

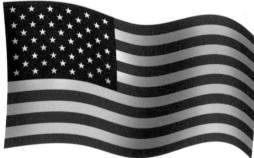

5 Because there's so much white in the flag, we need to reduce the overall brightness or our shading won't show up properly. Use the Curves or Levels dialogs to bring the highlights down slightly.

6 Basic shading is added in the same way as on our Euro banknote earlier in this chapter. This simply accentuates the gross waves of the flag, showing us which parts are rippling towards us and which are rippling away.

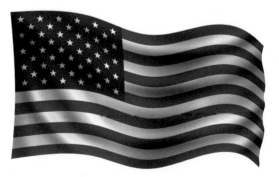

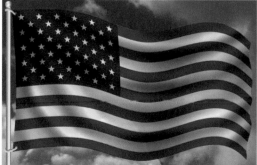

8 While the left edge of the flag looks convincing, the right edge appears too straight and uniform. This end isn't being held by anything, as the left was, and needs to flutter more. This is achieved simply by drawing a wavy path with the Pen tool, and hiding the edge with a layer mask.

9 When positioned on a pole and placed on a suitable background, the flag will still tend to look a little artificial. This is because flags are not solid objects: to blend it into the background, reduce the opacity of the layer slightly. Here, an opacity of 85% merges it in well.

HOT TIP

If you open an EPS illustration of a flag as a new Photoshop document, it will default to opening as a CMYK file. You may not notice anything wrong until you start to add texture, when you'll find that the Texturizer filter (along with several others) is dimmed out. Change the mode to RGB, or import it as an RGB file in the first place, to make these filters usable.

SHORTCUTS

Making custom fibers

T HE ONLY WHOLLY NEW FILTER to be introduced in Photoshop CS was Fibers, which creates natural-looking textures. Here are some ideas on how to make the most of this new feature, using different settings to generate a range of results for a variety of purposes.

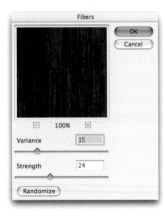

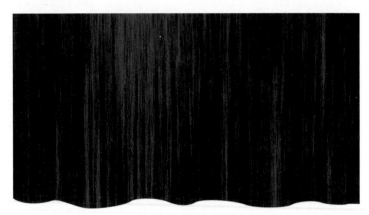

1 Starting with the basic black outline, above, we can use the Fibers filter to turn it into a reasonably convincing curtain. Set the foreground and background colors to red and black, and use a low Variance setting combined with a medium Strength setting.

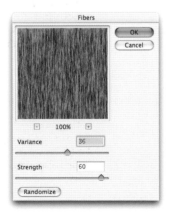

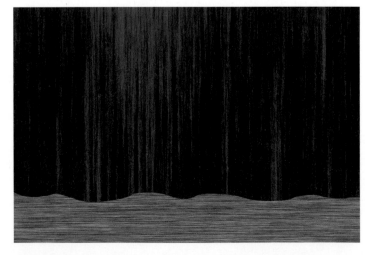

2 Now for the floor. To simulate a woodgrain effect, we begin by selecting dark and light browns as our foreground and background colors. To make the grain strong, we now want a high Strength setting to increase the contrast, with a medium setting for the Variance.

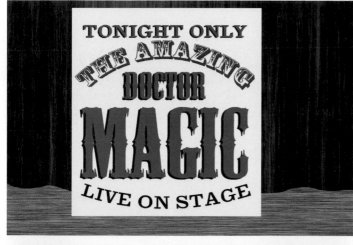

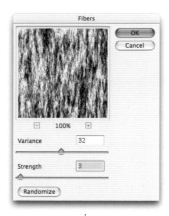

3 Now for the sign. This board is a flat, featureless object that looks entirely artificial. Using default black and white as our foreground and background colors, we combine a medium Variance with a very low Strength setting to get a lumpy effect.

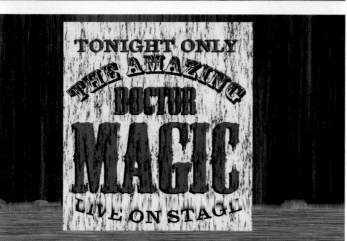

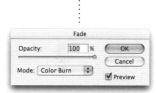

4 Applying the filter to the sign board made the whole thing disappear beneath the strong texture. So before doing anything else, immediately press ⌘ Shift F ctrl Shift F to bring up the Fade dialog: here, we can change the mode of the filter to Color Burn for a distressed effect.

5 All we need to do to complete the picture is to set the board in perspective and add an edge to it (see the technique in Chapter 10) and place shadows both behind the board and beneath the curtain.

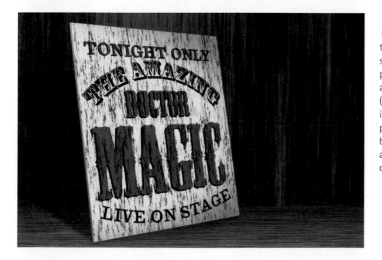

HOT TIP

The Fade command allows us to apply Fibers in a variety of ways. Experiment with the different modes, as well as the Opacity slider, to see how to change the way in which the Fibers filter acts upon the underlying layer.

SHORTCUTS

MAC WIN BOTH

305

Ribbon and tape

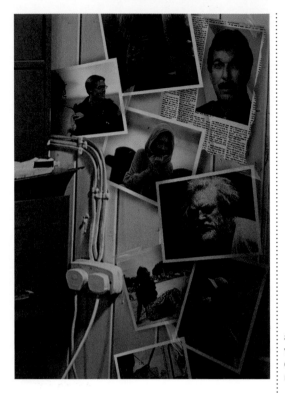

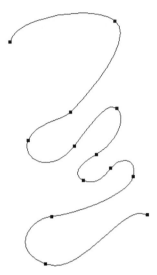 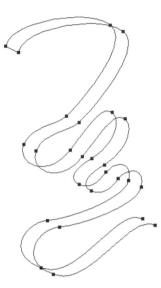

1 Begin by drawing a path using the Pen tool. Keep the curves smooth, avoiding tight turns and corners. When you've finished, save the path and duplicate it before continuing – we'll need this half of it later.

2 Now make a second path by selecting the original, and holding ⌥ *alt* as you offset it. Join the two starting points to make the two paths into one (holding ⌥ *alt* again, this time to force a corner at the join).

THE ILLUSTRATION ABOVE is part of a much larger montage for .net magazine about online stalkers. Dozens of photographs had to be fixed to the wall; shading on each one helped it look like it sat in place. The tape across the corner of some of the photos helped fix them to the wall in the reader's eye.

Ribbons can be used for a variety of purposes – from festooning partygoers to wrapping birthday presents. They're easier to draw than you might think; the trick is all in duplicating the Pen path.

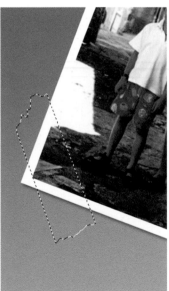 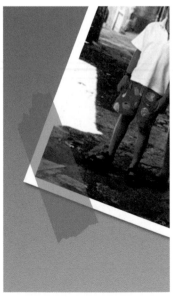

1 We're going to fix this photograph to the wall using sticky tape. Begin by tracing the outline with the Lasso tool, holding ⌥ *alt* to draw the straight lines between the sides. Keep these sides parallel!

2 We don't need to make this tape solid, since it's made of translucent plastic. Let's fill the selected area with 50% gray. (It would also be possible to fill with solid gray, then reduce the layer opacity.)

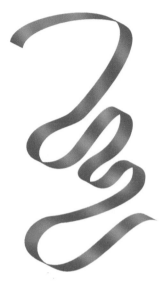

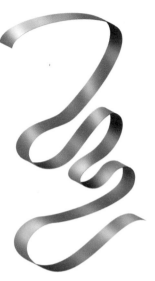

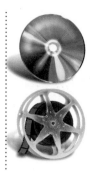

3 Turn the path into a selection by pressing ⌘ Enter ctrl Enter. The ribbon will have some bumps where the paths crossed; these need filling by just painting across them. Dodge and Burn add some basic random shading.

4 We now need to add shading in the hollows. Activate the original path and turn it into a selection: nudge the selection down, and you'll find that the areas beneath the folds are selected ready for Dodge and Burn.

5 All that's needed now is a bit of color. The Hue/Saturation dialog, set to Colorize, is one of the best ways to add dense color to a gray image.

HOT TIP

When the ribbon path was offset in step 4 of the first workthrough, I didn't align it precisely with the right edge of the ribbon. By offsetting it by just a pixel or two, it was possible to use the shading to give the ribbon a slight thickness simply by leaving the edge unshaded.

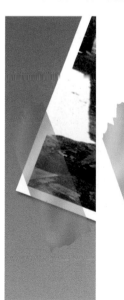

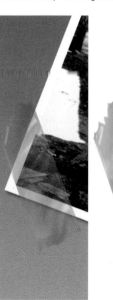

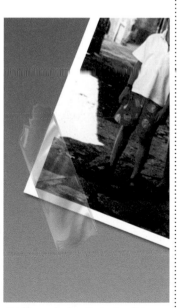

3 Now add a little random shading, once again using Dodge and Burn. This is only a preliminary stage before we apply the Plastic Wrap filter. I've shown the tape isolated as well, for extra clarity.

4 The Plastic Wrap filter makes that shading look convincingly like reflective plastic. This useful filter is covered in more depth in Chapter 9, Shiny surfaces. Change the layer mode to Hard Light to make it transparent.

5 Now color is added using Color Balance, which I find useful for subtle color effects; a lot of yellow and a little red does the trick. Brightness and contrast are increased slightly to make the tape shinier.

SHORTCUTS
MAC WIN BOTH

Upgrade and replace

THE FIRST COMPUTER I ever bought was a Sinclair Spectrum, which I purchased in 1980. It was a state-of-the-art machine, and I remember debating whether to choose the 16K version or opt for the massive 48K model. After much soul searching, I chose the 48K version: after all, I reasoned, this one was future-proof. Today, that computing power would barely run a singing greetings card.

The classified ads columns of newspapers and computer magazines are littered with advertisements from readers who have decided it's time to upgrade their equipment, and want to recoup the cost of their original purchase. Frequently, the prices demanded are well in excess of the aged computer's true value: often, readers will ask for more than it would cost to buy a new machine that offers twice as much power.

Their reasoning runs as follows: I bought this computer three years ago, and now it's obsolete thanks to the software developers, in league with the Devil and Bill Gates, who have upped the requirements for their new versions so much that they won't run on my old machine. And I'm damned if I'm going to shell out that much money simply to run Photoshop CS3, so I want my money back before I commit myself to buying a new computer.

It's a fallacious argument, for several reasons. The first is that there's nothing wrong with their old computer. It will still run the software they used on it when they bought it, it will still access the internet at the same speed and it will still enable them to do their job in the same way as they have for the last three years. If they want to take advantage of the tempting features the latest software versions have to offer, then they'll need compatible hardware; otherwise, they can just stick with the software they already have.

You can't blame software for needing a higher specified operating platform each time it brings new functionality: if this wasn't the case, we'd still be editing images one black and white pixel at a time on our Spectrums. The demands made by Photoshop are colossal in terms of processing power, disk access and chip speed; only the most diehard Luddite would advocate the withdrawal of new features simply in order to ensure compatibility with antique equipment.

But the main problem I have with those who complain about the cost of upgrading is that they rarely take into account how much work their computer has done for them in the intervening period. My Mac enables me to do all my illustration work, as well as letting me do my accounts, watch DVDs and play Call of Duty, for a relatively tiny cost compared with the revenue I generate from it. At the end of its three-year lifespan I reckon it now owes me nothing; the only hesitation I have in deciding when to upgrade is the knowledge that it will take a week for me to transfer all my applications and get the new machine running as smoothly as the old one. In return, I'll get a computer that's more than twice as fast, with a hard disk vast enough to hold the sum total of human knowledge in the 21st Century.

Many computer users resent the fact that not just computers but memory and hard disks now cost just a fraction of what they paid for them several years earlier. They feel cheated in retrospect: if only they'd held on another couple of years they'd have been able to buy more power for less cost. What they ignore is the amount of work their equipment has done for them in the intervening period, which can usually be valued at far more than the few hundred extra they may have spent on it.

I now consider the ownership of my computer to be more like a rental than an outright purchase. I need to top up my payments every few years, in return for which I get a pristine new piece of technology that has none of the grouchiness my old computer acquired over the years, and offers blistering speed in return. And I even have the opportunity to pass my old machine on to an aged relative or impecunious acquaintance – or, failing that, to convert it into a state-of-the-art fishtank. And I only resent the cost of the new one for a week or two.

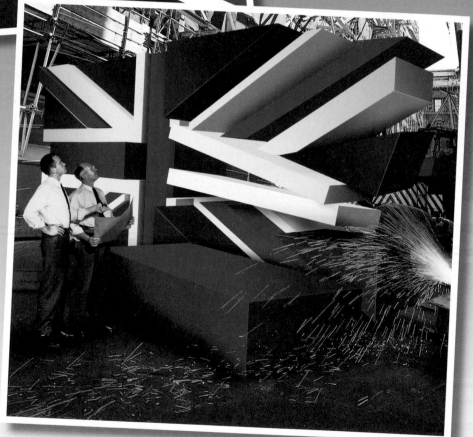

A simple flat image of a flag can become a dynamic, vibrant image full of life and movement when it's given that important third dimension. Whether you're using third-party applications to achieve the effect, or creating 3D images from scratch directly in Photoshop, you can't ignore the power of that additional element of depth.

12 The third dimension

Talk to many Photoshop artists about 3D and they'll start screaming. That's because the intricacies of conventional 3D modeling programs are so unforgivingly awkward that the mysteries of Nurbs and B-splines are better suited to engineers than artists.

But who said anything about convention? There's a lot that can be achieved directly in Photoshop, without recourse to any other applications. Simulating 3D needn't be a nightmare.

There are times, however, when Photoshop alone just isn't enough. Dimensions, that cranky old application ignored by Adobe for so long, can be just the job for creating quick and dirty 3D models: and Illustrator CS brings at least part of the process up to date.

Adding depth to flat artwork

ONE OF THE MOST common tasks the photomontage artist has to contend with is changing the viewpoint of an original photograph. Sometimes you can get away with simply rotating an object to make it fit in the scene; usually, it's a little more complicated.

The problem comes when an object has been photographed head-on, and you want to view it from an angle. Not all objects lend themselves to the kind of three-dimensional amendments shown here, but the principle used on these pages can be applied to a wide variety of source images.

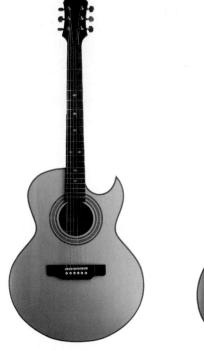

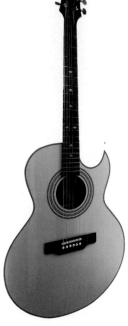

1 This guitar has been photographed directly from the front, in common with many objects sourced from stock photography collections. In real life, you'd hardly ever see an object in this position: and placing it in a montage will always look flat and unconvincing.

2 The simplest way to change its perspective is to use Free Transform, holding ⌘ ⌥ Shift ctrl alt Shift while dragging one of the corner handles to get a perspective distortion. The problem is immediately clear: there's no side to this guitar.

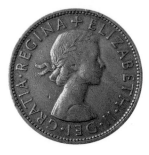

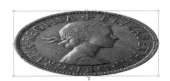

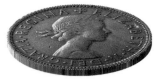

1 This old coin has been photographed directly from above; with close-up photography, an angled view would have made it difficult to keep the entire coin in focus. But we can create any view of this object we like with just a few actions.

2 The first step is to use Free Transform to squeeze the coin vertically: if you hold ⌥ alt then it will squeeze towards its centre. You may wish to add perspective distortion as well, but it isn't really necessary.

3 Then select the coin by holding ⌘ ctrl and clicking on its thumbnail in the Layers palette. Using the Move tool, hold ⌥ alt as you nudge this selection up one pixel at a time using the Arrow keys, and you'll create this milled edge as you go.

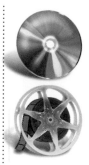

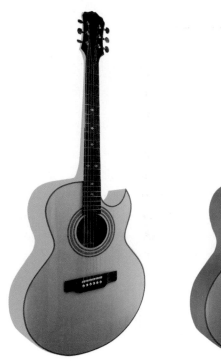

3 The side is best drawn with the Pen tool on a new layer, although you could also use the outline of the guitar as a starting point to get the curves correct. Here, the shape has simply been filled with a flat color to see if the perspective works.

4 A section of the guitar front is copied, duplicated and then flipped vertically to make a seamless tile. This is then used to fill the new side by clipping it with the side layer and repeating the pattern until it fills the space.

5 The key to realism lies, as ever, in the shading. The Burn tool has been set to Midtones to add the shadows – setting it to Highlights would have a more extreme effect, but would lose the warmth of the wood. Start slowly, and build up the shading.

HOT TIP

Boxy objects such as computer CPUs are easy to transform, even if photographed head–on. Simply copy a plain portion of the front of the unit, and distort it to form the side and top (if required). Adding appropriate shading means you can get away with a lot with little effort.

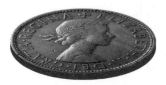

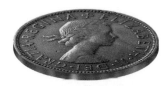

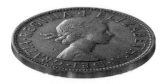

4 That milled edge is perhaps a little too strong. To fix it, use Shift ⌘ I Shift ctrl I to invert the selection and make a new layer from the edge. Preserve transparency with ⧄ and fill with a color picked from the coin itself.

5 Now use the Dodge and Burn tools to add highlight and shadow to this new edge, using thin vertical strokes to create the illusion of light reflecting off the edge.

6 Since this was created on a new layer, we can simply lower its opacity to allow the 'original' milled edge to show through underneath.

SHORTCUTS

An open and shut case

A TRICK THAT EVERY PHOTOMONTAGE ARTIST NEEDS TO learn is how to make photographed objects do what he or she wants them to do – which means ignoring the perspective of the original image and adapting it to suit the needs of the job in hand.

The ability to open a closed door is a technique that every Photoshop professional should be able to achieve. Opening the drawer of the filing cabinet in our second example takes a keener eye, since it's important to match the rather distorted view present in the original photograph. But in Photoshop, if it looks right then it is right: you just have to trust your eye.

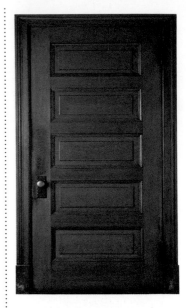

1 This door has been photographed closed, but opening it is simple. To begin, use the rectangular selection tool **M** to draw a rectangle that includes just the door itself, and not the frame. Cut this to a new layer using *Shift* ⌘ *J* *Shift* *ctrl* *J*.

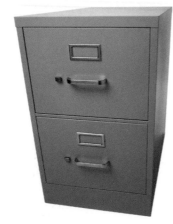

1 The technique used to open the bottom drawer of this filing cabinet can equally well be applied to a wide range of tasks. Unlike the door, above, the drawer front doesn't hinge, so we can't use the perspective distortion in the same way.

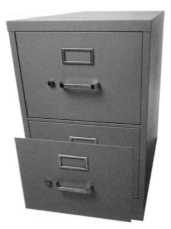

2 Select the drawer front, and make it into new layer using ⌘ *J* *ctrl* *J*. It needs enlarging slightly, since it will be nearer to us; and a small amount of perspective distortion is required to match the extreme angle of the original.

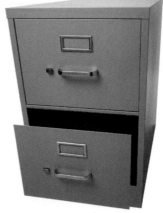

3 Now reload the original selection by selecting the path and pressing *Enter* (the advantage of having created a Pen path) and make a new layer for the inside of the cabinet. Fill it with a dark gray, and add shading using the Burn tool to give the sense of depth.

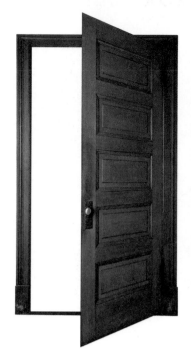

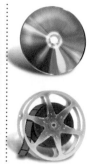

2 Now use Free Transform ⌘ T ctrl T to distort the door to its new position. If you hold ⌘ ⌥ Shift ctrl alt Shift while dragging a corner handle you'll get a true perspective distortion; use the center handles to make the door narrower.

3 The thickness of the door is easy to make: draw a rectangular selection that includes part of the front edge of the door (but not the handle), make a new layer from it and flip it horizontally. Drag it into place, and then just darken it up.

4 The doorknob didn't take well to its perspective distortion, but it's easy to make an elliptical selection of the knob and distort it back to its correct shape. Since the door is a separate layer, darkening the interior on the layer below is child's play.

HOT TIP

When you use perspective distortion to open a door, you'll also need to reduce the width of the door to match: the more open it is (and the stronger the distortion), the narrower it will have to be. There's no solid rule for how to do this – just make sure it looks right.

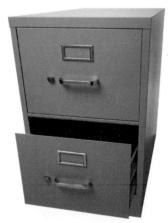

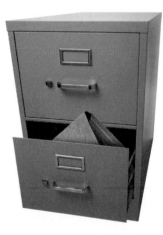

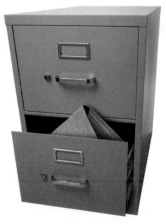

4 The drawer side is drawn on a new layer placed behind the drawer front by simply outlining it with the Lasso and filling with a mid gray. The three ribs are then drawn by selecting with the Lasso, and the areas between darkened with the Burn tool.

5 Once an object is placed in the drawer, the whole scene begins to make more sense. You need to choose objects to fill the cabinet that have a similar perspective to them; filling it with objects photographed head-on will look unconvincing.

6 The final stage is to add the shading – behind the folder in the drawer, and beneath the drawer itself. Make a new layer, grouped with the base cabinet layer, and paint on this using a soft-edged brush with black paint set to around 40%.

SHORTCUTS
MAC WIN BOTH

Opening the hamper

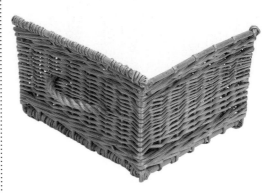

W HEN SEARCHING FOR IMAGES, very often we'll come across a photograph that almost meets our needs. Many such pictures can be adapted to suit our purpose without much effort.

This image of a closed hamper is a good example. We want a picture of an open hamper – but this is the closest we could find. Rather than continuing to look for the perfect shot, we can make good use of the resources available. This image includes all the elements we need to open the lid; all we have to do is to rearrange the constituent parts.

1 Begin by making a layer mask to hide the hamper lid. It's worth paying a little attention to the way the rolls of bamboo appear on the upper edges: the best solution is to hide the top edge with a straight line, then paint it back in lump by lump with a hard-edged brush.

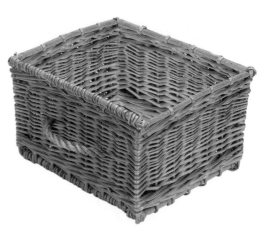

4 We can repeat the process for the remaining side of the hamper. To make the inner corner more convincing, I've used the Smudge tool here to pull out individual strands of bamboo and knit them into the corner post. It only takes a few seconds, and it's worth the effort.

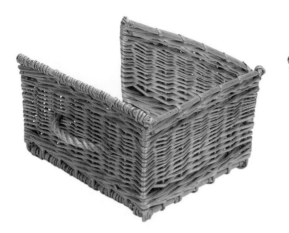

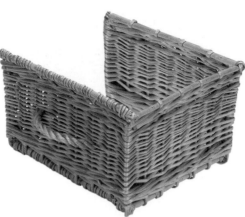

2 The front side has a handle on it, which we could remove with the Clone tool: but it's easier to use the handle-free right side. Duplicate the side to a new layer, move it behind the composition, and distort using Free Transform so it fits into the space.

3 The bamboo on the upper edge of this side is pointing in the wrong direction. We could have flipped the whole side horizontally, but this would have meant losing the tidy left edge, which will make a good join. Instead, we can take a copy of the original top bar, and flip and rotate it to fit.

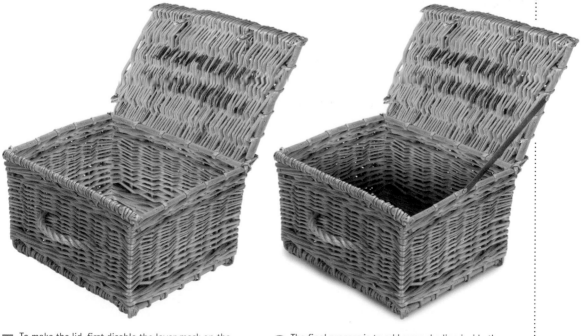

5 To make the lid, first disable the layer mask on the original hamper (Hold *Shift* as you click on the layer thumbnail) and select the lid. Use ⌘ *J* *ctrl* *J* to make a new layer from this lid, then enable the layer mask again. The lid is distorted into its new position with Free Transform.

6 The final process is to add some shading inside the hamper. ⌘ *ctrl* click on one interior side's thumbnail to load its pixels, then ⌘ *Shift* *ctrl* *Shift* click on the other to add it to the selection. When you now paint the shadow, the holes will be retained. Don't forget to add a strap!

Matching existing perspective

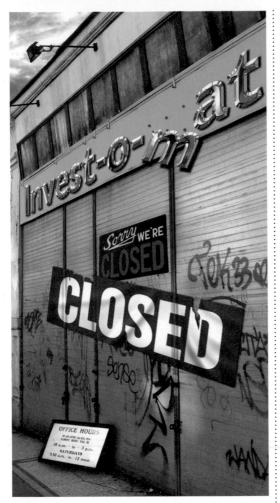

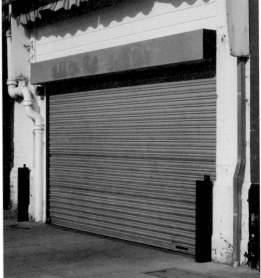

1 This shuttered shopfront is an ideal surface on which to place our sign. Not only does it have strong perspective lines, which will allow us to place the text accurately, it also includes a good bumpy texture that will make the finished result more convincing.

I N THIS ILLUSTRATION for the Sunday Telegraph, I aligned some of the elements with the perspective of the shutters. But the large Closed sign was placed at a deliberately skewed angle, to make it look as if it had been pasted on in a hurry. The sign still had to appear in perspective, but this was achieved by eye using Free Transform. (See Folds and wrinkles in Chapter 11 for tips on shading the paper sign.)

In this workthrough, we'll look at how to make a shop sign that looks like it was photographed with the original shop.

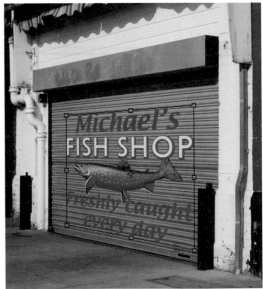

4 Select Free Transform (or press ⌘ T *ctrl* T). Hold ⌘ *ctrl* and grab a corner, then hold *Shift* as well after beginning to drag to constrain the movement to vertical. Align the top and bottom so that they line up with the ribs on the shutter.

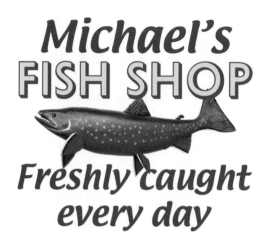

2 The sign consists of four elements: the three sets of words, and the fish. Although it would have been possible to create all the text in a single block, you get far more control over size and spacing when they're kept as separate chunks of text.

3 Select all the sign elements, and choose New Group from the pop-out menu on the Layers palette. Duplicate that set by dragging it onto the folder icon at the bottom (or choosing Duplicate from the pop-out menu), and then merge the new group so it becomes one layer.

Not all surfaces have as obligingly clear perspective lines as this one. To work on an image without these structures, it can help to place a simple grid over the surface first, and then use that to help align the text and other elements.

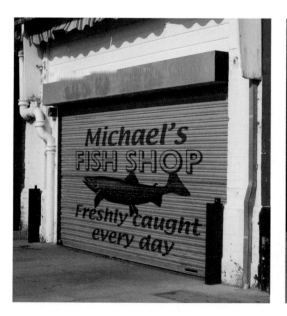

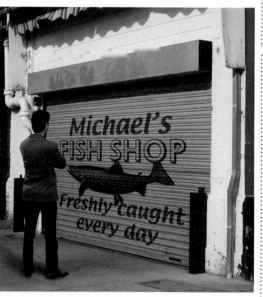

5 The previous step got the sign into perspective, but it didn't look as if it was part of the image. Changing the layer mode to Multiply (use the menu at the top of the Layers palette) allows the original texture to show through, which looks far more convincing.

6 Placing the figure in front of the sign achieves two things: first, it adds a human element to the image; and second, by obscuring a tiny part of the sign it makes the sign look far more integrated into the final image.

SHORTCUTS
MAC WIN BOTH

Building boxes

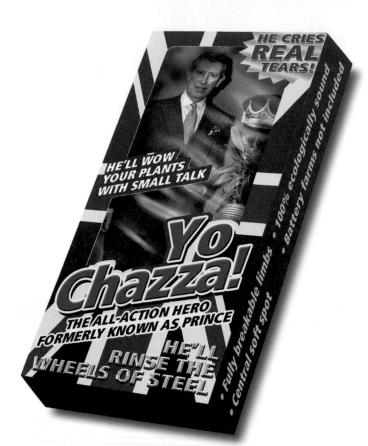

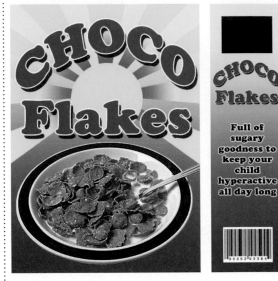

1 When preparing your flat artwork, remember that in most cases you'll be seeing the side of the box as well as the front, so you'll need to draw that as well. Keep a consistent color scheme on the side, and reuse some of the original artwork such as the Choco Flakes logo.

DRAWING BOXES IS EASY – it's simply a matter of distorting flat artwork using Free Transform, and adding a few finishing touches. The illustration above, for ES Magazine, was made slightly more complex by the fact that the box had a window in it, which meant drawing the polythene (see Chapter 9, Shiny surfaces) and giving the inside of the lid a little thickness (using the techniques described earlier in this chapter). But the principles are exactly the same as with the breakfast cereal box used to demonstrate the process on these pages.

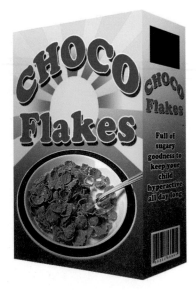

4 Darken the side of the box to make it stand out from the front. Then add some shading to the entire artwork using the Burn tool: a small amount of shadow helps it to look more like a real object and less like distorted flat artwork.

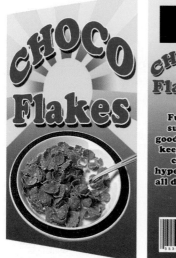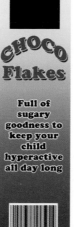

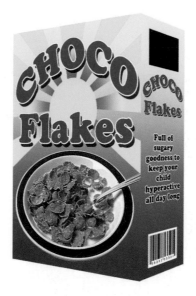

2 Create a merged copy so that you've got all the elements in one layer – that is, one for the front and one for the side. Then simply distort the front using Free Transform, holding ⌘ Shift ⌥ ctrl Shift alt and dragging a corner handle to make the perspective.

3 Now simply repeat the process for the side layer. If you only distorted the front of the box on the left-hand side, the side layer will still be the correct height and can be distorted in the opposite direction to make the box look three-dimensional.

HOT TIP

You can't keep text editable when applying perspective distortion – it needs to be rasterized first. So make sure you (and your client) are happy with the base artwork before turning it into a 3D object, or you'll have to repeat the process all over again after they've made the changes.

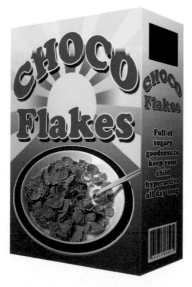

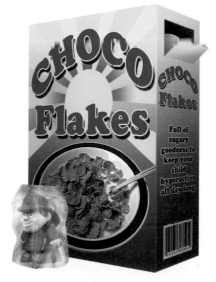

5 Since this box is made of cardboard, you won't get a perfectly sharp edge where it bends around the corner. Here, I've selected a couple of pixels down the left-hand edge of the side and brightened that strip up to give the impression of the cardboard bending.

6 What makes an illustration like this work are the elements that break out of the planes, such as the spout on the right. And where would any self-respecting cereal be without a plastic toy? The wrap for this was created using Plastic Wrap – see Chapter 9 for how to do this.

SHORTCUTS

Displacement maps 1

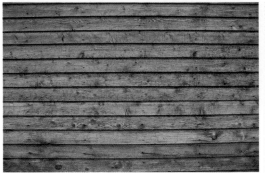

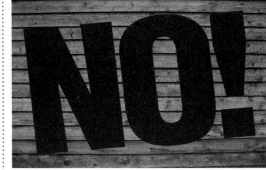

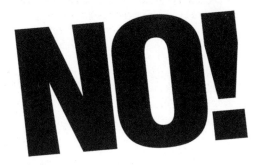

WHEN A DESIGN APPEARS on a three-dimensional surface, it needs to take on the shape and form of that surface. The most effective way to do this is by using a Displacement Map.

The approach is similar to that used for creating texture channels for the Lighting Effects filter, as seen in the Metal, wood and stone chapter. But rather than making the maps from scratch, we're going to simulate the bumpy effect of natural surfaces by using those surfaces themselves. Like texture channels, Displacement Maps use light and dark information in the image to distort the picture. By overlaying an image distorted with a Displacement Map with the source image from that map, we can create a convincing three-dimensional effect. Let's see what happens when we combine the two images above.

1 Simply placing one layer above the other does nothing to convince the viewer of the validity of the scene. There's no interaction between the two layers, and no sense that the lettering and the fence are co-existing in the same space.

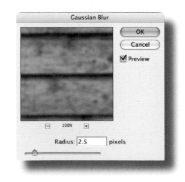

4 Select the text layer, and choose Displace from the Distort section of the Filter menu. You'll be asked for a scale: try 50 for both horizontal and vertical initially. When you press OK, you're asked for a Displacement Map: choose the one we saved in the previous step.

7 Open the Displacement Map file once more, and try some Gaussian Blur to smooth out the hard edges in the fence. The aim is to get rid of minor variations in the texture of the wood, without losing those knots and strong horizontal lines that define it.

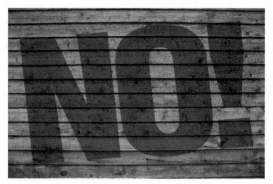

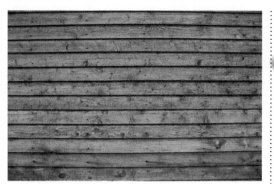

2 One way of making the text look like it's been painted onto the fence is to set the layer mode to Hard Light, and to reduce the opacity to, say, 70%. But it's far too neat a result: we can see the fence through the text, yet we don't get the impression it's really part of it.

3 Let's make a Displacement Map from the fence. First, duplicate the fence layer, and desaturate it using ctrl Shift U ⌘ Shift U. Now copy this layer to a new grayscale document, and save it as a PSD file – this is the format Photoshop will need in the next step.

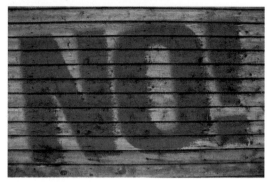

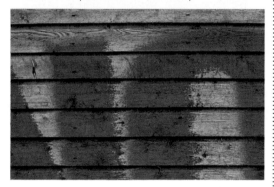

5 Now, the layer is distorted by that Displacement Map. Light areas distort the image up and to the right: dark areas move it down and to the left. With the layer still set to Hard Light at 70% opacity, the texture of the wood shows through the text.

6 The trouble is that the light and shade values have been taken too literally. Every slight nuance of shading is reproduced perfectly: the result is rather too ragged to be truly convincing. Undo the filter step, and we'll try again with a few changes.

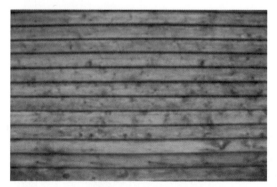

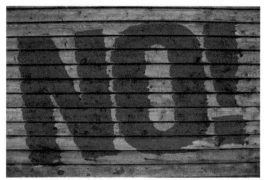

8 The amount of blur you apply depends on the image in question. Here, we've used just enough to soften the wood effect. Now save this Displacement Map, with a different name in case you want to return to the original, and run the Displace filter once again.

9 This time, the results are far more convincing. That raggedness around the edge of the lettering has gone completely, leaving a much smoother paint job; but the gaps between the wood slats now cause the text to be distorted through them, as if the lettering were really painted there.

Displacement maps 2

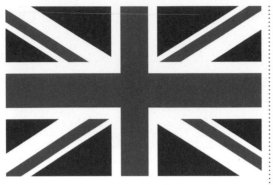

DISPLACEMENT MAPS can be used for placing many kinds of design onto many different surfaces. Here, we're going to apply the technique to a Union Jack flag, to produce two very different effects.

The map by itself isn't enough: it's important to decide how much of the original texture layer is shown, and in what way it should interact with the design layer. In the previous example, we set the text layer to Hard Light mode to allow the texture to be seen through it. But here, as we'll see, this isn't always the best technique when multi-colored designs are involved.

Displacement Maps can create the illusion of rough stone or smooth silk, depending on the application – and, to a large extent, the success of the project depends on the amount of Gaussian Blur used on the Map itself.

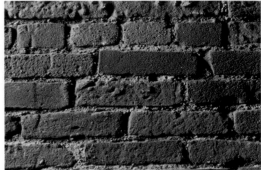

1 We'll start by mapping our flag onto this rough brick wall. The wall itself has a lot of texture in it, and will be the perfect base for accepting a design. We don't want the color of the wall to show through, though: it needs to be entirely painted over by the flag.

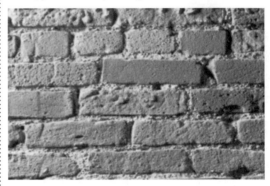

4 Duplicate the wall to a new document, as before, then apply Gaussian Blur once again and save it as a PSD document to be used as our Displacement Map. Once again, we need the blurring to prevent every tiny variation in shading causing fiddly distortions to the flag.

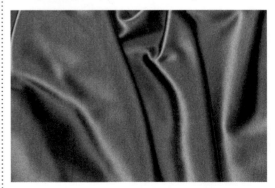

7 We're going to use exactly the same technique, but this time we'll map the flag using a photograph of some crumpled silk rather than the wall. Because this silk has a detailed texture, we need to blur it enough to hide that detail: it's only the folds that we want to retain.

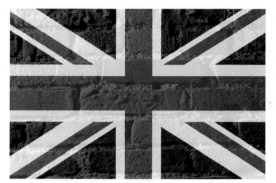

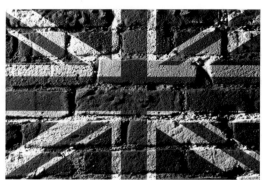

2 Let's begin by changing the mode of the flag layer to Hard Light. It's not nearly as convincing as the text layer on the previous page: and however much we experiment with the opacity settings, we're never going to get the showthrough to look as we want it.

3 Instead, duplicate the brick wall layer, and desaturate it using `ctrl` `Shift` `U` `⌘` `Shift` `U`. Now, when we move this layer above the flag and change its mode to Hard Light, we can see a huge improvement: even without distorting the flag, the wall texture has a tremendous effect.

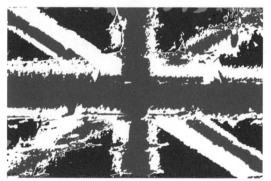

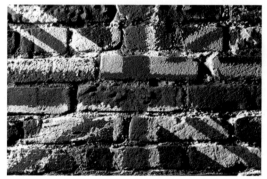

5 When we now use the Displace filter on the flag, it has a dramatic effect. Here, I've hidden the duplicated brick wall layer so we can see exactly what the filter has done to the flag. Although the distortions look random, they line up precisely with the wall.

6 Combining the displaced flag with the duplicated Hard Light brick wall layer produces this dramatic result. Look how the flag really does appear to have been painted on the wall, following the dripping mortar lines and disappearing into the cracks.

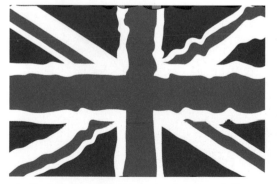

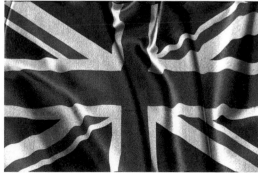

8 Here's the flag, as distorted using that piece of silk as a Displacement Map. Compared to the brick wall effect, above, the displacement is much more subtle: but this smooth distortion is exactly what we need to blend these two layers together.

9 And here's the result of combining that displaced flag with, once again, a copy of the silk layer set to Hard Light mode. The flag really appears to be wrinkling with the underlying folds in the silk for a thoroughly convincing fabric effect.

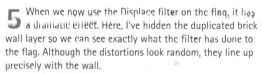

HOT TIP

You don't need to limit your Displacement Maps to existing photographs. Try creating maps based on concentric circles, for example, to create a rippling effect. But if you do draw your own maps, remember to apply at least a small amount of Gaussian Blur first: otherwise, as with Lighting Effects, the result will be harsh and unconvincing.

SHORTCUTS
MAC | WIN | BOTH

Wrapping labels without CS2

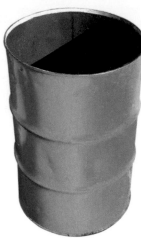

1 This view of an oil drum presents a tricky problem for label wrapping. First, it's a curved rather than a flat surface; and second, that surface has been photographed in perspective. So here's how it's done.

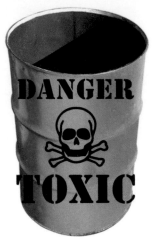

2 The label is created using suitable text and graphics. Although these were necessarily made on separate layers, it's important to merge them into one so that the distortions can be applied to everything together.

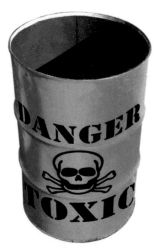

5 Now rotate the canvas back again, and use Free Transform to apply a simple perspective distortion to the label. Don't expect it to look perfect; a close fit will be enough at this stage. To avoid fiddling around, it's easier to apply final tweaking to the misfit characters afterwards.

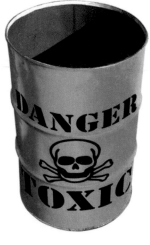

6 To make the lettering fit the perspective of the barrel, we need to select the troublesome letters (the beginnings and ends of each word) individually, and shear them vertically until they fit. A bitty font like Stencil is easiest to work with, as you can distort letter sections in chunks.

WRAPPING LABELS around curved surfaces was a tricky proposition before Photoshop CS2. The tutorial is included here for those readers who have yet to upgrade to the latest version of the program, and as a reminder of the dark days before Image Warp.

In the illustration above for The Independent, I had to break the text into several chunks and distort each one using the Wave filter in order to make it look as if it was wrapped around the plastic surface.

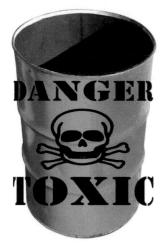

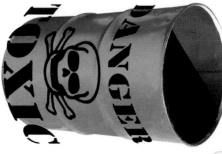

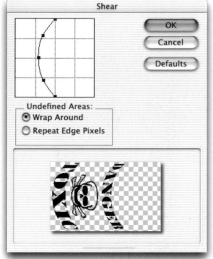

3 The first distortion is to Spherize the label, so it looks more as if it's wrapped around a cylinder. In the Spherize dialog, use Horizontal Only rather than the full Spherize, so that it's only distorted in the horizontal dimension.

4 Now to bend the label using the Shear filter. This filter will only distort horizontally, so we must first rotate the canvas 90°. The filter works by drawing points on the straight line, which can be dragged out into curves; the preview shows the distortion.

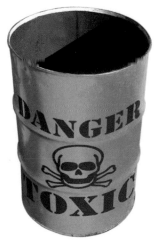

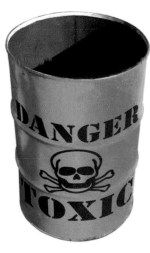

7 To retain the texture of the original, load up the area of the distorted label (⌘ ctrl click on the name in the Layers palette), hide it, switch to the base layer and float the selection using ⌘ J ctrl J. Now simply use Hue/Saturation to colorize the label.

8 The label still looks a little unconvincing, so to strengthen it up change the Layer mode from Normal to Multiply – this will accentuate the shadows, making the finished label look far more like it's sitting on the object in the real world.

HOT TIP

If you're working on a large document, rotating the whole thing 90° to apply the Shear filter will take an age. Instead, you can simply copy the base object to a new document, rotate that, and then copy the resulting distortion back into your original image.

SHORTCUTS

Drawing pipes and cables

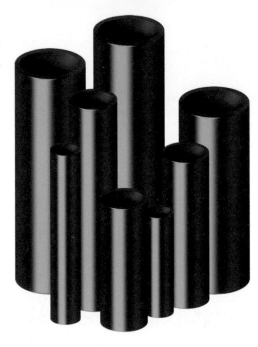

W HETHER IT'S MICROPHONE CABLES, sewage pipes or chrome cylinders, it's fairly easy to create any kind of tubular object directly in Photoshop.

Cables are drawn using the technique of applying a brush stroke to a Pen-drawn path: as long as the path is visible, any of the painting tools can be easily made to run a smooth stroke along it.

Pipes can be created at any length. Since the shading is applied evenly along the pipe by holding the Shift key as you paint with the Dodge and Burn tools, it's then easy to stretch them to any length you want simply by selecting half the pipe and dragging a copy where you want it to go.

Bending pipes around curves is another issue entirely, and the final step here shows a simple way to achieve this effect.

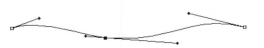

1 Drawing cables and wires is easier than you might think. Start by using the Pen tool to draw a Bézier curve that follows the line you wish the cable to take.

4 By nudging vertically and inversing the selection, only the feathered bottom half of the cable is selected. We can now use Brightness and Contrast to darken the edge.

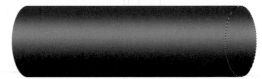

1 Begin your pipe by drawing a simple rectangle with the Marquee tool, and filling it with a mid-tone gray (you can always add color later).

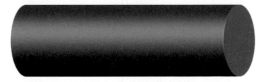

4 With the ⌥ *alt* key still held down, drag the ellipse to the other end: hold the *Shift* key after dragging to move it horizontally only.

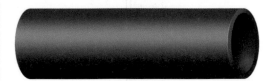

6 With the Marquee tool selected, nudge the selection a couple of pixels to the right and fill with the same mid gray. The bright rim looks better than a hard edge.

8 Draw a new selection with the Elliptical Marquee that's smaller than the original one, and add shading to make the inside of the pipe – darker at the top and on the left.

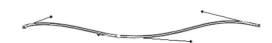

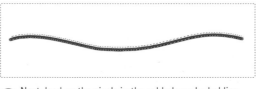

2 Now, with the Pen path still selected, switch to the Brush tool and choose a hard-edged brush of the right diameter – here, a 9-pixel brush was used. Now hit the *Return* key, and the path will be stroked with that brush.

3 Next, load up the pixels in the cable layer by holding ⌘ *ctrl* as you click on the layer's name. Feather the selection (a 3-pixel feather used here), and, with the Marquee tool selected, nudge the selection up 3 pixels.

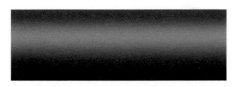

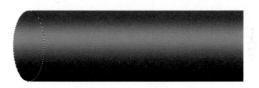

5 Now nudge the selection down twice as many pixels as you nudged it up (that makes 6, in this instance) and brighten up the top half in the same way.

6 After coloring the cable, it's time for the shadow. Modify your original path so that parts of the cable rise up from the floor, then stroke the path with a soft-edged brush.

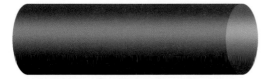

2 Using the Dodge and Burn tools set to Highlights, hold the *Shift* key to constrain the motion to horizontal, as you drag from end to end of the rectangle.

3 Now use the Elliptical Marquee tool to select an ellipse in the center of the pipe. Hold ⌥ *alt* to make a copy as you drag it to the left to form the end of the pipe.

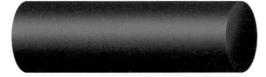

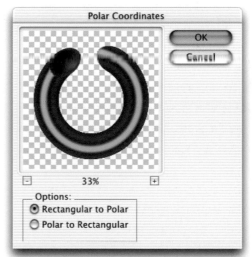

Polar Coordinates

OK

Cancel

33%

− +

Options:
- ⦿ Rectangular to Polar
- ○ Polar to Rectangular

5 Now brighten up the selected end of the pipe, using Brightness and Contrast or Curves. It's brighter than we need, but this will just form the rim around the edge.

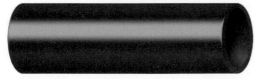

7 With the end cap still selected, add some more shading using the Burn tool. Bear the lighting position in mind: we want more shadow at the bottom right than at the top.

10 To bend the pipe into a curve, make a square selection around it and use the Polar Coordinates filter (Rectangular to Polar) to distort it. If the pipe is positioned at the top of the square selection, the result will be a very tight curve; if it's positioned in the center, you'll get a larger curve. Make sure the initial selection is square or the curve will be distorted. You can now take a section of this curved pipe to join two straight pieces together.

9 By applying a step effect using the Curves dialog, we can make this pipe look more metallic. See Chapter 10 for details on how to achieve this effect.

3D Transform filter: boxes

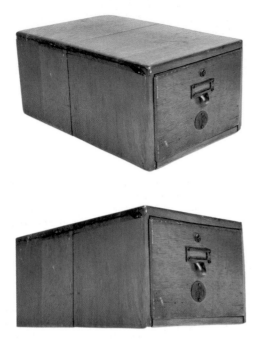

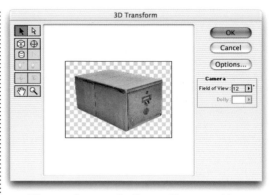

1 When you first open the filter, you'll see your object converted to grayscale. Make sure the object is in the middle of the document, or the perspective viewpoint will get horribly confused.

PHOTOSHOP'S 3D TRANSFORM FILTER, found under the Render section of the Filter menu, is a poweful tool for changing the perspective viewpoint of objects. It's also one of the hardest filters to get your head around.

The filter works best with boxy objects, such as this – er – box. But it can also be used to distort bottles, glasses and symmetrical objects of all shapes, as we'll see on the following pages.

In the dialog, images are shown in black and white, as they are here. The guidelines are shown in pale green, which I've changed to a thick red so they're easier to see in print.

The 3D Transform filter isn't loaded by default: you'll find it in the Extra Plug-ins section of the Photoshop CD. Drag it into your Photoshop Filters folder and relaunch Photoshop in order to use it.

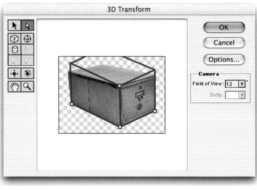

4 Now grab the remaining handle, the one right in the middle of the box, and move it into place. Nothing fits! And there are no more handles to drag! What can have gone wrong this time?

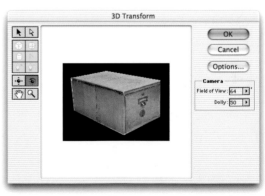

7 Drag on the Field of View slider once more until you can see the entire object in the preview window. At this point, it's worth clicking the Options button to raise the quality, and hide the background view.

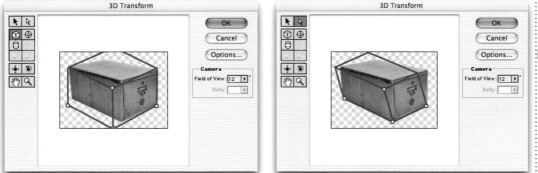

2 Pick the box tool and draw a box around the object, from corner to corner. It won't fit at all at this stage; we'll use the corner handles, shown as hollow squares, to adjust the fitting.

3 Switch to the hollow pointer tool and grab the bottom center handle and move it into place; then repeat the process with the bottom left handle, until all three lower handles correspond exactly with the corners of the object.

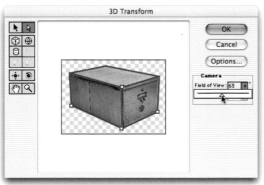

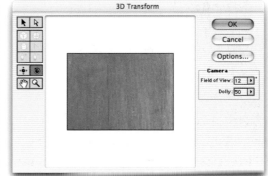

5 In fact, nothing has gone wrong – it's just that the perspective viewpoint is completely wrong. Drag the slider that pops out beneath the Field of View number and move it until the box fits the object.

6 Now click on the Rotate tool, which you'll find at the lower right. It's likely that you'll now see a view like this, showing a close-up of an irrelevant part of the object. We need to adjust that viewpoint again.

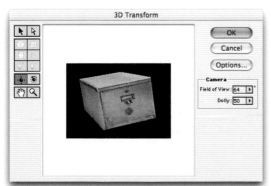

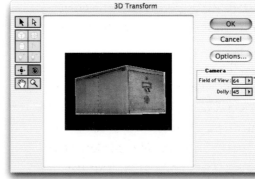

8 Now use the Rotate tool to drag the object to change its viewpoint. You can also use the Move tool, next to it, to move your object around within the preview window if your chosen rotation angle puts it outside the space.

9 You can even choose to view the object from an entirely different angle, as we've done here: in this case, the top face of the original object disappears from view as it's completely hidden from this viewpoint.

HOT TIP

This filter is one of the most fiddly you'll use in Photoshop, but more than any it pays to be precise. If your corners and sides don't match the original object exactly, you'll see bits of background distorted in the final render. One interesting feature of this filter is the way it creates unseen faces: if we'd turned the final example upwards, we'd see a plain gray base on the bottom of the object. It would be a simple matter to fill this with some of the original wood texture.

331

3D Transform filter: cylinders

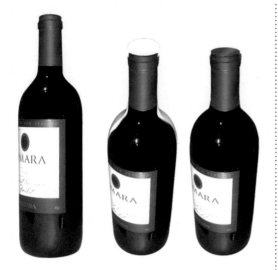

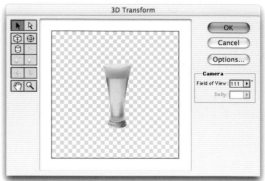

1 Objects opened in the 3D Transform filter can sometimes appear far too small. There seems to be no consistent reason for this; but as it stands, it's too small for us to see what's going on.

T HE 3D TRANSFORM FILTER, WHICH we looked at on the previous pages, is capable of applying different viewpoints to far more than mere boxes. But as the object in question becomes more complex, so the shortcomings in the filter become more apparent. The original bottle, above left, was distorted to produce the result shown center; but it didn't take a lot of retouching skill to patch it to produce the final result, right.

Irregular shapes take a little more thought than plain boxes, but the results can be impressive. It's worth pointing out that the restrictions of this filter mean it's really only suitable for use on symmetrical cylindrical objects, which have been photographed head on. Here, we'll look at how to change the viewpoint of a beer glass.

As on the previous spread, the original fine green outlines in the 3D Transform dialog have been replaced with a thicker red to make it easier to see on the page.

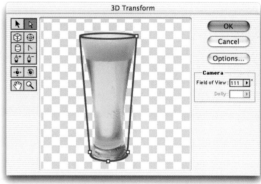

4 Grab the bottom handles and drag them so that they touch the base of the glass. The top corner handle shouldn't need adjusting if you drew the cylinder correctly in the previous step.

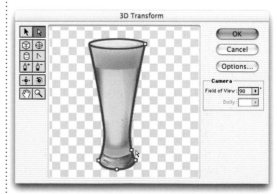

7 Next, change to the hollow Arrow tool and drag that new anchor point until it touches the side of the glass. With some objects, you may need to create several anchor points; the bottle, left, required three additional points.

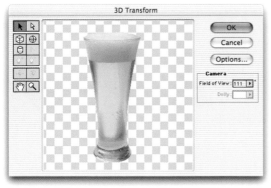

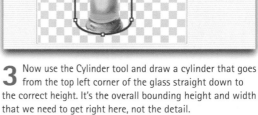

2 To see the glass bigger, you'll need to zoom in. In fact, you may have to zoom in and out quite a lot in this exercise, to make sure all the anchor points are placed correctly.

3 Now use the Cylinder tool and draw a cylinder that goes from the top left corner of the glass straight down to the correct height. It's the overall bounding height and width that we need to get right here, not the detail.

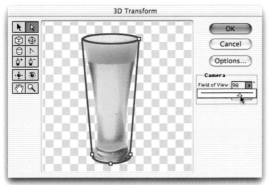

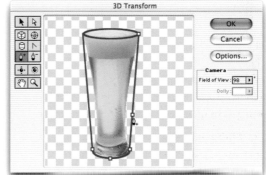

5 Now's a good time to adjust the perspective. As in the previous spread, drag the Field of View slider (it will pop up when you click the number) until the top ellipse matches the angle of the top of the glass. Nothing else will change.

6 Next, we need to make the outline fit the glass. Using the Pen tool, click to make an anchor point on the side of the cylinder. Don't drag as you click – the Pen tool doesn't work that way here.

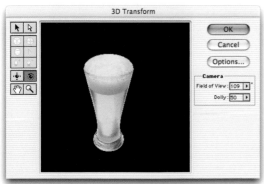

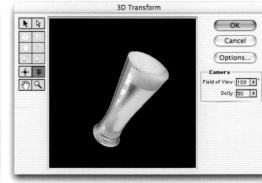

8 With the outline shape drawn to fit our object, we can click on the Rotate tool to enter this section of the dialog. As before, the glass can be rotated by dragging in the preview window.

9 One thing you can't do here is rotate in any direction other than directly forwards or backwards, or you'll be able to see a side of the glass that doesn't exist – and the tool isn't clever enough to wrap around the back.

12 The third dimension

3D Layers: the new approach

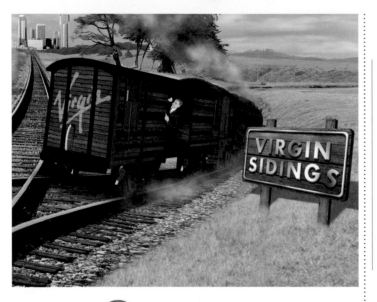

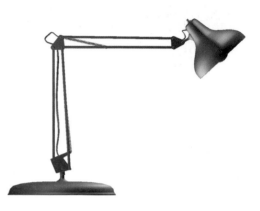

ONE OF THE MOST IMPRESSIVE features of Photoshop CS3 is the 3D Layers tool. This is available only in the Extended Edition, and doesn't appear in the standard version. We won't spend too much time on this technology, but it's worth a couple of spreads to show what it can do.

The 3D Layers feature allows you to import, rotate and scale 3D objects built in standard formats. It's not hard to find 3D models on the internet, and many of them are free.

The illustration above, for the Sunday Telegraph, uses two models - a train and a carriage – from the Taschen 500 3D Models collection, an excellent introductory set of 3D elements of all kinds.

Here, we'll use a desk lamp modeled for us by renowned 3D artist Simon Danaher. See more of his work at www.simondanaher.com.

1 This is our initial 3D model. Photoshop can currently import models in 3DS, OBJ and KMZ (Google Earth) formats; this OBJ model doesn't have textures mapped onto it, although other formats can.

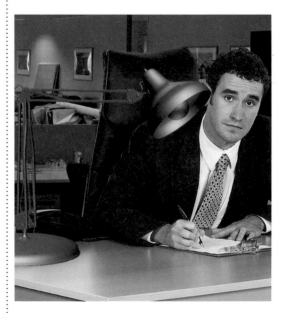

4 It can take a bit of fiddling to get the object into the right position for the scene. Note that if you want to make further adjustments, you'll need to enter 3D mode again: simply dragging the whole layer to the left will cut it off where it meets the edge of this frame.

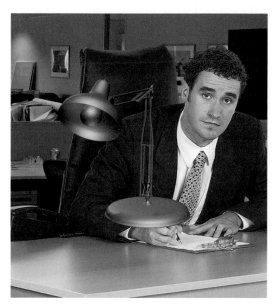

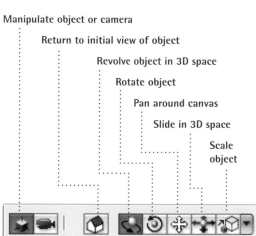

Manipulate object or camera

Return to initial view of object

Revolve object in 3D space

Rotate object

Pan around canvas

Slide in 3D space

Scale object

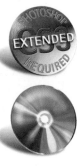

2 When we choose Layer>3D Layers>New Layer from 3D File, we can import the model into our scene. It appears, initially, in the middle of the screen. Although we can't alter the model directly - we're unable to change the angle of the shade, for instance - we can move it around in space.

3 When we double-click the 3D layer's thumbnail in the Layers palette, we enter 3D mode. Here, we can manipulate the object's position and scale, using straightforward tools. It's also possible to change the viewpoint numerically if you wish.

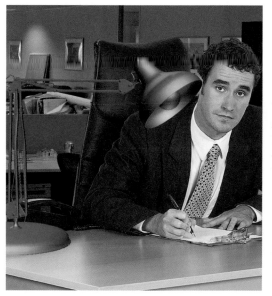

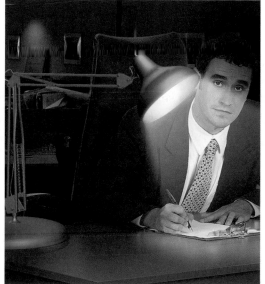

5 We can't paint on the 3D model, but we can add color to it by making a new layer, set to Color or Hard Light mode, and using the 3D object as a clipping mask. Of course, if you reposition the object, you'll have to paint the color on it once again.

6 When we add lighting to the scene, as described earlier in this book, the whole image comes to life. It would have been nearly impossible to find a photograph of a lamp from exactly the right angle; and photographing our own would have meant a tricky cutout. This is a perfect solution.

HOT TIP

3D models are available from a wide range of sources, both on CD and via the internet. The rendering engine in Photoshop is somewhat rudimentary, so you won't get beautifully lit renders directly within the application; some additional texturing and lighting is almost always required to achieve the best results.

3D Layers: using Sketchup

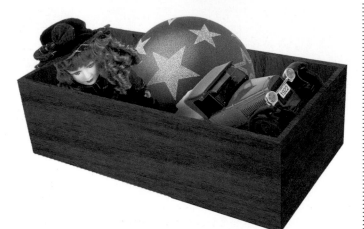

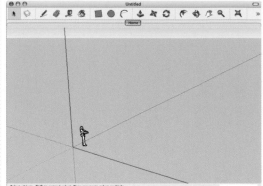

1 When you open a new document in Google Sketchup, you'll see this scene. It's meant for architectural modeling, hence the figure: click on it and delete it.

LTHOUGH 3D MODELS are widely available, you can't always find one that suits your requirements. If all you want to do is create a simple 3D scene, it can be just as easy to make your own model from scratch.

We can use the 3D Layers feature to make perspective drawing far simpler; in this example, we'll make an empty box. While it's possible to draw this box from scratch as a 2D object, it's a tricky task: manipulating a 3D object allows us to create exactly the viewpoint we want, with the minimum amount of fuss.

Most Photoshop artists don't have access to 3D modeling applications. Here, we'll look at how to make a basic box using Google Sketchup, which can be downloaded for free from the Google website.

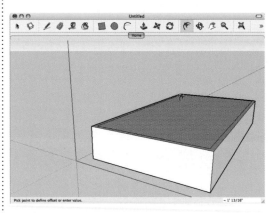

4 To make the inside of the box, click on the top face and then select the Offset tool. Drag a little way to duplicate the top face of the box.

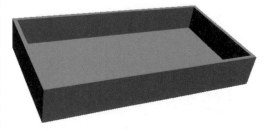

7 Back in Photoshop, choose Layer > 3D Layers > New 3D Layer from File and select the object we've just drawn. Double click this layer in the Layers Palette to enter 3D editing mode: we can now use the scale, rotate and revolve tools to manipulate the object in 3D space.

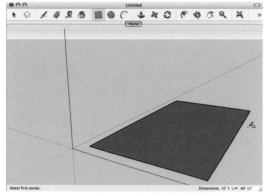

2 Select the Rectangle tool, and draw a rectangle to the shape of the box you want. Note how it's automatically drawn in perspective.

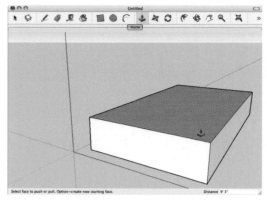

3 To add depth to the box, click on the Push/Pull tool, click on the top face and drag upwards: this extrudes the box as far as you drag.

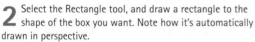

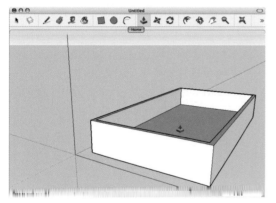

5 Use the Push/Pull tool once more to drag this top face downwards. This will hollow out the box: the sides are formed automatically as you drag.

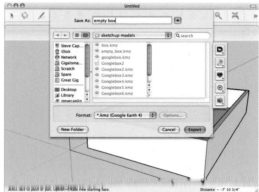

6 And that's all there is to it. All that remains is to export the 3D model as a Google Earth file, which can be read by Photoshop.

HOT TIP

Sketchup is far more powerful than we've shown here: check out the tutorials on the Google website for more information. It's hard to show how to use files to open and 3D Layers concisely in the space available on these pages: view the QuickTime movie on the DVD for a full explanation of how the technologies can be made to work together.

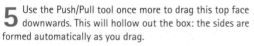

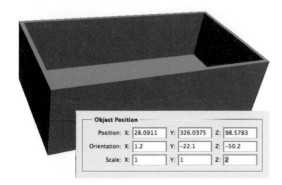

8 We can easily make this box deeper by clicking on the arrow next to the tool icons. Doubling the Z value makes the box twice as deep. We could change the X and Y values as well, so that this simple model can then form the basis for a variety of 3D boxes.

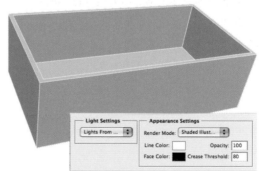

9 As it stands, it can be hard to select the box sides accurately: the top face is the same color as the base. By changing the Render Mode to Shaded Illustration we reveal the edges, making selection that much easier.

12

The third dimension

3D layers: cross sections

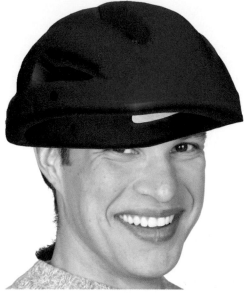

WHEN WORKING WITH 3D OBJECTS, we often want to place them around an object, rather than merely in front of it. That's the case here: we want this helmet to fit snugly on top of the head.

We could, of course, simply create a layer mask and paint out those areas where we want to see the head. But this would be a fiddle, especially when dealing with the cutout portions of the helmet.

Instead, we'll use an interesting feature of the 3D Layers function, which allows us to hide part of the 3D model selectively. This is done by specifying a flat plane through the model, with everything on one side of it hidden.

It sounds more technical than it really is. You don't need to type in any coordinates, as sliders allow you to fiddle with the settings while seeing exactly what's happening.

After the front half of the helmet is hidden, we'll duplicate it and restore it to its entirety in order for it to show up behind the head.

1 This cycle helmet has been rotated and sized to make it fit the head. We'll make it fit using the Cross Section dialog. Double click the 3D layer, then click the Cross Section icon.

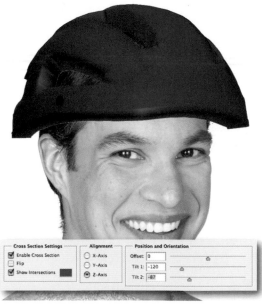

4 So far, so good: but we need to extend the visible portion of the helmet around the side more. To do this, move the Tilt 2 slider to the left, and the hidden portion will rotate around the side of the helmet. That's the front part of the helmet finished; now for the back.

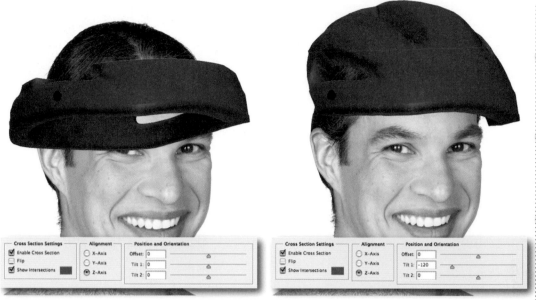

2 Check the Enable Cross Section box at the top right of the dialog, and right away the top half of the helmet will disappear. This is the default setting: the offset is half way through the object, and both tilts are set to zero.

3 We want only the front half of the helmet visible on this layer. Grab the slider for the first Tilt setting, and move it to the left so that the back side of the helmet, rather than the top, is hidden.

HOT TIP

Negotiating the two Tilt sliders in this dialog can sometimes be unpredictable. When moving the first slider, it may seem as if a setting of −75 gives us the best cutoff; but when we move the second slider, it's apparent that that won't make it fit. Change both sliders in combination to see what works best.

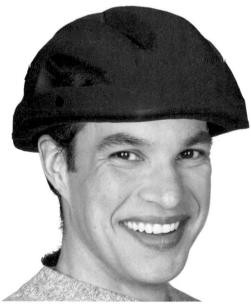

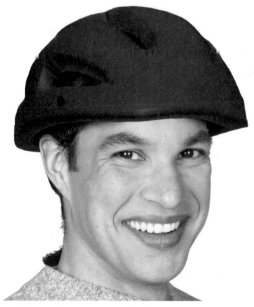

5 Creating the back is simple. Duplicate the helmet 3D layer, and move it behind the head layer. Now double click the layer's icon and open the Cross Section dialog again: all we have to do is to uncheck the Enable Cross Section box, and the full helmet will be restored.

6 There's often a little fringing where the two halves of the helmet meet each other. The simplest way of dealing with this is to create a Layer Mask for the top version (the front half of the helmet), and paint out the offending areas. Here, we've also added a slight shadow on top of the head.

Illustrator and Photoshop

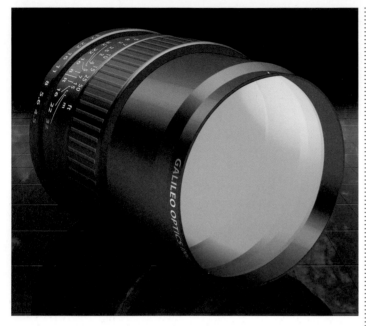

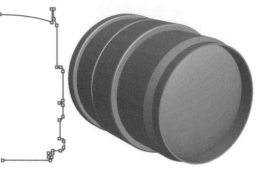

1 The basic outline of the lens was drawn in Illustrator, and then revolved using the 3D filter to create this perspective view. The final illustration was exported as an EPS file, and placed into Photoshop using the Open dialog.

OFTEN, THE MOST BASIC 3D MODEL can be used as the starting point for a realistic illustration. In this example, we've turned a simple outline of a lens into a solid object using the 3D Revolve feature found in Adobe Illustrator (version CS and higher). To achieve a measure of accuracy, I Googled a photograph of a lens taken head-on, and traced around one side to create the profile.

The results produced by Illustrator tend to be low contrast, plasticky and unconvincing – but it's the basic shape we're after, and we can use Photoshop to give it both realism and gloss.

One advantage of creating the initial model in Illustrator is the ability to view it from any angle, at any perspective. Here, the viewpoint of the initial model was then shifted slightly to make the reflected view beneath it.

4 Back in Illustrator, the text was saved as a Symbol and then mapped onto the lens surface. The surface was set to Invisible, so that just the curved text could be exported and placed in Photoshop on its own.

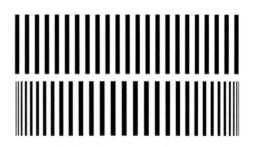

7 The trickiest part was not the modeling, but the ribs around the zoom ring. First, I drew a series of vertical bars; I then Spherized them using Horizontal Only, to give a front-on perspective effect.

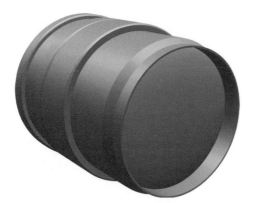

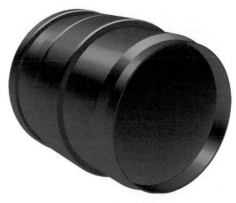

2 When placed in Photoshop, the lens looked too dull and flat. It would have been possible to adjust the lighting in Illustrator – but it's far easier to simply increase the contrast in Photoshop.

3 The metallic sheen is added using Curves, as described in Chapter 10. By creating the Curves as an Adjustment Layer, it's easy to see the result and preserve the ability to adjust it later.

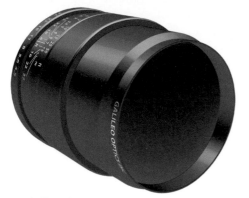

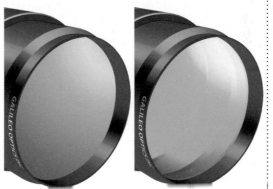

5 In Photoshop, the text was recolored and given a slight bevel using Layer Styles. This made it appear to be embossed onto the surface of the lens, for a much more realistic appearance.

6 The first glass element was drawn and on a new layer, and shaded appropriately. Multiple copies of this lens were made as a clipping group with the first one, their modes set to Overlay to allow us to see through them.

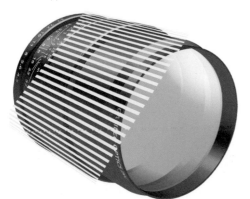

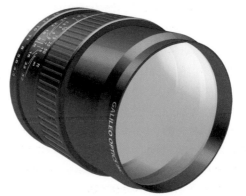

8 The ribs (here shown in yellow for clarity) now needed to be distorted to fit the perspective of the lens. This was easily achieved usign Free Transform, stretching the handles so the ribs followed the edges of the lens.

9 Finally, the ribs were cut to match the shape of the zoom barrel on the lens, by selecting the area with the Pen tool and deleting the ribs outside it. Beveling was then added using Layer Styles to give them some depth.

HOT TIP

While Illustrator is great at generating basic models, it would be folly to expect too much of it. There's little point doing too much refinement here, when such tasks are more easily accomplished in Photoshop. It would have been possible for example, to create the ribs in Illustrator by extruding a ring of dots; but the difficulty of setting an appropriate angle would have been far greater than the worth of the finished result.

The Poser phenomenon

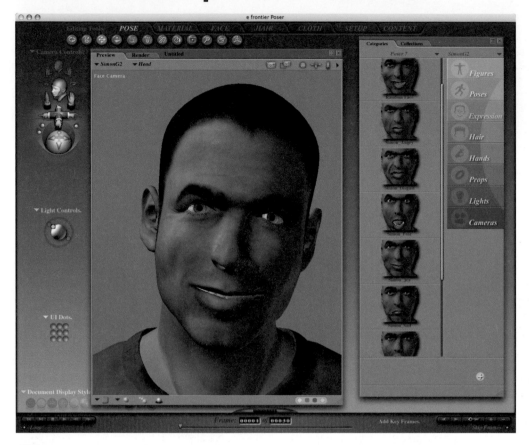

POSER IS A UNIQUE 3D MODELING application. It has just one purpose: to produce images of people, as realistically as possible. The realism of the application's output increases with each new release, and it's getting to the stage where the figures generated look almost real. Almost, but not quite: you can still tell that a figure has been generated rather than photographed. Nevertheless, with a bit of work in Photoshop it's possible to get acceptable results from Poser without having to go to the expense and inconvenience of hiring models (or the embarrassment of asking them to take their clothes off).

With its quirky interface, Poser 7 (www. curiouslabs.com) looks and feels like no other

program. As well as being a powerful modeler, it's also fun to use, as long as you've got enough RAM: the latest version requires at least 200Mb assigned to it, and is far happier operating with a whole lot more. Poser comes with a range of reasonably convincing figures of its own; but if you want greater realism, you'll need to purchase additional models from Daz3D (www.daz3d.com) who, under the name Zygote, developed the original Poser models.

For the digital artist interested in generating photorealistic images, Poser is useful in that it's quick and easy to model any pose you like; using the Daz3D models, you can even change the physiognomy of the faces and bodies of your models to suit your needs.

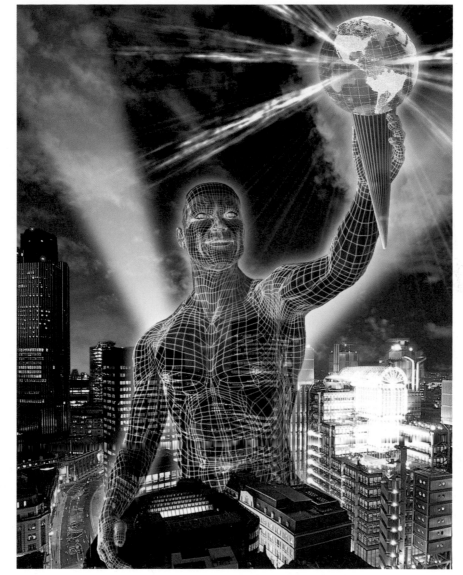

Poser's interface (left) may be confusing to new users, but it's easy to use once you get the hang of manipulating your figures using the modeling tools. Rendering the final image only takes a few minutes, resulting in a TIFF file with an Alpha channel that can be used to isolate the figure from its background.

This image (right) was for an awards feature for the Sunday Telegraph newspaper. They didn't want a real person, or a model whom readers might think they were expected to recognize; Poser provided the perfect solution in the form of this wireframe model. Setting its mode to Screen allowed it to be partially transparent so we could see the buildings behind, which greatly enhances the scene.

Each version of Poser has added more realism, greater flexibility, better animation, and a higher degree of user control.

The figures never quite look real enough to fool casual readers, even though it improves with each new version. But Poser is great for generating crowds of out-of-focus people to populate your backgrounds, for creating roughs or for building wireframe models for cases where you want a computer-generated look.

A wide range of clothing, hair and tools is available, both from Daz3D and from many third party and shareware sources – one of the best is www.renderosity.com, who distribute free and low-cost clothing, props and characters.

Reality overload

REALITY IS ALL VERY WELL, but it can be a little dull. Photoshop gives us the opportunity to make real life more exciting, more vivid and more dynamic. Throughout this book I've concentrated on techniques for making images look as realistic as possible; but we shouldn't let our desire for realism get in the way of a good picture.

We instinctively know when something looks plausible, and when it doesn't. We've all seen old films showing flying cars, rockets and men falling out of airplanes, and have sensed that the real thing wouldn't look that way. But how do we know what the real thing would look like? Most of us have never seen a rocket from space, or someone falling from a plane. It's likely that the 'real thing', when filmed, wouldn't look convincing either: in many cases, creating a plausible image is more important than one that adheres rigidly to the confines of reality.

Often, the way we remember an object or scene is of more importance than the prosaic reality. Let's say you wanted to draw a time bomb, to be incorporated in a montage. You could spend hours researching bomb construction on the internet, and end up with a dull, colorless device that readers would find hard to interpret. Or you could simply draw two orange sticks attached by curly wires to an analog alarm clock, and you'd have an instantly recognizable image.

Let's take a different example. You're creating a montage of the President of the United States at his desk in the Oval Office. Without suitable reference material, you must rely on your memory – and the collective memory of your readers – to make the picture work. So you assemble a large desk, a high-backed chair, and a window with flags hanging either side of it. But what of the view through the window? It's likely that, should the President turn in his swivel chair, he'll gaze out over a dull stretch of White House lawn. For the reader, though, such a scene wouldn't help to place the location. If you instead opt for a view of another government building, perhaps with a glimpse of a dark-suited man in black sunglasses with a curly wire over his ear, you'll give the reader many more clues to where your scene is located.

Cartoons, both in print and in animation, have educated us to recognize a host of artificial visual devices designed to accentuate the action. So we'll always see a puff of smoke as Road Runner suddenly takes off for the hills; and we're so used to seeing characters carry on running in mid-air as they leave a cliff top (before suddenly plunging to their doom when they realize their predicament) that we don't think twice about the logic. In printed cartoons, we've come to interpret a series of wavy lines behind a running figure as indicating speed, and straight lines emanating from a central point as a sign of explosive activity.

These metaphors have become so much part of the public consciousness that we can adapt them for use in photomontage. The result will tend towards illustration, and few readers would be fooled into thinking these were actual photographs. But, sensitively used, the cartoonist's techniques can add life to an otherwise static composition.

In real life, explosions are scenes of chaos and confusion, usually so wreathed in smoke that you can't see what's going on. In Photoshop, we can start with the elements of the destruction and add fire, smoke and sparks to illuminate the scene; we're not so concerned with recreating the effect of a real explosion as we are with communicating to the reader that an explosion is taking place. Which means dipping into the collective subconscious to retrieve the sense of exploding material we've gathered from action movies.

If what you want to do is fool your public into thinking they're looking at a real photograph, then none of these techniques will apply. But if your aim is to create an illustration that's entertaining and that tells a story, then don't let the constraints of reality get in the way.

In the next chapter we'll look at a few ways of making reality just that little bit more exciting.

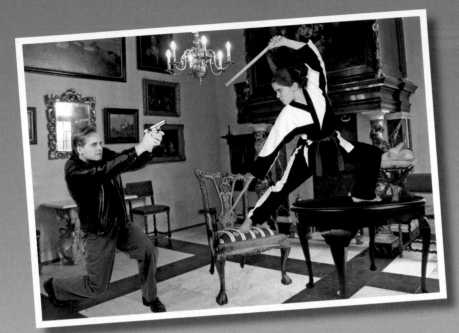

A mismatched fight between a man with a gun and a woman with sticks should make a compelling image. But the version above lacks drama: it's all too static and posed. By throwing realism to the winds, we can create a much stronger, more engaging image that really draws our interest.

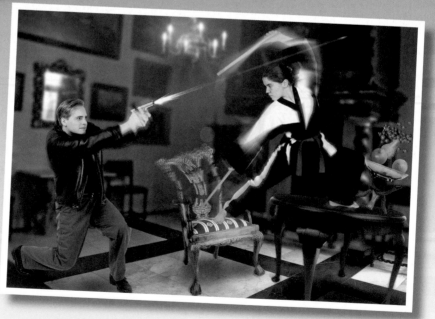

13

Hyper realism

FOR TIMES WHEN REALITY becomes too much to bear, we need to add illustrative elements that make a static picture look more dynamic. These move an image towards hyper realism: what we're depicting is no longer gritty realism, but a graphic illustration.

Real blurred photographs may give the sense of speed, but it's at the expense of clarity. By creating blurs and showing them selectively, we can give the impression of a fast-moving object without losing the detail. In this chapter we'll also look at how to make explosions and other scenes of destruction, as well as how to make complex scenes comprehensible.

Blurring for speed

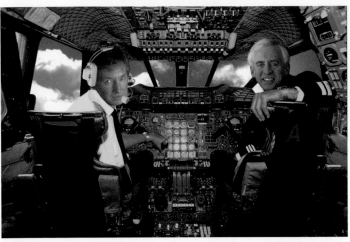

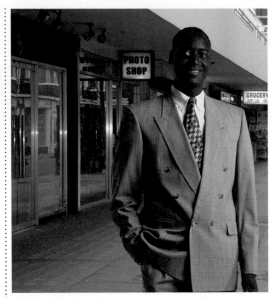

1 Here's the proud owner of a new photomontage shop, photographed outside his premises. He's been positioned so we can see the sign behind him, but it's all rather lacking in dynamism; the empty space to the left of him badly needs filling.

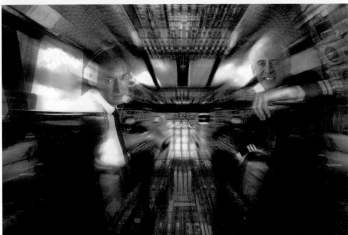

THE ILLUSTRATION ABOVE was to illustrate a Sunday Telegraph article on the proposed merger of American Airlines and British Airways. It was a simple enough job: fitting the heads of the two airline bosses to the bodies, and placing the logos on the backs of seats. But I felt that as it stood, the image was too static: so I added a Radial Blur to give the impression of speed.

In this section we'll look at how to use blur techniques to give the impression of movement, and how to get the best results from the filters.

4 Here's a model of a space shuttle taking off into the skies. It's clearly not the real thing, and looks little better than a child's toy suspended against an unconvincing sky. Motion Blur, once again, can help bring this static image to life.

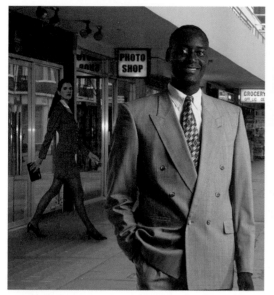

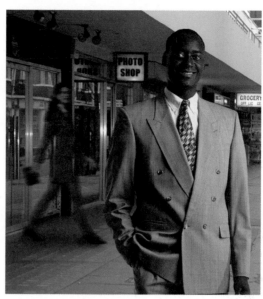

2 Placing a passer-by in the scene helps with the composition of the montage, and her bright red suit adds a much-needed splash of color. The trouble here is that she's too strong an element: she draws the eye away from the main focus of the picture.

3 Applying a small degree of Motion Blur to the figure makes it appear as if she happened to be walking past while the photograph was being taken, and knocks her more firmly into the background. Of course, in reality a person wouldn't be blurred as evenly as this; but the effect works.

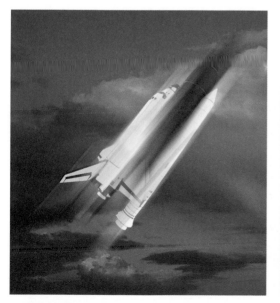

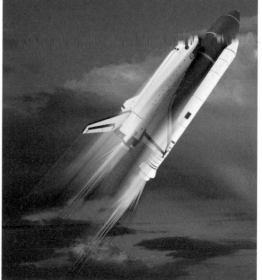

5 The shuttle layer is duplicated – we don't want to lose its sharp outline, only to add a blur on top. This layer is then blurred using Motion Blur. But the filter works in both directions: to make the shuttle look as if it's speeding forwards, we need to move either it or the blur.

6 By moving the shuttle to the top end of the blurred layer, the whole of the blur takes place behind it. The flames shooting out of the rocket boosters help: these are simply fireworks, merged in using the techniques described in Chapter 3, Hiding and showing.

HOT TIP

The Motion Blur filter offers no preview within its dialog – instead, the blur is displayed on the whole image every time you make an adjustment. Getting the angle of the blur right can be tricky: but rather than dragging the direction wheel, highlight the Angle field and use the Up and Down cursor keys to change the angle of blur in small increments.

SHORTCUTS
MAC WIN BOTH

349

More blurring techniques

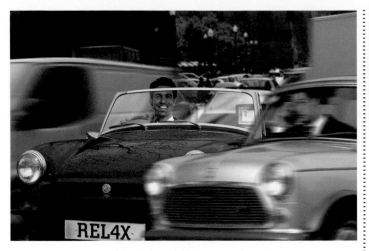

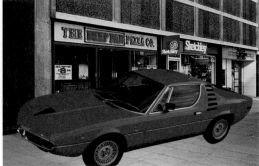

1 Here's our driverless sports car, careering out of control on a shopping street. The immediate problems are apparent: first, the car clearly isn't moving; and second, the angle of view of the car bears little relation to the street on which it's been placed.

BLURRING GIVES THE IMPRESSION of speed, but can also help to focus the reader's attention. The illustration above was for Men's Health, to show how wearing a hands-free headset would help to lower stress levels while driving (this was before it was suggested that hands-free headsets might fry your brains while you're chilling out). The car we want the reader to look at is buried amongst the traffic, but by blurring the vehicles around it I could ensure that the reader wouldn't be distracted by them.

On these pages I'll discuss how to make both Motion Blur and Radial Blur work together, to give the impression that a static car is really moving.

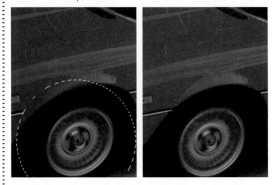

4 The first way to give an impression of movement is to add Radial Blur to the wheels. A circular selection is made into a new layer, which has Radial Blur (Spin) applied, as seen on the left; this is then masked (right) so that the car body is no longer blurred.

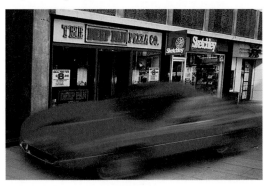

7 Motion Blur, as I explained on the previous page, works in both directions. But we only want the blur to show behind the car – not at the front, where it hasn't been yet. So the whole blurred layer is simply moved to the right so that it trails behind the vehicle.

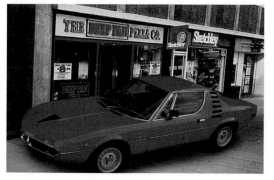

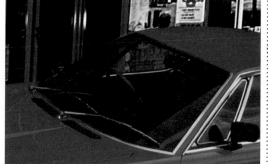

2 Cars are complex shapes, and distorting its perspective would have been a laborious and probably impossible task. But it's easy to change the perspective of the street to match the car: Free Transform is all that is required. The shadow beneath the car also helps to position it.

3 Although the car has been cut out, the original backdrop was still visible through the window. Making a layer mask, we can hide the view through the window so the street is visible. Then, by reducing the contrast of the mask, we can make it appear as if we're looking through glass.

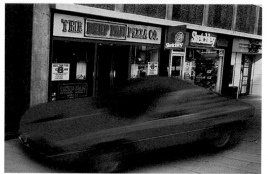

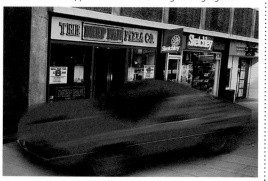

5 The whole car is then duplicated, and Motion Blur applied to the new layer. It's really easy to adjust the angle of the blur to match the dominant angle of the car, as the filter gives you a full-screen preview of its effect.

6 Because the car is shown in perspective, the straight lines of the blur no longer match all the angles of the car. Using Free Transform, we can distort the blur to make it follow the perspective of the car reasonably well.

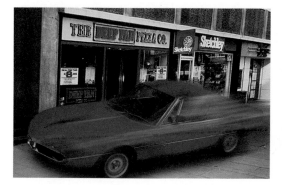

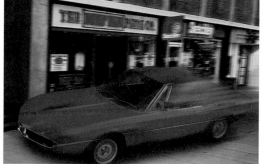

8 The blur hid too much of the original car, and blurred elements such as the wheels didn't look convincing. So we can simply make a layer mask for the blurred layer, and paint out those areas we want to hide: now we retain much of the car's detail, while keeping the sense of movement.

9 The whole image still looked too static: the car was clearly moving, but the sense of speed didn't come through. The answer is to add a little Motion Blur to the background as well, as if the photographer had tried to follow the car's motion but didn't quite manage it.

HOT TIP

Simply adding Motion Blur to a layer can have the effect of muddying the image, rather than adding a sense of speed to it. Blurred images will often need brightening also up to make them work more convincingly; it's also worth experimenting with setting their layer modes to Screen or Hard Light to enhance the effect.

SHORTCUTS
MAC WIN BOTH

351

Cartoon distortions

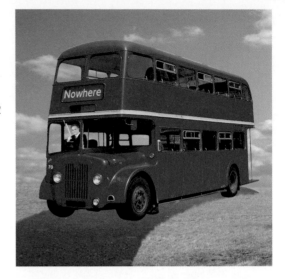

ONE OF THE MOST IMPRESSIVE FEATURES in Photoshop CS2 is the Image Warp transformation, which we discussed in Chapter 2. There, we looked at how to use it to make objects fit within a realistic environment.

Of course, realism is only one facet of this remarkable tool's abilities; it's perhaps at its most effective when creating distortions that take photomontage firmly into the area of illustration. Here, we'll look at how to replicate a technique commonly used by cartoonists to give the impression of speed and energy.

It's a playful, frivolous approach to photomontage that won't appeal to all users, and is certainly far removed from photo realism. But it's fun, and the results speak for themselves.

1 Here's our starting image: a British double-decker bus coming over the brow of a hill. The hill isn't the sort of road you'd see in everyday life: that curve is too extreme for the wheelbase of any real car, and would cause a cracked sump if not worse damage. It's a cartoon hill, and the bus looks too stiff in comparison.

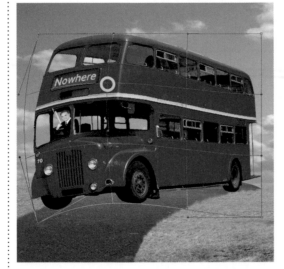

4 Raising the handle in the previous step lifted the wheel well, but the result is that the lower floor of the bus is too condensed, making the whole thing look top heavy. We can fix that by grabbing the top left center handle, in the middle of the mesh, and dragging it upwards. The upper deck is now more compressed than the lower, exaggerating the sense of movement and giving the impression that we're viewing the bus from slightly below.

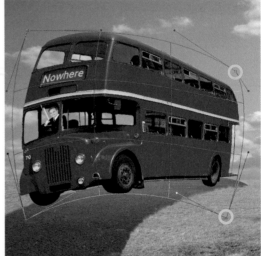

5 Now let's look at the rear end, which at present is too straight. Grab each right-hand corner handle in turn, and drag it down and in to add some curvature to the back of the bus, giving it a slight Spherized effect, as if it has been photographed through a wide angle lens. This also gives the illusion of the bus being closer to us than it really is.

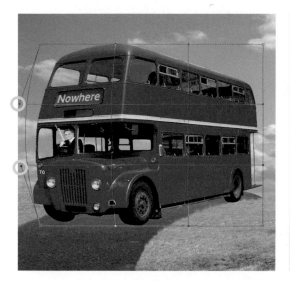

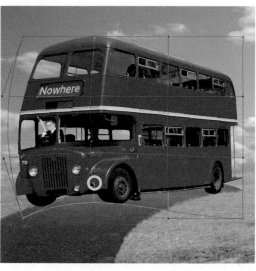

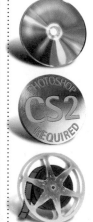

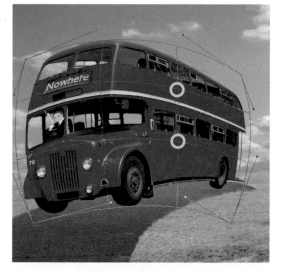

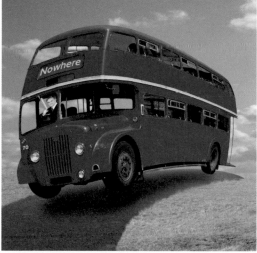

2 Let's make the bus suit its surroundings better. Begin by entering Free Transform mode using ctrl T ⌘ T as usual, and then press the Warp button on the Options bar to move to Image Warp. We'll start by ballooning out the front of the bus: drag both left corner handles (ringed here in yellow) so the bus distorts in the direction of travel.

3 The curved front helps to make the bus look more unreal, but we still have a way to go. Let's lift that front nearside wheel so that it raises itself off the ground a short way. Grab the handle closest to it, and drag it up to compress the area around the wheel.

6 Time for some fine tuning on the interior. To make more of a curve on those side windows, grab the remaining two interior anchor points on the mesh and drag them up slightly, to accentuate the curve and make it match the curvature of the top and bottom of the bus. That's it for the distortion: you can now press *Enter* to leave Free Transform mode and return to the main artwork.

7 Normally, shadows beneath objects lying on the ground would be touching the object at each point of contact with the surface. But here we can take another tip from the cartoon illustrator's book: by painting in our shadow at a distance from the bus itself, we give the impression that it's leaping up in the air rather than proceeding sedately along the road – almost as if the effort of coming over the hill has sent the bus flying.

HOT TIP

The difficult part of creating a cartoon distortion is, as is so often the case, knowing when to stop. You should aim for a final result that looks almost like a real photograph at first glance, but which on closer inspection proves to be impossible. Don't get too carried away: the image should look more or less plausible, if the object in question were made of rubber rather than metal.

SHORTCUTS

Breaking glass

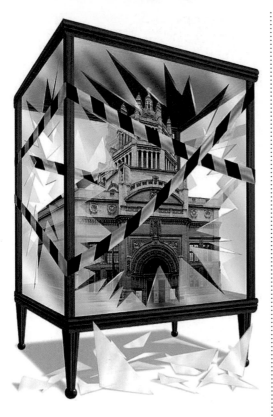

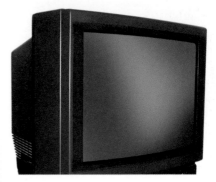

1 The original screen on this television has been replaced by a new layer, tinted blue and accented using the Dodge tool to make it more appealing. Since the days of black and white TV, we're used to screens looking bluish.

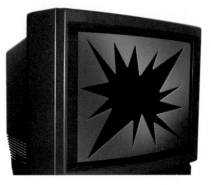

4 In the last step, we reduced the selection area to the original Lasso selection minus a thin border at the right edge. When we now exit QuickMask and delete, we're left with just the brightened edge of the glass to give some thickness to the broken edge.

BREAKING GLASS IN PHOTOSHOP has little to do with broken glass in real life, which tends to look dull and lifeless. We want to give the impression of serious damage, as in the illustration above for The Independent: the violence of the act must be more apparent than the actuality.

Here, we'll look at the process of smashing the glass on the front of a television screen: the glass will explode outwards to heighten the effect. In real life, of course, smashing a screen would cause the glass to implode inwards, to fill the vacuum inside the tube; but real life is sometimes too dull to reproduce.

On the following pages, we'll look at how to turn this broken screen into an explosion.

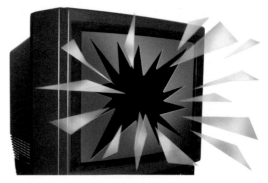

7 Nudge the selection down a couple of pixels (don't use the Move tool or you'll move the layer), and use the Brush tool set to Behind to add some thickness to the glass. There will be some awkward double spikes at the pointed ends; these can be removed using the Eraser.

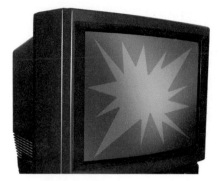

2 Using the Lasso tool, select an irregular shape on the screen and brighten it up. If you hold ⌥ *alt* while clicking points on the screen you can draw straight selection lines between the points.

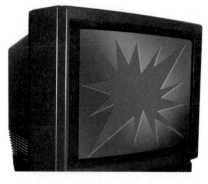

3 Enter QuickMask mode by pressing **Q** and select the red mask with the Magic Wand. Nudge the selection up and left a couple of pixels; then inverse the selection and delete, so only a fraction of the highlight remains.

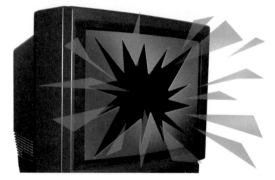

5 On a new layer, draw individual shards of glass with the Lasso tool – simple triangles work best. Using a soft brush at around 50% opacity, paint some color from the screen into these shards, but don't fill them completely.

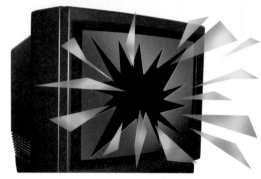

6 Don't deselect, but use the Dodge tool to brighten up those shards so that they look more reflective. Again, use the tool unevenly so that the pieces don't end up looking too uniform in appearance.

HOT TIP

If you don't see the broken screen highlighted in step 3, but see the inverse in red instead, it's because you've got your QuickMask settings set to default (Masked Areas). Double-click the QuickMask icon and change the settings to Selected Areas, which is easier to work with.

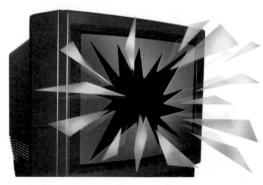

8 Duplicate the glass shards layer, and use Free Transform to shrink the new layer towards the centre of the screen (hold the ⌥ *alt* key as you drag a corner handle). Lower the opacity of this new layer to around 50% to give the impression of movement.

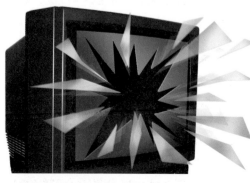

9 Make another duplicate of this layer, and reduce that in size even further – you can add a small degree of rotation as well if you wish. Reduce the opacity of this layer still further, to around 20%, to complete the explosive effect. Finally, paint a little smoke inside the screen.

SHORTCUTS
MAC | WIN | BOTH

Smashing things up 1

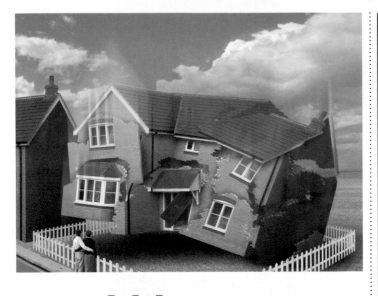

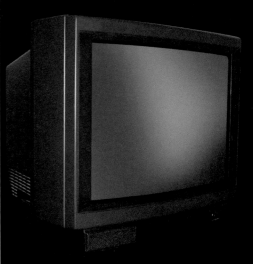

WHICH OF US HASN'T WANTED, at some time or other, to take a sledgehammer to our computer when it freezes? Or to our television during an election broadcast? With Photoshop, it's easy to vent your anger without voiding your insurance.

The illustration above was for a Sunday Telegraph article about the collapse of housing prices. It's a straightforward metaphor, but added more interest than the usual shot of a row of For Sale signs.

The principles of breaking up technology apply equally well to televisions as to houses: it's a matter of making holes and then filling the gaps. Following on from the previous page, we'll look here at how to make a television explode.

1 Here's the same television we used before, placed against a black background. If you're going to use explosions and flying glass, the effect always works best against a dark background; explosions rarely show up well against white.

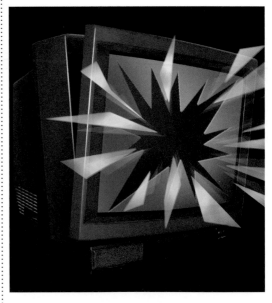

4 Now we can bring in the flying glass and broken screen from the previous page, rotating it to fit the new angle of the screen border. That's the basics of the television finished: all we need to do now is to add the elements that will make the destruction look more explosive.

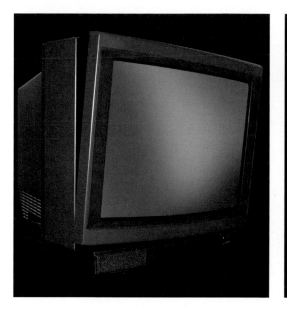

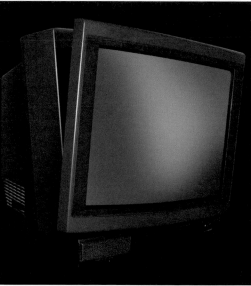

2 Begin by selecting the front panel, then cut it to a new layer using *Shift* ⌘ *J* *Shift* *ctrl* *J*. It's now easy to distort it to a new position: although I've kept it close to the original, there's no reason why you shouldn't have it flying halfway across the room.

3 Repeat this process with the side, rotating it in the opposite direction. Add some shading with the Burn tool to give the effect of a shadow. You'll also need to draw the inside of the frame, on a new layer: simply fill the outline with a color picked from the TV, and shade it.

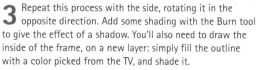

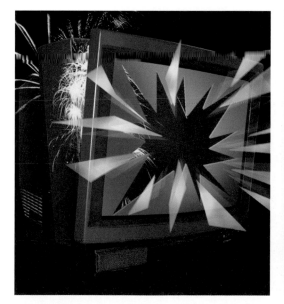

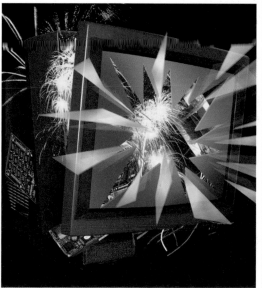

5 Fireworks make great explosions. This firework has been placed just in front of the rotated side, and the black background knocked out of it using the techniques described in Chapter 3. The back edge of the side was painted out on a layer mask so that the firework spilled out behind it.

6 The firework layer is duplicated to make a second explosion, and a bunch of other electronic material is added to give the impression of the guts of the TV flying out in disarray. Next time you upgrade your computer, remember to photograph the boards before throwing them away.

HOT TIP

In the introductory illustration (opposite), I had to build the interiors of the rooms visible where the brick wall had broken away. This was easily done by shading and distorting patches of wallpaper to match the existing perspective.

SHORTCUTS

357

Smashing things up 2

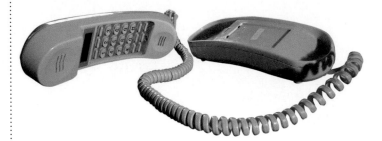

O N THE PREVIOUS spread we looked at an explosion in the act of occurring, complete with sparks and flying glass. Here, we'll step forward in time to view the destruction after it's happened.

This piece of artwork for the Sunday Telegraph was for a story about the break-up of the telecommunications company Energis, graphically illustrated by a smashed telephone. It's a fiddly job, as each of the buttons on the handset needs to be isolated and distorted individually; but it simply takes a little patience to ensure that all the pieces fit where they belong.

Never having studied the interior of a telephone, I have no idea if they contain printed circuit boards or this sort of wiring. But this is artwork, not technical illustration; such niceties as factual accuracy need not concern us.

1 To begin with, I simply photographed a phone with the receiver off the hook. By placing it on its side, a small sense of chaos is already achieved. I chose a phone with the keypad in the receiver so that I'd have the base free on which to place the Energis logo afterwards.

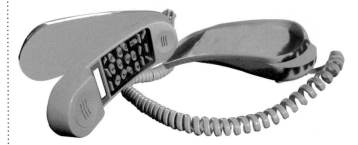

4 The interiors of the base and the handset were drawn and filled with a flat color to fill the gaps where the tops had been broken off. This was simply a matter of inventing the new shapes using the Pen tool to draw the smoothly curved outlines.

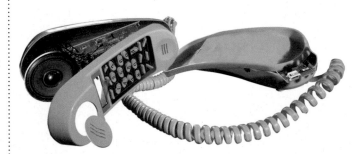

7 The speaker is simply a loudspeaker from a stereo system, photographed and distorted to fit; the printed circuit board is actually a computer logic board cut to fit the interior of the phone.

8 Opposite is the finished illustration, with background and shading added. The Energis logo was taken from their website and redrawn, then distorted using the Shear tool; the shading was added using the Emboss feature in Layer Effects.

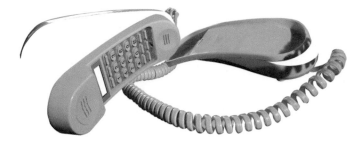

2 The first step was to separate the two halves of both the receiver and the handset, exactly as shown in the television example on the previous spread. While it would also have been possible to break the handset into shattered fragments, it adds to the sense of realism if the constituent parts remain intact. If you (or your children) have ever tried to break a telephone handset, you'll know how resilient they can be.

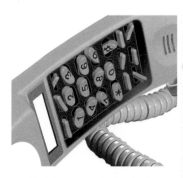

3 Each button was isolated using QuickMask, and then cut to a new layer using *Shift* *⌘* *J* *Shift* *ctrl* *J*. The button background was recreated, and then the buttons rearranged individually.

HOT TIP

Outlining the buttons was the trickiest part of this illustration. It would have taken too long using the Pen tool: instead, I entered QuickMask mode and used a hard-edged brush of the same diameter as the end of a button. Clicking at one end, then holding *Shift* and holding at the other end, drew a smooth lozenge that exactly fitted the shape of each button. If you're using a graphics tablet, this method will only work if you have pressure sensitivity turned off.

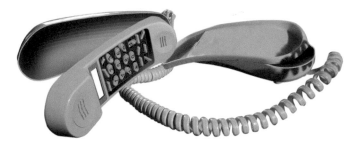

5 To make the interiors look more realistic, shading was added using the Burn tool to give a sense of depth and rounding. The horizontal ridges inside the back of the handset were added because the flat interior looked too dull without them.

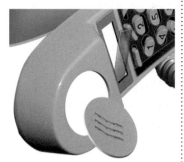

6 The disk covering the mouthpiece was cut to a new layer, and both the disk and the hole given depth using the techniques described in Chapter 12.

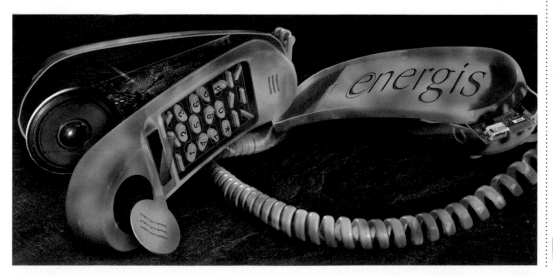

SHORTCUTS
MAC WIN BOTH

Chaos and complexity

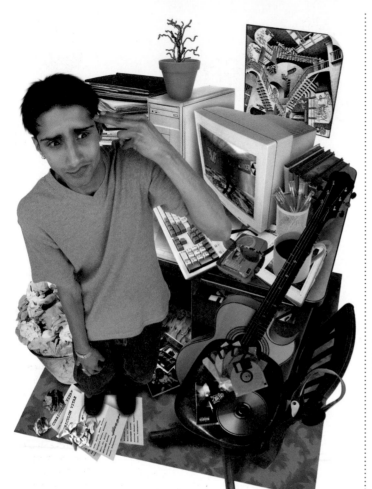

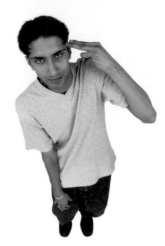

1 The student was clearly going to be the key figure in this image, so it was important to find the right one. Many royalty-free photographs of people are shot from up a ladder; this one had enough action to make him appear to be struggling with his task.

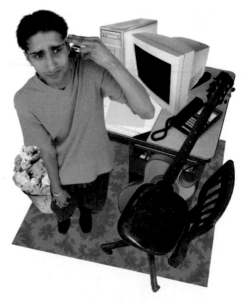

4 The next major props were the computer, the trash basket and the guitar. The guitar was given depth, and the desk drawer opened, using the techniques described in the first two sections of Chapter 12. With the big stuff in position, I could place the smaller items.

WHEN AN IMAGE IS TO BE PRINTED right across a spread, it can help to pack a lot of detail into it. This illustration for the student magazine Juice showed a student struggling to write his curriculum vitae (résumé) amid the chaos of his untidy living quarters.

I decided on the top-down view of this illustration simply to add dynamism to it: plus, I knew I had a picture of a desk and chair viewed from above. All the other props were either photographed or distorted to fit.

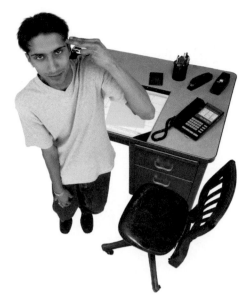

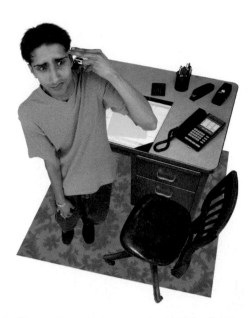

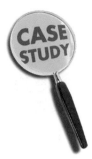

2 The desk and chair were the next major props. Originally the chair was facing the desk, but it didn't take much to move it; the only constraint was positioning it so that its perspective matched that of the rest of the scene. The props on the desk were too business-oriented, but they'd all be covered up later.

3 The carpet was simply a scan of a piece of wallpaper cut to an irregular shape. The image needed a solid base, but I didn't want to square it to maintain the visual interest of the scene. I also changed the student's expression and recolored his T shirt to make it stand out from the desk.

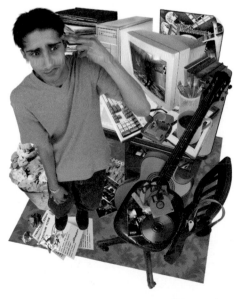

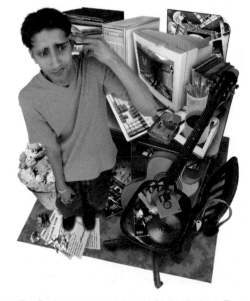

5 All the other props were added and positioned where they fitted best. You need a fairly comprehensive library of images in order to find all these elements; most of the elements used here came from the Hemera Photo-Objects collections.

6 The final stage, as ever, was to add the shadows. These were created on several layers – one above the carpet, one grouped with the top of the desk, and so on. There's no point adding shadows until the composition is more or less complete, since they can be awkward to edit afterwards.

HOT TIP

Creating an irregular outline for an illustration is an easy way to add life to the image when it's printed: this is far more appealing on the page than a squared-up picture would have been. The key is knowing which elements need to be included, such as the carpet, and which can be missed out: I originally put a wall behind the desk, but removed it when it became clear it wasn't needed.

The fall of the house of cards

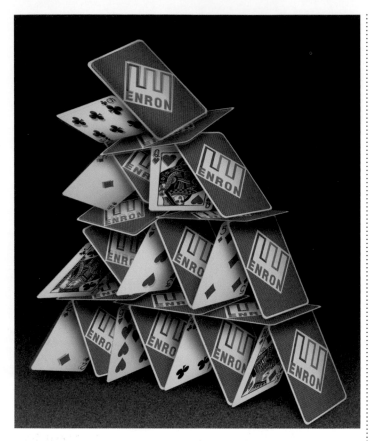

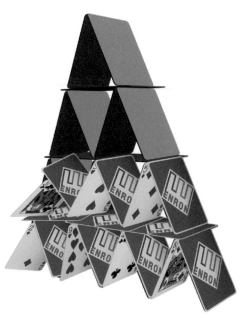

1 The Dimensions model showed the formation of a completed house of cards. While this wouldn't be used in the finished illustration, it made a useful template to show where to place the cards themselves.

MAKING THIS HOUSE OF CARDS appear to be in the process of collapse – while still looking like a house of cards – meant that each card had to be carefully placed to show it in the act of falling.

The illustration was for The Guardian, relating to an article about the demise of energy company Enron. Their distinctive logo, placed on the back of each card, tied the illustration to the story.

In this instance I made the original card house model in Dimensions (see Chapter 12), although these days it could easily be drawn in Illustrator. This formed the template around which the cards were built.

4 A few cards were added that break out of the line of the template. At the bottom of the pile, the cards were only slightly disarrayed: any misalignment here would cause more chaos higher up the stack. Each card was simply distorted to look as if it was falling.

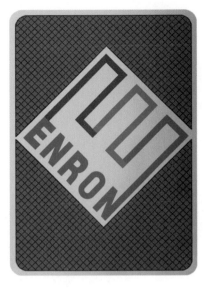

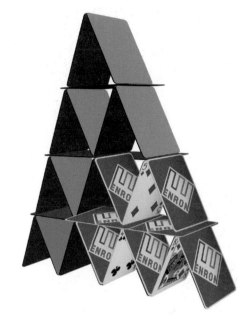

2 The Enron logo was placed on a card-shaped background, drawn with the Shapes tool. The patterned area outside the logo was filled with a cross-hatch pattern that I created for drawing fences, and colored.

3 The first few cards were put in place, following the template. Each card was distorted using Free Transform to fit the template and placed behind the card in front of it: it was easier to work from the front backwards.

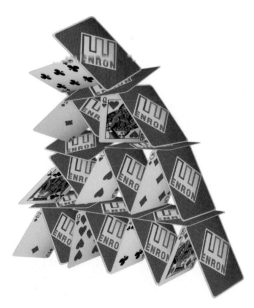

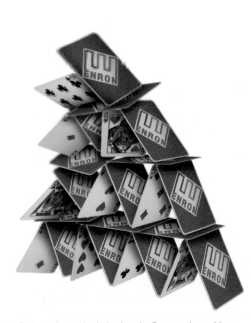

5 With all the cards in place, the template could be hidden so that we can see the full effect. No shading has been added yet, although the cards were given some thickness by selecting each one and holding *alt* ⌥ as it was nudged up and right a couple of pixels.

6 Each card was shaded using the Burn tool to add realism to the scene. In addition, the falling cards were duplicated and rotated, and their opacity reduced: those at the top were set to 30% opacity, reducing to just 10% at the bottom of the stack.

HOT TIP

Using a simple 3D model can greatly help in the placement of objects in a 3D environment, even when the template is discarded at the end. Matching this sort of perspective viewpoint would have been a much trickier task if the cards had all simply been placed by eye: I know this to be true, since this was the way I originally attempted to do the illustration.

SHORTCUTS

363

Zombie pensioners from hell

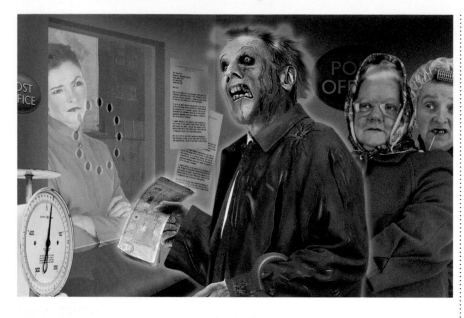

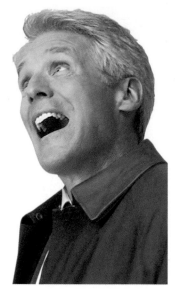

WHEN THE SUNDAY TELEGRAPH wanted to illustrate a feature on pension fraud, they immediately thought of zombie pensioners. It's not as daft as it sounds: it turns out that some unscrupulous relatives are continuing to claim pensions for long-dead members of the family, so the idea of a gruesome grandad isn't so far-fetched after all.

Whether or not you want to turn your own ageing relatives into creatures from beyond the grave, the chances are you'll want to inflict the scourge on *someone* you know, even if it's only a politician or the owner of Microsoft (for example).

It's not difficult to do, but it is an awful lot of fun. Here's how I turned Mr Average Gray into a grisly grotesque. The only really surprising thing is not so much that a conservative newspaper should want to inflict this sort of imagery on their readers, but that I actually get *paid* for doing this stuff.

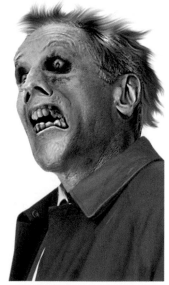

1 Here's our starting image: the head is a cheerful enough chap, placed on a raincoat body. The key thing here was the angle of the head, which let me see the open mouth clearly – all the better for drooling with.

5 The eye sockets and teeth are taken from a Hemera Photo-Objects image of a skull, photographed from a similar angle to the head. The rest of the skull is painted out on a layer mask.

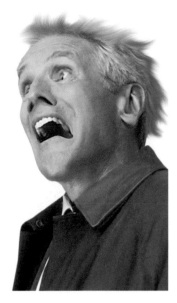

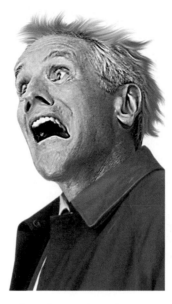

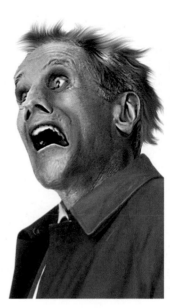

2 The first step is the basic distortion. The mouth, nose, ear and eyes are all distorted using the Liquify filter; the hair is then messed up using the Smudge tool for a more wild effect.

3 Normally, over-sharpening an image results in too much degradation of the original. Which is exactly what we want here: roll on Unsharp Mask, with the settings far too high for conventional use.

4 The grime is painted on a new layer, set to Hard Light, using the head as a clipping mask. Here, we can add both shading and coloring, using a soft brush at low opacity. Don't paint directly on the head layer!

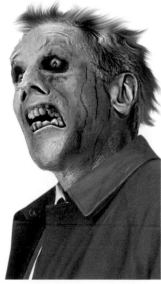

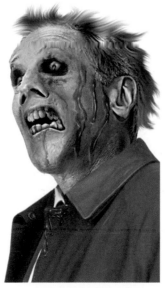

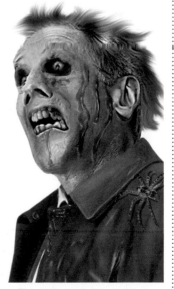

6 Irregular selections of the cheek are made using the Lasso tool. These are copied to a new layer with *ctrl* **J** / **⌘ J** and darkened slightly; a small bevel, added with Layer Styles, makes them slightly recessed.

7 The goo inside the face slashes, and that dribbling out of the mouth and down the chin onto the coat, are painted on a new layer, shaded and textured with the Plastic Wrap filter.

8 The coat is treated in much the same way, with irregular selections darkened and shaded; more goo all round with Plastic Wrap again, and a couple of nasty-looking spiders for good measure.

HOT TIP

The trick to making an image like this work lies largely in selecting the right original photograph. You need an open mouth, both to distort into a leer and to place rotten teeth into. If you don't have the right image, you can try opening a mouth by splitting it into two layers (upper and lower lips) and distorting each with the Mesh Warp feature of Photoshop CS2.

SHORTCUTS

MAC | WIN | BOTH

365

Carry on spending

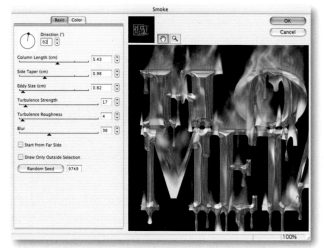

A combination of Alien Skin effects: www.alienskin.com

HOWEVER GOOD YOU MAY BE at using Photoshop, there are times when a particular effect is just too complicated, or too difficult, or too time-consuming to be worth the effort. Photoshop itself may not have all the answers: but you can bet there's a third-party tool out there that does the job. You'll find demo versions of these plug-ins on the DVD.

There's a huge variety of Photoshop plug-ins to suit just about any need. Among the best all-purpose sets are the **Nature, Impact** and **Texture** plug-in suites from Alien Skin software. All three are offshoots from the popular EyeCandy set, and they specialize in real-world effects: with these plug-ins you can create water, fur, scales, fire, smoke, chrome, glass and many more realistic-looking objects and textures.

Also from AlienSkin is **Xenofex 2**, which comprises surface effects that make your artwork look like mosaic tiles, shattered glass, crumpled paper or jigsaw puzzles. Again, the emphasis is on realism; in addition, all the Alien Skin plug-ins are easy to use, with a straightforward, uncluttered interface and plenty of presets you can use as the starting point for your designs.

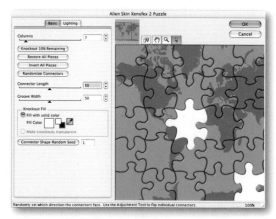

Puzzle, one of the Xenofex filters: www.alienskin.com

For those with a celestial bent, the one man band that is **Flaming Pear** produces a great range of low-cost plug-ins, including specialist tools to

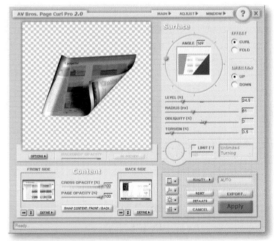

Flood, one of the plugins from www.flamingpear.com

recreate moons and planets (Lunar Cell), suns (Solar Cell) and starry backgrounds (Glitterato). Solar Cell makes great flares and haloes, so if you reduce the sun size to zero it can generate spectacular explosions. He also creates **SuperBlade Pro**, which adds intricate bevels and depth to any artwork (including a fine array of rusts, caustic distressing, and more) as well as the truly fantastic **Flood**,

which can fill a scene with rippling, reflective water in seconds.

New to the scene come two plug-ins from AVBrothers. Their **PuzzlePro** takes the creation of jigsaw puzzles to a new level, with an extraordinary degree of user customization that's capable of great results. Most spectacular of all, however, is **PageCurl**, a stunning plug-in that can turn any flat artwork into a 3D page from a book or catalog, complete with rolling-over pages, realistic lighting, creases and more. This one really has to be seen to be believed!

The one essential plug-in I'd recommend

PageCurl Pro 2 from www.avbros.com

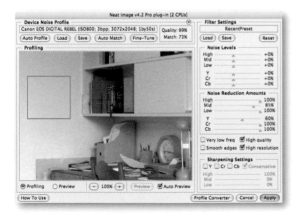

The best noise reduction: www.neatimage.com

to all Photoshop users is NeatImage, which does a fantastic job of reducing noise in digital photographs. It analyzes a clear area within the picture, and calibrates itself to remove the noise it finds there – and then applies it to the rest of the image. NeatImage also includes profiles for just about every make of camera available for download from its website, and can use this information to run automatic noise reduction based on the make and model.

367

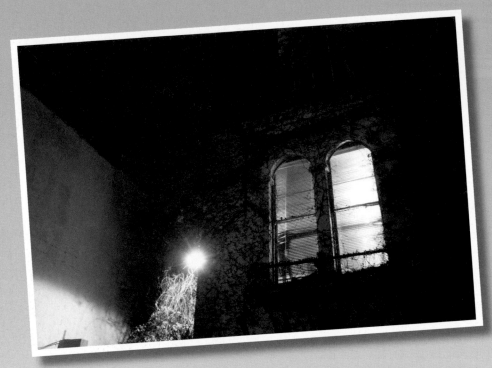

■ What's the difference between these two photographs of my house? Answer: in the top one I'm still hard at work in my studio. In the bottom one I've finished work and gone to bed. This is a simple message: the faster you can do your work, the more time you have for other things, such as sleeping.

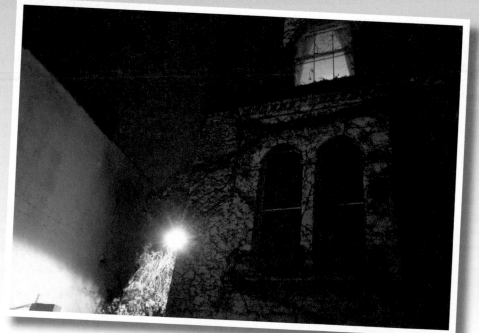

Time-saving techniques

YOU MAY BE THE MOST TALENTED Photoshop artist in the country. You may be overflowing with creative ideas, bursting to get them into print. But unless you can meet a tight deadline, you have no place in the frantic design studios of today's newspaper and magazine publishers.

Learning keyboard shortcuts is an obvious advantage. Some people take to them naturally, others find them more trouble than they're worth. And yet there are many other ways to speed up your work in Photoshop, from automating repetitive tasks to preparing artwork in advance. In this chapter, we'll look at a variety of techniques that will make you more productive, more efficient and more effective. And they'll also help you to get to bed earlier.

Front and back

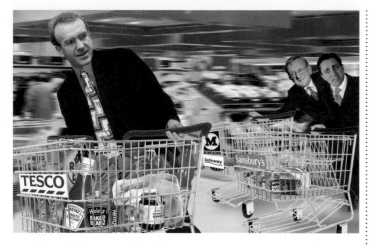

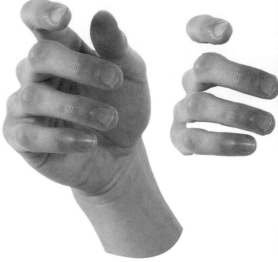

S UPERMARKETS ARE BIG BUSINESS these days. Which means the financial pages of Sunday newspapers are full of them. Which means shopping carts... aaargh!

Shopping carts are a nightmare to work with. They're about the most fiddly object in the world to cut out, and you can't use standard erasing techniques such as the Background Eraser because there's so much white in the chrome bars. So, after years (literally) of cursing the things, I bit the bullet and spent a couple of hours laboriously cutting this cart from its background.

Then I went one step further: I separated the front two sides from the rest of the cart, and saved the result as a layered PSD file. Now, every time I need one, I can pull it straight out of the folder and fill it with groceries, supermarket managers or anything I like. (I can't give you this one, though – it came from iStockphoto.com, and someone owns it.)

It's not just carts: plenty of other objects benefit from the front-and-back technique.

1 I use hands a lot in my work – holding pieces of paper, poles, placards, whatever. So my favorite hands are saved not as JPEG files with clipping paths, but as layered PSD files: the hand and fingers are on separate layers, one above the other. (They're separated here only so you can see them.)

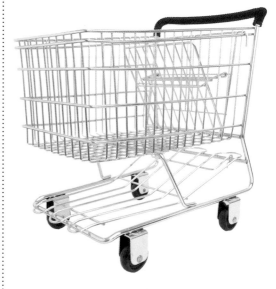

3 And so to the shopping cart. As it turned out, it was possible to remove most of the background from this cart with the Magic Wand tool; but it needed a lot of fine tuning to get it right. I created a new layer, filled with a strong color, behind the cart to see the cutout better.

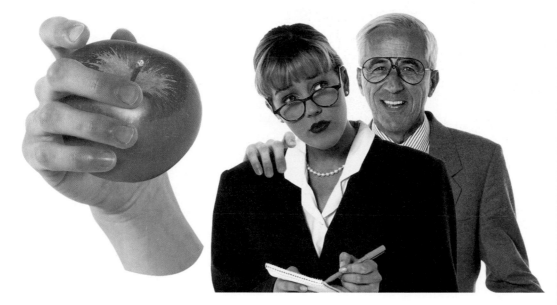

2 Now, every time I need a holding hand, I choose one from the right angle and drag it into my composition. This hand can hold just about any manner of object; that raised index finger makes it ideal for holding oversized elements that wouldn't fit into standard hands. The hand and fingers are linked together, so they move and transform as one. But it's also great for making two people look like they're in touch with each other: with the hand behind and the fingers in front, it's easy to position the assembly for maximum harrassment.

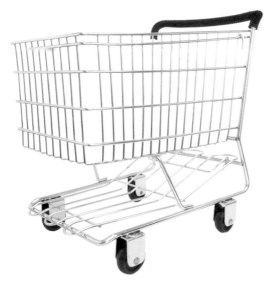

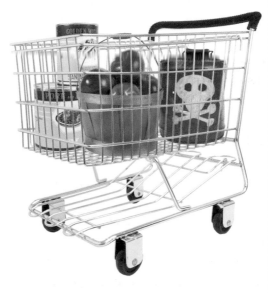

4 I then duplicated the cart and hid the original. Then the painstaking work started: erasing all trace of the rear of the cart from this view of the front two sides. It was often hard to see what was going on amongst that mess of steel tubing; QuickMask was a great help in this job.

5 Once again, the two layers were linked together and saved as a layered PSD document. Now it's an easy matter to drag whatever items I need between the two layers. Whatever I put in there looks convincingly as if it belongs in the cart – even if it's patently absurd.

Avoiding white outlines

MOST PHOTOSHOP USERS build up their own libraries of images that they've photographed. If they're objects, then it makes sense to save them with a clipping path, so that they can be easily lifted from their background at a later date.

The trouble is that when objects are saved as cutout images, with no background, the act of turning a clipping path into a selection will, because of the anti-aliasing process involved, include a thin white border from outside the object within the selection.

This is not a difficult problem to deal with, and we discussed several methods of remedying the situation in Chapter 1. But wouldn't it be better if the problem didn't arise in the first place? Here's a simple solution that can save a lot of time later.

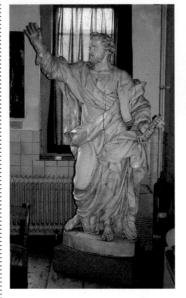

1 Here's a typical situation: a photograph of a statue in a dark corner of a museum. The statue's a fine piece of work, but all that background clutter is too distracting. It will have to go.

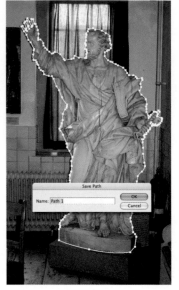

2 Drawing a path around fiddly objects like this is a tricky business, and it's not the sort of thing you'd want to do more than once. So we'll save the path we've drawn, to be retrieved later.

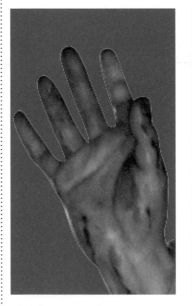

6 When we zoom in we can see a white fringe around the whole statue. This is exactly what we don't want: it makes the whole composition look ugly and unnatural.

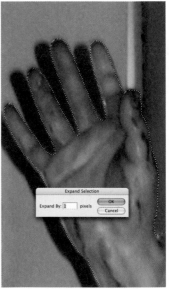

7 The solution is to stop after the initial path is drawn. Rather than inversing and deleting straight away, turn the path into a selection and then expand that selection by one pixel.

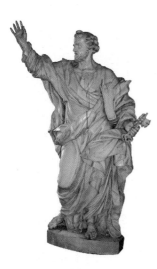
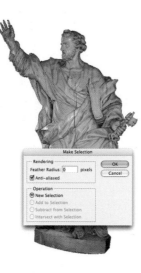
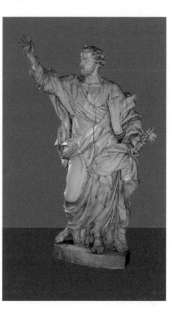

3 Here's the standard procedure: make the path into a selection, inverse that selection and then press *Delete* to fill the outside with white. (I've assumed we're still working on the background layer.)

4 As with all cutout images, this one is saved as a JPEG to be worked on later. When we come back to it, we take that path and turn it into a selection, so that we can lift the statue from its white background.

5 This is a much better background: it makes the statue stand out, but it's graphic nature doesn't detract from the image. When we look closely, though, it doesn't look right: is the outline as clean as we'd hoped?

If you're still using dialogs to turn paths into selections, you're causing yourself extra work. Instead, click on the path name in the Paths palette, then press *ctrl* *Enter* ⌘ *Enter*. The selection will be made for you. Better still, write a Photoshop Action to do the whole job with a keystroke.

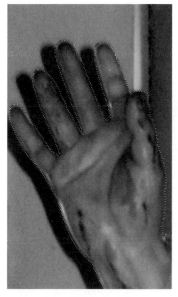
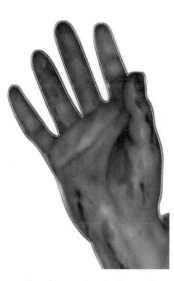
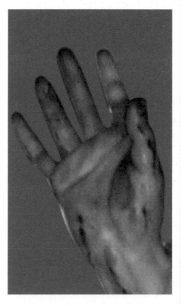

8 Here's how the expanded selection looks: there's now a fringe of background image, one pixel wide, all the way around the perimeter of the statue.

9 Now, inverse the selection and delete to fill with white as before. Note that the path itself hasn't changed – it's now one pixel inside the object perimeter.

10 The difference is that when we now make that path into a selection and place it onto a different background, there's no white edge. Problem solved!

Using Smart Objects

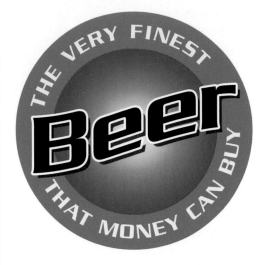

S MART OBJECTS are new to Photoshop CS2, although the way they work will be familiar to anyone who's used the same technology in Adobe Illustrator or Macromedia Freehand.

Smart Objects are a radical departure from the way we've treated Photoshop layers before. In the past, distorting a layer or group meant irrevocably changing it, and we could expect more degradation of the image each time we applied a further rotation or other transformation to it.

Now, we can group multiple layers together into new units that store the data for future reference (the layers are actually saved to disk in temporary files). This means that not only can we apply as many distortions as we like to layers without losing their integrity, we can also change the original Smart Object and then have that change reflected in each instance of it on the page. Here, we'll look at how to put this new technology to work for us.

1 Here's our original set of layers – a beer mat designed for an imaginary client. They want to see it not just in isolation, but in place on bottles, glasses and beermats. The trouble is, we know they're going to want to change their minds later. How can we avoid all that extra work?

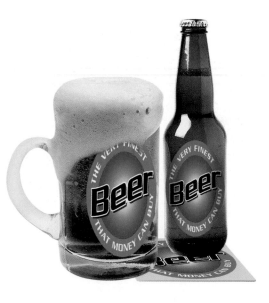

4 We can now duplicate that Smart Object layer, and apply it in different ways to our artwork. We can scale, rotate or shear it, and even apply Image Warp distortions and layer masks, to make it fit our bottle, glass and mat. The only things we can't do is paint, recolor or filter the new layers.

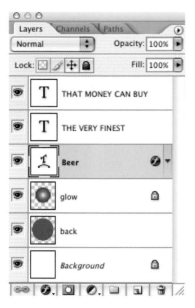

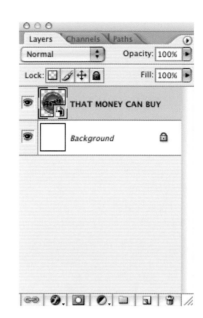

2 Here's the state of play so far. The label comprises five separate layers, including a text layer which has a Warp effect to make it rise. It's additionally complicated by a set of Layer Effects that includes a stroke and drop shadow. All the text here remains editable.

3 Select all the layers we want to include, and choose Group into New Smart Object from the Smart Objects section of the Layers menu. Now all the layers appear to have been flattened into one, except that their icon includes that custom Smart Objects corner icon.

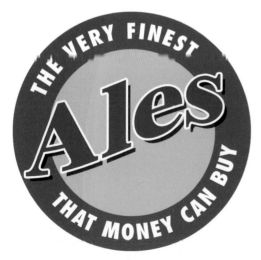

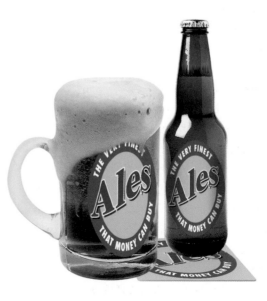

5 This is where it gets really clever. Select one of the Smart Objects layers and choose Edit Contents from the Smart Objects submenu. It opens in a new window, and we can make changes: the colors, font, lettering and any other factors can all be adjusted here.

6 When we've finished, we simply save the Smart Objects file that popped open in the previous step (it was a .psb file, a new format). The changes we made are instantly reflected in the artwork: all instances of the duplicated Smart Object are replaced with the new version.

Layer groups and layer comps

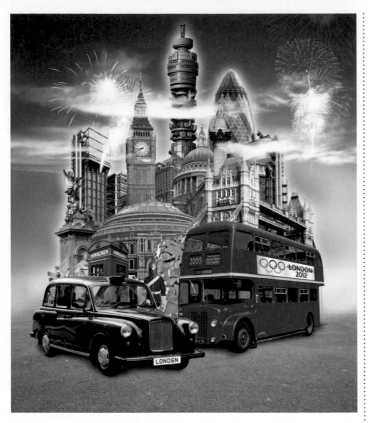

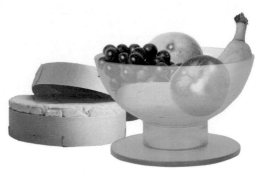

1 Here's a simple still life arrangement: a bowl of fruit and a Camembert cheese. The fruit bowl consists of a separate back and front, as well as individual layers for the apple, orange, grapes and banana. The front of the bowl here is simply duplicated and set to a low opacity.

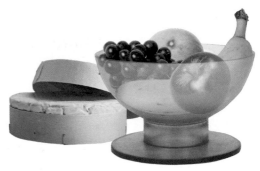

4 It's now easy to experiment with different varations without losing the original fruit bowl. By making a duplicate of that group, we can – for example – adjust the color of the bowl itself in one of the groups, while always being able to revert to the original group later.

WHEN WORKING WITH a large number of layers, managing them becomes a tricky issue. Layer Groups (known as Layer Sets in versions of Photoshop before CS2) help to organize multiple layers into logical groupings, which makes navigation that much easier.

The illustration above, for The Guardian, is a complex arrangement of buildings and other objects. During its construction there were several alternatives open to me: by saving each as a different Layer Comp, I was able to switch quickly between them to see which worked better with the new image elements as they were added.

This tutorial isn't about special effects or techniques, but about better working practice.

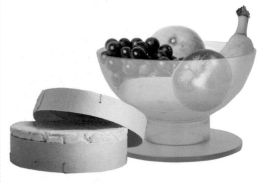

7 We don't know whether we want this cheese in front or behind the bowl group. Create a new Layer Comp (from the Layer Comps palette), then move the cheese in front and create a second Layer Comp. You can switch between the different comps by pressing the arrows in the palette.

2 For the sake of neatness alone, it makes sense to group all those fruit layers into a single set. Photoshop CS2 users should select all the layers and press *ctrl* G ⌘ G; those with earlier versions should link them together, and choose New Set from Linked from the pop-up menu.

3 One of the most useful things you can do with a layer group is to duplicate it. This gives us an exact copy of all the layers, so that we can create variations of the original group. In Photoshop CS2, duplicated layers within a duplicated group have the word 'copy' after their names.

HOT TIP

If you want to change the size or angle of a number of layers together in a large montage, it can help to make a group from them first, duplicate the group and then merge it into a single layer. Transforming this new layer will be far quicker than working on a large number of separate layers together: when you get the effect you want, you can always delete the new merged group and repeat the transformation on the group as a whole.

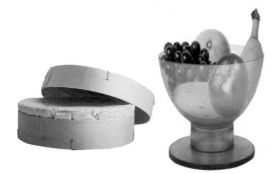

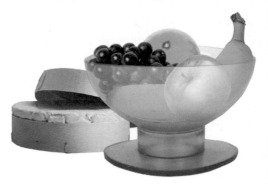

5 Layer groups can be scaled, moved or rotated as a unit. But you can't apply perspective or free distortion to the entire group, nor can you use advanced distortions such as Image Warp transformation on a whole group: to do this, you need to merge the contents of the group.

6 Make sure you're working on a duplicate of the original group, and choose Merge Group (pre-CS2: Merge Layer Set) from the pop-up menu on the Layers palette. Now, when the group becomes merged, you can recolor, distort or manipulate it as a single layer.

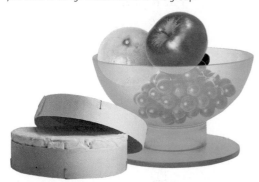

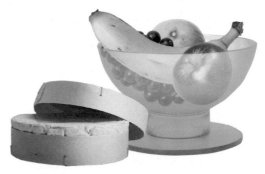

8 Layer comps can remember the position, visibility and layer styles for each layer. This means that as well as moving the cheese back and forth, we can move the fruit around and even hide the banana in different comps: we can then cycle through them all to see the difference.

9 What you can't do, however, is to rotate or otherwise distort layers between comps. Here, we've rotated this banana to sit across the fruit bowl: when we switch to an earlier comp, the banana will be rotated there, too. The only solution is to duplicate the layer first, and hide one or other.

SHORTCUTS
MAC WIN BOTH

Watercolor with Filter Gallery

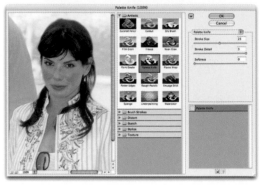

1 Here's our original image: Sandra Bullock, snapped at the Cannes Film Festival. I've already brightened the background so she stands out more.

PHOTOSHOP FILTERS are an easy and quick way to create a variety of special effects. But some techniques involve using multiple filters together: applying them one after the other would involve too much guesswork.

The Filter Gallery is much more than a convenient way to preview and choose filters. Its strength lies in the fact that multiple filters can be stacked on top of each other, allowing us to see the entire effect without committing to any one of them. We can adjust the sliders at any time, to vary the effect of each of the filters in the stack.

The Filter Gallery also allows us to change the order in which the filters are applied, by simply dragging them up and down in the list. This gives us tremendous flexibility, allowing us to fine-tune the final effect with ease.

Here, we'll combine multiple filters to turn a routine photograph into a watercolor effect.

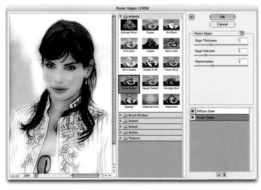

4 To add a new filter to the stack, click the New Document icon below the list of filters. This will duplicate the current filter, so here's Diffuse Glow twice – a very overblown effect.

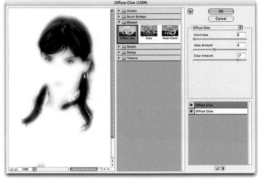

7 Because we chose Poster Edges after Diffuse Glow, it was applied on top of it. As well as changing the settings for each filter, we can also change the order in which they're applied: here, when we drag Diffuse Glow above Poster Edges, it's applied on top – for a softer result.

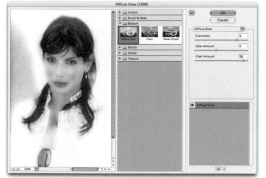

2 We'll begin by choosing Diffuse Glow from the Distort section. This adds an ethereal brightness, fading her shirt off into the background.

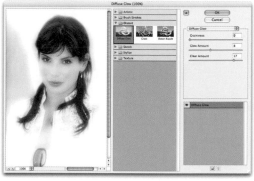

3 As it stands, the default settings include too much grain. We can reduce the grain amount to zero, and adjust the Glow and Clear settings until we get a vignette effect.

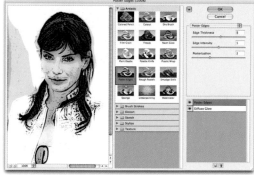

5 We can change this to any other filter in the set; let's choose Poster Edges from the Artistic section instead. These settings make her look like she has too much stubble, so we'll change the parameters.

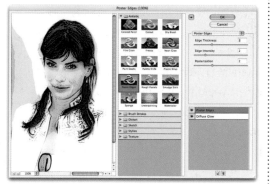

6 By reducing the Edge Intensity and the Edge Thickness settings, we can soften the effect considerably. You don't need to get it right first time: the setting can always be adjusted later.

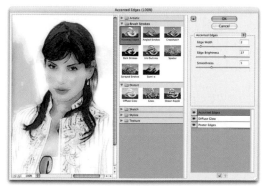

8 To smooth the image even further, we'll add a new filter – Accented Edges. This softens the skin tones, and removes all trace of the hard speckles caused by the Poster Edges filter. The image is now looking far more like it's been painted by hand.

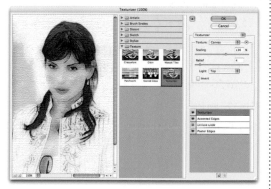

9 Finally, we can complete the watercolor effect by adding some texture: we'll add the Texturizer filter to the top of the filter stack, setting the scaling and relief amounts until we achieve the effect we want. All done within a single, editable filter environment!

HOT TIP

One drawback of the Filter Gallery is that it doesn't allow you to save favorite combinations of filters for later use. The best way around this is to start recording a new Action before you enter the Gallery; your settings will be preserved within the Action. If you then click to the left of the Filter Gallery item in the Action to set a 'stop' point, then running the Action will open the dialog with all the filters lined up for you.

Smart Filters

SMART FILTERS are a new way of working with filters in Photoshop CS3, providing an editability that wasn't present before.

Working with Smart Filters involves turning the layer into a Smart Object first. The advantage here is that a layer mask is associated with the Smart Object: this means that not only can we edit the overall effect later, we can also choose to apply it selectively by painting on the mask.

Here, we'll take this photo of Arnold Schwarzenegger and use the Smart Filter technology to revert him to his Terminator days by blasting away a portion of his face.

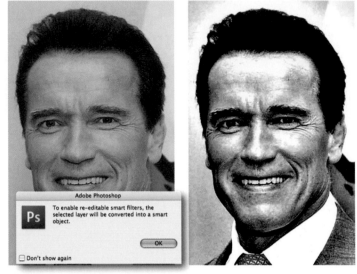

1 Before we begin to apply Smart Filters to the image, we need to make Arnie into a new (not background) layer, then choose Convert for Smart Filters from the Filter menu. Say OK to the dialog that appears.

2 We'll begin by applying the Unsharp Mask filter, to an unnaturally high degree: here, I've used an amount of 200%, at a radius of 50 pixels. We'd never normally choose this high a setting for standard sharpening work.

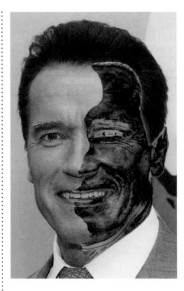

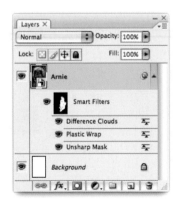

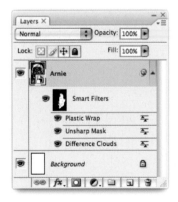

6 Let's add another filter: I've used Difference Clouds to make this solarized effect. As this is a random-effect filter, you may have to apply it a few times to get the exact result you want. Here, I used red foreground and white background colors.

7 As with the Filter Gallery, described on the previous pages, we can change the order in which the filters are applied. Unlike the Filter Gallery, though, using Smart Filters we can make this change at any time – even long after the filters were

originally chosen. Here, the Difference Clouds filter was chosen after Plastic Wrap and Unsharp Mask, so it's applied on top of them. By dragging it to the bottom of the list in the Layers Palette, we can make it the first filter that's applied to the image.

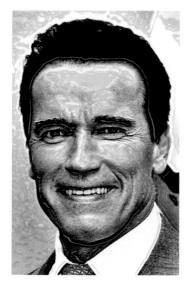

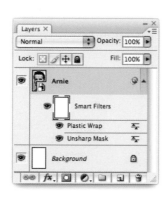

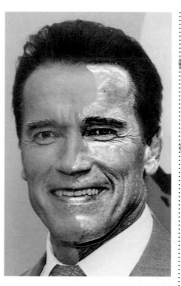

3 Next, let's apply the Plastic Wrap filter. Choose the settings that you feel give an appropriate amount of shine to the image – but remember, we can adjust these settings later.

4 When we now look at the Layers palette, we can see those two filters listed beneath the Smart Filters icon. This is actually a mask; by painting on here in black, we can selectively hide the filters' effects.

5 To make the job easier, we can first fill the mask with black to hide it entirely, then use a brush with a white foreground color to paint it back in where we want it. I've chosen a hard-edged brush for this effect.

HOT TIP

Although we've been working on a single layer here, multiple layers can also be combined into Smart Objects – which means that a set of filters can now be applied to several layers at once. As with all Smart Objects, if you want to edit the pixels on the original layer or layers, you need to double click the Smart Object icon to open its contents in a new window. When you're happy with the result, save the new document to return the results to the original file.

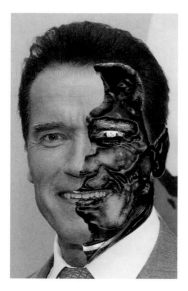

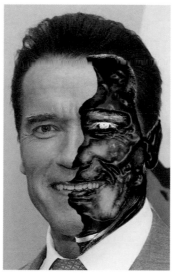

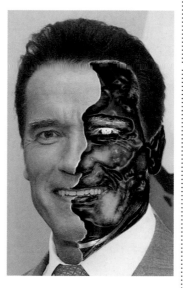

8 This is the result of changing the filter order. The Plastic Wrap filter, in particular, looks far more shiny when it has the Difference Clouds random effect to work on – and it brings out that glowing eye perfectly.

9 To complete the image, let's add a couple more steps. First, load up the mask area by holding ⌘ *ctrl* and clicking on its thumbnail, then paint some shadow on a new layer using that selection to limit its extent.

10 Finally, I've selected a thin rim of the original image, made a new layer from it and brightened it to give the impression of the thickness of the skin. These last two steps give a more convincing sense of the Smart Filter set appearing behind the skin.

SHORTCUTS
MAC WIN BOTH

Making the most of Bridge

Store frequently-used folders in the Favorites tab at the top so they can be accessed easily. Just drag a folder into this section to store it here; use contextual menus to remove it.

Step back and forth between recently used folders here, or click on the pop-up menu to view them all.

T HE FILE BROWSER was first introduced in Photoshop 7, and was greatly enhanced in Photoshop CS. Now renamed Adobe Bridge, it's come out of its shell and evolved into an application in its own right, running right across the Adobe CS suite.

Speed of generating thumbnails is now better than ever, and many new features have been packed in to make the program better and easier to use. It's now much more than a simple open dialog: Bridge allows you to sort, classify and annotate your images with greater ease than was previously possible.

Batch processing of images is also much easier with Bridge. Any Photoshop Action can be applied to a range of selected images – so if you find that all your digital camera pictures need the same adjustment and sharpening, it's easy to achieve this with a single click.

Adobe Bridge can save a lot of time when you've got a large number of images to sort through, and it's worth taking the trouble to learn what it can do.

Saving your images into subfolders makes them easier to browse: you can view your entire hard disk in this way, and even browse images on your digital camera card.

The Preview window shows the image as large as the window. But if you click within it, you'll see an 'actual size' pop-up – useful for checking whether an image is fully in focus.

houses6.JPG (100%)
89 items, 2 hidden, 1 selected

Click here to create a new folder. You can drag images between folders in Bridge to help you organize your files.

Rotate images taken with digital cameras using these buttons. Only the thumbnail will be rotated at first: but when the image is opened in Photoshop, it will be rotated as well.

The Compact Mode button minimizes the window to display just a small selection of thumbnails. It's really useful to be able to shrink Bridge down like this so you can drag items into other applications, and then push it back to full screen at other times.

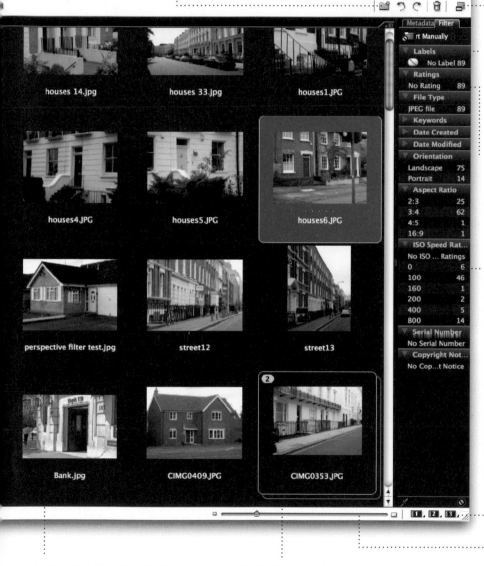

You can filter images by star rating, or by label. This is a useful way of creating on-the-fly selections for a particular job: images can be assigned temporary labels, which are removed later.

The Keyword feature in Bridge is a useful way to categorize images across several folders. It may take a while to specify the keywords, but it will save plenty of time later.

Metadata can show you when an image was taken, what camera and settings were used, and so on. You can also write your own information into the custom fields.

As well as the standard Thumbnail view, there are other ways of looking at your images. Filmstrip view shows thumbnails of all the images either below or next to each other, with the current one previewed much bigger: press the cursor keys to move around them.

Get into the habit of dragging images into natural groupings within folders. Here, for example, I've placed all the houses in perspective together for easy reference.

Multiple images can be grouped into 'stacks' – handy if you have several different shots of the same subject

Drag the slider to change the size of the thumbnails. Enlarging a set of thumbnails together can be much quicker than viewing them one at a time in the Preview pane.

Photoshop Actions

THE ACTIONS PALETTE in Photoshop is a feature that most users tend to ignore, and when you look at the Actions shipped with the program it's hardly surprising. They allow you to perform such sequences as generating plastic-looking wood frames, creating dodgy reflections of type on water and filling the screen with molten lead. Which are hardly the sort of everyday tasks that make you want to explore the system further.

But Actions are capable of far more than building questionable special effects. At their basic level, Actions can be used simply to create keyboard shortcuts for tasks that would otherwise have you reaching for the menu bar.

In the examples here, we'll first look at how to create an Action from scratch. The effect of this one will be to delete a 1 pixel border around a selection - my preferred defringing method.

Next, we'll examine the steps that make up a more complex Action, explaining the purpose and function of each stage in the process.

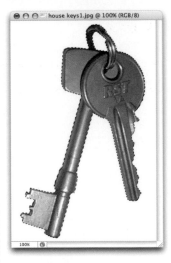

1 First, make a selection in your Photoshop document. These keys have been selected using a previously-saved clipping path.

2 Select New Action from the pop-up menu at the top right of the Actions palette. You need to choose a set in which to create the Action. Give the Action a name, and choose a keyboard shortcut; then hit the Record button.

3 The first step in this Action is to contract the selection by a single pixel. Choose Select>Modify>Contract and enter a value of 1 in the dialog that appears; press OK to apply the contraction.

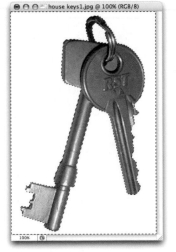

4 Two more steps: inverse the selection using ⌘ Shift I ctrl Shift I, and then delete using the Backspace key.

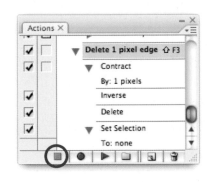

5 Finally, press the Stop button on the Actions palette (the square at far left on the bottom) and the Action will finish recording. Every step is now shown in the palette, and the Action can be played back on any image.

Anatomy of a complex Action

This is an Action I use several times a day, and it allows me to change the direction in which my subjects are looking. After I make a selection of a figure's eye region, the Action adds shading and color to a new layer, then opens a file named 'iris' and pastes it into the new eyeball, setting the mode to Multiply and using the eyeball as a clipping mask.

This is the name of the Action, together with the key command which activates it

The Action assumes I've already made a selection for the eyes; it makes a new layer called 'eyeball'

The foreground/background colors are set to default black and white

The foreground/background colors are swapped over

The selection is filled with white (foreground color)

A 'stop point' is placed here: this brings up a dialog asking for the feather amount. It depends on the size of the eyes in the image; the default is 8 pixels

The selection is then inversed

The colors are set to default black and white

The feathered outside of the eyeball is now filled with black, with transparency preserved so the effect remains within the eyeball area

The eyeball is deselected

A custom Color Balance setting is applied to add color to the shaded edges of the eyeball

The Action now opens a file called 'iris', located on my hard disk

The whole of the 'iris' file is selected and copied to the clipboard, and the file is closed

The 'eyeball' layer is loaded as a selection

A new layer is made to take the copied iris, with its mode set to Multiply so that the iris will take on the shading of the underlying layer

The iris, previously copied to the clipboard, is now pasted into the new layer

Finally, the iris uses the eye layer as a clipping mask

Actions ×

- ▼ eyes ⇧ F5
  - ▼ Make
    - New: layer
    - Name: "eyeball"
  - Reset Swatches
  - Exchange Swatches
  - ▼ Fill
    - Using: foreground color
    - Opacity: 100%
    - Mode: normal
  - ▼ Set Selection
    - To: transparency channel
  - ▼ Feather
    - Radius: 8 pixels
  - Inverse
  - Reset Swatches
  - ▼ Fill
    - Using: foreground color
    - Opacity: 100%
    - Mode: normal
    - With Preserve Transparency
  - ▼ Set Selection
    - To: none pixel
  - ▼ Color Balance
    - Shadow Levels: 0, 0, 0
    - Midtone Levels: 56, 0, -38
    - Highlight Levels: 0, 0, 0
    - With Preserve Luminosity
  - ▼ Open
    - Gigalomaniac:Celebs:Things: iris
    - As: Photoshop
  - ▼ Set Selection
    - To: all pixel
  - Copy
  - Close
  - ▼ Select layer "eyeball"
    - Modification: Remove
    - Without Make Visible
  - ▼ Make
    - New: layer
    - Name: "iris"
    - Mode: multiply
  - Paste
  - Create Clipping Mask

Self promotion

EVERY BUDDING PHOTOSHOP ARTIST needs to find a way to bring their work to the attention of art editors. In the past, this would have meant phoning to make an appointment, and then lugging a portfolio around the offices of newspaper, magazine and advertising offices.

Now, of course, we're able to use the internet to do all the legwork for us. Compiling a selection of our best images on a website is the easiest, most efficient and best way to show the world what we can do.

There are many tools available for website design: Dreamweaver and GoLive are among the most popular. PC users frequently turn to FrontPage to do the job for them; as a Mac user, my web authoring tool of choice is Freeway, made by SoftPress, which gives me the tools I need without my having to learn complex markup languages.

If the idea of learning a new package is daunting, then it's possible to use the built-in Web Photo Gallery in Photoshop to build a website for you, using a folder full of images as its starting point. Found in the Automate section of the File menu, Web Photo Gallery offers a range of different ways of constructing an image-based site with minimal pain.

Of course, you may have skill in building animated GIF and even Flash files, and have more definite ideas on the visual style you want your website to have. But before you start creating animations, give some serious thought to the impression you want to create. Do you want to appear serious, or playful? Efficient and workmanlike, or inspired and creative? There are many factors to be weighed in the balance, and the process needs to be worked out carefully.

One thing is for certain: your website will be viewed by people who are visually literate, who understand good design, and who will find any awkwardness in typography or layout painful to look at. If they didn't have such a sophisticated sense of design, they wouldn't have got the jobs they now hold. You want them to employ you because you believe you have a strong visual sense; to convince them of this, you need to make sure your website is as

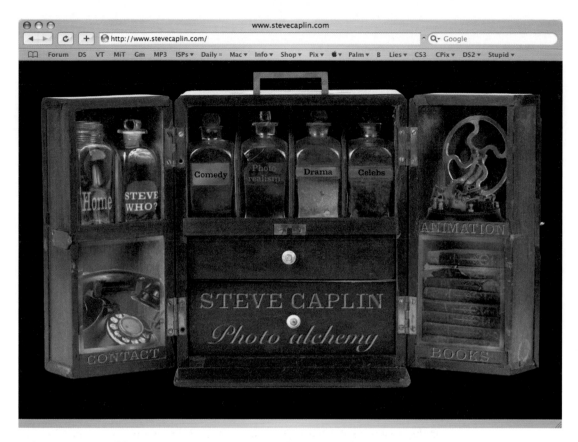

cohesive as possible. Mixing inappropriate combinations of images, fonts and other design elements is like going to a meeting wearing odd socks.

Unless you're absolutely sure of your design skills (which may be quite different from the skills required to compose Photoshop montages) then keep the site as simple as possible. If you do go for a more complex solution, then it's important to ensure that all the elements in your design are visually cohesive.

Websites don't need to follow any particular template, or have standard sets of menus and navigation elements – as my own website, above, demonstrates. But navigation does have to be clear: in my own design, each of the elements highlights as the mouse rolls over it, indicating that it can be clicked to proceed to the next section. Figures appear in the jars, the Contact and Books sections light up, and the wheel in the Animation compartment rotates on mouse over.

I'm not suggesting my own site as a method that would work for anyone other than myself: but your own site must reflect your personality and your skill set if it's going to sell your work to others.

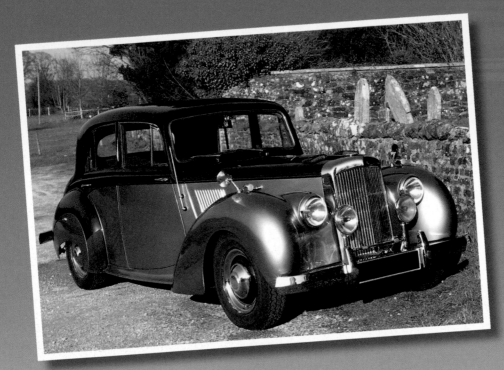

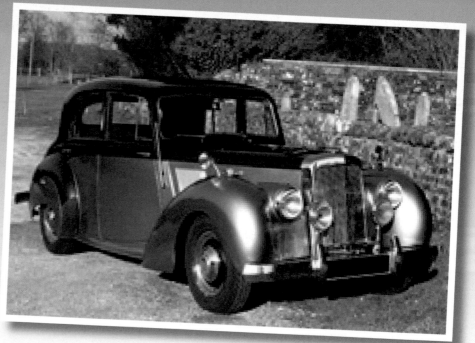

■ Two versions of the same photograph: both claim to measure 4³/4 inches by 3¹/2 inches. So why is it that the top one looks sharp and crisp, while the bottom one is fuzzy and indistinct? How can they be the same size, yet look so different? The answer is all to do with resolution, which we'll explain in this chapter.

15

Working for print and the web

Throughout this book we've been looking at how to get the best out of Photoshop, how to improve your workflow and how to make pictures that look beautiful.

But creating images that look stunning on your computer isn't enough. At some point, you need to break them out of the confines of your monitor and share them with the world – whether that's through the medium of print, or on the internet.

And that's where many people come unstuck. What is CMYK all about? How do you make files smaller without making the images smaller? And how on earth do people make those animations from Photoshop files? It's all a lot easier than you might think.

Image size and resolution

IMAGE SIZE AND RESOLUTION have long confused even the most Photoshop-savvy of digital artists. But there's no mystery: different media simply have different requirements.

The 'resolution' of a photograph refers to the fineness of the image: in other words, the number of dots used to make it. Image resolution is talked about in 'dots per inch', shortened to dpi. One dot equates to one pixel – that is, one square of unique color that combines with the squares around it to make up the digital image.

For images printed on paper, such as books, magazines and newspapers, the number of dots per inch required correlates directly with the quality of the paper. The better the paper, the less the ink spreads as the two come into contact, and so the finer the detail that can be reproduced.

Computer screens, traditionally, operate at 72dpi, although these days higher resolution screens are used for graphics work. There are no printing issues here: so anything destined for on-screen delivery, such as the internet, is created at 72dpi.

When you view an image in Photoshop at 'actual size', or 100%, it means that one pixel in the image exactly matches one physical pixel on your monitor. To see it at the size it will be printed, choose Print Size from the View menu. This reduces it on screen, and assumes that your monitor is set to display at 72dpi.

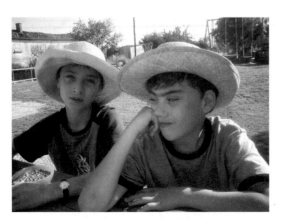

4 Here's a photograph taken with a standard 3.2 megapixel camera. The size of the image captured by this camera is 2048 x 1536 pixels: multiply those numbers together and you get 3,145,728, which is approximately 3.2 million pixels in total. It's from multiplying these dimensions together that digital cameras get their size rating.

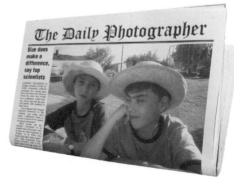

5 If that image were printed in a newspaper at 200 dots per inch, it could be used up to a size of roughly 10 x 8 inches. That's easily big enough for the main front-page photograph of most newspapers. Because of the lower resolution requirements, coupled with their speed, many news photographers now use digital cameras.

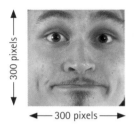

↕ 300 pixels
← 300 pixels →

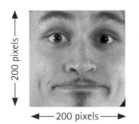

↕ 200 pixels
← 200 pixels →

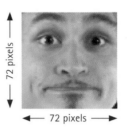

↕ 72 pixels
← 72 pixels →

1 This image has been scanned at 300dpi (dots per inch). The picture is exactly one inch square, which means it's 300 pixels wide by 300 pixels high. That makes a total of 90,000 individual pixels in this single square inch of paper.

A picture with this density of pixels is suitable for printing in high-quality magazines, which use 300dpi as their standard resolution. The higher the quality of paper, the finer the detail of photography that can be reproduced on it.

2 This picture has been scanned at 200dpi. Although 200 is two-thirds of 300, the image measures 200 pixels in each direction: this makes 40,000 pixels in all, which is less than half the 300dpi version.

This picture is suitable for printing in newspapers, which use coarse paper that doesn't take the ink as well and therefore require a larger, coarser dot screen. This resolution of image could be printed in glossy magazines, but the result would be too soft for demanding art directors.

3 This picture has been scanned at 72dpi. The picture is also one inch square. At 72 pixels wide by 72 pixels high, that makes a total of only 5,184 pixels in this square inch of image.

This picture is suitable for publishing on the internet, since 72dpi is the standard 'screen' resolution. It's far too low for glossy magazines, and even newspapers: you can clearly see the squares that make up the image.

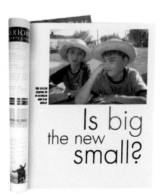

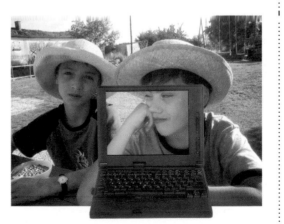

6 If that same image were used in a glossy magazine, it could be used up to just under half a page in size before the art director started to complain about the resolution. That's assuming, of course, that the camera lens was up to the job for high-end reproduction – size isn't everything when it comes to glossy photography.

7 If used on a website, the same image could now be used at a size of nearly four square feet – although an image this size would take forever to download. It's a matter of happy coincidence that the shortcomings of computer screens match the download and storage requirements of the internet!

Working for print

PREPARING IMAGES FOR PRINT involves working at a higher resolution, as we've seen earlier in this chapter. But it also entails an understanding of the difference between RGB and CMYK color models, shown below.

For most of the time, you'll work in RGB even if your final output is destined for CMYK. It's quicker in operation – the files are three quarters the size, for one thing, since they have one fewer channel – the dialogs are frequently more intuitive, and many of Photoshop's filters simply don't work in RGB.

But the RGB color range, known as its 'gamut', is far wider than that of CMYK. Which means there's a huge range of colors you can create on screen which simply won't transfer onto paper.

Even if you're only printing work out on your own inkjet printer, you need to understand why some colors print fine, while others don't.

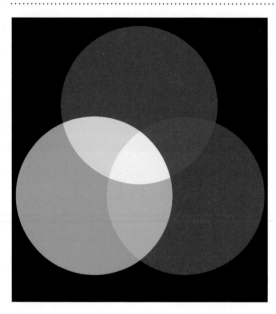

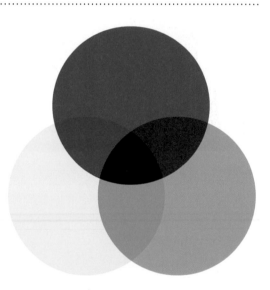

RGB Monitors display colors using Red, Green and Blue light. These are known as 'additive' colors, because the more light you add, the brighter the result: it's like shining torches on a sheet of paper in a dark room. You start with black, and each torch you turn on increases the overall light level.

Red and green added together make yellow; red and blue make magenta; blue and green make cyan. When all the colors are added together, the result is white.

You can see the effect of additive color clearly by creating red, green and blue shapes, and setting their layer mode to Screen, set against a black background. The file RGB.psd in the Chapter 15 folder on the CD includes these three disks of color: try moving them around, and changing their opacity, to see how all the intermediate colors are made.

CMYK Printing inks create color in precisely the opposite way to monitors. Cyan, Magenta and Yellow inks (with a little Black for the shadows) are 'subtractive' colors: you start with a white sheet of paper, and the more ink you add, the darker the result.

Magenta and yellow added together make red; magenta and cyan make blue; yellow and cyan make green. When all the colors are added together, the result is black.

You can see the effect of subtractive color clearly by creating magenta, yellow and cyan shapes, and setting their layer mode to Multiply, set against a white background. The file CMYK.psd in the Chapter 15 folder on the CD includes these three disks of color: as with the RGB file, try moving them around and changing their opacity, to see how all the intermediate colors are made.

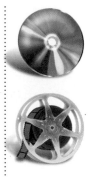

If you are doing work for print that will be sent to a magazine, newspaper or other publication, then work in RGB – and send them your files in RGB. There's a good reason for this: creating effective CMYK files isn't simply a matter of choosing CMYK Color from the Mode menu.

Professional publications will go to great lengths to print test images, comparing them with the original files, before producing their own custom RGB to CMYK conversion. A lot depends on the type of paper used, the printing method – sheet-fed or web offset – as well as the specific printing machine used. If you convert the files to CMYK first, they won't be able to perform their custom conversion and the result will look muddy when printed.

When you do have to convert work to CMYK yourself, however, make sure you get as much advice as possible from your printer first.

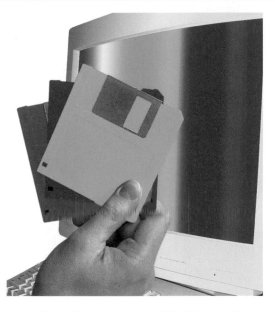

A fan of floppy disks (remember them?) held in front of a colorful computer monitor. Rainbow gradients such as the one on the screen are easy to make, and they always look bright and colorful – on screen, at least.

It's when you try to get them off the screen that the problems start. The RGB version of this image looks quite different to the dull CMYK impression printed in this book. There's no way of showing the RGB original in print – that's the point of this exercise, after all – but you can compare the two by opening the file RGB Gamut.jpg, which you'll find in the Chapter 15 folder on the CD.

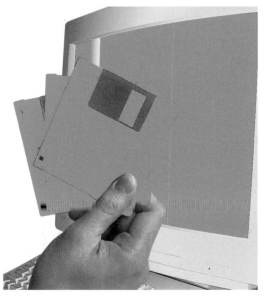

One way of telling how your images will look when printed is to turn on Proof Colors mode (*ctrl* Y *⌘* Y). This dulls colors that are out of gamut, giving a good impression of how their CMYK equivalents will look. Again, try this with the file RGB Gamut.jpg on the CD – you'll be astonished by the difference.

When working for CMYK, it's common practice to switch in and out of Proof Colors mode frequently, to check that the colors will work: any that look significantly different when proofed in this way will need to be changed.

Alternatively, you can turn on Gamut Warning mode using *ctrl* *Shift* Y *⌘* *Shift* Y. This turns all out-of-gamut colors to a flat gray, as shown here. It can be shocking to see how much of that bright color you'll lose!

Working for the web

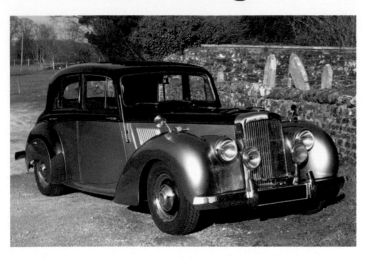

THE IMAGE ABOVE is 600 x 400 pixels, and has been saved at 72dpi for delivery on the internet. It includes a clipping path, which outlines the car – although we don't need this in the web version. Saved as a standard JPEG file directly from Photoshop, this results in a file size of 256K.

When you save JPEG images from Photoshop, you're trading quality against file size: the lower the quality, the smaller the file. If you're working for print, or simply to archive your own work, you should generally use a JPEG setting of at least 10, which gives the best compromise between size and quality. The maximum JPEG quality is 12.

Working for internet delivery, however, is a very different matter. Here, file size is all important: you need to make the file as small as possible, even if that means trading off a little quality.

Photoshop's Save for Web feature, found under the File menu, discards all such unnecessary elements as paths to produce the smallest possible files. Choosing Save for

Web opens the dialog shown here. At the top left are four tabs which allow you to view the original or the optimized image – that is, how the image will look after it's compressed. You can also choose to view the two side by side or, as shown here, four views of the same file with different compression settings. This is perhaps the most useful view.

You have the option of saving as either a GIF (Graphic Interchange Format) or JPEG (Joint Photographers' Expert Group) file. In general, you should only use GIF files for animations, or if you need to include transparency in your image, as these tend to result in larger files at lower quality.

A rather confusing aspect is that the JPEG settings are shown here as being ranked out of 100, whereas they're shown in standard Photoshop Save dialogs as being ranked out of 12. But a quality setting of 60 in Save for Web will roughly equate to a setting of 6 in the standard Save dialog, so just divide by 10.

The advantage of this split view is that you can see exactly how each quality setting will affect your image. You can zoom and pan in any of the views, and they'll all be synchronized to match: choose to view the most detailed area of your image when saving in this way.

In the example shown here, we can bring the quality right down to 30 without too much degradation: and this drops the file size to 50K, which is far more suitable for our purpose.

Save for Web always saves a copy of the original image, rather than overwriting it. So you can always return to the original (assuming you've saved it normally) if your settings later prove to be insufficient.

This is the original image. Its size is shown as 703K – which means the size in 'real terms' while the file is open in Photoshop. This does not equate to the size when it's saved as a regular JPEG file.

This is the size the image would be if saved as a 256-color .gif file. At 190K this is far too big for web delivery: the GIF format isn't really suitable for such complex images.

The information shown here depends on whether you've selected GIF or JPEG as the file format: each has its own set of controls. The settings for GIF files are described more fully on the next page.

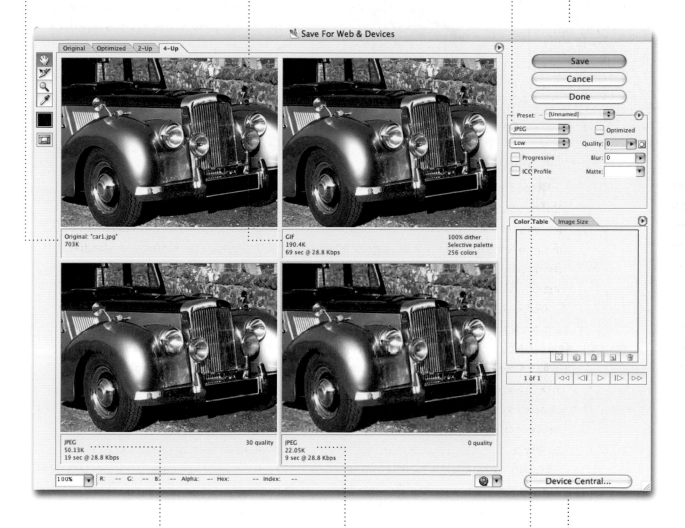

At a 'medium' quality JPEG file (which means a setting of 30) the image is still reasonably crisp and clear, but its size is reduced to just 50K. This is about the lowest we can reasonably get away with without the image looking ugly.

Here, just for the sake of comparison, the image has been reduced to its lowest quality setting of 0. This reduces the file size to just 22K. A lot of blockiness is now apparent, and the picture looks like it's been left out in the rain. You'd never normally use such a low quality setting.

A 'progressive' JPEG will load in stages, the resolution increasing with each pass. It's a good way of getting your images to appear more quickly, but can be annoying for the visitor.

Making it move

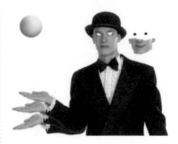

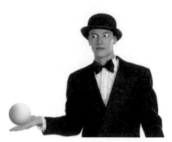

I MAGE READY, the web-authoring companion to Photoshop, has disappeared as of Photoshop CS3: its functionality has been bundled into the main application.

While it may not boast the versatility of Flash and other powerful animation systems, animated GIFs are easy to create, take up very little file space and can make web pages look that much more special.

One of the foremost practitioners of animated GIFs is Becky Fryer, known as 'maiden' on the How to Cheat in Photoshop reader forum. A selection of her work is included on the DVD.

1 Preparation is the key to successful animation. Here there are three arm layers at different angles, as well as separate smile and eye layers.

2 For our first frame, we'll use the lowest arm, move the eyes down in their sockets, and place the ball firmly on the hand.

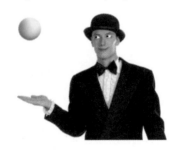

Tween
Tween With: Selection ▼   OK
Frames to Add: 3   Cancel
Layers
⦿ All Layers
○ Selected Layers
Parameters
☑ Position
☑ Opacity
☑ Effects

6 Now to flash that smile. Show the Smile layer for this frame only, and it will turn on when the animation reaches this point.

7 There's a jump between the third and fourth frame (steps 4 and 5 here). Select both, and press the Tween button on the Animation palette.

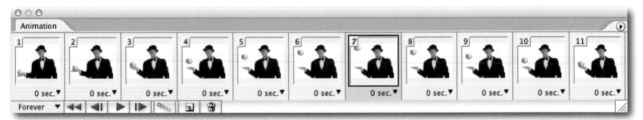

The standard Photoshop CS3 animation palette is shown above, detailing all the steps in the animation shown here. The Extended version of Photoshop also has the option to view animations as a timeline (below), which allows events to be moved easily to different locations. One further advantage of the Extended version is its ability to show 'onion skins' (below right) here, the previous frame is ghosted so we can see the difference between the two.

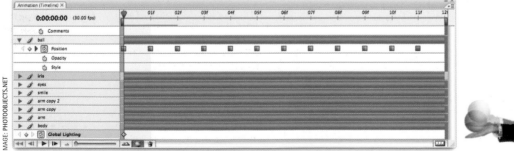

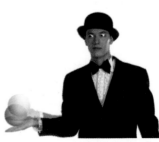

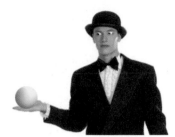

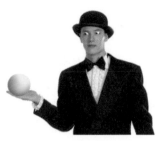

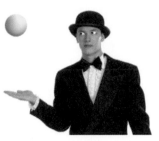

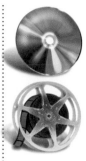

3 Open the Animation palette, and click the New icon for a second frame. Now hide the first arm and show the second, and move the ball.

4 Make another new frame, and show the third arm (hiding the second); move the ball once again so it sits neatly in the hand.

5 Make another new frame. To set the top of the juggle, move the ball (and the eyes) all the way up: the hand can stay where it is.

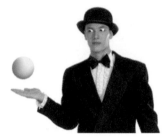

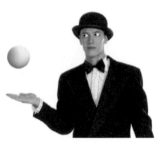

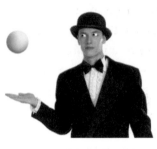

8 In the Tween palette we can specify the number of intermediate frames to be created. We'll stick with three, which gives the

illusion of motion. The frames shown here are generated automatically, with equal spacing placed between the first and last positions of each layer.

9 Duplicate the motion in the reverse order by holding *alt* ⏎ as you drag it to each frame new location in the Animation palette.

Save for Web: animated GIFs

Be sure to choose GIF rather than JPEG, or you won't see any animation (even if it's there in the original Photoshop document).

This menu selects the way colors are selected. **Perceptual** gives good results, with fairly small file sizes.

This determines the 'dither' method, or how intermediate colors are displayed. Diffusion is generally the choice here, but try None for smaller files (and a more graphic appearance).

The 'lossiness' is one factor that determines the file size. The higher this value, the worse your animation will look – but the smaller the file will be.

The fewer colors you use in your animation, the smaller the file size will be. Starting with 256 colors, you can reduce them in powers of 2 (64, 32 and so on).

When you use fewer colors, the remaining ones need to be 'dithered', which means using noise patterns to give the impression of colors that aren't there. The higher the dither amount, the smaller the file.

The web snap is the degree to which the colors in your document match the 216 'web safe' colors. This used to be more important when people had 8-bit monitors as standard.

Preset: – [Unnamed]	
GIF	Lossy: 24
Perceptual	Colors: 32
Diffusion	Dither: 100%
☑ Transparency	Matte:
No Transpare...	Amount: 100%
☐ Interlaced	Web Snap: 0%

TEST YOURSELF

W E'VE REACHED THE END of the book, and it's time to see how much you've learned. This self test section is a way to check that you've understood everything so far.

There are hints for each test, if you need them, in the Read Me file in the Test Yourself folder on the DVD – and that's where you'll find the source files, too. If you get stuck, visit the Reader Forum section of www.howtocheatinphotoshop.com where you'll find plenty of tips and advice.

For more tests, check out the weekly Friday Challenge section of the Reader Forum.

1: REBUILD THE WHEEL

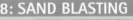

The ghosted image shows a complete wheel, but we've only got one whole spoke and section of rim. Reconstruct the entire wheel. **File: Wheel.psd**

2: CHANGING COLORS

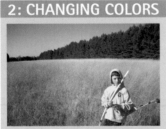

Joe liked yellow when I got him the sweatshirt – but now he'd prefer blue. Can you give him the color he wants? **File: Sweatshirt.psd**

3: FIRE HAZARD

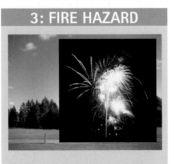

Your mission: to put the firework behind the trees, without any painting tools. **File: Fireworks.psd**

4: HANDIWORK

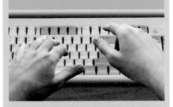

Can you make this mismatched pair of hands look like they both belong to the same body? **File: Hands.psd**

5: SPIN CYCLE

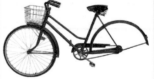

This old bicycle is in need of repair. Can you build a wheel to replace the missing one? **File: Bike.psd**

6: SNAKES & LADDERS

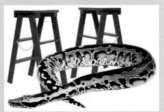

A snake. A couple of ladders. Weave the snake through the ladders so it looks realistic. **File: Snakes.psd**

7: PACK UP SMOKING

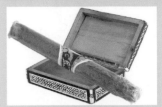

One cigar – but I want a whole box full of them. All placed inside the box, please. **File: Cigars.psd**

8: SAND BLASTING

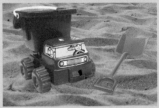

A bucket and spade at the seaside. Can you make them sit in the sand? **File: Seaside.psd**

9: ROOM WITH A VIEW

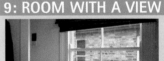
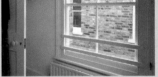

There's a great view through this window – or there would be, if that other house wasn't in the way. Can you fix it? **File: View.psd**

10: STREET SCENE

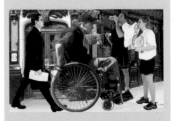

Can you resize all the people in this scene so that they're all located in the same street? **File: Street.psd**

11: DOUBLING BOXES

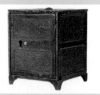

I'd like this box to be twice as wide, with two doors. I'd also like it arranged so both keyholes are together in the center. **File: Box.psd**

12: BANK JOB

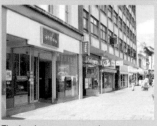

The bank nearest to us has expanded, and wants to take over the two shops next door. Extend it, while retaining its corporate identity. **File: Bank.psd**

13: SHADOW DUTY

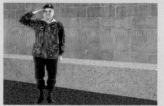

This soldier needs a shadow on the wall. But there's a bench in the way... **File: Shadows.psd**

14: FRUIT BOWL

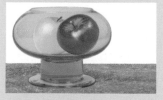

A couple of apples in a bowl. Well, they're not in the bowl yet – can you put them there? **File: Fruitbowl.psd**

15: BY THE BOOK

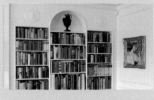

All those books get very dusty. It would be much better if they were behind glass. **File: Bookshelves.psd**

16: AGE AND BEAUTY

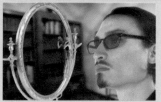

This woman is in her mid twenties, I'd guess. How will she look in thirty years' time? Will she still have a silver nose ring? **File: Ageing.psd**

17: REFLECTIONS

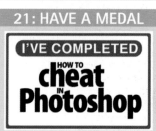

It looks like someone forgot to put any glass in the mirror. Can you oblige? **File: Mirror.psd**

18: METAL MALLARD

The artist Jeff Koons paid a fortune to have kitsch objects coated in chrome. Can turn this duck to metal? **File: Duck.psd**

19: STONE CARVING

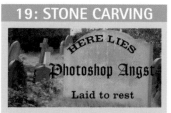

Here's the text I'd like to be placed on this gravestone. Carved, not painted, of course! **File: Grave.psd**

20: BLOW THE LID OFF

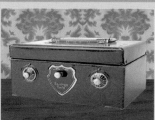

I'm sure there was something of value in here. But I've lost the key. Dynamite, perhaps? **File: Safe.psd**

21: HAVE A MEDAL

I'VE COMPLETED
HOW TO
cheat
IN
Photoshop

If you've got to the end of this book, you really deserve a medal. A shiny silver one. **File: Medal.psd**

22: SHUT HIM UP

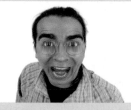

Why is this man yelling at me? I'd like him bound and gagged to keep him quiet. **File: bound.psd**

23: OPEN DOOR POLICY

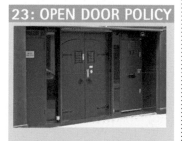

This nightclub has closed its doors. I'd like to see how it looks with them open. **File: Doors.psd**

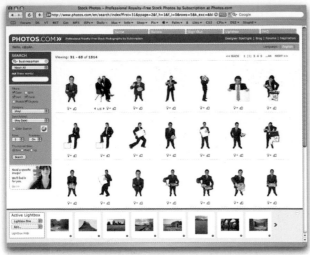

People in action

Good quality, large images of people in action can be hard to find just browsing the internet. Here's a hand-picked selection of people in a wide variety of interesting poses – just right for photomontage.

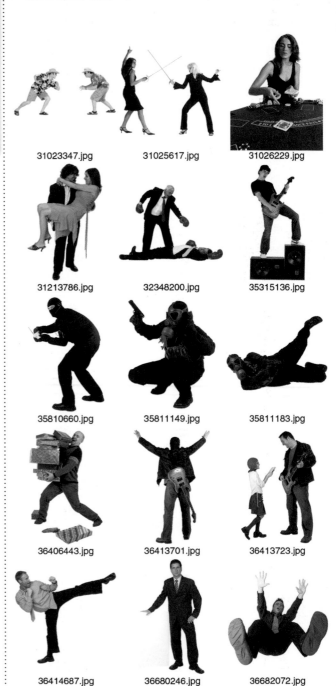

31023347.jpg   31025617.jpg   31026229.jpg

31213786.jpg   32348200.jpg   35315136.jpg

35810660.jpg   35811149.jpg   35811183.jpg

36406443.jpg   36413701.jpg   36413723.jpg

36414687.jpg   36680246.jpg   36682072.jpg

ALL THE IMAGES SHOWN on the next four pages are from the Photos.com collection of royalty-free photography. These high resolution images are provided for you to use for your own work: read the license agreement in the Photos.com folder on the DVD for full terms and conditions.

Photos.com features a huge range of people and objects with clipping paths for easy background removal, as well as many traditional images – over 235,000 pictures in all. All people and objects come with clipping paths.

Trial subscriptions start at $149.95 for one month, during which time you can download up to 250 images a day. Readers of this book get a special discount to just $99.95 for a trial month: see the web page in the Photos.com folder on the DVD for details.

Included here are 100 images I've selected as being of particular use for photomontage artists. To find out more, visit the website at **www.photos.com**

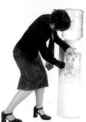

10052285.jpg

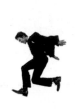

10055791.jpg

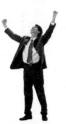

16320634.jpg

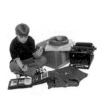

16447402.jpg

1935h1230.jpg

22774529.jpg

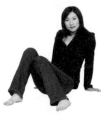

23306153.jpg

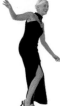

8034169.jpg

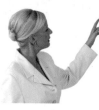

8034979.jpg

8035156.jpg

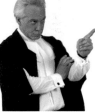

8035721.jpg

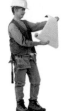

8035964.jpg

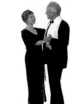

8038901.jpg

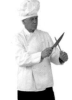

8039483.jpg

8041262.jpg

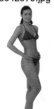

8042979.jpg

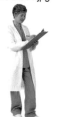

8044668.jpg

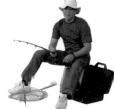

8045929.jpg

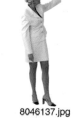

8046137.jpg

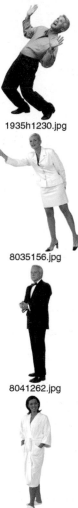

8070780.jpg

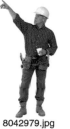

8075477.jpg

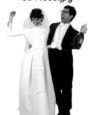

8248719.jpg

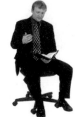

8250065.jpg

8250570.jpg

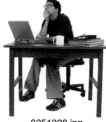

8251228.jpg

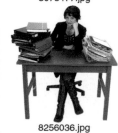

8256036.jpg

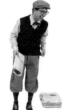

8258473.jpg

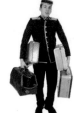

9819318.jpg

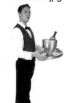

9820640.jpg

9821132.jpg

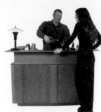

23440205.jpg

23650985.jpg

26559497.jpg

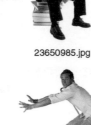

28562057.jpg

28563005.jpg

28563341.jpg

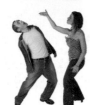

28564757.jpg

28709096.jpg

28710587.jpg

28710725.jpg

28711388.jpg

28714408.jpg

28716484.jpg

28719954.jpg

30746441.jpg

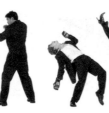

30838203.jpg

30838840.jpg

30846451.jpg

Things

Frames, boxes, furniture, dogs – we all need stuff. Here are some objects I've chosen with an eye to montage work.

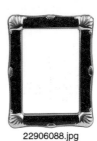

22906088.jpg

23109210.jpg

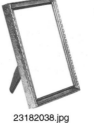

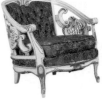

23182038.jpg

23339981.jpg

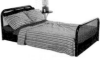

30844581.jpg

30844593.jpg

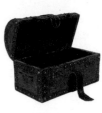

30893239.jpg

31215664.jpg

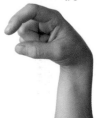

31215905.jpg

35811898.jpg

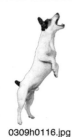

0309h0116.jpg

0414h0415.jpg

Places

A variety of rooms and locations, all empty so you can place your own figures within the scenes. No clipping paths, of course – but these are all high resolution images.

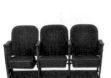

0742h0555.jpg

1244h0016.jpg

10017304.jpg

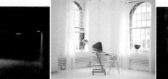

16475843.jpg

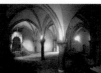

34644404.jpg

1367h1418.jpg

1378h0024.jpg

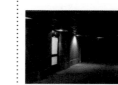

34734624.jpg

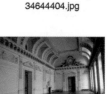

34769016.jpg

34769049.jpg

22510473.jpg

22521215.jpg

34821702.jpg

34832878.jpg

34837960.jpg

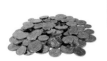

22710821.jpg

22713809.jpg

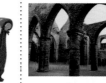

34838751.jpg

7308877.jpg

7379437.jpg

8028910.jpg

9814919.jpg

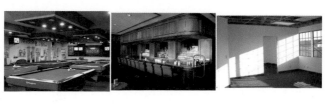

7634637.jpg

7721244.jpg

9829164.jpg

This symbol indicates that you'll find a Photoshop file on the DVD to accompany the tutorial. They're in a folder called **Photoshop Files**, and each one includes the starting point for each workthrough.

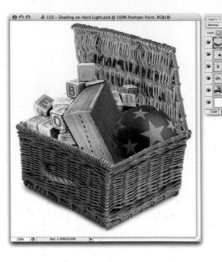

 This symbol means that there's also a QuickTime movie that shows the workthrough played out in real time. Sometimes it's easier to understand a concept when you see it acted out live, rather than just by reading about it. They're in the **Quicktime Movies** folder.

Additional folders contain 100 royalty free **Photos.com** images (see pages 404-407), a selection of animated GIF files created by **maiden** (see page 396), and a browser-based java applet that explains the mysteries of **two-point perspective** (see page 116). The **Test Yourself** folder (see page 398) contains all the relevant project files. In the **Bonus Content** folder, you'll also find a handy selection of high resolution skeletons that I rendered for you in Poser.

In order to fit in all the new pages in this edition, I've had to cut some tutorials from previous editions that I felt weren't pulling their weight, or which have been made redundant due to advances in more recent versions of Photoshop. If you feel you may be missing out, there's a folder called **Deleted Pages** containing PDF files for each of these missing tutorials.

Reader images

A number of regular contributors to the Reader Forum have generously donated over 200 top quality, high res photographs for you to use in your own projects. You'll find them in the **Reader Images** folder. They're provided here courtesy of Chris Martin, Gordon Bain, John White, Martin Guyer, Steve MacDonald, Stuart Cassels, Ted Eggs, Tom Murray and Vibeke Friis – thanks to all of you.